ENTEREXIT

EN TEREX IT

ENCOUNTERS AROUND TAROT
VOLUME ONE

ENRIQUE ENRIQUEZ

EYECORNER PRESS

© ENRIQUE ENRIQUEZ & EyeCorner Press | 2012

EN TEREX IT
Encounters around Tarot
Volume 1

The interviews are reprinted with the permission of the authors.

Published by EYECORNER PRESS
December 2012
Roskilde

ISBN: 978-87-92633-19-4

Editorial, cover design and layout: Camelia Elias
Image: Fabrizio Chiesa

Printed in the US and UK

To the letter V that sleeps
               with me.

CONTENTS

CAMELIA ELIAS: HE RECO ME / 9

encounters with

VITO ACCONCI / 18
JEAN-CLAUDE FLORNOY / 29
MICHAEL J. HURST / 42
ROSS S. CALDWELL / 68
JODY MELNICK / 109
SCOTT GROSSBERG / 125
JEAN-MICHEL DAVID / 141
MARY GREER / 168
TODD LANDMANN / 183
ERIC K. LERNER / 190
MARCO PONZI AND ROSS S. CALDWELL / 198
RONI SHACHNAEY / 204
MAJOR TOM SCHICK / 212
TONY EYE / 222
KAREN MAHONEY / 237
BRIAN HALLIDAY / 254
LENA RUTH STEFANOVIC / 260
RACHEL POLLACK / 274
ROBERT PLACE / 291
THOMAS HASTINGS / 302
PAUL NAGY / 307

HE RECO ME
ENRIQUE ENRIQUEZ'S POETICS OF DIVINATION

CAMELIA ELIAS, professor, cartomancer

Exactly a year ago I was vacationing in the Swedish woods. The whole atmosphere was conducive to reading oracles, walking between worlds, and appreciating nature in autumn. In the evening, in the warmth of the luxury log cabin, by candlelight and great internet-speed, I found myself marveling at how seemingly incongruous events mirrored each other. For instance, I found that there was perfect symmetry between the way in which nature communicates its power and strength in a very concrete manner and the way in which the writings of Enrique Enriquez on the Tarot de Marseille did the same. I found myself saying yes, yes, yes, and yes, on all accounts involving not only divination but also the poetics of reading visual texts. Here was Enrique, a good friend and first caliber scholar of magical texts, articulating what I was thinking. I was reading a number of interviews conducted by Enrique with a broad range of Tarot people around the globe. The conversations were very engaging.

As I'm in the position of being able to publish books that I like, I decided to proposition Enrique for a print version of these texts. He said yes, "but first I'll give you another manuscript." I also said yes. That has now also been turned into a book, *Tarology*, which came out last year, to many people's delight. One year down the road, and down Enrique's first book, I found myself in the same log cabin in Sweden, editing the conversations you are about to read here. I relish the result of our continued collaboration, which, in this case, amounts to a substantial work in two volumes (the second volume is introduced by Bent Sørensen). Here, Enrique gathers fresh voices and sharp tongues to speak of the art of Tarot as the art of living magically. Forty-seven tarot luminaries (readers, historians, philosophers, magicians, and scientists alike) gather to offer unique perspectives on what we can think of as divination with bones, human bones. Artists, deck creators, and modern-day neo-platonists follow Enrique's lead, letting themselves be enchanted by the piper at the gate of games.

What we are sitting with here is quite astonishing and a feast. Although the range of people contributing their thoughts is wide, we get the sense that Enrique picked his interviewees carefully. Full professors and magicians stand side by side with professional tarot readers; mentalist magicians stand side by side with artists; historians stand side by side with philosophers; and cultural theorists stand side by side with mystics. There is no quarreling. Historians in the business of collecting facts and weaving stories don't mind the high-end conceptual framework of the philosophers. Cultural theorists enjoy the mystical discourse of the poets, and the magicians allow themselves to learn tricks from the artists. What emerges is a careful consideration of and valuable thoughts around the history of the Tarot de Marseille, tarot in general, and contemporary modes of divination. Some of the central questions that Enrique deals with are: Do we read for the symbol, or the image? Do we read for the narrative that the cards create or their potential for transformation? Do we read for the plot, the poetry, or the formal properties? We find Enrique holding the torch and asking everybody the same questions: How do we experience the tarot? Through symbolic readings or through interacting with the image? While it is clear that he goes with the latter, he gives everyone a chance to state their preferences. But he doesn't stop there. He wants to see what the argument is for such preferences. What are the motivations in considering where images take us? How do the images do that?

What Enrique emphasizes in these conversations is the significance of the event of looking at the cards, before we search our memories for traditional set phrases that describe a card. Legends about secret codes inscribed unto the cards and occult systems of correspondences are all good from a narrative point of view. They make good stories. But how useful are they in a reading setting, when two people look at random images and try to get an answer for love-sickness, a loss of job, or lost vitality? For Enrique, whether the card represents an archetype, a symbolic world that promises self-governance and transformation, or an invitation to higher self-awareness is secondary to what he really wants to know, namely: how do we read images as images? What does following their composition, coloring, lines, rhythm, action, embodiment, do to our understanding of what's going on? After years of looking at these images, Enrique humbly discloses the secret to his own efficient and illuminating readings: he asks two questions of the cards. And he tries to answer these questions without making any compromises. I find his two-step mantra, 'what is happening?' and 'how do I feel about it?' as the most profound articulation of any method of reading cards. Here is Enrique aligning himself with the best scientists who also learned a thing or two about the significance of keeping it simple.

"One should make things as simple as possible, but not any simpler", said Einstein, reminding us of the value and good fortune of being able to penetrate the impenetrable, namely the obvious, or that which stares us in the face. Now, what does this mean in the context of reading cards, one might ask, and here I can think of a good example that comes to my mind as I write these words. And allow me now to enter the space where I not only try to formulate something about Enrique's poetics of divination, but also perform Enrique's teachings through a few examples taken from my own reading practice with tarot cards. I think of the card of the Chariot in Tarot, often associated with a winner. Now, what Enrique is trying to get us to understand is that it is easy to fall into the trap of imposing a set of symbolic meanings and norms on the cards which may interfere with their message on a concrete level. Thus, in a reading setting, one might be tempted to make symbolic analogies of this type, and convey this idea to the querent – sometimes even quite independently of the context of the question: Here is Charlton Heston in a gladiator movie, seducing us all with his will-power and victoriously heroic battle. The usefulness of such an analogy can be debated in a setting where perhaps seeing the charioteer as going, rather than coming, or as taking his farewell from the one embodied in a previous card, rather than showing his male prowess, would be more in line with what was happening on a concrete level. What if the chariot is a hearse, and the man in it is on his last ride? The point is that it helps to start with the descriptive level of a card and allow meaning to arise from that.

For Enrique, language itself becomes an oracle, and he insists that a word takes you to another word. A word contains answers to itself. Looking at the words that describe an image, rather than trying to transcend both words and image, is a way of paying attention to details that might escape our gaze. For Enrique, looking at the transformation line in the cards indicates that what transforms us is precisely that transformation. Looking at two cards in conjunction, we could say that the two chalices in Temperance transform into two horses in the Chariot. But what if we have Strength in between them? Surely, seeing that the water in Temperance, which traverses over the card's frame into that of Strength, but stops short at the lion's neck (in the Dodal deck), must put us on a track of considering that now the Charlton Heston of our symbolic world is not so powerful anymore.

The incredibly simple, yet most powerful lesson that Enrique teaches us is that following the lines of the card, looking at how elements between the cards rhyme analogously with each other, looking at the rising or falling tone and gravitas in a card, looking at what is tender in a card, is where meaning resides. Looking at how figures and characters embody different situations in the cards invite us to mimic their acts in the image. Follow the sign, not the rationale behind it, Enrique adamantly suggests, and demonstrates convincingly why this works. For once, the reader cannot be accused of being inaccurate. Secondly, the reader ends up delivering a concise, and verbally minimal message. Talk ruins everything, some say, and in the context of card readings one must grant that talk has consequences in a divinatory setting. For, what do we need so many words for, when we can all look at the picture on the table and get the picture by looking at it?

Enrique teaches us precisely that, to look at a picture, which is something that, paradoxically, most cartomancers have forgotten to do. Most are involved in reading book after book filled with personal meanings and random opinions about what the cards supposedly mean, and they convey this to the querent. But where does it all come from, when it comes down to it? It comes from looking at the cards. Not the querent, what she might wear, how she sits, or how she frets about her question. The useful meaning comes from describing the cards, looking at what's there right under your nose. And the querent's nose too. It is also for this reason that a good reader never makes any predictions. A good reader considers the cards on the table at the moment they are on the table. If they indicate a certain trajectory, then so be it. But what counts is the moment when the cards fall, the present moment of acknowledging what is happening right then and there in the reading session as it unfolds. If a woman gets the message that it's time for her to leave her abusive marriage, if she herself can see that in the cards, then she'll do it, regardless of what the reader may predict. Therefore, ideally, a good reader in a reading session should be able to observe and do this: Look at the cards and nod. Look at the querent and say nothing. This gives space to the querent to look at the cards and nod, and then say 'thank you' and leave. The only thing that gets lost in this exchange may be the symbol. But we can live with that. A symbol is, after all, only valid as long as we, as a community, decide it is valid. In and of itself a symbol means nothing. Therefore, again, the most efficient reading method must be this one: to arrive at meaning through questioning, and based on the querent's own question, another set of questions must be posed: what is happening in the cards, and how do I feel about it? Following Enrique, my own advice to those who want to learn to read cards is this: interact with the image first. Look at its indexical quality: what does the image show you, what's happening? Then you can go with your gut. Again, meaning arises from description, not the other way around.

One of the other lessons that Enrique teaches us in respect to the art of divination is that we don't need elaborate spreads, or set positions for cards with predetermined meaning. The popular Celtic Cross is an example. While it may be useful to know where we come from, what's ahead of us, what opposes us, what others think of us, what we hope and what we fear, we don't need 10 cards to get the gist of a message. Enrique suggests that 3 random cards on the table in a line create enough dynamics. If you read dynamically, it's about seeing all relations as part of a larger web of interrelations. If you read structurally, you're in a grid. The first one is more useful as a whole, and you see the querent as coming from different positions all at once. The latter is only useful from a narrative point of view. In this view you have teleological aims contingent on temporal chronology. The Celtic Cross has a card designating the final outcome, telling you, 'here's where you'll get' – maybe. In a dynamic reading you have a crossing of aims. This enables you to see things from multiple points of view, and then swerve. Swerving is not only playful but also more 'authentic'.

In the context of divination, swerving, turning away from our preconditioning to culture and symbolic order, makes us aware of how to appreciate precision in reading visual texts, and redefine accuracy in terms of predicting events. As suggested above, by linking tarot to poetry we can see how reducing universals to their concrete manifestation opens the door to meaning as it arises in context. If the cards turn out to have a correctly anticipated outcome, then it will be because the cards are right on their own premise. In this view it is never the diviner who is right about everything, but the cards. However, handing agency over to some pieces of carton with illustrations on them is not something that most diviners are comfortable with. So, traditionally, we are still dealing with claims to knowledge (higher or meta-textual) that most cartomancers stick to. But conceptual card readers, such as Enrique and myself, see the problem with accuracy as lacking both objective and subjective ground. As far as I'm concerned, I even go so far as to claim that there is no such thing as accuracy. People don't come to a fortuneteller for an accurate answer to some issue, but 1) to hear what they want to hear; 2) to dread hearing what they don't want to hear, 3) to fear the worst and hope for the best. It is quite clear that most of the professional tarot readers that Enrique interviews in these volumes also share these ideas. In other words, people come to fortunetellers primarily for the magic of narrative. They come to us because the cards create certain situations. And these situations have little to do with 'what is really going on' – though, we can point to the numberless spreads that purport to look precisely at that (the Celtic Cross referred to above is one of them). In truth, however, very few people come to fortunetellers to hear the truth. They want their fortunes told because that's the only place where they can indulge their regimented curiosity.

For all the talk against questions such as, 'what does he think of me?' that some diviners express for ethical reasons, insofar as people come to fortunetellers to hear just that, we all indulge. This is not to say that people come to us when they are all fine and not vulnerable. Their (love) pain can be as true as the water in my glass right now. So we address that. But it will hardly be from the vantage point of our making claims to accuracy. I'm suspicious of any such claims. If the cards work, it will not be because we are accurate, but because they are. On this issue Enrique is at his most brilliant, as he shows great care of and concern with how to divine in the name of staying true to the tarot as a tool, rather than seeing it as a medium for channeling higher powers. And he manages to put that across without offending either the querents or the other fellow-diviners who might expect channeling or prediction, thus entertaining opposite views. For Enrique, the idea that there is more between heaven and earth must come from the interaction with the images of the tarot alone.

But the very idea of swerving as a poetical move is something that is even closer to Enrique's heart and core method. Divination *is* a poetical act, he reminds us, and demonstrates it too by way of questioning, by turning the image aside from lending itself to the traditional *straight* reading of the symbol. Swerving, for Enrique, is a way of translating one element into another. A cup can turn into a coin, a sword into a baton. We look at 3 cards and we can assert: the swords coin the cups – if we agree that we can see how swords, by virtue of their being similar to the same elements in a card next to them can turn into the very thing that the swords *tend* to (for instance, 4 swords can turn into 4 cups)[1]. This in itself is a poetical act. But what does it mean? This means that what we are looking to achieve is not only to understand the place the image takes us to, but also to participate in its creation. By looking at how the space of an image expands or contracts – everyone can see that it makes a difference to go from the card with 2 swords depicted on it to the one with 10 swords depicted on it – we get a clear sense of the tensions in play. For such an understanding we need no metaphysics. Enrique finds the beauty of the tarot precisely in such simplicity, in the experience of the element as it presents itself to us.

What comes across in Enrique's questions about Tarot de Marseille is the way in which he creates space for traditional ideas to meet new ones. It is a thing of marvel indeed to realize that in spite of the vast range of different voices gathered here, they are all attuned to Enrique's own authentic, honest, poetic and deconstructive voice. And what does it mean to be authentic here? To pose conceptual questions. To ask meta-questions, such as, what does it mean to *look* at an image? What does it mean to make a *gesture* to enter it? Feel it, smell it, touch it, see it from within and from without. I believe that one of Enrique's messages here is that to be authentic in your approach to reading an image is to be able to participate in its construction, to participate in its message rather than its meaning. Every time Enrique reads a card he reconstructs its history *as is*, not as a representation of what *might be*. He looks at the image as if for the first time.

This approach of participation is therefore also very honest. Enrique doesn't merely invent stories based on set phrases and meanings, but creates stories based on the way in which even the names of the cards participate in their message. Such an act of participation is also a way of playing with both word and image. Wordplays and puns link to each other. To find Love in the card of Le Fol, for example, is an act of creativity. Reading Le Fol backwards fast enough gives us a sense of love, reading it even faster gives us a sense of floating. In his book, *Tarology* (2011), a feast and a masterpiece on poetic tarot, Enrique gives us such countless examples of what it means to participate in the creation of beauty. For there is a lot of beauty in such observations. Lof el lov el lov el lov el lov el

---

[1] See also Enrique's fascinating demonstration of this in the last text of Volume Two of this series of conversations, in which Enrique is interviewed by Paul Nagy on his method.

lov el. Love is flying. There is a lot of dedication in the work of this type of deconstructing word and image. It's clear that it takes time to sit and ponder about how an image might sound, where it might take us if we turned it around, and what it might tell us if we let it surprise us.

The act of swerving is an act of storytelling. Interpreting a traditional tarot spread creates one kind of a story. Interpreting lines, frames, color, smell, and taste creates another kind of story. Entering the space of the image on its own terms is a shamanic act. One approaches it with modesty and respect. It is the question and the image that dictates the outcome. The task for the reader is to listen and let herself be guided by the image. Storytelling in tarot is most efficient when it's based on the context of a question. Card reading without a spread is the ultimate individual and creative act. A querent *is* what a querent *questions*. A card *is* what it *shows*. Here, however, I'm fascinated by the interplay between fact and fiction. Often people come to a tarot reader because they need clarity. So the premise for their question is often anchored in a blind spot, or some fictitious relation that the querent projects. I think that the best approach in such a case is to trust the cards and the question, not the querent. As D.H. Lawrence aptly put it: "Never trust the teller, trust the tale." The fact is that the cards fall on the table whichever way they fall, so there's a story right there already, and that is the most honest.

Generally speaking, are we influenced or affected by art, by images. Here I would have to emphasize again the act of participation. Art is a way of mirroring. And when we mirror ourselves in art we participate in how we can reflect ourselves in colors, the situations created by an image and the embodiments in the cards that can derail our sense of reality. Derailment is yet another of Enrique's key concepts. The mere fact that we can shuffle a deck, and let random cards create a story on the table, indicates that we can use tarot as a window to other alternatives. 'Now, why didn't I think of that!', most people often exclaim, whenever they are presented with the possibility of derailment. So, what begins as a fiction – cards telling a random story, such as Strength struggling with the Fool – can easily become a woman's reality: 'I'm going to go home and ditch the fool', some declare upon seeing how easy it is to put the hassle behind them. Thus, art, and the art of tarot *par excellence,* can give us a sense of how involved we want to be, first with ourselves and then with others. If we can play with our reflections we can also change things, and it is precisely for this reason that art is important. Art is like a gate into our higher or other selves.

Throughout these conversations, although Enrique stresses the importance of art, a form of spirituality emerges as well. Given also his poetical and philosophical inclinations, one can argue that he is already much more in touch with the creative powers of his unconscious than the average person. To me, one can't get more spiritual than that. When one makes creative leaps, one expands one's field of vision. One expands one's consciousness. I think Enrique communes with the spirits of the tarot in the best shamanic way, which is the way of drawing our attention to the fact that the universe is bigger than our minds and bigger than our physical brains. His contribution here is a most generous gift. But I also understand why, in places, Enrique resists being associated with spirituality. As spirituality needs a material body to manifest within, so there is an economy of exchange there. Economies are based on power relations, and power is easy to abuse. In other contexts of magical worlds people have learned ceremonies and rituals because this gave them power over others. When power is exercised without consideration, the first thing that goes out is the spiritual. The magicians contributing to these volumes know all about that. However, what we can all agree upon is that in order for divination to work, one would have to be opened to walking between worlds, the world of logical thinking and the world of analogical thinking. The two are not mutually exclusive. Being consciously between worlds makes us prone to reading signs. And reading signs is an interesting operation. It enriches our lives and makes us aware of what it means to relate to others. Tarot is indeed the instrument of negotiating with our desires.

Roskilde, November 2012

"Maybe everything has already been done. But you can twist something in a way no-one has yet twisted it. You can look at it upside-down and see if it takes you to a place where you haven't been before".

A conversation with VITO ACCONCI, designer, landscape architect, performance and installation artist.

So, tell me again, what are we doing here?

Let's have a conversation. But let's leave it to the cards to dictate what we talk about.

THE EMPEROR

This first card you drew is The Emperor. If we look at it we notice that he is all about keeping control. I am not just talking about the idea of an emperor as a representation of power, but about this character's body posture. He is sitting in a relaxed yet solemn way, as if pulling back from whoever is in front of him. He holds a scepter in his right hand, a symbol of power that often signifies a distance between the person who holds it and everyone else, but he is also holding his belt, or his pants, as if suggesting self-control. This is an interesting image to speculate about with regard to your work, and I wonder: how much space for chance is there in what you do? How much room do you make for the unexpected?

Those kind of initial schemes were probably totally controlled, totally about control. I mean, the performances always had a direction, they always started with a set of directions, but I will never plan what something was, visually. Those directions will then allow for... if I was doing a performance, I would know what to do, but I wouldn't know what people were going to do. I always saw my performances as a way of putting myself on the spot, so that I wouldn't be able to plan how I was going to react. I never knew what people were going to do. My attempt was to set up an occasion where I could deal with stage fright. I didn't know if I could do this. My performances were never repeated. That wouldn't make any sense. To repeat a performance would mean that the previous performance was a rehearsal.

That is interesting as The Emperor is all about projecting a sense of confidence that may very well not be real. That is at least how I see the difference between having one hand hold a scepter, that is, an object intended to be a symbol by means of its public exposure, while the other hand holding the pants, an intimate, self-composing gesture which becomes ridiculous when made public. So, in a way, that stage fright could have been there even if you were pretending that it wasn't.

Of course! Even in things that weren't so much performances. I did a number of photograph pieces at one time, but the photographs were an attempt to take a photo no so much of an event but to take a photo through an event. So, the method of the piece would be to hold a camera while going through the exercise of, say, touching my toes: reach my hands above me, snap photo one. Reach my hands down to my toes, snap photo two. So, I had no idea necessarily about what was I photographing. The desperate attempt was asking: could the combination of an activity and a place produce an image? I didn't care what the image was. No work I did was ever based on the final images, but on a method that would, of course, produce an image.

Your method was a structure and the end result was a piece that responded to the method but wasn't necessarily expected, just like this interview, or like a tarot reading.

Yes.

How does this method and the unexpected translate into your architecture?

When we plan a piece, when we plan a project, when we plan a space… It is interesting because I think it is easier to talk about this with regard to performances, but I think the same kind of activity is happening with the architecture.

I guess it is similar in that you don't start with the idea of a final shape in mind.

But we do start with a kind of method. We started to work on a project now, in Santiago de Chile, and the site we have is this kind of plaza in the middle of the city that has some particular meaning for people in Santiago, since it seems to separate the wealthier sections from poorer areas. It is a place where people gather in masses on a variety of occasions. It could be for an argument against the government, or it could be for a soccer team. Whenever people are gathering they now have some kind of power, and they block some streets around the plaza. So our starting point was that we like this idea of a crowd, but part of the problem with a crowd is: do crowds become unindividualized? Is there a way to make a crowd of individuals? We haven't figured out how to make it yet, but we are trying to make a space in which we take the whole plaza and we don't necessarily separate the people but we create different kinds of 'bubbles' for them. We don't know what these bubbles would be like yet, but as you are in the space you are part of a crowd, and yet you are also semi-contained in the space – contained is a strong word – with three people, or two people, but of course, as people move about, these associations change, so temporary cocoons are formed.

In a way it seems as if you are seeing the crowd as your sculpting material, and you are trying, as a sculptor would do, to impose an order on that material and articulate the details of that crowd, almost as if you were reminding each individual of himself.

Yes. As much as I want people to do things, I think that when you have people gathered in masses they are very easy to be lead, while if you have little groups of three or four, you make it harder for them to be lead.

XIII

There are several reasons I like this card. Although the Marseille tradition has it unnamed, we can see in it a typical depiction of Death: a skeleton with a scythe cropping life – or the living – from the land. The Grim Reaper. Death brings to mind the idea of putting an end to something or finishing things, and I wonder, when, or how, do you know that a project is finished? What is your relationship with that idea of endings? Poets say you never finish a poem, you just abandon it. Are deadlines your Grim Reaper?

Not necessarily. A deadline means that this is all we can do now, but we can always add something later. This is something we can do now because we have to submit a proposal, but there is always the possibility of adding something later. Second thoughts are very important to us. One of the best things about working with a group of people is that, although it is possible to say that four or five people may not think better than one, they certainly think more than one. Once you have people thinking more, there is almost no reason for it to end.

I remember something you said about how a project that starts individually dies alone, but a project that starts within a group always becomes something else.

It always becomes something else. It usually becomes something better, and when it doesn't become something better it is because one person is taking too much control, or the other people are giving up. Here we have been working together long enough. I often start a project off with a general method, but once we start working and designing together, things take a different shape. Everyone here is very computer apt, while I am obviously not. But after a while everybody here says that I think within the same kinds of rules a computer imposes, like a computer script. Even though we may not know where something came from, it always becomes something else. Maybe not completely different, but is has become expanded, it has become twisted, it has become... Maybe the initial idea came from me. It came from one person. I am better at general ideas, but I am not so great at details, I am not so great at specifics. I love specifics, but what thrills me about a project is that initial grasp at something. You know, when you are trying and trying and trying to feel your way around something. That's much more interesting to me than saying "O.K. Now that we think we have the general feel we need to think how to perfect it". I love the idea of perfecting but I don't know how to do it. I have no idea. So I probably don't like the idea of perfection. I love the idea of perfection with a crack. I like cracks. I like second thoughts. My first literary hero was Faulkner, very understandably because he had lots of trouble making a sentence end. Because a period is another version of Death. With a period you are ending something, so, you better be ready, you know? That's why Faulkner would add another subordinate clause, another parenthesis, you know... keep it going, because you really need to be ready to be as final as all that.

And what is Death to you?

Well, physical Death means something to me, you know. I don't want it (laughs) but then again, who does? I heard someone saying: "I really don't want to get old, but then, when I consider the alternative... getting old isn't so bad!" But yes, I think of death as a kind of final, final thing. Maybe that is why doing work is so important to me, why having some kind of possible influence is important.

In terms of the tarot, Jean-Michel David has pointed out that if we were to put the whole series of trumps in one straight line, Death would cut that line at its golden mean, which is a beautiful thing in terms of design. And of course, there is the idea of Death being an unavoidable step. Death as life's golden mean almost suggests that our whole life is structured around it. Within the tarot, if we were to speak from an iconographic point of view, there is an idea of transcending Death by means of an afterlife, which I understand is something you don't believe in.

No. I don't. I mean, I thought I did, once. I grew up as Catholic, and I went to a Catholic school for a very long time. This was my choice more than that of my family's choice, and I guess I felt I belonged there.

Yes, but now I feel you are talking more about understanding the immanence of Death as something that makes this moment, whatever transpires before Death, precious. I find that interesting because, if we put these two cards together, with The Emperor looking at Death, we get this idea of controlling certain processes, certain projects, as a way to fight Death through a different kind of transcendence, that of the influences that will keep going afterwards. That seems to be an important way to face Death, wouldn't you say?

Yes. What interests me in setting some kind of directions, some kind of rules, is that, if you really set the right kind of rules, you can make almost the opposite of an organized space. If you set the right kind of rules you can establish a kind of swarming, twisting space that you really don't know how to get around; and that is a kind of goal. My goal is that I want rules to take me to a place where I am turned upside-down, upside-down and inside-out. I hope a project will get us thinking: wow! how did we get here? Or how did we ever get in this mixture of 'heres'? Because when a project really works it is not so much that we are 'here' or 'there'. We are in different places at the same time. But I have never been able to get to a space like that. I have never been a proponent of drugs or drinks. I want to think as clearly as possible because thinking as clearly as possible can lead to some kind of rules, and suddenly you find yourself in a state where you can control the method, but not necessarily the state itself.

ACE OF COINS

Besides the 22 famous symbols everyone associates with the tarot, we have these other four symbols that we can anchor to four different kind of relationships: two of those are relationships of closeness, such as, when we do business with someone, as is the case with Coins, or when we celebrate with someone, as is the case with Cups. Wands and Swords suggest a distance with the other. Wands are scepters, symbols of power, like clubs. I actually made a little social experiment back when I was studying graphic design. I was 18 and I was starting to look into the tarot. I decided to spend a whole day walking around the city with a huge stick, like a club, and see what happens.

Of course, what happened was that people became aware of me from a distance: that distance was necessary for them to feel safe from me!

So, this is a scepter, and this is?

A Sword. Which is an even more confrontational symbol.

But it has a crown, like the crown of a king.

Yes, it is quite suggestive, because this is the Ace of Swords and the sword seems to be entering this crown. It is a beautiful image! It is tempting to see all the crowns in the tarot as representing the established mindset of the rational mind, right in place, controlling and limiting what 'it' is, like a helmet. The crown as symbol of whatever has been institutionalized. So, it is intriguing how this sword can be seen as scraping off whatever seems to be stuck inside that crown, or poking that crown, almost like a thought that doesn't want to leave us alone.

Is there any inherent connection between sword and crown?

Well, I guess that from a medieval point of view we can see the sword as a prerogative of the crowned heads. Peasants and common people had to manage with the club, or the stick. Only the wealthy can wield a sword.

Could it be the opposite? What if one wants to kill the father, or kill the king?

I guess it is an option, sometimes. Treason was one of the things crowned heads feared most. Now, the oldest text we know about the tarot was written by Francesco Piscina in 1565. In it he speaks of the connection between swords and severe punishment, saying that punishment can only be inflicted by the powerful. For an offense like betrayal, the powerful could even punish members of their own caste. I find it amusing that Piscina considers clubs 'softer' than swords.

Talk about the soft Death. What is a 'soft Death'?

Well, it is a very bizarre thing: being clubbed to death is more painful than being decapitated!

But I guess he is referring more to a reprimand, hitting someone with a club rather than actually making one's head soft by clubbing it! Of course, if you are very good at clubbing people you may very well need only one blow to get the job done! Which takes me to the idea of focus and back to the Ace of Coins. We can see it as the foundation of our material dealings with the world: a coin growing roots. So I feel inclined to ask: what is your relationship with money? How does that work? Because you are part of that generation, and I don't even know if 'generation' is the right word, or of that moment when some artists decided to use their tools in ways that no one had used them before. You were trained as a writer but you went on to do performance art, which was just emerging at the time. I am very interested in that abstract leap. It was certainly not a safe bet, and I can't imagine you did all these performances with the idea of becoming rich by doing them.

Well, at the same time, the Time was doing that. It seems everything was being overturned in the late '6os. There were demonstrations against the Vietnam war. It was a time when we really thought, for a long time, that there could be a revolution in the United States. It was this incredible time in which it seemed possible for a person, for one person, maybe not alone, but a person talking to another person, meeting with another person, to be instrumental in bringing down the government. And we had no choice. With Nixon there we had to bring the government down! And it is no mystery that the revolution started in universities, but in particular universities: Columbia, and Berkley on the West Coast; because these universities were built almost like city streets. They were built with a lot of intersections, so the intersections meant that inevitably one student will cross another student. Once you cross another student you start to have a conversation. Once you have a conversation you start to have an argument. Once you start to have an argument others start to gather around. It was an amazing thing. After that, it obviously wasn't a revolution, but it was something that happened all over the world: it was happening in Paris, all over the place, but the actual revolution didn't happen.

Yes, but somehow you, and those who were making art at that time, actually revolutionised the way art was made.

Well, yes.

But then again, you were taking pictures of yourself without concern for the actual visual result. I can't imagine you were actually aiming at selling a bunch of those pictures in a gallery.

No. One of the things that people of my generation reacted against was that idea of the 'artist's signature', you know? It is not that we hated De Kooning, but a 'De Kooning signature' seemed reprehensible in that it certainly separated those who could afford it from those who couldn't. I remember when in 1970 the Museum of Modern Art had a show called 'Information'. That was the first show – in the United States perhaps, but certainly in New York – that started to deal with conceptual art. I remember Dennis Oppenheim saying to me: "I wish they won't put names on that stuff. It isn't our names that are important". I think most of us felt that the Time was doing something, you know? What else could we do but use ourselves in our pieces? Because the language of the time was 'finding oneself'. We were doing what people were doing in music: Neil Young, Van Morrison... long songs... and, you know, maybe it wasn't an accident that it was a male voice. There were some females, but aside from Joni Mitchell and Carly Simon there weren't many others. So, it was basically the male voice that had the luxury to devote a seven minute song to the 'contemplation of 'self'. I mean, the '60s was a weird thing. On one hand there was a kind of escapism, and on the other it was "let's change the world", but also "let's escape from the ordinary, everyday world. We have to contemplate the Self". It was a strange combination of absolute sensuality and hippieness mixed with the monk.

This brings to mind something that takes me back to the Death card. I read somewhere that Allen Ginsberg, when he was taken to the hospital because he was dying, asked someone to bring him a book of Mother Goose rhymes.

Seriously?

Yes.

Well, he found his lost child in Death.

Indeed, his last poems feel very playful, they have a child-like sound. What do you think about that? Do you think that Death would bring up the child in you?

I wouldn't know. (Laughs). Actually, I would know. Two years ago I had heart surgery.

That's hardcore!

Yes. The last time I had been in a hospital was when I was a kid and I had my tonsils removed. I once went in for a hernia operation too, but that seems like candy store surgery now. My doctor told me I had a 99% chance of success and I thought: "O.K. but, how many people does he operate on every day? If he operates three patients a day he loses one patient a month!" I really thought that was it. Well…A hospital is not a place I particularly like to be in, but while in there I kept thinking that there is a person I have been with for a long time now. A person who is still with me. And I thought "Well, if this is it, at least it is good to know I was with this person. At least it is good to know I had love in my life". I think that thought helped me. Knowing that I have been with this person for so long and feeling grateful about it helped me.

THE HANGED MAN

This is quite an interesting image, one we can trace back to Italian shame paintings.

Shame?

Yes, shame. If you were accused of treason you would be hung by one foot, just like this. As a matter of fact, that is how they hung Mussolini just 'yesterday'. But if you managed to evade conviction, if you escaped, they would paint your portrait like this and post it all over town, so everyone would know you were a traitor.

So, that is an historical reading we can make of this image: see it as a form of punishment or torture. But, what do you find interesting about it?

What intrigued me is that he was looking at things upside-down.

Well, that is another reading we can make of it. I have to admit, this is all a misreading. The moment we decide to take up these cards, cards that were intended for a game of chance, and use them for divination, we are misreading them.

I like misreading. I think misreading is very important. By misreading something you create something else, you know? Misreading is what we do.

Exactly. I believe it was Omar Calabresse who said that Postmodernity was the result of people misreading Baudrillard!

Actually I didn't even notice he was hanging. I didn't even look at that rope. But I looked at his head, upside down, and I even wished he was standing on his head.

See? Here is something I have been discussing with people recently: the importance of going beyond information. We are obsessed with information, but information stays at a superficial level. When we can only go after the information in things we lose all kind of possibilities. If we look at a chair, if we look at an object only to confirm it, it is a chair and we leave it at that, we get nothing out of it.

Maybe you need to turn the chair upside-down. Maybe you need to sit on one of the chair's legs. Maybe you need to spin on the chair. By misreading it you can try to make something that hasn't been done before. Maybe everything has already been done. But you can twist something in a way no-one has yet twisted it. You can look at it upside-down and see if it takes you to a place where you haven't been before. That is what is important about any kind of… any kind of art production.

Perhaps misreading is what defines the job of the artist, and I am afraid this question will sound lame but I have to ask it anyway: what is Art to you?

Most of us… we have become disenchanted with what the art market has become… but the making of art… the making of some kind of artistic production… I wish sometimes that 'art' could be less of a noun and more of a verb. I can think of the books I read when I was young, the movies I watched. I remember when I saw *Last Year in Marienbad*. That initial scene in which there is a long corridor and the narrator's voice takes you into the movie… at the time, I thought of myself as a writer. I was an undergraduate. That opening scene taught me that, as a writer, people would follow me if I had the right voice, the right intonation. "This is what being a writer is" I thought. But even now I can see in that same scene that all architecture is about passing through space. When you look through a window you aren't in the space, but when you enter a space you aren't anywhere, you are passing through. So, I guess that movie is still teaching me things! (Laughs). Now that we are talking about movies, I have to talk about Godard. Godard had a great influence on me, you know? When I first watched his films… Godard was the one who said: "A story should have a beginning, a middle, and an end…but not necessarily in that order."

THE WORLD

I thought of picking this card. I like this character in the middle... it seems connected with all these angels and things... but I don't like this element. It makes me feel that this person is confined, isolated from the rest. I am not interested in confinement.

That is called a mandorla, after the Italian word for Almond. It is cool in that to make a mandorla you have to intersect two circles.

Ah! I see. But then I wonder, what happens if you intersect three circles, or four, or six?

I guess you create more and more confined spaces. But it is interesting to see this woman standing between two circles, between two realms. So, I wonder, how many realms does Vito Acconci inhabit? Is the studio space separated from the private space, or from the art space, or from the architecture space? How many mandorlas do you have in your life?

Hmmm... There was a Time... I often wondered, you know? I wonder from time to time... There is this person I have loved deeply. This person I love deeply... We have been together for a long time. We are still together. She is still with me. But I wonder sometimes, is the space this person shares with me... Did that prevent me from some sort of artistic production? All this time... Did it prevent me from creating something no one else ever did? Or has it helped me? Do I create in spite of this love? Can artistic production and personal life be separated? Should they be separated? Do I create because of this love? Has it helped me? I wonder about that sometimes, you know?

That was kind of a messed-up answer!

New York, February, 2010

"For a craftsman/artist, the more you make beauty, the more your soul is beautiful!"

A conversation with JEAN-CLAUDE FLORNOY, historian, artist, and restorer of the Marseille tarot

Let me start by asking what everyone in the tarot world is wondering: do you remember your first kiss?

Oh yes!

How did that first kiss compare to the moment in which you 'got' the tarot? I mean that moment in which the whole tarot suddenly made sense to you.

These are moments of exceptional intensity, rare in a lifetime and much alike. Suddenly the sky rips open and you are sent into a state of fusion with the surrounding world: it suddenly becomes meaningful and it is understood. You hallucinate, give thanks for the beauty of the world and fall head over heels in love with the tarot, or Britney Spears.

Now, you probably didn't marry the first girl you kissed, but you became a master card- maker. How did that come about?

First of all, on December 6, 1986, the day I experienced this moment of fusion, I started to write an autobiography. In my vision, all my life had recapitulated before my eyes to the rhythm of the tarot, in precise, quasi-surgical slices of life. So I wrote my experiences, while "remembering myself," according to the arcana. The basic link between experience and image, essential for the tarot, was accomplished. The rest was easy. "Remembering oneself" means to relive the past as an observing/observer, with the savor of the moment's energies. It is a "Madeleine of Proust". This book is finished, but I have given up on finalizing it.

At about the same time, I started doing readings using the deck I had stowed away when I was twenty. Each arcane is a graphic programming of a "place of consciousness", or as Castaneda might have said, a precise "assemblage point". So, when my visitor drew the Lover card, I could break into the tears of a 16 year old. If Force was turned up, I felt again the ambition of my 30 years. I was in sympathy (in the Greek etymological sense: suffer with) my visitor, and it was therefore very easy for me to evoke and transmit the energetic quality needed for finding a way out of her existential crisis.

Then, in 1995 a Parisian theatre commissioned me to make a scenery using the 22 majors of the Marteau tarot. Each measured 2.50 x 1.20 m. The theatre had financed the materials and I had got as far as Temperance when the production was cancelled. I was left with my work and a surfeit of the Grimaud tarot. It was then that I began a serious historical study, painted my canvases white and started over with the Conver. I enjoyed the work very much, and the year and one-half immersion changed me. Among other things, I was able to observe the incredible operativity these images exercise in such formats. Then I took on the first 8 majors of the Noblet. Since the ektachromes for the others wouldn't be available from the Bibliothèque Nationale for a year, I did the Dodal majors and then went back to finishing the Noblet. In the course of these projects, four completely "unusual" Viéville (XVI, XVII, XVIII, XIX) were also produced in large formats.

You have given us restored versions of the Noblet and the Dodal, first in limited, hand-stencilled editions and now in full, mass-printed versions. I know how important it is for you to preserve the correctness of the original decks, but how much of you do you think there is in these decks?

The minimum! I see none in the Noblet. And a little in the Dodal: the reversible back, still a debated question, and two errors in color placement: one accidental (on The Moon), the other deliberate (The Sun). Of course, an industrial edition requires that the card dimensions be standardized. The original inner-frame dimensions vary by 2mm in height and by 1mm in width. I chose the the maximum height as reference. Around this is a 1mm black frame and then an outer band of 3mm. This last space is imposed by the printer for technical reasons, and is not determined by whether the corners are to be square or round.

In your reconstruction of the Dodal you had access to the two only existing originals: the one at the Bibliothèque Nationale in Paris, and the other at the British Museum. Did you work with both of these decks?

Yes.

What differences did you find between the two?

First of all, the colors on the English copy are in better condition, but soiled and dull. The English print is more charged with ink, as well. Then, three cards come from another, probably earlier block: the Ace of Batons, Ace of Swords, and the **Valet of Batons.** For our edition of the Dodal, the choice was made according to which card was more carefully engraved. The English copy was selected for the Ace of Swords, while the French deck was retained for the two others.

How is it technically possible that three cards came from a different block?

The stocks! At that time, people didn't hesitate to re-compose complete decks from disparate sources, even using decks from diverse workshops. Worse, they were often re-cut. We will probably never know if the tarot moulds controlled by the office of the *Généralité de Lyon* marked *«français pour l'étrange»* ("French for export") were included or not in the royal destruction edict of 1701. We only know that Dodal began a new production in that year. In those days, little was wasted: everything was used and re-used. So, leftovers from an earlier edition could have been used in another.

As for the inscription "F.P. LE.ETRANGE", T. Depaulis suggests it could mean either "Franc pour L'Etranger" or "Fait pour l'Etranger", both appellations exonerating, from French taxes, decks destined for export. Could Dodal have added an 'i' to his name in order to promote the sale of his decks in Italy?

How long did it take you to finish this re-construction?

More than two years.

How long do you think it could have taken for the original engraver to create these plates?

I would imagine a maximum of two to three months, but I'm not sure.

I often wonder how much care was really put in the manufacturing of these decks. What is your feeling about that?

The engraver as free and independent person always worked as cleanly and conscientiously as possible.* In the workshops, printing the black line was mostly carried out by highly qualified professionals. Colors, however, were often put on negligently, sometimes by children in deplorable conditions. I have read in the Sainte-Suzanne archives that in 1792 the local carterie started stencil work at midnight, employing children who applied the colors by candlelight.

When printing your version of this deck, you had to settle for a color palette. Would you say that the final result is closer to the French or to the British deck?

Closer to the French.

I find a strong graphic resemblance between any of the Dodal images and the images in the Noblet. I am talking about the posture of the characters. This is especially clear in the court cards: Pages, Queens, Kings and Knights. The Dodal knights seem like loose versions of the Noblet's horsemen. Do you think that it is possible that the Dodal was made by copying from the Noblet?

No, the graphic style and significant details are too dissimilar. They draw the same thing, the same theme, but each has his own personal style. On the other hand, one can use the word copy for the later tarots made in Marseille from about 1720/30. As elsewhere, there is no more re-actualization.

When I showed the restored Dodal to a couple of people their reaction was "So... it is the same deck you already have, only bigger, right?" In a way I understand what they are seeing, but at the same time I think they are missing the point. In your view, why was that restoring the Dodal made sense? What are people going to get from it that they won't get from the Noblet?

The Dodal generates a flash, or energetic short-circuit of the unconscious, different from that of the Noblet. A tarot image opens a door, and the landscape behind it is different depending on the door. As I mentioned before, the image is a programming of a "place of consciousness", the precise assemblage point of a particular inner regard. Depending on the arcane and the engraver, they resemble each other a bit, much, or not at all. It's like a chocolate Charlotte made by two chefs: one will be sweeter, the other juicier.

Tell me a little bit about the term 'companion'. Is that a term you use to define all medieval guilds, or do you mean something else by it?

The "companions" entered into a "Compagnonnage" fraternity in the same way one joins a religion or the Communist Party. Work was organized in the modern way, almost as a trade-union would, with sectors devoted to mutual aid, recruitment or intense in-house techno-spiritual training. As a craftsman you must have manual skill and a highly-developed feeling for materials, but also practice, all at the same time, and in addtition to 6 other basic traditional qualities: courage, patience, generosity, humility, obedience and a sense of responsibility. With time and application these 6 qualities progress together with one's skill.

But what was it that these fraternities were asked to build? Athanors, alchemical crucibles: collective trance machines intended to transform a whole population and carry it to God! We are in the realm of technological shamanism! So the "companions" within "Compagnonnage" on their building sites, whatever their trade (mason, stone mason, carpenter, sculptor, glass-maker) are part, whether they know it or not, of a permanent school of wizard/technicians worthy of Harry Potter. The companion becomes Master when he *knows* he is one. We are a far cry from the later guilds which only served to structure the privileges of professional castes.

I was talking to a woman who has restored a few Thangka paintings from the 12th Century. We were talking about how there is an underlying visual knowledge in a Thangka painting that we can also find in the stained-glass windows of a European cathedral, or the illustrations in a Medieval manuscript. I am talking about an understanding of shape, namely, that it is also an understanding of how to use shape to move the human spirit. At a technical level, a Tibetan artist and an European draughtsman knew the same things, which they just applied to different belief systems.

Exactly!

In your text accompanying your restorations you wrote "the wisdom underling the tarot is a pragmatic professional philosophy". Are you talking about that same knowledge?

Yes, but not only that. There is also the idea of progressive improvement in which work and the spiritual world are inseparable. For a craftsman/artist, the more you make beauty (the beautiful is operative, direct like a punch, it creates an astonished destabilization and opens the doors to paradise), the more your soul is beautiful!

How would you describe the "operative science" you see in the tarot?

Operativity is what the apprentice is learning to acquire. For the image-maker in a sacred period it is a question of using an image to program the unconscious to a precise meditation. The state it focuses on, the arcane under consideration, is defined by graphics and above all by colors. Thangkas and the tarot function on the same operative level. Whether we like it or not, colors manipulate us. The art is to consciously distribute them in a meaningful way.

Now, mandalas invite our mind to take a spiritual/psychological voyage. Would you say the tarot does the same thing?

Yes.

In this case, do you think the tarot intends to take us all to a specific place?

Yes, it it has been doing that discreetly for centuries. It would seem that today there are still amateurs for this variety of shamanism, and a very modern one it is. The source tarots behave like a GPS. They all lead us to the same place, but for some it will be springtime in a crowd while others will experience loneliness and winter. The tarot is above all experimental, so I have often chosen to use the word psychonaut (or tarotnaut!) to indicate this "spiritual-psychological voyager". Aren't we all sailors on the ocean of the soul?

There is an idea, behind contemporary art, about taking our mind for an illicit spin.

"Art" and "illicit": these words remind me of the interminable and highly Parisian discussions I participated in when I studied philosophy in university. "Illicit" seems to stand for the courage, which would like to see itself as exceptional, to accept crossing the barriers of conventional regard, and to let oneself be carried on towards an unknown. Illicit, in my opinion, simply means "random". The GPS precision is lost, and one is tossed about wherever the emotional winds choose to carry us. I fear that with contemporary art we are certainly operative, but like a crazy compass!

Materials and symbols have an experiential meaning, –

Meaning isn't exactly the right word; power would be more appropriate.

– but although each artwork would set some collective coordinates to start our trip, the arriving point is both individual and unexpected. How do you see that happening with the tarot?

With the tarot we approach precise states of consciousness, valid for all and validated by many generations. This is not the case with highly egocentric and anarchistic contemporary art. As long as we are discovering a territory, the landscape varies according to the seasons, to our position, our mood and the taste of our first kiss. It is a permanent innovation in perpetual motion. The goal of the tarot is to indicate an itinerary of the soul, undertaken one foot in front of the other, and not to toss us about on the tides of emotion.

In your writings I detect a notion that interests me a lot, but I would say it has been more developed in the Eastern world than in the Western world: any craft can be a spiritual path.

Yes, but let us not forget that culturally we are descended from a quadripartite system of social organization :

> Producers : artisans/peasants: batons
> Merchants: shopkeepers/financiers: coins
> Warriors: aristocrats/soldiers: swords
> Savants: doctors/priests: cups

The tarot is its reflection. What fundamental difference can we perceive between the castes of the Hindu orient and the "colleges" of the occident? None on a theoretical level, more with respect to action. What characterizes a fraternity of the Middle Ages is the recognition by one's peers, through ritual and ceremonies, of a progress towards excellence, as much technical as (we would now say) shamanistic or spiritually operative. Modern western Sufism comes closest to this genre today.

When you say, for example, that The Star card shows an eye in the belly of the woman as an allusion to the stone cutters' "eye of the master", their ability to feel the stone and know how to place it, are you talking about a craftsman's ability to intuitively understand the nature and limitations of the material he is working with?

Still more, to feel them physically! In the course of an apprenticeship comes a moment when you are taught how to place your attention, both in the here and now (seeing the instant as it occurs; letting it happen while observing it) and in a particular corporal sensation, a sort of attraction/repulsion, related to the sense of the stone. This trick is useful to a craftsman, but the essential thing is learning to attain a state of observing/observer. One can also call this state "second attention", and its automatic practice is what makes you a master.

I would think of Jackson Pollock, and how he understood painting to such an extent that he could take it beyond the limits of representation.

He seems to go beyond symbol or meaning and speak directly to the unconscious. All depends on what he has to tell it!

Pollock is an interesting example in that some physicists have now established that all of his paintings follow a fractal structure. He seemed to have painted in tune with the rhythm of nature, and as such one could see his action painting as the by-product of some sort of spiritual momentum.

The golden section had this function. To me, certain modern artists seem to have gained the worlds of operativity by breaking and entering, in an illicit way, loaded down with a whole pack of more or less convoluted, neurotic and egotistical material. Others open the Doors of Paradise for us.

But I am also thinking about Chang Canasta, a magician who devoted the last decades of his life to painting. When he was asked why, he answered: "I believe in something called talent. Once you have it, you can apply it to everything."

Idries Shah named this "learning how to learn". Once you've learned how to learn, in 6 months to a year you can achieve excellence in a profession previously unknown to you. He went on to say that in a well-filled life it was necessary to have practiced at least 6 trades at the highest level! Serghiu Celebidache was a celebrated orchestra conductor and a respected mathematician and rug expert and pheasant breeder and an exceptional linguist speaking 7 languages...

Talent here is, again, an understanding of form, rhythm and pattern that a man like Canasta could use to present a card trick or to paint a landscape. As soon as we understand proportion, balance, symmetry and contrast, we can apply that knowl-

edge to all areas of our experience. Is it that the tarot intends to teach us, beyond the iconographic choice of imagery: mastering your craft is mastering yourself?

You have perfectly summarised the mission of the tarot. It goes even further: 'mastering yourself' in order to participate in the Soul of the World.

You also mention in your text that "All master engravers during the second half of the 17th century were instructed in the inner meaning of the tarot – Mermé is their last representative." How do you relate that affirmation to the idea of the Dodal, being the last tarot that was consciously permeated by the companions' intention?

It is the flame of *La Maison-Dieu* which induces me to say that.

The tarot emerged from a Platonic-type mental world of philosophical immanence: the individual can, by his own achievements, put himself in a position to join the worlds of the Spirit. The flame is thus ascending, and to my knowledge Dodal's is the last tarot to depict it in this way. All the other significant details confirm how well-understood the "pilgrimage of the soul" was, and how at that time the procedures of transmission were fully-functioning and conscious.

Later, the flame billows down from above, raising the question of divine grace and its intercessors: we are in a philosophy of the Aristotelian type. The inner meaning is lost; what remains is reduced to recollection and hearsay. The same applies to the other meaningful details. At best one installs them by copying, while at worst "fantasy" takes over. The engraver of Nicolas Conver went so far as to settle his accounts with nascent freemasonry by placing 3 dots on the chest of the Devil: freemasonry is a she-devil! These mid-eighteenth century quarrels mean nothing to us today. Respect for a tradition vanishes, the overall consciousness of a civilization shifts and the pre-industrial era dawns.

Dodal furnishes only meaningful details and signs with the Master's chrism. Resembling a stylized 4, this figure evokes measuring instruments and has been the prerogative of image-makers, carpenters and stonemasons since the Middle Ages.

I am asking you this because I am not familiar with the companions' tradition, but I am familiar with what I would call the 'Marseille Lore'. To me, this lore consists of a series of footnotes added to certain images, without their necessarily being in accord with the image's original iconographic intention. I take that lore to be a funda-

mental part of the Marseille tradition, and by tradition I mean the narrative/divination use we made of these cards. To mention a couple of these footnotes, there is the idea that The Fool is the card without a number and Death is the card without a name; so when you overlap both, Death becomes The Fool's skeleton.

If I remember correctly, it is to Tchalaï that we owe this idea. That lore is the reason Jodorowsky said, in a preface to his first deck edition or in one of his books, that having been raised on classic Marseille lore (Grimaud), "killing the father" was the condition on which he could produce his deck. Numerous bad "good habits" had been acquired because this was the only historic deck on the market. Along the same lines, there is Tchalaï's fine discourse concerning the comma on Force's hat. But this comma was the result of damage to the woodblock!

When I began work on the Conver, after having painted over the Marteau images, I underwent the same temptation: make my own deck. For example, at first I painted the figures in Soleil naked, then put on vines with green leaves...then became annoyed with myself and dressed them back in their shorts! When Jodo liberated himself from the Marseille/Grimaud lore, he went into an egotistical creation frenzy. Considering his talents, this choice was regrettable.

There is also the idea of the person who is emerging from the grave in Judgement being, graphically at least, composed of two halves of two visibly different persons, or the idea of The Hermit containing a visual pun in that a man who looks at his lantern blinds himself instead of finding anything.

This pun is part of the essence itself of the Hermit. But within this lore, some details are significant, like this androgynous figure in Jugement, or the Hermit's cane which resembles a spine, while others are not.

Your book is full of these great "narrative spells". I call them 'narrative spells' because they are these little stories that validate a detail in a card, but at the same time they get validated by that same detail, in some sort of symbiotic loop; but these little tales don't seem to amount to a coherent code that one can use to read through the whole sequence, –

These stories are there to bring into relief a particular perceptive state, explain certain experiences, or highlight a detail. They don't add up together, and are indeed like footnotes.

– but I am a little bit septical of their historical validity.

You are right to be sceptical. Certain stories come from my own stock of experiences and I can validate them, while others are visions drawn from the memory of the world. These are from time to time corroborated by other people in strange ways. For example, I received a mail explaining that the "caterpillar trance" was an exercise practised in simplified form by people studying phosphenism.

For one thing, these descriptions can't be found in books. They spread by word of mouth, it seems. So, what I want to know is, what is your take on that lore?

For the last 150 years, and it is barely older than that, this Lore has been fed at best by visions, at worst by the analyses and pronouncements of its spokesmen. The word-of-mouth transmissions have been interrupted for centuries. Only the world's memory remains, that strange source phenomenon which is the tarot's gift to its faithful enthusiasts. The memory of Jean Noblet or Jean Dodal is present still, and the path has been cleared of underbrush. These ancient masters can still flood you with their spirituality. It is for us to make contact. The stories issued from the world's memory have an incomparable savour, leading you into a consciousness where doubt doesn't exist. Here direct transmission comes into play; it is the storyteller's talent. As a tarot reader, you often enter into visions and know how to share them. You already exercise this talent.

It is that lore part of the message from the companions, –

Yes, direct transmission was part of the Compagnons' teaching in times past. Today the younger generation is thirsty for stories, as it is these that transmit. In any case, what choice do they have? There is no longer any techno-spiritual instruction available through a profession.

– or is that an embellishment on the way we describe the images that happened later? Do you think that such lore may have influenced the way the images were drawn?

Significant details were transmitted and utilized. The other details, those nourishing the lore, are late and intellectual, mostly dating from the middle of the 19th century.

I like that lore a lot. In fact, at some point I mentioned to Roxanne, your wife, that one of the reasons why I enjoy working with the Dodal more than working with the Noblet is precisely because many of these footnotes can't be seen in the Noblet.

Noblet is a bit dry, and close-fisted with details, while Dodal's engraver is savory, his details are numerous and imaginative! Compare their versions of the lady in the *Star*: Noblet made her half adolescent/half man to illustrate the virginal-purity/force-maturity of the master, a very strict and masculine definition of the canon. Dodal makes her pregnant to emphasize the transmission of essentials, and gives her a double regard to signify that she understands from within and without — a very supple and feminine description of mastery.

This leads to my next question: you make a distinction between the Noblet, the Dodal, the Viéville, and the rest of the decks within the Marseille tradition. For you the Dodal is the last deck within the Marseille tradition in which some details were purposefully added.

Yes.

Now, for the untrained eye, like mine, when it comes to certain details the Dodal, it is more similar to the Conver than to the Noblet. The Noblet seems to be the odd one.

That is exact, and I feel the same way. I think the answer has mostly been covered: it is the "Marseille lore". Noblet undoubtedly is part of it, but from afar and in a strange way. He gives the impression of being an ancestor from another planet! One sees that the basic teaching is the same, but the two seem not to have had the same professor.

How do you manage to see such distinction between the Dodal and the following decks so clearly?

Dodal's engraver knows what he's talking about from experience, or transmission, or (as I believe) both. After him, one speaks of things because, at best, one has heard them spoken of. It is hearsay: my cousin told me that his brother had heard this or that... As long as the engraver has not lived the inner process of transformation to mastery, he doesn't know what he's talking about, and can only copy. With Noblet and Dodal, we are in the same world, but not with Conver and even less with those who follow him. We know their mental world by heart, and let me say we are very glad to be rid of them.

Finally, I wouldn't like to end this interview without knowing: what will be next? I imagine that right now you and Roxanne may be feeling ready to rest a little bit and rejoice in the enormous accomplishment you have made but, what will you do when you get restless again? What is next?

Viéville, if I manage to extract myself from the historian's quandary I'm mired in. I am convinced that this tarot was made "as mirror" by necessity, by an impossibility to do otherwise, and not to confer a particular meaning. Furthermore, why perturb and confuse the coming generations with all these images conforming to the Marseille pattern, but reversed? As for the 4 or 5 unusual arcana, they alone justify the effort. These 'exceptions' confirm the rule and are the major interest of this tarot. The question deserves reflection by the community of historians and enthusiasts. So yes, I would like to edit the Viéville in the classic Marseille order and direction. This would indeed be an illicit act. Will I have the courage to deliver myself up to massacre by the purists?**

New-York / Sainte-Suzanne, February 2010

---

* "An engraver of 25 years named CLAUDE MERME born at CHAMBERY to the family of a Master Card-maker of CHAMBÉRY (His father was JOSEPH MERME) declared at the time of his marriage (which took place on April 3, 1714); to have worked for JEAN & JEAN PIERRE PAYEN in AVIGNON. He declared to have also worked for another Master Card-maker JEAN-JOSEPH REVEST at CARPENTRAS. At the date of his marriage, he worked for another Master Card-maker from AVIGNON, ÉTIENNE BLATEROND. JEAN PIERRE PAYEN and BLATEROND confirmed his declarations on that day."[1]

** Unfortunately Flornoy did not live to realize his last project, the reconstruction of the Viéville tarot. He died on May 24, 2011. We honor his memory and are grateful for his work and legacy, which has been taken up by his wife, Roxanne. So we are actually fortunate that she completed this project, and presented us this year with a beautiful Viéville reconstruction, which is also available for purchase from their website (C. Elias).

---

1 Archives Départementales du Vaucluse. Étude Charrasse.
  Posted by Yves le Marseillais here: http://traditiontarot.com/forum/viewtopic.php?id=110

"The confusion between a historical poem and contemporary poesis is, of course, a central problem."

A conversation with MICHAEL J. HURST, tarot scholar

There is a quote from Louise Bourgeois I want to share with you. I like it a lot, as I have been working on my intro for the event I will be doing on March 10th, and something I am interested on stressing is precisely the trans-verbal nature of the tarot:

> You cannot fool me in the visual world, but you can take the better of me in the verbal world.

So we're talking about a difference of opinion and the fear of being put down. That antagonistic framework is interesting, but it is not clear what the choice pertains to.

What are we doing via words or pictures?

I think Bourgeois's phrase says a lot about iconography vs. wishful thinking!

I think you are right, although I hadn't quite thought of it that way before. It's a different take on Tedesco's "truths" versus "facts" line, both of which seem to be stating a preference for subjective versus objective approaches, although making the arguments in very different ways.

On that topic, I want to share a couple of more examples that came to mind. In both cases, words (facts) got the better of me, but in what I take to be a good sense. The first (which I'm pretty sure I've told you before, but I've lost my email archives) is from eight years ago, in early 2002. *The Tarot Journal* was still being published and I had written a deck review for the *Templar Tarot*. In that review I analyzed one card in detail.

"An outstanding example of the way in which the artist blended themes to create a unique and fascinating Tarot card is the High Priestess. The booklet identifies the figure as Mary Magdalene. That identification neatly connects some common themes of the HBHG (Holy Blood Holy Grail) literature to Tarot. The

Magdalene is often considered the "Apostle to the Apostles" and Jesus' successor to leadership of the mystery cult that was allegedly at the heart of his true teachings (6). This makes her, rather than Saint Peter, the first "pope," which corresponds with the historical title of the card, the Papess, and justifies the occultists' gift to her of the Keys (7-8). This association with the secret teachings of Jesus can also be easily (perhaps even appropriately) related to Arthur Waite's description of the card as "the Secret Church,"(9) a connection which is alluded to in the Templar Tarot booklet.

The High Priestess shows the figure of Mary Magdalene in front of a large cross, a conventional emblem of Faith. (A small cross was a common attribute of the Penitent Magdalene iconography.) Also behind her is a large anchor, another ancient Christian symbol and an emblem of Hope derived from Hebrews 6: 19.(10). (The cross and anchor, representing Faith and Hope, take the place of the High Priestess' conventional two pillars (11), and the Temple veil has become a fisherman's net (12), draped to suggest wings, or the letter "M".) (13). Mary's pose and ornate circular halo are reminiscent of a Madonna (14), a conventional allegory of Charity or Love, thus completing Saint Paul's trio of Christian Virtues (15). The artist has arranged conventional Christian symbols into a design expressing a conventional Christian motif. On this level, it seems to be a Magdalene Madonna, which links the card to the Magdalene legend of the Black Madonnas (16).

However, a Madonna design implies a baby Jesus, which is absent. Instead of a new life held to her breast, Mary cradles a skull, an emblem of death. The skull, as a memento mori, was a conventional attribute of penitent saints including Mary Magdalene. (Another common attribute of the Penitent Magdalene iconography was an open book. For some reason, this conventional attribute of both the Magdalene and the High Priestess card was not included.) With its biblical connection to the place of Jesus' death, ("Golgotha" is the Greek version of the Aramaic *gulgalta*, meaning "skull," while "Calvary" is from the Latin *calvarius*, meaning "bald skull") (17), the skull suggests another interpretation. Instead of a Magdalene Madonna, we see a Magdalene Pieta. (In fact, the face and the attitude of the head of the High Priestess figure are similar to those of Michelangelo's sculpture, even with the figure's headband mimicking a band across the forehead of this most famous Pieta.) The conventional image of the body of Christ, taken down from the cross and lying in the lap of his mother Mary, has been replaced with a symbol of the dead Christ in the lap of his (now gray-haired) widow Mary (18).

This identification of the implied infant Jesus in the arms of his mother Mary, (which would complete a traditional motif of the three Christian Virtues), with the actual image of a skull in the lap of Mary Magdalene, is in the best tradition of Renaissance symbolism (19). It offers varied avenues of comparison and contrast, (particularly via the association of Love and Death), inviting reflection on a variety of profound themes, complex and subtle relationships. It does this while remaining focused on the central theme of the deck, the contemporary "tradition" of Templar-related legends within the context of Tarot.

One other noteworthy symbol on the High Priestess card is a nautilus shell. The nautilus takes its name from the Greek word for sailor, nautilos. According to legend, Mary and a group of persecuted Christians were set adrift in the Mediterranean, and "saved by a favorable wind" that took them to Marseilles (20). Saint Ambrose compared the Church to a ship, with the Cross as its mast (21). The background of the card suggests an enormous wave, from which Mary is shielded by the Cross. An example of a modern Christian use of the sailor reference comes from Leonard Cohen's 1968 song, Suzanne.

> Jesus was a sailor when he walked upon the water; And he spent a long time watching from a lonely wooden tower; And when he knew for certain only drowning men could see him, He said, 'All men shall be sailors then, until the sea shall free them.'

An outstanding analysis of a brilliantly designed card, I was sure. I pointed out that most of the deck was not nearly so coherent and systematically suggestive, but I really thought that some parts were carefully designed. After publication I had the opportunity to talk to the artist. He never designed anything in his life with that kind of analytical content! I was completely mistaken – he just liked the bits and pieces without knowing their history or how they might work together.

Words or facts, an authoritative "you're wrong", got the better of me.

That only shows that the artist is a moron. You cannot make images and use symbols while being unaware of what they mean. That is naive, at best, and basically unprofessional.

The second brilliant analysis/blunder is from last week. It follows much the same pattern even though the initial misreading was of a text rather than a picture. The text was in a language which I don't read, so my "reading" was actually speculative reconstruction, and schematic, at best. Like reading a picture, I could identify parts of the work and I could associate some external parallels with those parts to interpret the passage. Like my *Templar Tarot blunder*, the passage was partly about the Popess, one of the most inherently ambiguous subjects in the deck. As with the Templar Tarot, the part which I selected for analysis seemed incongruously analytical compared to the scatterbrained blather of the larger work and, although mentioning that warning in both cases, I ultimately dismissed it in both cases. And as with the Templar Tarot example, I was naturally quite pleased with myself for a successful effort. You can read it for yourself – I appended it to an earlier post about female allegories with papal attributes, along with a correction (and justification for leaving it online) that Marco was kind enough to provide.[1]

In the second example, I had the entire known world of pictorial Popess examples on my side – literally all the pictures in the world. There has never been, as far as I know, an image of a papal consort shown enthroned with papal attributes such as tiara and keys. And yet, the words (facts) got the better of me again.

Both the "truths versus facts" and the "pictures versus words" seem to be good ways to look at aspects of the larger problem/benefit of Tarot's inherently nebulous meaning. Having chewed on the line a bit, I agree with you that Bourgeois' (great name) statement says a lot about the difference between subjective "wishful thinking" versus more objective iconography. However, with regard to my own characterization of the "trans-verbal nature of Tarot", I would reach for an older psychological framework. The trumps, to the extent that they are detached from their historical moorings, are adrift in a sea of acculturated meaning and motivated arbitrarily by the winds of personal projection.

Moreover, as indicated by the variety of early decks and orderings and by appropriati, including the Invective of Lollio and Imperiali's *Rejoinder*, this has been the

---

1   Pre-Tarot Images of Pope Joan
    http://pre-gebelin.blogspot.com/2009/03/pre-tarot-images-of-pope-joan.html

case from the very beginning of Tarot's voyage. And that view coincides with what I've often argued, that the meanings that I seek – explanatory or intended meaning of each deck's designer – would be incidental trivia even if it could be compellingly established. Historical meaning was binding on no one, ever. *Homo Narrans*, telling the best story he can, comes up with something a bit different in each telling. Each person made of Tarot what they wanted, just as did the 18th-century Freemasons and fortune-tellers. That's why I've never cared about the pseudo-historian's dodge, "what would a 15th-century cardplayer (or magi, etc.) have read into the trumps?" That is a dodge because it is used as an excuse to impose a preferred modern interpretation, a subjective imagining of a subjective imagining. How profoundly self-indulgent is that project?

I want to know the very thing that no one else cared about, what the designer was thinking. The Bourgeois quote characterizes this interaction of one person fooling another, on the assumption that one's subjective take on pictures – which is unarguable except via words – is essentially valid in some way that transcends the objectively argued take on the pictures. The subjective should, for some reason and in some way, triumph over the objective.

What makes me such a misfit in the Tarot community is that I've never had my own take. I privilege external facts over any "truths" I might prefer, which is why I simply change "my own" view whenever it is pointed out to me, convincingly via evidence and argument, that I'm wrong. So "my view" is really a composite of other people's views (the views of scholars) on Tarot and on related works of art and literature.

Yes, but there is something else in your take. You are interested in the objective intentions of the designer. (Perhaps the word designer is key here). Not in the designer's state of mind.

It is difficult to pinpoint. If you say "focus on the text, not the author", then you are already in the Postmodern morass of relativistic readings. If you say, "authorial intent" or the (usually ironic) "author's message", then you have the mind-reading problem. If you attempt to articulate it as precisely as possible, it gets messy. It's something like "the author's message as best it can be reconstructed via the most objective study of the text and relevant historical context," which leaves everything very slippery. But that is, unfortunately, the project.

I have lots of problems with anybody who argues that every single Marseille deck conceals a different intention: "This eye, a little bit bigger in the Conver than in the Noblet, is talking about a different thing..." I simply don't see it. But I can see how the whole 'family' of decks has a definite intention.

That's a big point. That is absolutely an occultist point of view, regardless of the specifics that are imputed.

Even the notion that every family of decks must have a coherent meaning is not a plausible *a priori* assumption. It has to be demonstrated, and that has to be done essentially the same way the Church argued that doctrine could only be argued from the literal/historical sense of Scripture. It's not that the other senses are not legitimate; they just aren't legitimate for that purpose.

It is like the commentaries on Petrarch's *Trionfi*. Love, Chastity, Death, Fame, Time, and Eternity is a really weak cycle to match with an Ages of Man paradigm. Only the first half is technically an Ages of Man parallel, so it becomes a psychological parallel. In middle age one thinks about Death and Fame, while in old age one thinks about the *ubi sunt* and Christian view of life. These allegorical readings of Petrarch's triumphs were not only longer than the poem itself, but – like the iconographic tradition of the Trionfi – actually a separate work of art/literature that was only loosely tethered to the original. These are how people knew Petrarch's poem, but if you REALLY want to know the poem you have to read Petrarch himself, going back to the literal sense of his work, his actual words.

Now let me contradict myself. I believe I can read points of confusion in the mind of whomever carved the Dodal. There are several 'moments', details in each image that are completely abstract. Those abstractions, made in a moment when going beyond representation wasn't an option, show a confused mind that didn't know what it was copying.

That is another crucial point, the textual criticism approach to sussing out lines of transmission. We have very few (relatively) early TdM (Tarot de Marseille) decks and only two of them, Chosson and Noblet, seem to have any claim to being a close descendant of what came from Milan in the 15th century. We know that Tarot went from Milan to France in the 1400s; from the Cary Sheet and the Sforza Castle Two of Coins we know that it was pretty much like TdM in some form or other; it appears that the only big changes made by the French were the addition of the border frames and the names. The fact that a number of the TdM trump figures either overlap the borders or are cut off by them is a clear indication that these are direct descendants of a deck without those borders and names.

Noblet's claim to Italian origin is based primarily on the two Sforza Castle trumps, dated to about the same period as Chosson and Noblet. We can see that Milan had a tradition that was almost exactly like Noblet in the 1600s, except without the borders and names! This tells us most of what we can know (with current evidence) about the missing years of TdM, whether *Trionfi da Milano* or *Tarot de Marseille:* the Noblet was an Italian deck. The Noblet has a few neat details, most notably the Fool's privates being batted by the cat, that are not in most other decks and which suggest originality. However, it also has some obvious corruptions, such as Justice having not a throne, not wings, but just something behind her that was neither clearly conceived nor executed.

Chosson's claim to Italian origin is based on 1) the beauty of the draftsmanship, 2) the fact that it was the most widespread and successful model, suggesting an early start, and 3) the additional detail it has is not idiosyncratic, (like Geofroy or Viéville, etc), but could easily have been the model for all the others. Of necessity, we know that these decks are all from a common ancestor. Equally certain, just by chance, some of the surviving decks are going to be more similar to that ancestor than others – we just don't know which ones are which, *a priori.* We need to find the one(s) that appear to be good copies of something, as the sloppy copies are inherently corrupt, and we need to find the one(s) that are not oddly out of step with the synoptic character of the TdM family. That's Chosson/Conver.

We know from Sforza's 1450 letter that decks of varying quality were being produced and sold at that early date. My own guess is that Chosson (aka, the TdM II style) is probably our best surviving fossil of the original *Trionfi da Milano,* based on a rather high-end deck, while Noblet (aka, the TdM I style) is also a direct Milanese descendant but from a later and cheaper deck. To me, it appears that the Fool, Fortune, the Devil, and especially the World cards in Noblet had intentional "rectifications" from an assumed Chosson-style original. The Fool is made more playful, a crude change for a deck aimed at a lower-class market. Fortune and the Devil were stylistic choices of no apparent significance, presumably simply because the woodcarver preferred a different model. The World is the most dramatic revisioning, and it is a huge step in the direction of a traditional Christ in Majesty image. This is exactly the kind of change one would expect in a deck designed for the hoi polloi, away from a sophisticated allegory toward a more direct representation.

That is why I love them both – I think they are both "best surviving examples" of the Trionfi da Milano.

I can't help but feel that what I am saying is some sort of heresy.

Among the historians, of course, it's a commonplace.

A priori, there necessarily was an Ur Tarot, although we may never know what it was.

A priori, the Ur Tarot may or may not have had a coherent design.

We don't have that deck. We have only copies, variations, copies of variations and variations of variations. The odds are great that most of the changes were ad hoc rather than systematic, (excepting complete re-designs like Boiardo and Sola-Busca). For example, the Sicilian Devil replacement (a ship) and its odd Tower (a coastal fortification against naval warfare) are directly related to each other and vaguely related to standard Tarot. However, it is too much to ask that they also contribute to a coherent overall narrative. Sure, a story can be constructed, but this gets back to fanciful readings. This is the same situation, in all probability, with most of the intentional variations and all of the sloppy-copy corruptions.

Anyway, that's one of the things I most appreciate about your approach. Whatever Tarot was is not the living question. It may or may not be interesting in an historical sense, but whatever it meant to others, whether courtiers in the early 16th Century or New Age nimrods in the late 20th Century, is no more relevant to the moment than the original intent of the various deck designers. That vitality, as I understand what you've been saying, is part of what separates art (in the honorific sense) from glorified illustration. What you are doing with your interviews and the *Bookshop of Crossed Destinies* is about living meanings, with Tarot being brought to life anew rather than the cards being held by the dead hand of history.

Thanks for that!

Your primary interests and activities in Tarot are wildly different from mine and, as demonstrated below, you sometimes seem to lose track of basic distinctions and make statements that sound like radical Postmodern platitudes. However, even when I don't quite know what you're up to, even if I would probably disagree with your premises, you seem to have a clearer and more rational take on both historical Tarot and contemporary Tarot usage than 99% of the people writing about the subject.

At one level I think Bourgeois is addressing the problem of form vs. the problem of interpretation. Those who understand forms understand a language of proportion, balance, symmetry, contrast, rhythm, and pattern. So, as you look at a visual object you know if the image works or not. I think that what she is saying is: "As I see, I know. Then you can rationalize something as much as you want, and you may confuse me, I may overlook what I know, but when I see, I know". The moment when a person looks at an image and the image sends them back into their bodies is very powerful in that it has an essential quality that makes words very unlikely to work with. I have seen his happen many times and I find these moments to be the most extreme examples of the a-verbal nature of the cards. When a person is locked in whatever the visual language of the card is eliciting in them, it is almost impossible, in my experience, to take them out of it. So, at that moment, it is as if the person is quoting Bourgeois: "you can say whatever you want, but I know what I am looking at".

There is a well-known body of phenomena termed "mystical experience". They are undeniable, but then there are the words that different people use to describe or explain their experience, or to justify some beliefs or doctrines based on that experience. The great insight of Zen, epitomized by the Sixth Patriarch tearing up sutras, is that mystical experience does not translate into words, nor vice versa. Wittgenstein took an essentially mystical approach to his lectures and writings, calling them a ladder that, once climbed, needed to be thrown away.

The problem with most people who embrace that immediate reality of personal experience is that they cannot distinguish between that "truth" and historical "fact". The belief in universals and dismissal of convention makes people profoundly ahistorical rather than a-verbal. That would be fine, of course, except that very few of them understand that their personal epiphany is not scholarly history, and instead they impose an anachronistic sensibility on the past.

This takes me to my next point: in the somersault from visual to verbal, the notion of misreading is fundamental.

This is the point of Harold Bloom's book, *Agon*, referring to the contest between meanings. (That's where I learned the word "misprision" as something other than "misprision of felony".) Excellent book, by the way.

As you pointed out, even from the earlier appropriati, these verbalizations of the tarot images are misreadings whose value applies only in the moment. Moving a little bit forward, the whole idea of using the tarot as a divination device is a misreading of that artifact. So, one has to be aware of the fact that any interpretation of the cards is a misreading. It may make sense in the moment, it may be useful, but it is nothing more than a misreading. I find that proposition very sobering.

I find it very misleading. In absolutist terms, every reading is a misreading because no absolute norms can be established. That is absolute relativism, and that is what is implied by "nothing more" than a misreading. There are a number of ways in which an interpretation can be more than that. It can be historically sanctioned by having specific historical examples. It can be historically sanctioned by having historical parallels. An interpretation can be supported with relevant evidence and rational argument and, if anyone claims that these things are not significant, they cannot rationally argue against those points because they have begun the fight by cutting off their own arms and legs. There is no rational argument against reason.

As a matter of fact these days I suspect that one can consider the tarot a visual poem that stops being a poem and turns into a game as soon as one reads the cards aloud.

That rejection of a privileged reading can be (and has been) asserted with regard to all of art and literature. (By the way, are you playing off of my old line, "Tarot de Marseille is an architectonic masterpiece, an elaborate poem of medieval Christian views of salvation"?)

But most tarot people find it problematic.

Actually, the view that Tarot's meaning is a living thing has been asserted emphatically. Robert V. O'Neill insisted in his *Tarot Symbolism* (1986) that this was the intended design of Tarot. Let me try to find a quote or two... here's one, from his introduction to a final reading of the trumps.

> Throughout this presentation, we will be analyzing the images on a very intellectual plane, on the level of the philosophical systems of the Renaissance. However, it must be remembered that the Tarot has meanings at a more fundamental level. They are archetypal symbols as well as expressions of a philosophy. Therefore, the cards may convey special meanings to the individual reader. We will not deal with this level of interpretation here, but the reader can be assured that such meaning was very much within the intent of the designers. The personal meaning of the symbols can never be analyzed completely, and that too was very much the intent of the designers. The reader should feel free to find his own meaning in the cards and realize that the designers fully desired him to find those meanings. (364)

Thus, the designers did not inadvertently create an endlessly flexible Rorschach-like game of projection, they did that consciously. They had no intention of communicating a particular message (which O'Neill could not find in any earlier analysis and could not find himself), but they intended to suggest whatever you might perceive there.

I am going to try to explain myself in a different way. Imagine you draw a dog. Before the image of a dog we can be quite confident that this image intends to say "dog". So, if you were to get in my mind to elucidate my intentions while drawing it, guessing "dog" would be a good guess, unless... Lets say I drew that dog while running along a topless woman who carried a bow and wore a helmet, or along a bunch of ridders on their horses, or while running along with a few other dogs and a wild board. Then you will rightly guess that I intended to say 'hunt' with that dog. But imagine I didn't draw any more dogs, nor a topless woman, but a tombstone in front of a dog. Then you could rightly guess that I am saying 'Fidelity' with that dog. Why? Because you have seen a bunch of images in which dogs are used that way. I may be wrong, but I believe that is what you, or any serious researcher, have done with the tarot.

Extremely well put. Context counts.

You have explored the intended meaning of each image by finding cognates that tell you how that image was used at the time the tarot was created. At this point, I understand those who are open to debate if the whole sequence had an intended meaning as a sequence, or not (although I would argue that you have shown how the context of each image within the sequence reinforces each image's intended meaning).

Exactly right.

But I can't accept the notion of each image being a "purposeful Rorschach", as O'Neill suggests. In other words, I can't think of any single work of art from that period that had a "think what you want" kind of message. Do you know of any? As far as I know, images weren't used that way.

Exactly right. On the other hand, it is a cool idea, albeit an anachronistic one. However, the whole "layers of meaning" idea is largely folklore. As used by O'Neill it is routinely a Holy-Blood-Holy-Grail type of dodge, to impute the opposite of the obvious meaning. Even when restricted to the four senses of Scripture it is somewhat speculative to attribute it to works of art and literature. Dante, an early and influential writer, made that point, so it can be defended... but it is not clear that this was intended even in that limited sense, even in most of his famous *Commedia*.

Now, if I show you a dog that means dog I can foresee that your subjective experience of a dog may be different from mine. You may like dogs (I am recently discovering they piss me off!) or you may not like dogs. I am willing to accept that my image of a dog may take your mind into a cat, as that would be a culturally accepted opposite of a dog, but I cannot see how can you think 'butterfly' is the meaning of my dog. Again, I can see how my image of a dog may take your mind to that experience you had of your Golden Retriever chasing butterflies in a field, but still, my dog will be a dog... is a dog... is a dog...

Also, in the context of the Fool as a fool, or a pauper, or a vagabond/vagrant, the cat playing with his junk is easily (mis)read as a dog, and even turned into a dog by later copyists.

I am inclined to think the tarot has one specific meaning. The cards mean what they mean (they mean whatever people assigend to them when they were created) and there is no way around it. I am also inclined to think that those who say the tarot has no inherent meaning simply don't like that meaning. Same thing happens with those who try to find the meaning of tarot outside Europe. But I also think that once we start using these images outside their original purpose, that is, as a game, we step into a poetical realm.

Exactly right.

On one hand the image will mean the use we make of it today.

Exactly the words I would use – it means what we use it to mean.

On the other hand, that meaning may be in conflict with its intended meaning, and therefore, it becomes a misreading.

Bingo. That's the part that is incomprehensible.

So, what I meant to say is: all readings of the tarot that ignore, negate, or overlook the way these images were used when the tarot was created, are misreadings. I find the proposition sobering as long as it helps me not to 'read back', forcing today's meaning into the tarot's original intention.

Or the other way around. Tarot's history and historical meaning are not adventures in modern practice, and nothing about Tarot history or iconography is in any way constraining of contemporary practice.

This is key, as most tarot people need the historical validation for their nonsense. They cannot come to terms with the fact that the intended use of an image today may not be 'ancient' and still be useful. I believe that's the mistake most tarot authors make.

Wishful thinking, speculation, "exploring", and "possibilities".

Now, an argument can be made in that all mystical experiences are the same.

Right. And to the extent that they are inherently ineffable, beyond adequate translation into any form of expression, they are at least to that extent the same even if there are seven distinct kinds of mystical experience. If we can't identify them in words well enough to make the distinctions clear, then from a rational (symbol-based) point of view they are the same. Empiricism requires observable differences.

I mean, the non-verbal quality of the experience may be the same. In that regard, a mandala can be as effective at prompting mystic ecstasy as a tarot card is. BUT, I disagree with those who like to equate that with the idea of the intention behind the mandala and the tarot being the same. I don't buy the "international sacred brotherhood" scheme. That is another misreading in which people are imposing a new-age view of religion unto the past.

Exactly right.

I make the same mistake when I impose my liking of poetry unto the tarot and conceive it as a poem. (By the way, in order to experience what I mean by that, compare Judgement in any Marseille with the Ace of Swords. To me, the Angel's wings visually rhyme with the vines we see inside the crown: they are Visual Homophones.

Actually, one has its "wings" up and the other down, which was clearly a significant design consideration for TdM, given the contrasting styles used in the Empress and Emperor. So it's an off-rhyme. But I get the idea...

I can craft a narrative from that rhyme. I can experience the rhyme as movement and for me that is a story, and I can translate that story into words. Now, the mistake I won't make is to say that such visual rhymes were intended by the tarot's designer.

At least, not in most cases. It remains a possibility, and that can be explored and, if something appears supported by additional context and is reasonably congruent with the overall design, then maybe...

My approach (for readings, not for historical research) has the merit of being visually verifiable by my listener, and since any analogy I map can be seen by the listener, it is more likely to be taken as true, heightening my chances to affect that person's mind. By the same token, as my words are all anchored in the images, they are easier to remember.

As opposed to most Kabbalistic correspondences, astrological correspondences, even a lot of numerology depends on a pre-existing body of associations that doesn't exist in most people's mindset outside the cult. Even a lot of the supposed archetypal meaning is in fact acculturated among the neo-Jungian enthusiasts rather than actually apparent.

I know why what I do works, and I use this knowledge intentionally, but let me reinforce this here: I will never claim that it has anything to do with the intention of those who created the tarot.

The most amazing thing is also the simplest thing, that you even recognize the difference. Some people, including O'Neill, James Revak, myself, and sometimes Ross, have taken pains to make that distinction in a variety of different ways, and yet it remains not just unseen but seemingly unimaginable to many people. The idea that different decks with different images in different order might be intended to convey different stories is difficult, but it's becoming more commonly accepted, yet there is still an undercurrent that there must be a true Tarot and that all the others are in some sense "really" telling that story.

My view is that there is or was an original Tarot, and that it was more coherent than later copies and variations, but even if we had that deck, and a designer's manual to go with it, it would not somehow overwrite later decks. They overwrote it. As such, each deck is necessarily telling its own story, whether that is simply a corrupted version of the original, a "rectified" version of the original, or something with really cool new bits and pieces, or even something like Boiardo and Sola Busca, a wholly new design.

This is a difficult topic, as I am willing to consider that all draftsmen, from all cultural backgrounds, know how to use symbols to affect the human mind. So, I will be willing to say that there is a secret knowledge – secret for non-draftsmen – common to all draftsmen. But it is not an occult knowledge, and it is not metaphysical in any way. It is craftsmanship and you learn it in school, or by apprenticeship.

And many things that are today claimed to be secrets known to only a select few, as you pointed out, were in fact not secret at all but conventional, including a lot of color and number symbolism.

Some people argue that the Marseille tarot has a different occult meaning than the Italian tarot. That is, any change in the images alludes to a secret code. I simply wonder how can we see that evolution in the pips. No one knows. Then I wonder if many of the decisions, from a hand-painted deck to wood-engraved decks, couldn't have been economical. That is, to me it is obvious to think that a Marseille deck is a cheaper deck. The idea of a Marseille deck being 'cheaper' seems like another blasphemy.

That is a significant element to consider when looking at our meager supply of early decks. Some were very high-end, some were stylish engraved works, others were very sloppy. It takes a much better artist and a lot more work to create the Cary Sheet deck or Chosson than it does to create most of what is seen in woodcut decks. The Metropolitan-Budapest deck is a pretty decent cheap deck, probably a standard pattern for that locale, while something like Geofroy is mid-range, and a creative mix by someone familiar with a lot of imported cards. And so on.

Now, how do we know if these details, or these rhymes between images, were intentional and not a default part of the process? We would have to find the same language being used elsewhere, just as we know what a dog means because we have seen it being used in other contexts.

Cognates, establishing a convention in other works of art and literature. Facts/evidence rather than intuited truths.

Where has this been used in a similar way we can discern? We don't know. I will use the example of the language of the birds. Not because I can prove it has anything to do with the tarot, but it interests me for two reasons: first, the French have a history of playing with verbal homophony they like to call 'langue des oiseaux' that takes us into the realm of folklore. Second, and more importantly, verbal homophony is fun. So, could it not be possible that any change in the images was about making the game more amusing? I am not saying I am right, but I am saying: wouldn't it be possible to explore these design decisions from the perspective of the tarot as game, instead of the perspective of the tarot as an enlightening tool?

That is one of the reasons why something like Rom's alleged code is, *a priori*, interestingly plausible. Although trivial in any case, it would be the kind of playful exercise that a bored cardmaker might have done. Same with Filipas abecedarium idea, although a Hebrew(?!) abecedarium is wildly far-fetched, just another recycled occultist cliché. These things might actually have been done by someone at some point, so the ideas need to be checked out. It was a good idea, and it didn't pan out – move on. However, people like Rom and Filipas can't do that, and new myths are born.

I am sold to the idea of a narrative intention being present in the whole cycle. In fact, I find the contrary hypothesis quite puzzling: how could someone, originally, have played a trump-taking game with non-numbered/named images without having a sense of narrative? Knowing what comes before and what comes after is a narrative act. It is also indispensable to know if you can win the game or not. So, in my view, the logic of the text behind the tarot has to have been apparent to those early players, and that logic had an intentional design.

Now, here is what I am skeptical about. Yesterday I had a woman pulling several cards from the suit of Swords, alternating with The World and The Devil. It was SWORD-WORLD-SWORD-DEVIL-SWORD. The scimitars in the suit of swords form an elliptic shape that mirrors the World's mandorla, just as the rope tying the two creatures in The Devil mirrors half of that same ellipse. Jodorowsky, Jean-Claude Flronoy, Camoin, Unger... all these authors will tell you that this is part of the tarot's intentional design. I am skeptical about that. More surprisingly, to me, was how this sequence brought the blue up. In the Dodal, the two points of contact between all these scimitars is of the same color blue as the devil's body and the World's mandorla. It was actually remarkably beautiful how the proximity of the cards made the color blue relevant, but I would be skeptical of this being due to the tarot intentional design. I would love to be wrong. I would love to find evidence supporting these visual coincidences. I am ready to jump the fence and say: "Wow!!! This is a great design!" because I love the visual rhymes I see. But I don't think that such a reading of the author's intention would be accurate. Most TdM lovers do.

As background justification for the basic premise, I would point to both the medieval theory of pictures as the text of the illiterate but also to medieval examples of this in practice. I've discussed both of these background subjects repeatedly, but let me point out one of the most dramatically obvious examples of multi-layered conflation of motifs. *A Complex Wheel of Fortune*.[2]

By authenticity, I mean a relatively direct copy of the assumed original, coherent design. There are more than a dozen different orderings of the trumps, and there are dozens of iconographic variations. Perhaps the original design was coherent,

---

2   see: http://pre-gebelin.blogspot.com/2009/04/complex-wheel-of-fortune.html

perhaps not, but it is virtually certain – both *a priori* and after years of examination – that most surviving decks are crap, a hodge-podge of ad hoc variation and corruption. It is virtually certain that the original design is not among the surviving designs, but it is also virtually certain that some are closer to that original design than others, hence "relatively" direct copy. The assumption that the original was worth knowing about, a work of serious value, is necessary to justify any study of Tarot as other than a Rorschach-like projection game.

So we need to at least consider all orderings and decks which might have some claim to reflecting that Ur Tarot.

Ordering, for example, can sometimes identify changes: placing one of the three virtues, Justice, between the Angel and the World, is an obviously intelligible design, but also an obviously derivative one. If it had been originally intended for that role it would have shown Michael rather than a weak substitute that clearly belongs with her sisters, in the middle section. Draftsmanship is an obvious clue to corruption – a sloppy copy is by definition a sloppy copy; QED. Being widespread is another possible indication of early origin. The earliest designs had the best opportunity to become established in many places, to be known as a standard from which the many more localized variations were created. The point is that some decks (e.g., those with the three virtues either adjacent or equally spaced) appear instantly more well designed than others (e.g., those with the virtues placed less systematically); one deck, the Conver/TdM II style, appears to be by far the most widespread; one deck closely related to that, the Noblet/TdM I style, is almost certainly a direct descendant of the 15th-century Milanese standard pattern; and so on.

If we can find a 17th-century or earlier deck which does not appear to be too corrupt on its face, and in which we can discern a coherent story, it is evidence – far from proof, but evidence – of a connection with the original design, whereas obviously corrupt and apparently incoherent designs, regardless of our fondness for a given deck, do not have that same plausible connection to an original coherent design. If that deck were either the popular TdM II or the better attested TdM I deck, it would have even more plausibility as the best surviving example of the Ur Tarot.

OK. It occurs to me: what happens with danse macabres? Are all of them identical or do we have several different representations of that subject?

Excellent example – there are many variations, even in what might be called the archetypal form. Just like Tarot, there are copies, variations, and a number of families of obvious relationship. Lydgate even added a Bagatto (Tregetoure) to the list of figures. He doesn't have an appropriate image for that, so he uses the Visconti-Sforza Magician card to illustrate. (He also uses the fake Cary-Yale Magician card.) I don't know of a picture of one, but here is a gambler that looks similar to what would be expected. Gamblers, musicians, and fools were common, but not magicians. In any case, this guy's luck has clearly run out.

Why not to consider the tarot in a similar fashion: a theme treated slightly differently by different authors. (Caveat: 'author' is a tricky word for 'cardmaker'. 'Author' implies intention in the content of a work, when in fact a cardmaker could have copied blindly without intending anything). It is hard to make a distinction between authorship and draftsmanship, I guess, but I would suggest that the difference between authorship and draftsmanship is at the basis of detecting an 'original' tarot from a cheap copy.

The nebulous term 'theme' works better with the Dance of Death, where the number of images varied from one to many dozens, where sometimes there were biblical framing elements but more often there were not, and so on. The Tarot trump cycle is much more like a single family of works from the Dance of Death tradition. (As usual, this is excepting the great exceptions, Boiardo and Sola Busca.)

I see...

The TdM sequence, the composition of the cycle, is the only one for which I can find a detailed, card-by-card structure, so I rule out all other designs on that basis alone. Both these decks, Noblet and Chosson, are apparently from the 3rd quarter of the 17th century, and the comparison is wildly self-evident: one has detailed, meaningful, and well-executed designs and the other looks like a very poor copy. It seems reasonable to believe that one is a good copy of an earlier good design while the other is a poor copy of an earlier good design.

So IF there is to be a poem in Tarot, before we read our own song into it, it seems that it would probably be in the Chosson/TdM II pattern of deck. In the old *Mendicant's Tale* essay, I had the following tables illustrating the stanzas of that poem. The cards are arranged by what I termed affinity patterns, i.e., a rhyme scheme. The Fool and Deceiver are paired, as are the Empress and Emperor, while religious figures rhyme at the end of each line. Triumphs in Love and War are paired, as are reversals of both voluntary Asceticism and involuntary Fortune, and downfall, both the deserved end of a Traitor and the Reaper who takes the rest. Again, each line ends with a rhyme, the three Moral Virtues. The Devil and his downfall, Fire and the fall of Babylon/Rome, are triumphed by the adventus Star, herald of the self-proclaimed Morning Star of Revelation. The Moon and Sun, symbols of Time as well as the lights of this world, are triumphed by another herald, Angel of the Resurrection. And what do the heralds proclaim? The true Light of the World. My argument was (and is) that this is as close to a poem in pictures as one could possibly create: three stanzas with a AABBBCCD rhyme scheme. I see it as literally and historically a poem, whereas I think you are saying that only the process of bringing it to life in the moment is one of poesis. Am I right about your more limited use of the term? What do you think of my more extravagant claims?

I find your analysis of all these triads brilliant and iconographically sound. To me it is the best understanding of the meaning of the tarot I have seen. There is of course one big assumption that people who like to use the word 'belief' while doing history won't like, and that is to assume that coherence in design can be evidence of these tarots being more 'truthful'. That is a gesture that goes over the heads of many. Your analysis is something I am more than happy to buy into, because it is both beautiful and meaningful. By 'beautiful' I mean that it makes evident a great design. By meaningful I mean that it still holds truth (at least the moral part). That is what I define, even in my workshops, as the 'TAROT'S DISCLAIMER' when I quote you: this is what the iconographical evidence suggests that the images meant. Ignore that at your peril!

Expressed in an AABBBCCD rhyme scheme, it becomes very clear!

I'm glad you find it believable as an intended design and general meaning, with that structure. It is the TdM ordering that creates the rhythm and rhyme, which other orderings don't have. The idea of interwoven meanings, two layers in each section, each related to the same overall design, is also best appreciated by analogy with a poetic (and especially, allegorical) use of language. I just wasn't clear about your use of the term poem.

I use the term on several different levels. At a content level I suspect the tarot trump cycle to be a canto, some sort of narrative that in the TdM case you have outlined as a visual poem. Then I have a totally literal take on the idea of the poem based on the symmetries that emerge when you create rows of random cards.

Sort of a magnetic poetry project, with archaic but vaguely understandable pictures in place of common words.

Then, the process of the reading itself is an act of poiesis, in which the client creates meaning both from the images arrangement and my narration of it. The original poem, the original narrative intention of whomever created the tarot co-exists with the poetics of chance and with the poetic nature of the brain.

The living poetry being created as opposed to the original textual poem being reconstructed. The confusion between a historical poem and contemporary poesis is, of course, a central problem. Part of that problem appears to be self awareness, being alert to how much we impose. Most of us have serious failings in our self-awareness. That need for self awareness is one of the reasons why I stayed active in the online forums for so long. They provide a basis for comparison and contrast, a mirror for self awareness in addition to whatever other functions they serve, or that I might serve in them. What strikes me as the most interesting aspect of your readings is the use of pip cards.

Working with the pips is a choice I have made based only on my liking of these images, even when I suspect the actual message of the tarot is contained in the trumps alone. I understand there is an occultist tradition of assigning meaning to the trumps, but I don't think that that is necessarily right. That is another retroactive misreading.

When we talk about meaning, in my current understanding, the tarot is composed by 22 + 4 symbols.

And each of the four is sub-divided into two ranked groups, seeming to correspond to four social hierarchies, nobles and nameless ones who are nonetheless ranked, if only by quantity.

My own view is that originally the Mamluk (or other Ur card deck with those suits) represented four societies, each with an identical social structure. It is easy to see that kind of meaning, which parallels the two "suits" of Chess, as the basis of pips and paints.

The idea of ranking the pip cards on the feminine suits backward, however, seems like a kind of mixed metaphor. It doesn't make sense of the four societies, two of which count more people as worth less than fewer. It seems to make nonsense of any rational reading of even the standard deck before the game came to Europe, suggesting that the first ad hoc changes were somewhere "lost in the mists of time".

The trumps plus four other symbols: coins, cups, swords and scepters. I have no indication to believe that the four of Coins, for example, means something different from 'coins'. Four coins or ten coins are that: coins. It is only that ten is more than four. (As you may see, I have a PhD in platitudes!) Numbers qualify something in a very similar way adjectives do. So, I see each one of the pips suit as one noun advectivized ten times. I work with a meaning for these four symbols that comes, half from Psicina, and half from the tarot itself: when you look at the characters' hands you see how they use these symbols. That way you understand that coins and cups experientially suggest some intimacy: they are hold inside the hand and they can only be shared in close quarters; while sword and scepters are extensions of the arm and therefore suggest distance. Given that we use these tools to keep people away from us, or to hurt people remotely, 'distance' can be seen as opposition or antagonism. That division of four symbols into two opposite kinds of relationship is consistent with Piscina. Having them is very useful to make more precise narratives.

Brother John's 1377 (1429) *Tractatus* suggested that two suits were considered good and two were evil. The identification of two suits as masculine and two as feminine might be the only authentic symbolism intended in the original European/Arabic suit-signs, with two of them being linear and ranked in natural order, the other two being circular and ranked in reverse order. The two parts of Brother John's analysis, 1) that the cards represent a "status mundi" (the four societies, each ranked appropriately), and 2) that the suits represent good and bad, two of which are ranked in reverse order, seem flagrantly contradictory. At the end of this exchange, I'll include an article I found on Brother John's *Tractatus*. As for the later writers…

Meister Ingold associates all the suits with sin, which doesn't seem particularly helpful.

Boiardo created his own deck with suit-signs representing the four Passions of the Soul. This would be more useful, except that his suit-signs are non-standard. There is no obvious parallel. In a deck with the standard suits, Swords and Staves are weapons of war while Cups and Coins are weapons of the grog shop. Arrows and Whips might seem to be the masculine suits, parallel to Swords and Staves in being cruel weapons, while Eyes and Vases seem feminine... but that was not the way they were ordered. In the game, as described by Viti, "Among the numeral cards, the higher-numbered beat the lower-numbered in the suits of Arrows and Vases, but, in those of Eyes and Whips, the lower-numbered beat the higher-numbered" (421), as Michael Dummett wrote in his *The Game of Tarot* (1980). The masculine suits were associated with the attractive Passions, Love (Arrows) and Hope (Vases), where more is better; the feminine suits were associated with the repulsive Jealousy (Eyes) and Fear (Whips). No direct parallel.[3]

The named Court cards of the French suit system, established in the late 15th century, suggest the possibility of allegorical associations with the suits, but I don't know if anyone has pursued that, figured it out and published the answer.

Galcottus Martius, (*De Doctrina Promiscua*, circa 1488), seems to recall Brother John's simple division into two kinds of suits: those in which greater values are beneficial and those in which greater values are detrimental.

Aretino's *Les Cartes Parlantes* says "that swords recall the death of those who have become mad over gaming; batons or clubs, the chastisement that they merit who cheat; coins or denari, the food of gaming; cups, the wine in which disputes of the gamesters are drowned". Again, all pretty negative, associated with sin.

Virgil Solis may well have had symbolic intent behind the choice of suit-signs, (which were subsequently used by Catelin Geofroy in his 1557 Tarot deck), but again I don't know if anyone has sorted that out.

---

[3] see also: *Boiardo's Poems and Viti's Commentary*
http://pre-gebelin.blogspot.com/2007/12/boiardos-poems-and-vitis-commenary.html

1551, Innocentio Ringhieri associated the suit-signs with the four Cardinal Virtues. Cups symbolized Temperance, Columns showed Strength, Swords represented Justice, and Mirrors [Coins] symbolized Prudence. Like Boiardo's analysis, this seems to give more to work with.

Piscina has the masculine (properly ranked) suits as weapons of War and the feminine (inversely ranked) as emblems of Peace. This seems to be similar to Boiardo's passions, with two obviously negative themes and two ostensibly positive (but actually negative, representing Avarice and Intemperance) themes, but based on the regular suits.

A 1582 book by Gosselin associates the four suits with the four elements, (also mentioned by Piscina), with which they are commonly associated by occultists today (although the correspondences are different).

Perhaps the most well-known interpretations of the suit-signs comes from Menestrier, writing in 1704. He interpreted the four suits as social allegories: Hearts represented men of the Church, Diamonds the merchants, Clubs were symbols of the peasantry, and Spades represented the "Noblesse d'epee". Menestrier's interpretation was familiar to the first occultists who took an interest in Tarot, in 1781.

So, at a symbolic level a pip will anchor a trump into a specific kind of relationship, but I don't stop there. That may give me a theme for the readings, but then I explore the symmetries I notice between all these cards and compose alternative narratives that may add up or not. Using the pips are kind of chasing a wild card. Sometimes I feel they just water the reading down. Some other times they create very sharp messages.

Take for example a woman who pulled the Two of Coins, The Tower, and The Ace of Coins. Look at them if you have a chance. They scream 'divorce', and divorce was indeed what the woman had in mind. When something random comes up with that precision, there is a sense of 'truth' of a profound psychological impact.

I like that, especially the part about them being a kind of wild card.

If we have Temperance, for example, we can describe an action: she is pouring liquid (water into wine, water into water) from one jar into the other one. I can read more into the image, as her body posture suggests taking a step back to look at things from a certain perspective, as we do when we need to calm down before making a commitment. To me, the whole image physically says 'moderation'. What I think is important is that I can read the pips in the same way. If Temperance were paired with, lets say, the 2 of Coins, I would read the same action in the pip card: these two coins stand in balance, like Temperance's jars, by a sense of flow that is being expressed through the S-like band that unites them both. That band's orientation in space is symmetrical to the motion of pouring water from one jar into the other one. In the 2 of cups there is a scene that I can read by mapping a relational analogy: each coin is a 'person' and the whole scene is analogous to a certain kind of relationship. Two people stand one in front of the other, creating balance.

Temperance paired with the 2 of Coins will suggest then moderation in business, or material-related matters. It would be the same it we paired Temperance with 2C or with 3C, except for the fact that the 3 of Coins presents (I cannot say it represents) a different kind of relationship: we have the same two persons, represented by the same two coins, and then, the third, new coin comes to redefine their flow.

While Temperance paired with the 2 of Coins will suggest 'moderation in business' in a dynamic with a partner we know, Temperance paired with the 3 of Coins will suggest 'moderation in business' in a dynamic where new factors are entering into play. Bottom-line the message is the same, but some of the circumstances in the narrative become more precise in two different ways.

By mapping relational analogies from a pip card to human interaction one can always read a scene in a pip card.

Going over our conversation this whole week I got an idea. Would you be O.K. if I put an edited version online?

I was just thinking of your earlier comment about packaging "conversations" as "interviews". There was a lot of rambling, bordering on babbling, where I tried to get a handle on some things that are second nature to you as well as things that you are currently trying to sort out – the trickster vs. the charlatan thing... there was some Ages of Man stuff... a couple examples of my blundering over-interpretation... my view of early standard patterns from Milan to Noblet and Chosson... babbling about mystical experience vs. how they are interpreted and reported. I threw in some political ranting and some anti-Pomo abuse, Frankfurter's analysis of "bullshit"... some Dutch Tarot links... While I've gained a lot from our excange – thank you very much! – and I've tried to return the favors as best I can, tossing in some old tidbits I thought might be relevant or interesting, there doesn't seem to be much there of general interest. That's partly because of the nature of the potential audience. Even though I enjoy these little micro-studies, I can't quite imagine an audience outside a particular individual.

However, if you think you can, and want to, pull something out of that random collation of comments to post somewhere, then go for it. I would love to see what you can create out of such a mess.

New York, February, 2010

"I think *tarocchi appropriati* is the pre-eminent "form" that modern tarotists should be inspired by. Occultism has really run its course; it's a dead vessel."

A conversation with ROSS SINCLAIR CALDWELL, tarot historian

I would like to start by sharing with you a quote from painter Marlene Dumas:

> Images don't lie. They cry wolf.

I find it as fascinating as the Louise Bourgeois's quote I shared with Michael Hurst: "you cannot fool me in the visual world, but you can take the better of me in the verbal world"; but I also think Dumas is contradicting Bourgeois. Don't you think? While Bourgeois trusts that first spark of 'truth' we experience when we connect with the forms of an image, Dumas suggests that all images can be red herrings. So, my first question would be: can an image lie?

I don't think an image can lie, but it can portray a lie, or cleverly conceal its real purpose.

I'm not sure I agree with Dumas's statement, at least in the way I understand the meaning of "to cry 'wolf'". The boy who cried wolf really believed it, as I understand it. People were worried, but no wolf appeared, so people forgot about it. He cried wolf again, and again no wolf appeared. People began to get annoyed. He cried wolf a third time, and a third time no wolf appeared. People beat him up. He cried wolf a fourth time, and people ignored him, and again, no wolf appeared. The people were right. But he called wolf a fifth time, and people again ignored him, but this time a wolf DID appear, and attacked the sheep (or was it the people?). So, finally, the boy was right – or was it just a lucky-unlucky guess?

I think the lesson is about wanting to get attention by extreme measures, or about abusing fear (the "bogey man") for trivial purposes, when it should only be invoked in real emergencies. If invoked too often, when real danger comes, the "wolf-crier" will be ignored, sometimes with fatal consequences. But it's also a lesson about complacency. Lies? I guess so, if you think the boy was lying just to get attention.

I don't know what that has to do with images. But she must mean something by it, and she doesn't mean lying, so she must mean seeking attention in a way that might or might not refer to something real or true. So maybe she means "Images don't lie. But they might be pointing out something different than the most obvious interpretation, and if you miss it, you will say they are lying."

So, I guess I would answer your question by saying that an image can't lie, but it might be, accidentally (through the ignorance of the observer) or deliberately (there's the author's deceptive intention), misunderstood. The purpose of it might be misunderstood. The boy was lying for attention, or sincerely confused (not lying).

One thing that popped into my mind when considering your question was the *trompe l'oeil* method, optical illusions, or M.C. Escher-type visual paradoxes. Are these "lying"? I think they come the closest to lies, as images go. They are really trying to fool you, or confuse you. Escher raises aesthetic and philosophical questions, which is really a Socratic method of doing art.

Then there is the question of forgeries. An artist who really tries to make you believe that his work was made by someone else. These are also lies. But I don't think Dumas means either forgeries or optical illusions. Perhaps she means that images will suggest a thousand things to us, only one of which is right. All the rest is "crying wolf". But you can apply this insight to things like forgeries and illusions. If you miss a forgery, for instance, the forgery isn't lying, you just aren't looking closely enough to see how it is deceiving you. It is crying wolf in a thousand ways, but really it is just seeking attention, and its obvious meaning distracts all but the most insightful and knowlegeable observer. If it succeeds in crying wolf, its real truth will be ignored, and its false message accepted as truth.

I wonder if I am missing your point. And her point. Does she mean "meaning"? As in a painting of a couple holding hands, walking on a beach, for instance? We take it for love, but perhaps there are other things in the painting that indicate sorrow, conflict, or a non-erotic interpretation – perhaps leading by the hand to some nefarious purpose? In this case, I guess my understanding of looking closer than the surface gets to the point of the statement – the obvious, first-glance meaning is crying wolf, but a slower observation will show what is really going on.

Now, a trompe l'oeil, or a forgery are conscious attempts at making a deceitful image. But I suspect Dumas is not referring to that. I guess she is saying is that an image may not necessarily deceive you, but it can throw you off in an unexpected, or even wrong, way. Let me share with you something that happened to me this morning. I was at a coffee shop, reading one of Calvino's stories from his Castle of Crossed Destinies. This is a story in which the woods take revenge and claim back the cities. The final line of that story reads:

> And another card's announcement has also come true: 'the day will come when a feather will knock down the tower of Nimrod'.

The card the text is alluding to is The Tower. The book actually shows The Tower card from a Marseille deck. So, I am there, looking at that image, and I look up to the next table, where a man is reading the front page of the New York Times, and there is a picture of a couple crying in front of a collapsed building. The caption below the picture said: "As the devastation sinks in, Chile requests outside aid". I went back and forth from the New York Time to The Tower several times in total awe. The symmetries were uncanny! I guess Jung would have had a field day with that! Something I have been discussing recently is precisely that sense of 'truth' that comes from a happenstance. I walked away from the coffee shop, savoring that moment of chance, and thinking on how tempting would be then to believe that The Tower is the tower of Nimrod. I guess I could go and try to find any possible evidence to corroborate that idea, always inspired by a happenstance. So, here is my question: which tools does the tarot historian have to overcome ignorance and self-deception?

I had trouble answering this question, Enrique, but now I realize what the problem was: your example was one of the interpretation of an image, not of Tarot history per se. You can be a superb Tarot historian without offering an interpretation of the sequence or any image in it.

So the first part of your question, about ignorance, you'd address ignorance with knowledge. The only cure for ignorance is knowledge. The only cure – albeit always partial – for self-deception is to have external, objective, standards by which to judge your subjectivity – perhaps in this case, your "opinion", "understanding", "interpretation", etc.

You can look at any academic discipline through the lens of the classical "Trivium" – Grammar, Logic, Rhetoric. Grammar is the primary material with which you work; Logic comprehends the principles of how Grammar's structures work; Rhetoric is the application of Grammar and Logic to convey an idea (classically, to persuade).

Applied to History, by analogy, then, the Historian's "grammar" is the body of evidence, the facts. The Historian's "logic" is methodology, the principles of interpreting the evidence, and for discovering more. The Historian's "rhetoric" is the marshalling of the evidence, according to historical methodology, in making an argument or interpretation of how all the facts go together. This is often presented in the form of a narrative, the success of which will be determined by the Historian's mastery of the grammar and logic of his discipline as they are combined with the full range of rhetorical strategies in presenting them. The Historian is telling a story, and the scientific Historian wants to tell the best story possible – possible within the factual and methodological bounds that constrain him.

So, to overcome ignorance, the prospective Historian first has to learn all the evidence. For the Tarot Historian, this isn't very much really. It is so little in fact, that only knowing the evidence that is directly and explicitly related to tarot cards will be hardly any mastery at all. It would be like learning only one part of speech, or a few isolated words. To make it worth anything, the Tarot Historian has to seek context – contextual facts for the moment. Tarot is a family of card games, and is part of a much bigger family – playing cards and card games. Learning everything relevant suddenly becomes quite a bit harder; in fact it is an inexaustible subject. Tarot games is a huge subject – probably the richest single family of related card games there is – but while they may occupy a lifetime of study, they must be placed in the context of the bigger family of card games in general for any kind of perspective to be possible. So the Tarot Historian has to become an expert in card games, in the same way that a linguist has to become an expert in languages. The Tarot Historian doesn't have to become an expert player of hundreds of card games, just like the linguist doesn't have to speak a thousand languages – but they both have to know the principles upon which all games/languages are based and how they work in principle, sufficiently to identify a particular object by its class.

All of this is only the class of card games – which are obviously part of the much bigger family of games in general. Suddenly the Tarot Historian emerges from the forest of card games to a clearing on the crest of a hill – he sees before him on the vast plain below, stretching as far as the eye can see all around, the universe of human play. Now THIS is a field worthy of a philosophical mind; at the realization of the vastness of it, we scurry back to specialization in a sub-domain, where technical mastery is still possible.

So the Tarot Historian sees the big picture, the biggest picture of all, and now can sense the bounds of the field that will be relevant for the specialized study. Besides the raw facts, he meets the names of those who collected them and presented them – the authorities in the subject, and the sources. From them he learns, both by passive reception and active engagement, the methodology of the field. He passes from Grammar to Logic by studying and discussing with the experts, not just taking the facts like nuggets of gold that he's mined from their writings. He can't just memorize where Cicero uses the ablative absolute – he has to read and understand Cicero. The context in which the fact is presented is equally, if differently, as important as the fact itself. He must think like an archaeologist or geologist, learning everything in situ as well as extracted and replaced in a hypothetical former place or condition.

You'd address self-deception – trying to keep it in check – by developing principles and comparing yourself to external standards like other very smart people who have tried to interpret what you are interpreting. Naturally, you'd also use "common sense" – it's a late medieval Italian card game – I take it for granted that this obvious truth will help you avoid a lot of possible avenues for self-deception. By "developing principles" I mean establishing premises, like whether the trump sequence – any extant trump sequence – has a coherent meaning in principle; some people, like Michael Dummett, seem to believe that this is not necessarily so. They await a compelling argument that it does. The first rule for not deluding oneself is to constantly remind oneself of this basic uncertainty. Never take your interpretations too seriously, since by the time you get to the point of making a thorough-going interpretation, you'll realize how easily something new could come up that would completely change everything. In the absence of the original designer's notes, it's all speculation. So remember that great minds, authorities in the subject, differ.

The interpretation game really is a game. As long as everyone involved knows all the rules – i.e., has mastered all the relevant facts – then the game is played in the standard rhetorical, argumentative way. Unless some new fact comes up that really does change something, then "winning" and "losing" in this game is impossible in an objective sense. Even if an interpretation of a trump sequence won universal acceptance on the basis of a brilliant argument, it could still be wrong.

This is why the best arguments will suggest avenues for further research, they will be "theories" that will make "predictions" that will enable testing – to use the scientific model. History differs from science here in that even a correct theory may lack all positive evidence, which could have been lost, whereas phyiscal science tests real things, the present world. But a good historical theory of origin for something like the game of Tarot will suggest at least some new avenues for possible discovery (predictions), if not definitive proof. For instance, my preferred theory at the moment predicts that more information on the earliest tarot might be discovered in archival sources of the University of Bologna. From experience in old libraries, I imagine that there may be in some volume, manuscript or printed, a sheet of paper inserted on which someone has written basic rules, maybe a list of trumps. I have seen a lot of "lost papers" stuck into very old books, and I suspect I might have been the first person in hundreds of years to see them.

But imagine the immensity of the task! In fact, it is almost impossible to test my "theory" in reality – you'd have to go through every volume of archives and old printed books in the various buildings of the University (although I suggest that the first place to look should be the Law school), just hoping to stumble on something. So really, we have to rely on chance, and the occasional directed search, to advance earlier than 1442 in our knowledge of Tarot history. In the meantime, we argue theories.

About interpreting the Tower as the Tower of Babel, if you accept the premise that a sequence has a coherent narrative, you'd have to see how the Tower of Babel might fit in such a narrative. Why is it flanked by the Devil and the Star? Why is the name never "Tower", but "Fire" or "Thunderbolt" in the early Italian sources, and "House of God" in the French? Why do some early decks, like Viéville, not show a Tower at all, but preserve the thunderbolt in a different context? Is this trying to tell us something about the meaning of the card in the sequence in the most abstract way? How do we tell if a given sequence has an intended meaning, a coherent icongraphic narrative, or not? All of this comes down to argument, establishing premises for further deductions. These are games that few experts engage in, and none are in complete agreement on.

Thus it seems to me that every expert will consider every other expert to be self-deluded or ignorant in some way, missing something obvious or at least, if subtler, more persuasive. There is no absolute cure for self-deception, but the most basic errors, such as anachronism, can be mostly avoided.

Now, you are pointing out something I think is very important but gets constantly overlooked among tarot lovers: the difference between the history of the tarot as an artifact, and the history, or provenance, of the images. I suspect that what most tarot enthusiasts take for tarot history is a quest for the origin of the images we see in the cards. This of course has to do with the fact that the tarot experienced some sort of false-start in its narrative. The tarot was 'born again' around 1781 when it was proposed as the carrier of an occult philosophical message, and the popularity of this tale overlapped its 'firts coming', its original invention as a card game. Now, before we move forward I want to ask you: why the tarot? When did you know that you wanted to give your time and attention to the tarot's history?

"When" was in early 2002. I had just arrived in France, was learning the language, and remembered a book I had seen in Fresno State's library (UC Fresno, Henry Madden Library) when I lived in California in 1990s – *Tarot: jeu et magie*. (I didn't remember the name of the book at that time). I didn't have a historical interest in Tarot in the 80s or 90s, and I couldn't read French, but I remembered that the book had some intriguing pictures of a deck I later found out was called the "Charles VI" deck. So I went online looking for information, which led me to *TarotL* at yahoo groups… Rather quickly, I got hooked on Tarot history. I started frequenting libraries in my region and building a little file. I had been a long-time student of the "Holy Blood, Holy Grail" genre, so being in southern France was the perfect place to get to know the Templars, Mary Magdalene, Rennes-le-Château esoteric mix better, and I tossed Tarot in there too.

One constant theme in my intellectual and academic life has been the search for origins. This is why I majored in History as an undergraduate – my aim in studying history was to learn about the Bible, biblical literature, and Christian origins, naturally the first century, but also the background (Second Temple Judaism) and up to the Council of Nicea. In graduate school at Harvard I focused entirely on Biblical literature and Christian origins. It may seem strange that I could suddenly start studying the European Middle Ages, but seen from the angle of Tarot origins you can see it makes perfect sense. I think many people who study ancient history partly do so in the hopes of getting a grasp on the origins of some important things – the origin of writing, the calendar, various mechanical technologies and sciences, whatever. In fact in my last year at Harvard I was planning on doing my doctorate in the Near Eastern Languages and Civilizations (NELC) program, going as far back as written history allowed. It was always going back, back, back – to the original writings, the original stories, the "original versions" of things. So the Middle Ages, and then later the Italian 1300s and 1400s, wasn't exactly on my radar when I began this study. But when I came to realize that the Quattrocento was the time when Tarot was invented, that's what I had to study if I were to get to its origins.

The methodology of historical research is the same whatever period you want to study, but I imagine that for any scholar traces of their formative training will show up. In my case this happens when I use analogies for the Tarot like when I call the "three families" of trump orders – A, B and C or Southern, Eastern and Western – the "synoptic tarots", or compare the standard playing card deck to the "Old Testament" and the tarot trumps, being added to it, to the "New Testament". I find them actually quite useful and instructive analogies – most people can grasp immediately that a regular deck of cards is therefore older, broader, and has a more complex and obscure history than the Tarot. But, conversely, for Christians – in this analogy, Tarotists – the arguments over Tarot will be more immediate and intense than arguments over the origins and history of the four-suited deck.

For the question "Why the tarot?", the simple answer is that I had been an esoteric user of the Golden Dawn tarot tradition – primarily Crowley and Waite – since 1979, and so that kind of Tarot was already a familiar friend. Once I turned my historical gaze toward the real history of the Tarot, it was a foregone conclusion that I wouldn't stop until I got to the bottom of it all.

Here is another version that I wrote about 4 years ago, explaining how I changed from a believer in the esoteric myths of the Tarot to coming completely around to reality. Michael Hurst called it a "conversion experience", and I think that is an accurate description. It wasn't an about-face, just a nudge onto the right track after a long journey towards it, but conceptually that "nudge" spanned an incredible gulf that few true believers ever cross, no matter how educated they become in the true history of the game. They hold on; I let go.

I began historical tarot studies in early 2002, and made my first post on *TarotL*. Before that, I had 23 years of occult tarot (on and off), and had even been a professional tarot reader (in 1996). I hadn't thought much about the history of the cards, but since I was trained in historical methodology from '86 to '94, it didn't take much to apply it to tarot. The only hang-up I had was believing, like so many before me, that the cards *had* to have some occult significance, had to have arisen in the "mists of time", or at least, be very exotic and not "simply" some kind of early 15th century Italian game, etc.

Tarot history provided an escape from the pressures of being in a new country, with a foreign language. Secondly, here in southern France is "esoteric" territory – Templars, Cathars, Mary Magdalene – it was a good place to be, to explore all the half-baked ideas I had been consuming as an Anglo-American. Tarot as an esoteric text from the middle ages? No better place than here to research it. My entry was to explore the Charles VI deck, and I took umbrage at the assertion of the "authorities" that it was late 15th century Italian! Clearly, there was prejudice at work on their part...

Those blinders were eroded away when I applied myself fully to the study, and left no stone unturned to get every scrap of information (this was the only time I think that I went through some of Kubler-Ross' "stages of grieving" for a theory – or at least, a prejudice). I can remember the very day that I finally let it go (not the date, unfortunately, which I didn't record, but the moment, place, reason etc.) – early April, 2004.

My notebooks show the process fully – my natural skepticism, trained in sound methodology, battling against the slow and regretful loss of the tarot mystique – which was being replaced by a much more exciting and very real historical investigation. The loss was for times past, not of faith, because I had already lost faith (in the early 90s – yes my professional tarot reading was half-cynical, if compassionate). It was the death of an old friend.

After two years of "hard research" and collecting sources, I had found the title of a book that should at last demonstrate that someone who knew about esoteric stuff, thought that tarot had some esoteric significance. It was by Claude-François Ménestrier, from 1694, titled *La Philosophie Des Images Enigmatiques, Ou Il Est Traite Des Enigmes, Hieroglyphiques, Oracles, Propheties, Sorts, Divinations, Loteries, Talismans, Songes, Centuries de Nostradamus, De La Baguette* (to see why I thought so highly of his erudition, judgment, and particular qualifications, see the Catholic Encyclopedia article on him – in particular, he had made huge studies of heraldry and emblems, and was born, educated and lived his whole life in Lyon – *the center of French tarot production*).

This book was not in Gallica's vast pdf. collection, and no previous scholar of tarot cards had cited it, so I presumed it had been overlooked or not yet examined, and I had to make a special trip to Montpellier to read it in the original. Of course it was a test – I must have already long realized that the esoteric idea was dead – I just needed a final proof. What I found that afternoon was that in nearly 500 pages of discussion of the most arcane of esoteric subjects (all the stuff in the title of course, hieroglyphs, alphabets, enigmas, iconology, lots and divination, geomancy, lot books, Malachy, Nostradamus, dreams, Cabala, talismans), Menestrier did not mention Tarot cards, nor even playing cards, even once. Not a single time. I got up from the table with a sense of relief. Finally all the tendencies of the previous two years of studies came to rest. I felt now that I had read everything I needed to – the certainty of a PhD student at the end of coursework who knows he's read every relevant thing – in order to be able to assert that at the turn of the 17th century, tarot had no occult significance. I was free to devote myself without prejudice to a *new* (to me) study – the purely historical tarot. No more shadows, no more dark suspicions. The process of this liberation may have been gradual, but the moment of release is precise. It is when I read Menestrier's 1694 book.

What I personally hope from history is to deliver me from madness.

I find that an extremely odd way to think about the value of history! I think that as long as the stories we believe about the past don't impel us to evil acts, then it really doesn't matter what we believe. Of course, many of the stories of the past, especially religious and political ones, do come with moral imperatives – they are often designed that way, to arouse a sense of entitlement or injustice that has to be righted. Sometimes it's good, sometimes not.

There is a sense of sobriety in the facts of the tarot's history I cherish. There is a cognitive dissonance between what comes to my mind when I say the word 'tarot' and to what comes to most people's mind. In most people's mind the tarot is associated to bad taste, old creepy ladies, lots of purple, ignorance and deception. In my mind the tarot brings the austerity of pure color and simple shapes whose rhythms and patterns can make me experience that kind of truth we know as 'beauty'. For me, knowing the facts of the tarot's history equals cleaning the mind from all sorts of fringe garbage.

I agree with the value of cleaning the mind, getting the plain truth. But for me, once the separation had been made, and I had established a new, clean space or point of view in the real historical world, I could appreciate the spooky trappings and tarot mystique in its own place. It's a phenomenon too, it's telling us something, it's worthy of investigation like any other subject. It's another way Tarot is played.

Do you feel, today, that there was still something to gain from all your incursion in the 'occult'?

Absolutely. The occult, esotericism, was formative in my spiritual life. It ran parallel to both religion and science as a way of approaching the ultimate truth, which has always been a driving force for me, at least since early adolescence. Maybe as long as I can remember, depending on how I look at it. I always wanted the big picture, I wanted to know everything; I started writing a history of the world at age 10, and saw the future of humanity in giant space colonies, going out to distant stars. My view is very different now, but that was the early part of what has really been a continuum of thought throughout my life – the desire for the big picture.

The esoteric tree for me started growing in 1978, when I read a book called *The Zarkon Principle* (1975), by "Zarkon", which was a kind of summa of Von Däniken, Berger and Pauwels, René Guenon, a mixture of Theosophy and the western mystery tradition, Crowley, Hitler and Nazi occultism, mystical physics (a la Fritjof Capra), etc. leading up to the author's theory about how by vibrating at a certain rate humans could achieve immortality and survive the big crunch (the collapse of the universe back to the quantum vacuum before the next big bang). You can see, with my imagination, the desire for a "big picture", how this appealed to my 12-year old mind, and of course I had no critical faculties in place to judge it. I also read things like *The Exorcist* and *The Amityville Horror*, which made me believe in demons (I also drew my own pornography, since I had none... I wish I could see those drawings now, to see how I imagined things!).

In the summer of 1979, I had to move from Lanark, Scotland, to Calgary to live with my paternal grandparents, because my stepmother and I couldn't get along any longer (2 years of hell for me). It was an emotional shock, and in the new environment I found myself estranged and a stranger, both with the family and in the new school. Faced with benign neglect in the one place and bullies in the other, I withdrew to my fertile imagination and sense of uniqueness. In September 1979 I picked up (in a bookstore called "The Laughing Rooster" in North Hill Mall – just to show you how precise the memory is) a book called *The Satanic Bible* by Anton LaVey, and read it in a single afternoon. I was converted to Satanism! It allowed me to be arrogant, to laugh at the stupidity of my peers. It gave me an identity, and a philosophy.

At the same time, naturally, being curious about everything, I got into other kinds of occultism. Palmistry, astrology, tarot – and Aleister Crowley. By the end of '79 I had memorized the Little White Book for the Rider Waite deck, and was reading Tarot for anyone.

In 1980 I had a hunch that the trumps might be related to the chapters of the Book of Revelation, so I started reading the Bible, and books about the Bible. The Bible was so down on divination and vivid in its threats of punishment for diviners, that I began to get scared. I was also ashamed of my masturbation – I'm not sure how that happened, since I was never lectured about it, and I don't remember reading about Christian attitudes towards it, but somehow that shame grew in me. The fear of being a sinner going to Hell finally led me, in the night of August 19, 1980, when I was visiting my mother in Newmarket, Ontario, to "give my life to Christ" – getting down on my knees by my bed and promising to change my life. The next day (my birthday), I went out to buy a study Bible – I wanted a Hebrew-Greek English version (being a scholar, you know), and a kind stranger (an alcoholic, "sober for 90 days") in the store bought one for me. I still have it – the *Ryrie Study Bible*.

That fall, back in Calgary, I publically (in a park during the day) burned all my occult books and books about other religions, like Buddhism and Hinduism (about 200 books all together), along with all my occult paraphernalia, including 27 packs of Tarot and oracle cards. At school I gave away all my other possessions, like comic books (wish I'd kept some of the complete series' I had) and electronic toys. I started watching TV evangelists like George Vandeman on "It Is Written". I got a couple of friends invovled with my new found faith, and started seeking out churches to go to. I wanted the "oldest Church" (the historical purist in me), which of course meant the orthodox traditions, Roman Catholic and Greek Orthodox. That fall I went to several of them, but never joined. Instead, I went, with my friend Dave Bergeron, in December to a revival at the Seventh Day Adventist Church. A visiting pastor from Spokane, Washington was preaching, along with his wife and two attractive daughters, one of which was certainly my age. They sang beautifully... seductively... "Does anybody here wanna live forever? Say 'I do'. Does anybody here wanna walk on golden streets? Say 'I do'. Is anybody here sick and tired of livin' like you do? If anybody here wants a home with love forever, say 'I do', say 'I do'". I said I did and was the first up for the altar call. I joined the Seventh Day Adventist church (after getting permission from my official guardians, my grandparents, since I was only 14).

My friend Dave didn't follow me in this. I was active in that church for about 6 months, and began drifting away in my mind. Something was coming back, some dark urges... that fall of 1981 I was cutting down trees with my grandfather and uncle in Canmore, and the radio was always playing Juice Newton's "Playing with the Queen of Hearts":

> Playing with the queen of hearts
> Knowin' it ain't really smart
> The joker ain't the only fool
> Who'll do anything for you

The Tarot was coming back... I couldn't resist it. All of the imaginative power, the romance, of the occult flooded back into me that fall. I stopped going to church (but they kept calling, believe me), and started buying – and stealing – back my occult books and stuff. I tore up a Bible in school and announced I was a Satanist again.

I had a brief relapse into born-again Christianity in January 1982, but my journal shows that I was reading the cards again in early February. I guess I didn't burn my books this time. When I came back to occult this time, I still wrote "Ave Satanas" as the cry of liberation. I was living in the basement of my grandparents' house, and decorated it like a Satanic Temple, with the Baphomet head in the pentagram on the wall. Rumors began to circulate about me – that I had sacrificed a cat, that I dug up graves – I met strangers on the bus who said "Aren't you the guy who sacrificed a cat?" But my occult studies were mostly intellectual, and wide-ranging, although I did some regular rituals and meditated, and did wander in the night. I was still growing up, and with that kind of teenage energy it's hard to stick to a discipline for long. I tried to arrange a schedule for myself, based on a monastic model – for several months that spring I rose well before school time and did a shamanic dance to the Police, then read and meditated. I didn't want to think I was just living for school. I shaved my head (and the first time, my eyebrows as well) to look more like Anton LaVey – a shaved head on a teenager was unusual in those days, and the school Principal called me in to ask why. They thought of suspending me, but cooler heads prevailed. I scrawled blasphemies like "Mary was a whore" and "Jesus was a bastard" in a Bible and showed it around. I was very much a tortured soul, not only intellectually, but also because I was in love – obviously frightening the poor girl (and yet also obviously fascinating her). Later I would marry her.

By spring of 1983 I was in deep depression, and designed a way to kill myself. Note that I absolutely did not use drugs or drinks; this was an intellectual depression. I looked up the lethal dose of acetysalicylic acid (aspirin), and kept a slightly higher number of the pills on me at all times (150). Finally, on the night of February 23, 1983, in the basement of the new house, I decided to do it. 10, 20, 30, 40, 50 – I couldn't do any more, I gave up trying to kill myself. I knew I'd be harmed by it, get quite sick, but something stopped me from taking the necessary 120 or so. I crawled out of the window into the snow, and lay looking at the stars. I promised them I'd live.

I was sick – I vomited a few hours later, but hardly anything came out. It was a three-day daze; during it, I walked into my Social Studies class and told the teacher I was dropping out of school – I hadn't been going much anyway. She looked at me in a strangely knowing way. So I dropped out of Grade 11. My grandparents finally noticed something wasn't right, and arranged to get me out of the setting that was depressing me. In March they sent me to live with my great uncle and aunt in North Bay, Ontario. It's a small north Ontario town surrounded by forest and lakes, where I had spent a few weeks every summer since 1975.

There the wound healed. I was enrolled in the Catholic boys' school there, Scollard Hall, to finish my Grade 11. I took up piano lessons, swam and sailed, and most importantly, took up the Crowley-A.A. meditation regimen outlined in *Libers E* and *O. Magick in Theory and Practice* became my bible; I was determined to achieve the Great Work. Although suicidal thoughts stayed at the beginning – I found my uncle's hand gun and kept it under my pillow, and I used to act out Pink Floyd's "The Wall" in front of the mirror – the healthy air and later, sunshine, purified my soul. By August I was ready to go back to Calgary. When I got back I was so changed that the girl whom I had suffered so much for and who had rejected me, barely recognized me. I was no longer in love with her. But when she saw me she fell in love with the new me – so I agreed. We started dating.

I enrolled in Alternative High School for Grade 12. I kept up my serious exercises with the A.A. work, meditation, ritual, and exercises, as well as esoteric study. In the spring I decided I wanted to marry my girlfriend, but since she was Mormon, I had to be too. She had no idea that I went to the LDS church in my area and started the process to be baptized. This was entirely calculated on my part; I decided to do it as if I were going into "deep cover" – I wanted to be so good I could even fool myself. I believed all beliefs were interchangeable anyway, and Thelema was compatible with Mormonism. I stopped masturbating for six months – until one night I had a dream of ejaculating like a fire hose, such was the pent-up desire.

In the fall of '84 she went off to Brigham Young University, and I stayed behind, working at the hospital in the dietary section. I had long stopped caring about the Mormon church and was just pretending for her parents, but they could tell and had doubts about me. My mother-in-law to be did some snooping and found out I wasn't going to Church where I should be (the Ward for young adults – I was going to go on a mission the next year, so I was not to promise myself to any girl, nor she to me), and also not taking some extra classes I was supposed to at Alternative High School, to make up for my matriculation. In reality I was working the A.A. system intensely, had contacted the OTO, and began smoking pot and taking mushrooms. I went down to see her in Provo twice – once in the fall of '84, and once in the spring of '85, where we had sex for the first time – kind of, since everything but vaginal penetration was allowed. Back in Calgary I had already had my first sexual experience with a friend, Robert Cawley, who was the one whom I had introduced to Crowley and Thelema, and the one who introduced me to drugs.

My girlfriend came back in April of 1985, and quickly ascertained that I had changed. My daily letters in the beginning had become weekly and finally only one or two for the last couple of months; she knew I was back in the occult and had left the church. Somehow, she agreed with this and left the church as well, much to her family's chagrin. We had proper sex for the first time in the woods of Edworthy Park, and we moved into an apartment in May, where we had sex 5 times a day, smoked pot, burned incense, and I introduced her to the rudiments of Thelema.

In June we decided to take a trip around the world, starting with working for the summer in Toronto and then taking a boat to Iceland. But first, we had to get married – in the pagan way, by handfasting. Up to Edmonton we went, where the local OTO Lodge was headquartered. Since they were also Wiccans, we got handfasted. The day before, I was initiated into the OTO, taking the Minerval degree.

Then we were off on our adventure – three of us driving to Toronto in a car (I can't remember what type) my friend Steve had rented. It broke down in northern Ontario, and we camped out for the night, and had to take a bus to North Bay to ask for further help from my relatives. They let us stay for a few days and fed us, but no more. Our only option was to hitchhike to wherever. Of course we had to split up – who's going to pick up three people? After a few hours in the sweltering sun, we got a ride to Peterborough, while Steve had gotten a ride to somewhere. Our ultimate destination was Montreal, where Steve had relatives, and we would all meet up. After Peterborough we got a ride to Quebec City, where we again camped, in a thicket on the Plains of Abraham. Finally we got to Montreal, and lived for two weeks in a camper behind the house of Steve's uncle. There I painted, with a brush made from own hair, a copy of the Stele of Revealing, 26th Dynasty funerary stele that had been part of Crowley's inspiration in writing of the *Book of the Law* (I gave it to my friend Craig in Fresno in 1998). We also tormented poor Steve, who was sleeping just a few feet from us on the other side of the small camper, with loud vigorous sex. God, it must have been terrible – what inconsiderate, arrogant assholes we were!

Finally we decided to leave and go to Toronto, to work at the Canadian National Exhibition, which takes place in late August to early September. With this money, we would start our world tour. We arrived first in Newmarket, where my mother lived. It was night so we set up our tent outside. In the morning she was overjoyed to see us, and said a fortune-teller had predicted it by tea-leaves. Our plan was to stay with her for a few days while we looked for jobs at the CNE. She must have been wiser, looking at these two 18-year old ragamuffins, planning a trip around the world! She asked if we were really married, and although we said so – because to us a handfasting was real, although not legally married – she finally got us to agree to get really married – for tax purposes of course. Days turned to weeks, and the CNE idea was gone, and so was the idea of leaving for the trip. We were stuck with working, at least through the winter. I got a job at McDonald's, as the night janitor. That lasted about six weeks, when I quit out of frustration at the manager. I got another job, also a janitor or "caretaker", at the school where my father-in-law worked, Pickering College. This was full-time and would last 7 years.

We didn't last long under my mother's roof – only until November. Jamie – my father-in-law – had probably seen one too many midnight rituals in the fields beside the house, and they hated us burning incense. We had to find our own accomodation, and finally did find a reasonable appartment in Newmarket. My mother, and my wife, began to convince me to go to university instead of on the road, and I relented, entering York University in September 1986. I was working full-time at Pickering College and also going to school full-time (my job was Monday and Tuesday nights, 4pm to midnight, and Saturday and Sunday 8am to 8pm). At Pickering College I had few duties, and could devote most of my time to meditation and ritual; this is where I developed the habit of saying the four daily adorations; I also managed to write an exhaustive concordance of the *Holy Books of Thelema*, and memorized the *Book of the Law*. At home our house was a library and pagan shrine, and dedicated to all kinds of ritual and debauchery. My wife had become a priestess in her own right, and we developed a little "coven" in Newmarket in the late '80s.

My academic interest was erratic – it took me six years to get my degree. But in the final two years, I stopped all occult and esoteric studies and focused entirely on getting my academic life in order – I got perfect grades in those years.

Once at Harvard in the fall of 1992, I began to hear the drumbeat of the mystical once again. This time it was serious. It began with dreams – a presence in the woods, coming for me; a hill I was just about to surmount, beyond which lay uncertainty and terror; dancing in tight black leather in a red room for a witchy woman; the dreadful fear that we were going to get divorced. At Christmas '92 we went back to Newmarket to visit. During a party I took LSD (I had been doing it since 1987, without ever finding exactly what I was looking for) and finally "came to myself" – I realized who I was, the figure in the dreams and what they meant. I was turned on and I turned on the whole party – just like the dancing figure. Everybody got to writhing and swooning, although it didn't break out into an orgy like I'd hoped – there were some minors present, one girl I kissed who was only 16, and she seemed willing although I had enough presence of mind not to go further. But the point was "magick" – I knew what it was and where it came from within me.

When I got back to Harvard I had changed, and indeed within 4 months we were separated (and divorced in September '93). I kept my studies up, but it was my social life, as a magickal life, that drove me. Suddenly girls were everywhere, and I loved the "alternative" music of that time. One of the powers I had long sought was "fascination" – being able to command attention and get people to do my bidding, and it seemed I had it now. Life was an orgy. My practices began to include Voodoo – which I learned from a priestess (studying Law and Theology!) at Harvard. Although pleasure was often the aim, I realized that I lacked my true desire – that ever elusive "Great Work". I decided to go back to basics, and "initiate" myself through the Golden Dawn rituals, memorizing them and then going through them in ordered sequence, until the 5°=6° – symbolizing the grade at which the Aspirant achieves "The Knowledge and Conversation of the Holy Guardian Angel." After this, in the winter-spring of '93-'94, I prepared to do the ritual "Liber Pyramidos" for Easter, in order to establish myself on the path to attainment. After a whole-night vigil, I did it for Easter morning, ending at dawn, and swore myself to the work.

My lover had given me a magickal name, told her in a dream – "Zapapaias". This is the name I used in my self-initiation. In June, my father, along with my stepmother, came to visit me at Harvard. We took a nice trip up to Salem and generally got along well. They invited me down to Rio de Janeiro, where they were living, later that summer. I had a girlfriend I wanted to take with me, but she refused to go. I went alone, in August 1994. I had made contact with a Brazilian church that used Ayahuasca, a "tea" made from a hallucinogenic vine, the Uniaô do Vegetal – this was one of the things that brought me to Harvard, Timothy Leary's legacy, and by divine coincidence a man who knew him and had contact with the entheogenic community in California came to Harvard in '93. Through him I got to talk to Dennis Mackenna, who put me in contact with the UDV and set up a meeting for me in Rio.

I took a long walk from the tip of Ipanema beach all the way to the end of Copacabana beach, often going into the sea and praying to Yemenja, the goddess of love and the sea. That night I had a dream in which a woman came to me, and we were about to make love, when I said "No, I want a real woman". She skipped away, laughing, "I'm disappointed in you, Ross". My father took me up to Macae, where Schlumberger's people are based. He took me out to a local bar and introduced me to his friends, many of which were women. I would have three of them; Yemenja indeed blessed me.

For the UDV, I went to their service and drank the tea. I hadn't taken the precaution not to eat seriously, so when it began to kick in I had to go out and vomit. It was a common occurrence, judging by the others doing the same thing. But afterward, for about 45 minutes, it was quite an experience of visual and emotional grandeur. They sing hymns, passed down orally, during the peak of the tea's effects. I asked if I could get recordings, and my guide said they are never recorded. But I had a trick to memorize it – I had a song, written by Crowley in a vision, that I had long used in my rituals to Babalon. I had a tune for it, but I hated it. But what the UDV's songs did for me was so profound, I knew that THIS was the music for my song. I had only sing my song with their music, and it was a perfect marriage. I had learned their mystical and transcendent songs, which sound like ancient longing. I felt like Prometheus stealing fire from Heaven. Later I would have a private session with members of the UDV and the tea, which I properly prepared for and did not have to vomit. In any case, for the song, I sing it to this day. It is one of my most cherished possessions.

In Rio I also fell out with my father and step-mother (in part due to my girlfriends); I stayed on for the last 4 weeks only because I knew I had to squeeze every moment out of this trip, and I would probably not have the chance again. I haven't spoken to him since 1994, and don't even know where he is.

When I landed at JFK I had 27 cents in my pocket. I had to make a collect call to my girlfriend at Harvard, and told her to sell a set of my books (the *Theological Dictionary of the New Testament*) and buy me a plane ticket. Back at Harvard, I had a dorm room for the fall term, but I spent most of my time in my girlfriend's house. During the summer, when we were officially broken up, she had been using Ecstasy (MDMA) – in a pure form, from a "source" who made it – and wanted to introduce me to it. Remember that we called such drugs, used in certain contexts, "entheogens" – "engendering god within". The powder was bitter, and she dissolved it in a glass of port, giving it to me like a sacrament.

It was like the opening of the heart chakra. It was everything, all love, no fear. Everything that had happened to me in Brazil came pouring out, all of the insight was present, the mystical verses, I started singing Crowley, and reciting passages of the Holy Books that I had never understood before, or seen the profundity. I knew exactly what they meant. I knew exactly what they felt like. I felt like I was almost there, to the Great Work, I saw at last the possibility of it.

That fall, my last, at Harvard, I started to try to "correct" the *Necronomicon*, based on the original sources. I found out it was impossible, since the work is fiction and barely has any mesopotamian sources in it (I was preparing to apply for the doctoral program in NELC). But the work opened something in me – a Babylonian current. I began to understand Crowley's Babalon as really Inanna, Ishtar, the goddess of Babylon. As I turned to Babylon, my magickal life turned too; I found myself working harder, deliberately, in visionary states and dreams, for the Knowledge and Conversation of the Holy Guardian Angel. This was the one barrier I had never crossed; I couldn't do the Great Work without it.

The work progressed, school progressed. One of my girlfriends from Brazil, sadly smitten with me, had come up to Harvard in October. Since my Harvard girlfriend and I weren't officially together, still maintaining an open policy, I was free to see the carioca (who really did live across the street from the restaurant where Jobim and Moraes wrote "The Girl From Ipanema" (then called Veloso but now known as Garota de Ipanema). But I felt horrible; she was in love, I was just having fun. I had to break her heart; it broke mine to break hers, and it seemed my two years of mindless adventure were coming to a close. I had to settle down. But I had found what I was looking for, and for that I was grateful.

There was a close conjunction of Venus with the Moon in November; it was beautiful and glowing in the sky one morning; it seemed like a good omen. One morning I awoke from a night of turbulent dreams, the phrase I thought of was from Genesis, 32: 24ff – Jacob wrestled with the angel. I knew this was my Angel. Later I demanded to know his name. I had achieved the Knowledge and Conversation.

But it wasn't finished. In a similar half-dreaming state, where I was conscious, I received a new name "Master Murru", from a certain lady. I couldn't take it seriously – I was no "master"! I didn't know what to do, what sort of practice or ritual or meditation to perform, so I chose to look at my old name Zapapaias, for clues. I analyzed it by the Golden Dawn Kabbalistic method, where the letters stand for processes and ideas, deities. A is Apophis, a period of destruction, and I found the correlations for the periods in my life up the final "a" of the name. The next letter, S, is the letter of Saturn, and today was a Saturday. Saturn is the planet of Binah, which is the grade $8°=3°$ in the Golden Dawn Tree of Life grade scheme, "across the Abyss", the Master of the Temple.

I realized what it meant – I had to take the Oath of the Abyss, traditionally held to be the most insane thing an unprepared person could do. I was hesitant, indeed. But I realized that's what the signs were saying, and I had spent 15 years of my life preparing for it, and lately I had been very successful... so I took it. Behind Andover Hall, in the bright sunshine, in the middle of the parking lot. I don't know and didn't care if anyone saw me – it would be good to know there were witnesses.

So I took the name "Master Murru" and began an entirely new life in magick. I would become the founder of the school of Babylonian Magick. But my involvement with occult tarot didn't end until 1996, when I read professionally a little in a Fresno bookshop. I did occasional face-to-face readings, which I had been fairly good at. But the owner had a franchise for the Psychic Readers Network as well, and I decided to try it – the hourly pay was good, and depending on my ranking after the two week trial period, the money would be even better.

Around 10pm every night, I'd log in and wait by the phone for random callers. My preferred method was Tarot, but really any method was fine, under the rubric "psychic". I put on a fake accent, that I'd borrowed from a Romanian friend I knew at Harvard (who was a follower of Carlos Castaneda), and gave my advice – the longer they stayed on, the more the PRN got paid and the higher my ranking went.

It was tiring, of course, but I generally got by with just about any old bullshit – intuitive bullshit of course. But I slowly began to grow a conscience. For instance, one time a guy phoned me from somewhere in Florida, in a hurry – he was on a hot date and wanted to know if he had any STDs (sexually transmitted diseases). I asked him if he thought he did. He said no, so I just said "I don't see any either" – and that was it. I realized what I might have just done. Then another time a woman phoned, from Louisiana. She was worried about some family matter, her poverty, and she just wanted to keep talking, so I did – it was great for my ranking. When her fears and questions had been thoroughly answered – about 20 minutes at 3 bucks a minute, I thought she was about to go when she started asking about her children's futures, one by one – there were three or four of them. If I remember correctly callers got automatically cut off at 40 or 50 minutes, but whatever it was, she spent the maximum. When our time was up, I thought about this poor woman who had just spent at least 120 bucks talking to me. I felt literally unclean.

There were surprises that shocked even my jaded outlook – one time a guy called, a "tester", who wanted to see if I were really psychic. So he said he had something on his mind, and wanted to know if I could tell what it was. I gave my "Vell, let me see... let me look..." kind of talk, while doing my damnedest to guess, then to intuit, what it was he wanted to talk about. Nothing. I drew out the sighs, the "hmmmm"s, and thought – let me pull a card. I pulled one – I think it was the King of Swords, Crowley's deck. Whatever it was, I intuited "blood". Quickly I said "Somsing about your blood" – and there was silence on the other end. A stammer, then he said "Wow – how'd you know? I have a rare blood disease and want to know about it." That was a rare true success.

But in general, I got burned out and disgusted with myself. One night I couldn't face it anymore – there was no more intuition to draw on. The phone looked like an Inquisition rack. I decided to call a female friend, Patricia, a very psychic, intuitive person, to ask for her help. She offered – "if you aren't getting anything, try this: get them to say their name slowly three times, and take what you see, like this 'P a t r i c i a … P a t r i c i a … P a t r i c i a…' – so?"

"I get a wilted rose" I blurted out. Almost immediately I knew what I had done, but it was too late and she said good bye and good luck and hung up the phone. But I might as well have shot her in the heart.

I tried to call back later and apologize, but no response. I left messages. I wrote two letters to her and her partner David, but never heard back. I knew I had done irreprable damage to this sensitive, poetic soul. Of the heartbreaks I have caused, this remains the worst. Because we were not romantically involved, she had no defenses, no sense of betrayal to fall back on. She respected me immensely, she was at that moment the most vulnerable. I just shot her straight through the heart, one psychic to another, blunt and unforgiving, with my true feelings.

It was after that that I gave up my stint with the PRN, just short of my ranking period. And I gave up reading the cards altogether. I guess you could say that my "incursion" into occultism has influenced me a little!

I recently read a book about Aleister Crowley written by John S. Moore. Moore hoped to reinstate Crowley as one of Modernity's most important thinkers. I don't know… I think that comparing Crowley to Ezra Pound is quite a long shot. Crowley was a colorful character, but I think that his expressive material, magic and esotericism, is fundamentally at odds with modernity itself. Most importantly, 'the occult', as some call it, is a realm that stands for all these things our culture at large rejects when it comes to define itself. Now, if we were to contrast Crowley with a contemporary of his, like Marcel Duchamp, (Crowley was born in 1885 and died in 1947. Marcel Duchamp, was born in 1887 and died in 1968) things don't really look up for Crowley. In a sense, I would grant that, in the 20th century, the so-called magician attempted to do magic, but it was the artist, the one actually pulling of the tricks that succeeded.

Despite my deep involvement with Crowley, I wouldn't call him one of modernity's most important thinkers, by a long shot. He's in a category by himself – maybe he belongs with Casanova or Richard Burton, or Cagliostro; there's a bit of them in him. You might also compare him to William Blake. His poetry is too deep in me to give an objective impression of its worth. I think I'm being objective though, when I say that his best work is in his pornographic poems and prose. Then some of the *Holy Books*, *The Book of Lies* and a few others. Then his work with George Cecil Jones in creating the curriculum for the A. A.

What relevance do you think all that occult tradition really has in today's world?

That's a good question – I'm not sure it has any more relevance than it ever did. It is a way for some people, like I did, to take control of their lives and try to progress. But for many more it becomes a labyrinth with no exits; they become like any fundamentalists, lost in the text. It's dangerous, not only because of the charlatans who take advantage of weak minds, but also because it leads to self-deception and the emptiness that brings. I know both sides, so I can't dismiss it entirely – it can work, but there are other ways.

I guess its relevance is the same as any kind of religion – what does it provide to the believer, the practitioner? What are the risks? Are you being taken advantage of? A good tradition, a real mystical tradition, has a door that says "Exit" as well as one that says "Entry". You should be able to reach that Exit door within a reasonable time. From what I've read, my 15 years are pretty fast, but I was hardcore. I took the advice "If you meet the Buddha on the road, kill him" seriously. I feel it was too long, but I was growing up at the same time, so maybe that explains a lot of things. I can only say that I can't imagine I'd be who I am without "magick" – I can't imagine I would have taken so many risks and gone on so many adventures without it.

Ross, before I forget, my favorite part of your story is the fact that you carry with you a song as one of your most precious possessions.

Wonderful. I'm glad I emphasized it then. Song has always been an important part of my spiritual life. You could probably tell already. It's also an important part of religion in general – like the UDV shows, that's how the tradition is transmitted and expressed. More than sermons and discursive theology or philosophy, song is what gets to the heart and stays there. I can sing you some of my grandmother's United Church of Canada hymns, the Seventh-Day Adventist song I wrote for you, and some Mormon songs even. Song is for the heart, that's for sure. Whatever the words mean. If a church gets to dancing, it goes even deeper.

I am very interested in the idea of other currencies. A dear friend of mine almost came down to blows with a guy on the street. Then, a couple of days later, he was at another friend's apartment, looked down through the window and saw the same guy he had fought with, in his own apartment, naked. Seeing his opponent buttnaked and below him was a form of victory my friend cherished!

I can appreciate that. Revenge sometimes comes in strange ways. At Alternative High School in 1984, I was doing a Thelemic practice called "Liber Jugorum" – the *Book of the Yoke* – which aims to control speech, actions, and thoughts. First step is speech, so you chose what you can and can't say – certain words, letters of the alphabet – for a certain time, usually a week. This teaches vigilance. Every time you break your practice, you punish yourself – the book, in typical Crowley fashion, prescribes cutting your arm with a razor. I didn't have a razor, but I had a razor blade, so I used that. I didn't go too deep (most people today will tell you to wear a rubber band as a bracelet and thwack yourself instead, or some other bloodless method, but I told you I was hardcore), but I drew blood each time.

During an art class on Friday, I was doing a drawing – this one of a nursing mother. A student came in and complimented my drawing – I was trying to figure out a way to respond to him without breaking the rule of my practice (it might have been the word "I" or some letter of the alphabet), and it took so long for me to say anything that he just turned and left.

That evening I was taking the bus home – it was a long ride, at least an hour, with a transfer, and I still had a half-hour walk to get home – and I saw this student with some of his friends at the back of the bus. He was a big guy, much taller than me, and obviously "bad", in the drinking and drug using sense. I sat in the middle, in my own seat, and was lost in my thoughts. All of a sudden, this guy swung around on a pole and said "hey asshole" and punched me several times in the face. Then he went back. I was bleeding all over – nobody did anything – and pulled the cord for my stop. I went to the front of the bus instead of the middle door – the driver was a guy we called "the god", because he looked like Zeus, and

I felt he wouldn't let any further harm come to me. I saw the big guy and his friends get up to follow me off the bus at the middle doors. I got off at the front and looked back to see my assailant and his friends banging at the middle doors, which the god had refused to open for them. He really had helped me!

But I was shaken. I was pissed off – I didn't know (at the time) what I had done to deserve this attack. My only aim was revenge, so I sought magical revenge. I went home and prepared a ritual from the grimoire Goetia, which has some vengeful demons. In the best way I could with my meagre apparatus, I drew the circle and triangle, lit the candles and incense, and invoked the demon. I didn't expect an "appearance", I just said the ritual and when I thought it was time, I told him to wreak vengeance on that guy (I'm not sure what I said exactly, but you can bet it was much worse). After I was exhausted, I banished the space, cleaned up and went to bed.

On Monday, I didn't know what to expect. I half-believed he might be dead. But there he was, standing in the hallway. As soon as he saw me, he rushed towards me and begged my forgiveness for what he did, saying he didn't know what he was thinking and telling me how much he liked me and wanted to be my friend. Holy shit! Later he became kind of like my "muscle" for forays into the badder parts of Calgary – after I needed it, of course. But I never knew what changed him – what happened to him that weekend? What had pissed him off in the first place was that I didn't respond to his compliment, and I explained why – but I never learned why he had a sudden change of heart, so I believed that it had something to do with my "curse" – maybe he had a nasty dream. As I said, strange ways.

There is a question that immediately came to mind in response to your biographic recount and has to do with suicide. Given your experience, do you think you would have something wise to tell to someone planning to commit suicide? I had an experience once, with a client who came for a reading because his wife forced him. I was doing my readings at a café and I saw this man's family, a wife and two kids, sitting at a table nearby while he was telling me that he was about to kill himself due to some debts he had. His family didn't know about his financial problems, but they were about to lose everything, and he had decided to kill himself. I looked at his family and told him "yes, but you need to kill your children first". That guy never saw it coming, of course. I guess he was expecting for me to give him the usual "life is so precious" nonsense. But I told him he had to kill his kids first because otherwise he would leave them with this permission to fail, a permission to quit, embedded in their psyche forever. I took a gamble and I got his attention, which was what I wanted, but in retrospective I think it was crazy for me to say something like that. But thanks to that we got to really talk. We got to engage emotionally. I told him the story of these lizards that will sever their own tail to confuse a predator. The predator grabs the tail and starts eating it while the lizard runs away to safety, and eventually, the tail grows back. "The tail grows back" he repeated. To be honest, I couldn't help but resent this guy's family. I remember that his mother in law was also at the table, with his wife and kids. They were eating and chatting... gulping this guy's money, while he was talking to me about killing himself because he had no more money to give them. I managed to make him think about how losing a house may not be the end of the world. If you lose a house today you can get another one tomorrow. The tail grows back... I don't know what possessed me to tell that guy that, but I wonder of you have any insight on how to reach a person who is entertaining suicidal thoughts.

I think you handled it perfectly, and understand how you could "resent" the family, unknowingly driving him further into despair.

The only thing that works on people contemplating suicide – casually (as a test) at least – is sincerity. You have to be direct and blunt. You understood perfectly that the "life is precious" schtick wouldn't work – precisely because they have heard it a thousand times before and *already* decided that their own life isn't so precious. They wouldn't share their suicidal thoughts if they hadn't already decided their own life was worthless, and – most importantly – if they weren't ready to hear something new, that they hadn't heard before, that might deter them, they wouldn't reveal the thought to you. Hearing "but life itself is too precious" again will just turn the receivers off – you really don't care, you don't understand. But in revealing it, it shows they still have hope – hope that someone outside of their own tormented head might point to a better way that they couldn't have thought themselves.

Suicide because of debt is something I don't personally understand, but I think I can imagine why – it has to do with shame. Shame for failure. But unless he's in deep debt to ruthless criminals who might kill him and go after his family, there's no reason for fear (and even if he killed himself, they might still go after his family).

The worst that can happen is bankruptcy, and the loss of pride. As well as the hurt of starting from nothing. I think your analogy was perfect – the lizard who loses his tail. I know it from experience – in Spain as a child one summer, I used to try to grab the lizards I saw in the greenhouses – I'd grab the tail, and voilà! – I was left with a twitching tail in my hands, the amputee scampering off. I even saw one with two tails – I guess one almost got broken off, and the genetics kicked in, but the other healed too.

His mother-in-law was there; it seemed to me, just by your words, that she was the "Queen" of this situation. She was spending his money. If his wife is second to her mother, it could be that he is very angry with his wife, and the relationship she has with her mother. He might be thinking to punish his wife, and indirectly the cackling hag, by stealing what is making them so content – to show that it was all a facade anyway, built on nothing. He is trying to punish them. Who's laughing now?

Punishing people is a big motive for suicide.

When I was contemplating suicide I don't think I let on much, but I guess I told my grandmother because she mentioned it once when my grandfather was present. He was (and still is) a gruff old man, and only said "Well, let him do it then, we have enough mouths to feed". Pretty cruel, but although I felt worthless enough, what it did was turn me still more towards my inner strengths – I don't know, but it could be partly because of cruelty like this that I refused, finally, to go through with it. I had to prove them wrong. They gave me "spine".

I don't know if that kind of harsh "go ahead" approach would work for a grown man, whose problem is shame, not deep-seated depression – I doubt it, and I've never said it to someone who told me of their suicidal thoughts. All I have ever done for confessedly suicidal friends is made myself available and spent however much time it took – even taking time off work – just to be there and make sure they didn't have the time to go off and listen to the demons in their heads. In my experience, it always passed when better times came around, and I'm always up for a few long-nighters. I know this is not always the case.

For strangers who put their trust in me, I can't say I know. I'd hate to be the position like yours, knowing that someone's life might be in my hands, and that I had no further control than a short session over the cards or a cup of coffee. I'd do like you – go straight to my gut, to my intuition, and come up with good survival story, knowing that there is a light at the end of the tunnel and letting them know that. You can't erase a lifetime of (mis-)education on real values in a short session, but you can bring up a story, like the lizard's tail, that will resonate immediately and perhaps, just perhaps, plant a seed that will stop them from doing such immense damage to their family.

Oh, by the way, I liked that part even better – true instinct on your part – "you'll have to kill your kids first". I'm sure that stopped him – he'd probably thought of it already, and was ashamed that a perfect stranger might think it a perfectly innocuous observation.

Old school solution – what kind of a man kills himself to leave his family with debt and no place to live? Straightforward guilt. Might work too. Maybe he has no men around him to tell him things like that.

Now, if I were to look at the name ZAPAPAIAS something peculiar happens. The 'soul' of that word is AAAIA. If you look at the letter A, it stands like Le Bateleur, with its feet strongly planted on the ground, as if saying "this is who I am". That succession of letters A feels like a set of false starts A... A... A... it even sounds like stuttering. Finally, we arrive at the letter I, a door, a mirror or a membrane, separating the false starts for the final stand, the last letter A. The 'body' of that word is ZPPS. It is kind of symmetrical in that both the letter Z and the letter S suggest a communication between above and below, separated by these two letters P, as two banners standing for ideologies that fill our heads 'up there'; but the letter Z feels too abrupt, almost like a slide that takes an idea, not yet completely digested, down into the world. The letter S certainly feels like an improvement from the letter Z in that it suggests a softer, more fluent, form of dialogue.

I like your analysis – I understand the vowel=soul and consonant=body way of looking at it. I especially like the "false starts" and "stuttering" – I can relate to that. The P's as banners I like, and the "I" as a "mirror or a membrane". Sure – not bad. You need to know the context of my life and thought – as well as that Zapapaias was a name linked to a certain time, not a "true name" or "True Will" or anything like that. It was just an initiatory name, with a temporary message. It was just a step to help me to the next one (although, as you can see from searching on the internet, like any real magickal name, at least a euphonious one, it is completely unique – what are the chances of that?).

On the other hand, in chanting, sequences of vowels are often written that way to show the number of breaths – "breathings" or "vibrations" in magic chanting that you are to take. The shift from an A to an I, if done in a single breath, is quite a violent change (if you look at what has to happen between the nasal cavity, throat and tongue) – but I back to A is not so violent – it's a relaxation.

Here's how I thought of it at the time – my method was dogmatically Thelema-Golden Dawn: letter/tarot card/ritual. A is the Fool, not the Bateleur, and Apophis the crocodile (one of his manifestations, which came into the Golden Dawn teaching on the Tarot) – I didn't even know the Marseille Tarot in those days, and I certainly wasn't advanced enough to just go with free association. I needed concrete reality, or doctrine.

But first, it's interesting you point out the three A's (followed by an I). I never noticed that pattern. In fact three A's were part of my very first magical motto, chosen at age 15, well before I received formal initiations or "given" names.

Here's something I just recently posted to Aeclectic Tarot, on the topic "The Magickal Motto".

> I think magickal mottoes can be a key to initiation; but at first they are just statements of your magickal understanding, or self understanding, as that happens to be when you choose it. Later they become refined, and finally "granted" – a name becomes something you grow into rather than out of. Choosing it announces the birth of your magickal self – it's how you are known "in temple", whether physical or astral.
>
> I think t.town.troy is right that it should be not your native language. It should be foreign, suggesting the journey you are beginning (even if you don't know the destination).
>
> When I first started on the magickal path, as a teenager, I chose a very pompous name – "Ego Sum Qui Sum" – the Latin translation of the Hebrew "Ehieh Asher Ehieh" (all beginning with Aleph) – i.e. the name God called himself when Moses asked what his name was on Mount Sinai (Exodus 3: 14).
>
> Later, at my first real initiation (into the OTO), I shortened it to Aleph-Aleph-Aleph, calling it "Aleph Shalosh" (Three Aleph), both because it was like my first name, and because it was 111, the number of Aleph and the Fool.

At my second initiation, a few years later, I wanted to identify with the 93 current, so I chose "Jack Allah", which adds up to 93 as IAK ALLA, and also coincidentally contains the three Alephs.

About the same time (1987) I saw Crowley himself for the first time in a dream. When I went up to talk to him, he pointed at my chest and said "I know you, you're Spaceboy". Where he pointed on my chest there was a symbol which I had invented for myself when I was about 11 (Saturn and rings lit on one side, dark on the other, and a five-pointed star in the dark half). I took myself much too seriously to adopt "Spaceboy" as a motto. It became a kind of secret motto for myself, one which I did in fact grow into when I finally grew up and stopped trying to be a grown-up.

I didn't get a new name until 1993, when I had begun to rededicate myself to the Great Work in earnest. My lover one morning told me my name was "Zapapaias", and I took it as the first step in understanding how to progress in initation.

Long story short – the crisis or major initiation happened a year later, when I had to make a choice, do something, but didn't know what. I had received a new name that Saturday morning, after a Genesis 32: 24-29 experience. It was "Master Murru" – obviously I didn't want to call myself "Master", and I had no idea of what "murru" meant other than that it was vaguely semitic.

My method for going forward was to analyze the name Zapapaias in a Crowley-Golden Dawn Kabbalistic fashion, like that done in the Lesser Hexagram Ritual (Yod-Nun-Resh-Yod... INRI etc.) and by Crowley throughout his life. I came to the conclusion that I was in the last "Apophis" (last "a") phase of the name Zapapaias, and was going on to the "S". It was Saturday, after all. Saturn is the planet of Binah. The next step became obvious, and I took it with "fear and trembling".

This name "Master Murru" would be the final one in my magickal initiations, although when I understood it I adopted the Babylonian word for "master" (or "lord") – Bel. So it became "Bel Murru" as a name/motto. Master Murru for me corresponds to V.V.V.V.V. for Crowley – he is the Master of the Temple.

Funny, isn't it?

Here is my diary entry for how I interpreted Zapapaias that day:

"Dreamt of relating Crowley's trips to Aline (or someone – it wasn't Homer who wrote the Odyssey, but someone else with the same name). Must have been inspired by reading a snippet of Symonds yesterday. Awed by the breadth of view he would have had, for a man in his twenties in that age.

Somehow we found ourselves in a bathyscaphe – again, I saw this in the dictionary yesterday while playing Scrabble – the mind uses the symbols it can to illustrate the light within – and contemplated the depths of the abyss to which it could go.

I don't know how, I don't know who, I don't know when, I don't know where, and I sure as hell don't know why, but I got another name. Master Murru.

Maybe all these dreams of depths and butterflies and travels means I have to take the Oath of the Abyss – but it's all wrong! Then again, everything I've done has been wrong.

(— M U R R U ——- MURU < AMURRU?

silence son breath —— 252

—— 452

AMORRU – Breath of Love – could be a title of Binah.)

First, this is all too chaotic – there has been no stateliness, no order, no from-on-high commands. I can't even scry properly! Second, I can't test my visions properly. I have no external confirmation. Third, my life hasn't changed enough. What significant event marks this passing? It's not enough to say I have endured utter chaos – well, relative utter chaos – since my divorce.

I feel it's a test – it's either feeding my inflated ego, of They really want me to jump – to recognize I have come across. I can't believe I'm at such a silly impasse – worried about whether to take a grade and a name, when I think I've been there already. When I was born with this knowledge.

Let's see our Zapapaias, and what kind of cycle he might expect.

I started, when JARI came forth with the name, by saying it suggested "Master of Incantations".

Have I made good? I have written the music for my songs from the 2nd Aethyr, and I sung them unceasingly in Brazil, and attracted three nymphs. Thanks and praise be also to Iemenja!

On the other hand, spells for money have not worked (mostly VIII° & IX° – what I think I know of them). So I have not, even should everything else be correct, succeeded in mastering the task of my own name. (Path of [Resh], "power of acquiring wealth").

Moreover, the "Infernal Adorations Of OAI" are not Love-spells. Not merely to get conventional lovers, that is. It is a paean of attainment, of the supernals, of the Great Work. Singing it brings one across.

Furthermore -

Z———A———P———A———P———A———I———A—S

Lovers Fool Tower Fool Tower Fool Hermit Fool Aeon

————————————————————————————————very good;

This is a cycle of destructions, punctuated by phallic or intellectual action, finished by a bright firing-forth of will.

Z was the stage of living with Aline

A was the decay of that relationship / as it was

P was Kris, reawakening in the spring

A was the destruction of that, as of everything (Aline and I became lovers again)

P was either loving Aline again or Brazil

A was either leaving A. for Brazil, or the loss of my academic career.

I was Brazil or is the current stage, withdrawal from action for contemplation.

A is then the loss of my career, or the next stage

S is the attainment of the Aeon, mastery.

(10 minutes later, sitting outside – warm day!)

If these considerations aren't enough, it's not aesthetic – I'm too young a man to be claiming 8°=3°, or even the attainments that mark it. True, I have been on the path for 15 years, and Crowley was on it for only 12 by the time he claimed the grade – and he received the name in '05 or '07. But then, he was a better man than I am. At least, he worked harder.

The problem with an analysis like this is that it's best done in retrospect – anticipation of the next part of the formula might obviate its potency – well, on second thought, everything is providential of They who guide initiations, so we can make no missteps. I suppose the best that can be said is that it's nice to look back and see the plan.

So – there can be no doubt that this is an initiation.

And there can be no doubt that I am far from prepared to receive it.

And finally, there is no doubt that I will be put through it anyway.

(Asked myself the mental question – "The real question is – am I prepared to help others do this task?" At this moment my eye fell upon a penny, with a speck of oxidization. It is my custom to pick these up, with the ditty "see a penny, pick it up, all day long you'll have good luck". This time I also asked that the date on the coin be significant. "1994" it said. As soon as I had picked it up, my eye fell on a pile of pennies, 7 in number. I take these signs as confirmation of my guidance, and affirmative to my question.)

The upshot is that I should quit worrying and let things unfold as they should, as they will. And I must concentrate on the elemental work and the perfection of clairvoyance.

How strange this record must seem to an average person – this man prating of Grades & revelations, while his life crumbles around him. No – how normal! To seek in magick an escape from the duties and burdens of a normal life. I am living in a fantasy world, trying to distinguish amongst phantoms – all the warnings are correct."

ROSS (RSS + O) is a more straightforward name because the letter R sounds like a force pushing you forward, and these two letters S at the end reinforce that idea of a vertical dialogue. The letter S suggest the motion of the infinite, the lemniscate, which is also implicit in the 2 of Deniers. The soul of that word is the letter O. I am reminded of one of my favorite phrases from Italo Calvino: "A strength that cannot control itself in time creates a dessert around it"; which would sum up my main criticism to the 'occult': it feels too extreme and vertical to me, too focused on the individual wanting or finding 'power' in a way that alienates him from his surroundings: the head affects the heart, the heart feeds back the head, and your own process spirals up while everybody around you has no clue of what's going on.

When it comes to magic, my main criticism to all the 'secret doctrines' is how they sadly miss the point because they confuse symbols with concepts. I tend to suspect that 'Power', in terms of magic, doesn't comes from the individual understanding of nature, nor from occult forces, but from the individual's capacity to suggestion himself and then, to suggestion others. A ritual is only as effective as the suggestions carried by its symbols. Yesterday I was explaining to my kids how I was lucky to study graphic design. I should have gone to study art, but the art schools in Venezuela at that time sucked, and the usual gambit was to enroll in this great design school.

There was this great design school and your best bet was to get in, which was not easy, and then trick your way through it while knowing that you would probably never work as a designer. But now I see how the trick was to me, a good way. I think I was lucky in the sense that being trained as a designer, and being asked to teach design afterwards, gave me a designer's mind. I think of everything in terms of design, which is to say that I think of everything in terms of the relationship between form and function, but it also means that I always start by understanding my material. Any material has certain qualities, and a good designer has to be in dialogue with these qualities to use them in his favor. You need to understand what a material is, and you need to understand what a material says. Everything carries a suggestion and a good designer, a good artist, a good magician, knows how to articulate the suggestions carried by the substances he handles. Looking at the tarot as my expressive material, history is an important notion. I would go as far as saying that it is a liberating notion, for it allows me not to think of 'divination' in the usual terms. As a matter of fact I can only relate the tarot to poetry because of the tarot's history. I have basically built all my understanding of how to use the tarot on the notion of 'tarocchi appropriati.' So, I understand what you are saying about all of your experiences informing who you are and how you do what you do.

I like that, yes, I think *tarocchi appropriati* is the pre-eminent "form" that modern tarotists should be inspired by. Occultism has really run its course; it's a dead vessel. Some people keep trying to use its methods, as if new insight can be gained from it, but all that has been done. Crowley and Waite created the greatest esoteric Tarots that will ever be done, and there is enough in both to keep you occupied for a lifetime and to bring you all the wisdom possible through such a system.

Back to your words, I wonder if we should read that letter O – isolated at the center of the word ROSS – as wholeness or loneliness. Is it full or is it empty?

For a mystic, that question is simply a pleasant paradox, of course: fullness is emptiness, emptiness is fullness. Stretching it out on the chronological scale of my life, using the name Ross to express something intrinsic about me, then the O starts out emptiness, and becomes fullness. I roar on the one side, and hiss (or, "sparkle"!) on the other, however you take me.

MURRU (MRR + UU) is perhaps more intriguing as a word in that it still has the impetus of the letter R, doubled, but we have a letter M that suggest two letters I holding hands, this is, finally, the presence of the other, and we have those letters U, also doubled, and totally receptive to 'above'. The letter U functions as the suit of Coupes: they are ready to be filled, ready to contain substances or sounds.

Thanks very much for that. Yes, I like the "U" as receptive – that perfectly accords with the grade-meaning of the name, since Binah is "Understanding". I also like M as the "presence of the other". That's one way of seeing it – but what about "V" in the middle? Is that just the two I's growing arms? What is the difference between this and H then? Generally I take M to be a "letter of silence", since it is pronounced with closed lips.

So, you have been Ross (first letter A), Zapapaias (second letter A), Master Murru (third letter A), and I want to ask: what is that letter I? Have you crossed it yet, and if so, who are you now?

The attainment of 8°= 3° marked a break with Thelema and Crowley. We left for California at the end of January, 1995, and I spent the entire following year writing Bel Murru's magnum opus, Babylonian Magick. During the fall at Harvard I had madly copied text after text of primary and secondary sources relating to mesopotamian magic and language; I absorbed it all like a sponge. At first it was for "correcting" the Simon Necronomicon, but after Babalon became Inanna and Zapapaias became the Master Murru, it was all about this new identity. I had identified a plausible mesopotamian origin for the name Zapapaias, as if it were a Hellenistic form of the Sumerian Zababa, the patron god of Kish, consort of Inanna. So I understood the syncretistic nature of my identity and mission – it was to cover the entire mesopotamian tradition, summed up as "Babylon", from the earliest cuneiform sources up to the end of the Hellenistic period (in other words, it wasn't just to be a "reconstruction" of a particular period, such as Sumer or Assyria).

The book was a system of initiation, based exclusively on these sources, as much as could possibly be gleaned from them about the "theurgic" or initiatory-wisdom structure, in turn informed by my own experience in the AA initiation system, to give the whole, unformed mass of cuneiform magickal texts a place in a dynamic system. Through David Hulse (author of a book about magical alphabets, *The Key of it All*), I got a contact in Llewellyn to publish my book, but as soon as I began applying for the various copyrights, I ran into a frustrating catch-22 that made me give up trying to publish it as a book – the copyright holders of images and texts – that were essential for the system, since I couldn't expect readers to have access to one of the best libraries in the world, as I had, wanted to know the precise details of the publishing contract – publisher, number of copies, market, etc.... ; and of course Llewellyn wasn't going to give me a contract without knowing that I had obtained all copyright permissions... so I just gave up in frustration after getting a half-dozen such letters from copyright holders.

I would begin publishing it later on my first website[1] in 1998. It's a mess now, so out of date, and so many texts remain to be put up – but the system is laid out there.

In any case, by early 1996 I had drifted away completely from Crowley, and the Babylonian Magick system was put on hold. My fiancée and I became ordained in a lineage of the Jacobite Syrian tradition, which had come to the US via India in the late 19th century; one of its descendants had become the Patriarch of the Federation of St. Thomas Christians. It's a fairly complex story, even crazier than

---

1 http://www.angelfire.com/tx/tintirbabylon/nam.html
(old-school html entrance page, which was my own design for the book cover – http://www.angelfire.com/tx/tintirbabylon/)

what you have read so far, so I'll leave it there. As far as my relationship with magickal identities, from then on I have tried to figure out how to put it in context and understand it. But to sum it up – it seems I had got "magick" out of my system. I had found the "Exit" I told you about earlier here.

The value of it seems to be to put on a name on inner sources of creative inspiration. As much as I tried to create a world-view with room for beings separate from myself, directing everything, even my Angel being a distinct being, I have come to understand them all in a classically psychological way. The analogy I use is the Earth – the Ego is the crust, and underneath – or all around – is the unconscious, the mantle, which cause the plates of the Ego to move. The mantle is always breaking through, causing volcanoes and earthquakes, creating new crust and changing the shape of the Ego. The magician is trying to explore the "mantle", the unconscious, which is much vaster than that of the Ego, and goes down into levels of pure instinct and automatic physical functions where consciousness as we know it is impossible. The purpose of this exploration is to harness the power of these unconscious forces, for any purpose possible – artistic creation is one of the most obvious and frequent results, with music, dance and poetry – often of an "inspired" quality – the first things to happen. This is the level where people get "possessed" as well – all in a controlled setting in some traditional religions. But as you know, this is where shamans draw healing powers from – at least diagnostic powers, and in some cases the ability to "see" the illness is sufficient to heal it. Similarly, since the unconscious is vast and operates according to its own rules, learning about the properties of plants and stones is easier when on a visionary trip into those levels of consciousness. What the "name" of such a figure or force gives to the magician, which makes its way up in the form of an image to the borderline mind in trance or dream, is a way to invoke it, and thereby learn from it, create from it. The name is a direct path to the well-spring of creativity, to that state of mind.

If you think naming parts of yourself, and creating distinct personalities, sounds dangerous, playing with insanity, I'm sure you're right. But that's the way it's been done since the beginning of time. Artists do it all the time. Learning how to do it systematically, in a religion or school, is the only safeguard against permanent "possession" or classic psychosis. You can go in, you can come out. You can even be partially in for a long time, and still function in the "normal" world.

So at present, who I am now, is just somebody who has gone through various experiences, seen and lived with various parts of my being, and continues to live with them and try to put them in the context of a greater whole. There are some aspects I have touched, that I have not touched since, and have no intention of ever investigating. I'd prefer to let sleeping dogs lie. But I am grateful that I know it is possible, and that I can still conjure up communication through the name of some of them, and take inspiration from that source. The Master Murru is still there, in some distant, timeless place, an ancient master wandering from oasis to oasis, sometimes breaking his silence with a song of wisdom.

Otherwise, the only inner relationship I have is with a woman who comes in many forms, in dreams and half-dreams, and for whom I always have the profoundest love. I consider her my "anima", in the Jungian sense. Here is when I first recognized her, on May 8, 2002, shortly after I began studying Tarot history.

> *Tarot as a woman.*
>
> *I had a dream, and in the dream the Tarot was a woman – a young woman, whom I found attractive, although I can't describe her face or form, though I think it was slight, but really my attraction was intellectual – intellectual and spiritual. Nonetheless, my wife was jealous, as she has been complaining for days that I must have a girlfriend, and when I rose (in the dream) to visit the young woman on the couch, my wife got in between us with a ruler, so that we couldn't sit together – I began to wake up . . . and it was then, in these warm feelings I had for the form I had seen, that I realized who this girl was – because all tonight I was awake with the cards of the early decks in my mind, and did rise and come to the couch to write everything down and meditate with the images beside me – and the feeling for the young woman in my dream and the meditating in the Tarot are the same feelings – I am in it now.*
>
> *I have not studied Jungian psychology, but from what I gather this is my anima, and it is not unusual that an archetypal toy should*

bring her to me. But I have seen her before also, when I rebuilt, with love, patience, tender compassion and true interest, a very old machinist's lathe. I knew and cleaned every screw and bolt, every gear ; I brushed off every speck of rust from the lovely smooth steel, got all the shiny handles turning, arranged all the accessories in a cabinet I built, shined the plate with the name and gear ratios, and finally levelled the bed, and oiled it to perfection. I knew and touched every part of this old tool – 1919, I phoned South Bend lathes in Indiana and found its history through the serial number – and one night I spent all night with a lovely young woman, and found myself tenderly rubbing oil over her back for an eternity, and when I awoke I knew it had been the spirit of the lathe, brought out by tender love and compassion, unconditional surrender to the thing itself, to only learn its ways, and not to impose on or hurry it, or rule over it, but to serve it. And isn't this what "tender" means, to tend to with love and patience ?
And now I've understood again how it is with "men and their cars", although I have never had this in particular – that's why the swimsuit model appears on the hoods of cars and beside chrome-sparkling Harleys, not because "sex sells", but because she IS the machine, the soul of the machine, the anima of every man who lovingly tends and toils over his machine, the humble servant maintaining her perfection.
And this must be why ships are "she", since the men who sail it look after it so well, tend her, so that the spirit of the ship comes out and guides them, and they make an image and put it on the very front to show everyone her soul.
And this must be why the early scientists called the World Soul a woman, because they were falling in love with nature, and finally

not imposing rules on her but learning her ways through patient observation and unconditional love of it for itself, tender love, and it became to them a woman, the spirit of the world, and this dream made its way into the engravings and paintings of the scientific awakening.

And finally, (but it has been quick) I understand a little, although I am not a poet, of the beloved of the sufis, the troubadors, chivalry and the Fidèles d'Amour like Dante, who so rigorously studied and observed the rules of their art, that the art itself became a woman to them, their soul came out, through their patient absorption in the contemplation and performance of their craft. And I am not a musician, but it must be the same with an instrument – now I see !

And so last night the Tarot came to me as a Woman, after I had given up trying to impose upon or drag something out of the cards (these are just words, I don't know if I was doing that), I just studied them in themselves, tenderly contemplated them and lovingly arranged them, and with rapt attention heard their story told through time, a new story, at least to me, but

in a way which must resemble what humble men, all servants of love, have always done through the ages, which is to open up unconditionally to understanding, to become empty so the beloved can fill you up. Last night Tarot came to me, and She filled me up.

New York / Béziers, 2010

"I put my body in place somewhere and that provokes a memory."

A conversation with JODY MELNICK, artist, dancer

SEVEN OF WANDS

All the other cards from this suit show this kind of cross, as if several scepters had been lowered and crossed before us. They become some sort of screen, or door. There is red in the center, but we aren't allowed to touch it. This makes me wonder: in your work, how much use do you have for obstacles? I mean, I envision your dancing as a form of flow, and I imagine that flow only moving through openings in space. Is that relevant to you, this idea of closure or obstacles?

Oh! I guess in the sense of conflict. I think conflict is very prevalent and provocative in my life, in my work... I mean, that is how I relate to it. You know, there are the normal obstacles, I was going to say oftime, obviously, of making work and all that. But I don't think I am ever burdened by them. I am more burdened internally with how relevant the work I am making is, how possible it is, how translatable it is...

I was having that same conversation with a young artists who told me she is now completely paralyzed. She feels that her work is not relevant.

To whom?

To the world I guess. How do you see this idea of relevance?

I think that we live in a very concrete and tangible world. As an artist, I mean. I don't consider myself more of an artist than anyone else. Being an artist is just the way that you see things. It is not only that you produce objects or interesting and provocative works, but it is about how you think about the world, and life, and work... I think it is definitively a mindset. So, I am not going to say it is a job that I do. I think we live in a world that is very tangible, very production oriented, and art is very process-based. Things with relevance or meaning work for me as a prerogative that translates into a narrative. I guess a narrative would be, in my work, equal to something very tangible and concrete that has work and movement make sense. So the work I am doing, instead of being something that emerges from my imagination, has to be understandable, it has to be about a narrative, it has to be about a story. That is when I get caught up in asking: " Is what I am doing relevant?" I always have to remind myself – which is very strange – I have to remind myself of what I believe in. Even when I know I believe in something and that's what I do, I have to constantly remind myself of it.

And what do you believe in?

I believe that the form I have chosen to express myself, through dance and choreography, is profound in and of itself. The body as an abstraction is profound, in the same way a tree is profound. Do you walk by something like that and ask yourself "what is that?" No, you don't. Do you look up the side of a tree and ask yourself "what is that?" No, you don't. And I actually feel that way about a painting, about visual arts and obviously about what I do. I recently had this experience... I teach a class now at Columbia and Barnard in which the students evaluate you. They send me everything they write. I feel very fortunate, I guess, in that all they write is very positive. One student this year wrote: "we love your class. We learned so much about the body and about dancing; but sometimes I wish you would tell me: What am I supposed to feel?" I want to answer: "Am I also supposed to tell you what to feel? I am already busting my heart, and soul to teach these classes and give you all these tools, just so you can feel something for yourself!"

Well, if I were to punch you I wouldn't really need to tell you what to feel. But I find very beautiful what you are saying about the essential nature of things: they are what they are.

Yeah, I do believe that's what it is. I think I get caught up in the relevance issue when I have to articulate what I am making in order to get grant money for a fellowship, and I find that very daunting.

In a weird way that reminds me of an interview with Jackie Chan I saw the other day. I believe it was Conan who interviewed him. What caught my attention was that Jackie Chan couldn't answer a single question without using his body. Every time Conan asked him something, Chan jumped off his chair and used his body to punctuate his words.

I believe I read something about Jackie Chan: he doesn't read. He is illiterate that way. Look it up. I read that about him: he doesn't read a script.

That's fascinating.

Which is also why I am so attracted to words. Poetry, for good reasons, but even fiction and non-fiction, because what I get is not the idea of the book but how it was written, how these words were put together, how these two words look next to each other, and how they look together with the next sentence; and then I realize that I am not reading, I am not understanding what I am reading because I am so caught up in the organization of the words and their forms.

That's the way I understand the tarot: as shapes talking to each other. So sometimes it is very hard for me to put what I am seeing into words as it is so obvious to me what these shapes are saying in terms of movement and expansion, etc. Shapes have their own language that we then translate – or betray – into words. Now, you mentioned poetry and I believe it was Allen Ginsberg who told his students: "Quarrel. Quarrel with yourselves!" in order to make poetry. This takes me back to the idea of obstacles and conflict we saw in that Seven of Wands, and I wonder: How does that apply to your work? Is any of it the product of you quarreling with yourself?

I am so sure it is. I mean, although I write a lot about myself. When I am working, about thoughts and ideas that often turn into a narrative in my head, but the work will never look like that. I never use dancing or making art as a therapy. I never go out there and spill my guts out about the world and politics and racial issues, love and loss... You know, a good example is the death of Pierre, my fiancee. There is no way that is not going to affect my work. It is not about me being morbid, it is just that things affect me. You know Doris, she is a very, very, very important dear friend, and she is always part of my work for some reason. She always affects my work. All these things affect me.

It is beautiful because if we go back to the tree-metaphor, a tree is affected by whatever happens in its environment, but it never stops being a tree. It never stops meaning 'tree'.

Yes.

SIX OF COINS

Oh! Pretty!

The first thing I notice in this image is how it is crossed by several symmetries. That generates a sense of balance.

Does symmetry represent balance to you?

In this case, yes. Why?

Because I don't look at this and feel assured or relieved. This for me doesn't say harmony or symmetry in that sense.

What is symmetry to you?

I mean, I am talking visually.

I find that intriguing. I feel I have a corrupted idea of symmetry that is modeled after a medieval notion which supposes that one element in a work will have a response in another element. So, it is not so much being able to cut an image in two halves and see them mirroring each other, as it is about an analogical sense of correspondence.

I guess I think of symmetry as value.

Value?

Value. I couldn't be more different from my brother and my sister, we are just so different, but I think we were loved equally by our parents. To me, that is a symmetrical metaphor, like the value or weight of something.

Yes, but I think that kind of symmetry has to do with attention, with paying the same kind of attention to two different things so that they are balanced, like you and your brothers, two people in a relationship, two lovers. Symmetry is a state of correspondence, a kind of relationship.

Yes.

I can see a symmetry between the Seven of Wands and the Six of Coins, in that this X created by the scepters mirrors this vine surrounding the coins...

When you put something down like this and talk about symmetry, that is not what I do. When I think about my work, there is a little bit of chance in it... when I am making work for other people, I mean. My own work is a little bit more... not organized, but I am constantly measuring it and changing it, because I am on it. When I am doing work for other people it is a little... sometimes vague and chaotic and sometimes this happens [she is pointing to the Six of Coins] unintentionally and kind of jolts me. So in one sense that is a nice image, a great image.

Symmetry is a touchy subject. Some artists hate symmetry, some others love it. At design school we were discouraged to create symmetries. It was thought to be somehow predictable or naive. We were always asked to disrupt these symmetries with some kind of additional element. But then there are cultures where symmetry is equated with the sacred. Where are you in all that? Are you pro-symmetry or anti-symmetry? [Laughs]

Like I said, I think I don't start out that way, but I am also really intrigued or attracted to all those scientific notions of natural symmetry: rock formations, cell divisions... I sort of like that idea. Or I remember when I was much younger, opening a bottle of soda and it goes shhhhhhh.... and from the top part of the cap burst all these little bubbles and I thought "Oh, I think that's how people plan gardens", because it looked to me like a garden or an Italian piazza...

What you are describing is what I was talking about with regard to medieval symmetry! That would be symmetrical thinking. You connect one thing to another by mapping an analogy between them. Then you say "this is like this", just as the vine in the Six of Coins is like the crossed scepters in the Seven of Wands.

Oh! O.K. O.K. So, I like when that comes out of something I don't expect or plan.

You are interested in symmetry as happenstance. Perhaps it resembles the unconscious impulse towards order we like to see in nature. We somehow equate that with truth.

Right. And I think that if I were to describe the way my brain works, I'd say it doesn't work in a symmetrical fashion, but in concentric circles. When I am confronted with symmetrical formations I am a little taken aback – "Oh!" So, for that reason I trust it. Because I think I am clever enough to make a formation that will go like this. I think we just don't take a little brain-mapping which tells us to "do this and do this and go there", but when symmetry occurs in a non-planned, chaotic way, and is more part of anorganic trust in your instincts, it makes more sense.

I find that so beautiful. The idea of finding symmetries in randomness is precisely what orients my work with the tarot: truth is a happenstance.

Right. But also, plant life to me is symmetrical. I have the trunk of a tree and I have the roots, and the thing at the top will make sense with the thing on the bottom, so there is all this sort of ingrained symmetry.

Ah! Here is something: I have seen you dancing, and perhaps this may sound a little bit 'out there' but let's borrow that tree metaphor. When you are dancing on the floor, what is below you?

There are several ways I think about what is below. Most likely you are on a hard surface, and for me, I am barefoot. So in practical terms I like to change my idea about what I am standing on. Instead of being on cement or some old linoleum, I can have this idea of thick grassy moisty secure thing. It just makes your body fall easily. And then I always imagine that the floor rises up to meet you. When you are partnering, doing physical work with a partner, something I often think about or teach is that you are not grabbing or holding or supporting. It's really skin to skin, bone to bone, blood to blood… So it is almost as if you are of them and they of you, and I don't mean that in a romantic way, I mean it in a purely physical sense. When I think about the body and I think about the heart, or the lungs, I am not thinking about a romantic idea of my heart, but about where my heart is physically, the pericardium around it, the weight of the organ, the function of the organ. This is what provokes me, not sadness and happiness… So that's one way I think about the floor: that it is coming up to support you, so you have to give into it. The floor is giving into you, you are giving into it. As you are going down, it is coming up to meet you. That's how I think about the floor, pretty much a necessity when you are dancing on cement.

That's absolutely beautiful, and it takes me back to this idea of contraction we see in the transition from a Seven to a Six. When you describe your relationship with the floor you are suggesting a dialogue, and wherever there is dialogue there is contraction and expansion: something pushes, something gives in.

Contraction has a couple of different meanings for me: going away from... something being taken away... What do you think when you think of contraction?

Well, my idea of expansion and contraction is very much inspired by Joseph Beuys's theory of sculpture. Do you know Joseph Beuys?

Yes. Actually, he is right outside your door. You are so lucky!

Indeed. You know, it is funny because I always think of Beuys when I see these basalt columns outside my building, but I never look at the trees standing beside them.

The trees?

Yes. The basalt column marks the place where a tree has been planted. That block in Chelsea is an extension of Beuys's 7000 Oaks project. For each Oak they planted they placed a basalt column, but the important thing is the tree.

Oh! It marks where the tree should be on the street? I don't even think about that!

The basalt column is kind of guarding the tree. At the beginning the Stone is huge and the tree is small, but as the tree grows the stone shrinks in proportion to it. There is a nice metaphor of how the stone, the basalt column, contains all the nutrients to nourish the tree.

Wow!

That 'dialogue' is consistent with Beuys's theory of sculpture. In his view, all materials exist in constant transition from expansion to contraction. For Beuys, this natural behavior of matter is a sculpture process in and of itself. That is why I loved your idea of the meaning of a tree being the tree itself, because it takes us back to the true nature of matter. The meaning of a tree is our experience of the tree, just as the meaning of an image is our experience of the event it depicts. Obviously, I apply the same process to people: we are all in transition, either towards expansion or towards contraction. Our experience of life comes down to our experience of these transitions, and these transitions are narratives in themselves. So, a sequence of numbers is always telling a story of either expansion or contraction, as in this case, when we contract from the Seven of Wands to the Six of Coins.

Right. I love what you say about his sculpture, and the tree. I am becoming aware of how important, personally, culturally and historically Nature is in life and work. And as someone who grew up in the city or who loves being in the city, it really refreshes my being to be in nature, or to go by a lake or a mountain. I have always been drawn to sculpture and architecture; and they never make as much sense as when nature and architecture are juxtaposed. I like being on a mountain, it is beautiful to me, but something incredible happens when you juxtapose it with sculpture or architecture. When you place a Calder in nature, or witness that Joseph Beuys project, it somehow resonates more with me.

I guess it has to do with the use we make of contrast to understand things. We understand one thing in terms of its opposite. Now, is there anything else you would like to say about these two images?

I am just thinking about contraction, and I think that for me the attitude to things taken away is more of a mindset. You must realize what you are gaining from it. It is very hard not to think that things have simply been taken away from you, either professionally or personally.

Yes. It is very hard to let go of things without feeling a sense of loss. I once read Ann Demeulemeester's definition of 'luxury'. It was something like: "To have nothing is the ultimate luxury".

Yes. Or to really love everything you have. I like that too. If I could name everything I own [laughs]. If I can name it, that would mean I really like it. It would mean it is really important to me.

XIII *[L'Arcane Sans Nom]*

Oh! Oh… Ay Ay Ay… I have been dealing with that a lot! Oh my God, it is so interesting! Can I just talk quickly about it?

Sure!

Really... Really... My father just died. In the Jewish religion, after the burial the rabbi asks every member of the family to take a shovel and put soil into the grave. Only, my sister and I refused.

Why?

I think we were in shock; and I think it really meant that we would be putting our father away.

You and your sister were rejecting a symbolic act, which in itself is a symbolic act.

We were rejecting a symbolic act, and I think we also wanted to be witnesses. There was neither bad nor good, but it was interesting that we both had the same idea. [Jody Melnick talks without taking her eyes from the Death card, and when she talks about her sister and herself, she taps with her fingers on the two severed heads we see at the bottom of the image]. So, since then I have been thinking that I will need to revisit that event sometime; like talking to my sister about it or visiting my father's grave. I don't mean to say: "Oh! It is all good and beautiful." I feel totally neutral.

This may very well be my favorite card in the tarot. Not only in terms of what it means, but also because I find it beautiful. Here I differ from most people, in that I believe that, for us to appreciate something aesthetically, we must not be stopped by our moral judgements. If we can manage to take our opinion of Death out of the picture, what we see is a beautiful image full of blue, with red emphasis here and there, and the flesh kind of keeping it all together.

It is beautiful. I am so interested in the body, and here we have the spine and the skeleton, with red representing blood and veins, and the ligaments. I like all those colors and shapes.

I remember doing a reading for someone who got this card, and she showed me some pictures of her taken the day before. She had been working with a scythe and she was very aware of the motions involved. It is a kind of movement that can be quite soothing, both physically and metaphorically: the idea of severing. There is also the idea itself of Death. I guess that a big part of Life consists of making up a story about Death that helps you cope with living.

I have that. Yes.

What is your story about Death?

About Death, that makes me want to cope? Well, you know, losing my husband.

[I once asked Jodi Melnick's fiancée to draw me an animal and he drew me a cracked egg. That took me aback, because it forced me to deal with the unavoidable half-glass choice all ruined things present. Were we supposed to cry the loss of the egg, or cheer the birth of something? I got my answer a couple of months later, when he died. It is always so easy to connect the dots backwards!]

That's one of the most strangely amazing things that have happened to me, I must say.

Really? He was a strangely amazing man.

It was so provocative. I love cracks. Cracks are always hinting at something.

Did you tell him that you loved cracks?

Yes.

Good.

But how did you create your story about Death from that event?

No, no, no, no. I will say what is not, first. It was not the realization that you should cherish life and not take anything for granted: people, work, relationships. I don't think there is one person or relationship or situation in my life where I haven't felt "this is great, I understand it, I am present". I am very fortunate I grew up that way. So it didn't teach me "Oh, you have to live each day to its fullest". You need down days as well, you know? You sort of need to be in misery, too. I am fine with that.

Yes!

I guess it changes you, or hits you, this enormity of a feeling, the realization that there is this tremendous love, and loss. Back to symmetry: I remember writing... I am not a journal-keeper... When I write it is very cathartic and then I throw it out. So I don't have journals and journals and journals; but I do remember writing about Pierce: the feeling of losing him, and his death, was no more nor less great than the amount of love I shared with him. I don't understand that. I don't get how that can be. In a sense, it is the same. It is so symmetrical, it is so equal to that feeling. And then I thought, "Well, I might not have felt like this if it hadn't been such an amazing experience being in love with him and having this astonishing relationship with his death." And then, something that has not been part of my way of life or thinking is the idea of faith, not fantastical belief but reality-based: to have faith. It is more of a belief in yourself than some idea about faith. It is only recently that I understood the idea that I had two years with someone. It is easy for me to say "It is so unfair. He was taken away from me and I am devastated". But now I realize that it was just supposed to be for two years. There was a reason why I was supposed to experience this relationship. It has changed me. And I also have to be grateful that I have no regrets. I feel a little bit guilty in saying that. I understand why it couldn't go on longer. It makes sense that it was just for that time. While understanding that I am very grateful for it. I guess that I can't avoid understanding now that Death, no matter how tragic and unfair it is, is a real part of your life: one cannot exist without the other. The act of burying someone is very true and real: they go into the ground, they decompose, they fertilize the earth.

I guess that is also part of my story, the physicality of decay as a tangible way to become one with the world, not in a mythologized way but as fertilizer. We are a micro-organism inhabiting a body we call "planet", and in that respect we aren't more important than an amoeba that goes around categorizing between food and poison. So, at a very basic level, life has no meaning other than survival, and Death is the ultimate loss of meaning, unless we count fertilizing the soil as a form of transcendence. So, we inhabit the world to eat and procreate and die, and we fill in the gaps with fictions.

What happened is not going to go away. But with that there is also something else: this amazingly, incredible, beautiful experience is over. It will always be within me, and something will happen again.

In other words, you will survive.

Yeah.

There are several things besides the actual, physical, event of Death that come to my mind when I see these cards. We started with the interconnection of these scep-

ters, then with the expansion of these coins and now we have Death severing or cutting things down. I see an idea here about memory, or more precisely, about the memories in your body. Are there memories in your body you would rather erase, or forget?

Oh, I would love to erase a lot of physical memories! I think it would be easier to get through the day! No, I can't intentionally erase any of them. You can't be cognisant about your physical memories, just as you can't be cognisant when you wake up in the morning and have that first thought... you can change it, but that is what your head and body are telling you.

Would it be possible for the body to lose its memory?

Absolutely, with age, of course. But muscle memory is very, very strong, especially if you are someone like myself who is very tuned into it. It is also a practice that stays with you. I don't want to sidetrack, but I can actually remember...I may not be able to remember what I read or what it meant, but I remember physical feelings exactly, movements in my body from the 80's ... I put my body in place somewhere and that provokes a memory. I think my only experience stronger than a physical memory is linked with the sense of smell. I don't know how it is, but it is a huge part of my life.

Can you recognize your different choreographies by smell?

I could equate them to smells. The Fanfare piece, for me, has a more metallic kind of smell. Not because of the colors. If sunshine had a smell, some of my work would smell like that. Not only because "Oh, the sun is out!", but because of its intent and the radiation from it. If I were to describe the color yellow, there is one dance that will do yellow. If I were to describe the color green if you were blind, maybe one of my choreographies will feel like the color green.

Good. Now, in this card Death is looking out towards the right, so please take one more card to see what he is looking at.

You don't want to say anything more about Death? Should I be concerned about this card?

No. I don't think so.

EIGHT OF WANDS

It has flowers.

We started with the Seven of Wands, this is an Eight...

Look at the Symmetry!

Death is charging against these scepters, now more numerous than before. There is no crack so you have to make an opening, you have to make room, clean up life.

To me, this represents the importance of Life. You are remarking that you have this life, and you are important to people and you are being buried, you are being revered. So, it is not a big negative thing.

No. Death is there, and it is opening space to other things.

I have this image in my head, when I was talking about the tree growing up and growing down. Here we have these two flowers, up and down...

I feel that the thing with pain is that we all try to avoid it at all costs. We move away from pain all our lives, yet we admire those who have endured pain. They acquire this glow. We don't want that pain for ourselves but we admire the pain others have endured. Pain inspires respect.

That's so strange and so true! I guess there is a little bit of comfort knowing that someone went on that route and experienced that before, and that at some point you may experience what someone else has already been through. There was a short period of time... this is a horrible thing to say, but after Pierce's death, other catastrophes were a comfort to me. Even world events, or deaths or shootings, made me feel "Something else in the world is worse than what I am feeling". Because it all can become very narcissistic "It is all about me, me me, and no-one else could have experienced this". Those events help to put things into perspective. The good side of that is when you start realizing that there is also a huge amount of joy which you are allowed to feel as well. So, in that sense, witnessing pain or feeling pain have affected me. And I think what comforts me is that a painful, hard, experience does bring a certain amount of peace; like now I feel you can rip off my arms and legs and I would get through it.

I relate to what you are saying in that I have always tried to dialogue with pain. So, if I am feeling some sort of physical pain I won't run to have it fixed, but I will stay and let it get to me to see what it is all about. So, when the pain comes back I can recognize it and say, "Ah! I know you!"

Yes. But you know, there is no scale. My pain and suffering is not deeper and heavier than yours or anyone else's just because I have gone through this. Of course I think that sometimes, pain is pain, hell is hell. Hot coffee can be hell for you and not for me.

Well, that's interesting because, when my brother died last year...

Oh, I remember... How old was he?

He was two years younger than I, and that disrupted my narrative: younger people aren't supposed to go before you do. And if this didn't make sense to me, it made even less sense to my parents. Parents aren't supposed to bury their child. Of course, it really helped me to understand it all as senseless. But something I found extremely important is that my parents only found comfort in the words of those who had experienced something similar. They were polite to everybody, but you could see in their eyes that they were only really paying attention to those who shared their pain first hand. In other words, they paid attention only to those who knew what they were talking about. They could intuit that only they knew how to overcome the pain my parents were feeling.

I have amazing friends and all that, but it is very true that if you have lost someone you may experience a little bit of frustration.

Yes, I remember people telling me "Oh, your brother is with God now", or "Your brother died because the world's energy is unbalanced and it needed that beautiful energy to be released" and nonsense like that.

Oh my God!

And this is something I can see happening all the time with the tarot: I can enjoy and celebrate the poetics of chance, the beauty of the senseless being made sense of, but I don't feel I need to force meaning into everything. Now, there is something else that comes to mind when we are looking at the Death card. It has to do with the medieval tradition of danse macabre, the dance of Death, in which a skeleton just like this one would dance with all people in a society: the workman, the maid, the pope, the beggar, the princess and the emperor, as if to say: "No matter who you are or what you have achieved, Death is there for all of us". But the theme of the danse macabre motivates me to ask you: have you ever 'danced Death'?

Ah... I don't know. I don't think consciously, no. Have I danced Death?

Have you ever made a piece about Death?

No. But at the same time I made two works, that time you came to The Kitchen... There was no way I could avoid my experiences of the last year and a half. Everything I did was soaked with my experiences of recent death. So in that sense, yes, I have danced Death. If I do that piece again, that is how I would associate it. There is one section of that piece that was very deliberately constructed around this feeling, that sort of heaviness and blue, the feel of a body bag and the physical idea of Death, of seeing that person dead. That is what I carried into the studio in order to make this material. The steps themselves were not indicative of dancing with Death; it was just how that idea had affected me. On the other hand, the opposite occurred with Fanfare. While making that piece, as soon as anything was introduced that had to do with the idea of Death, or what I went through, or any kind of emotional connection, I would stop. I wanted it to be very different and I wanted it to be strictly form-based: a relationship between the structures on stage, the fans, the screen and the light. It was very important that I was an element. My body was an element, my brain was an element, the fans were an element, the lighting was an element... all a very minimalistic way of thinking, but something as an artist I am truly interested in. I go to the studio every day with all I have gone through, so I had to be really diligent about it. If any posture, muscle memory, body memory evoked this [she taps on the Death card] I would start over: "Form! Form! Form! The body. The abstraction of the body. The body".

Have you ever died on stage? I mean. Have you ever felt a failure to connect with the people in the audience?

Yes, I am sure. But for a while now... I guess that when I was much younger... I had an experience on stage in Madrid. I was by myself, and there was a moment when I was out of the dance and back into my life. When you are a dancer and you dance, that's your world... but I was out of it and there was this terrible light and it was horrible for me but nobody really knew. I was alone on stage. But the experience of performing is so important for my work that I don't manipulate it, but can control it in a sense. As it is happening to me I am very present. That is what interests me most about doing solo work, or being a dancer or a performer. With rehearsal, rigor, and technique I can go on stage and have an experience and know what to do. I can understand the audience's response and go with it to have another experience about the same thing, over and over and over and over and each time it will be different.

Finally, if there is a theme I detect in these four images read together it would be 'breaking ground'. I am not sure about how that applies to your life, but I wonder: Are you at a crossroad now?

I think just in terms of getting two feet back into the world, after experiencing Pierce. At my age, I think I would really like a big change, but I know that I don't always have or perseverance. So sometimes I wish I was just forced at a crossroad – and I don't mean to wish anything bad – but I would like to be at a crossroad and have to make some big directional change. I would welcome that.

New York, February 7th, 2010

"Quite frankly, I spend a great deal of time finding out whether people believe in their own magic."

A conversation with SCOTT GROSSBERG, magician

Last year, for the first time in its history, the world-famous Magic Castle (Hollywood, California) allowed one of its members to lecture on the subject of tarot readings. That lecturer was you! This was quite an accomplishment as the relationship between magicians and readers is 'tense', to put it mildly. There are those magicians who do readings, but I would say a huge majority among them equates readings with some sort of criminal activity. You are both a conjurer and a reader, which means that you constantly walk on that tightrope, albeit elegantly so. And here is the question I want to pose to you: do you think that it is possible to be a trickster without being a charlatan?

Both of the terms – "trickster" and "charlatan" are crowded and clouded with a disapproving connotation and moral significance. Alas, most people hearing these words consider them interchangeable. Without knowing their etymology, the general public inevitably thinks of swindlers, frauds and snake oil salesmen. Let us come together, then, and first answer the real question we all truly want to know: "Is magic real?" To that, I offer a decisive "yes."

The mystic and poet, Rumi, said it best:

> Magic makes a straw a mountain by artifice; again
> It weaves a mountain like a straw.
> It makes ugly things beautiful by means of sleight;
> It makes beautiful things ugly by opinion.
> The work of magic is this, that it breathes and at every breath transforms realities.

When a parent tenderly kisses a child's hurt to make the pain go away, the existence of the injury is made to disappear as if by magic and yet nothing more than a trick of the power of love and comfort was used. When a teacher confidently tells a student how easy learning can be to overcome a prior belief that a topic is difficult, an arduous task is wondrously transformed into a fantastic learning experience with a spell of words. And when an accomplished actor gives a riveting performance, we are entranced. In that momentary bewitching, we are transported from our everyday world. With the maneuvering of light and still images, we momentarily suspend our belief of what is real and what is not.

In each case, a "ruse" has been employed. In each case, the audience has been "misled." And yet in each case, realities have been transformed because our parent, teacher and actor all know the same thing – "believing makes it so." Perhaps it is best not to examine the labels of "trickster" and "charlatan" from the viewpoint of actions then. Perhaps it is useful instead to focus on the intent and perception involved. When that is done, you get to the root of the matter you have asked about; namely, that our illusionists/tricksters (parents, teachers and actors) have honorable designs (to nourish, to empower, to entertain) and their audience perceives them as rewarding.

On the other hand, using this same standard to examine what you have called a "charlatan," we find someone who has a disempowering intent (he or she wants nothing more than money, fame or some other advantage) and will use deception or quakery to achieve those ends. Contrary to our parent, teacher and actor, this fraudster sells worthless goods, ideas and services with little or no intent of fulfilling his claims nor care for the negative effect of his actions. For someone to be viewed as a charlatan, they must have been found out. So, their audience also realizes they have been cheated without any benefit.

O.K. Working with the tarot I am often presented with that moment of awe in which the images will tell the perfect story about a person. Take, for example, this woman I saw yesterday, who kept asking me if I saw a third person in her cards. During the reading a story emerged: The Pope, the Six of Coins, The Knight of Cups. The way I told that story was: "The Pope and the Knight of Cups met at a business meeting. Six people sat around a table, but The Pope only had eyes for the Knight of Cups and the Knight of Cups only had eyes for The Pope". She commented that, in fact, she had met this person at a business meeting. She was The Pope in that she was the one running the meeting, and the other person was there to actually pitch something, just as the Knight of Cups is offering his cup; and she experienced an unusual, unexpected attraction towards this person that had her losing track of everything else. The story in the cards was a perfect mirror of all that! As I have said elsewhere, I think my work consists in making room for these things to happen, but I will never claim nor even hint at the idea that I can make that happen. So, back to your proposition: "magic is real." I think magic is only real if we don't name it, but it becomes some sort of empty label when we invoke it. Don't you think?

Your statement astutely delivers us to the third part of our fantastic formula; namely, the role of confidence and conviction. I have introduced the themes of "intention" and "perception." When you now add the ingredient of "belief" you have an astonishingly palpable "magical" experience. It has been said before: "Believing is the magic." For me, it is not whether the actual word is invoked or not that gives it potency; it is whether the recipients of the "magic" – ourselves or others – consider the experience truthful. And the bringers of the experience (people like you and me) have a great many tricks and tools that can be employed to awaken and conjure a wondrous and empowering reading (in the case of Tarot).

I find that a belief is born when we first hold a thought or an assumption (a suggestion is planted) and then that opinion or expectation is somehow confirmed for us through one of our senses (the suggestion is apparently shown to be true). A firmly rooted way of thinking now takes hold. In your case, for example, you have written of your belief in the magic of serendipity and the stories that good fortune delivers to you. Thus, you leave a place for this in your reading style. And it works . . . because your programmed thinking makes it so. Should you happen to change your conviction, I have no doubt your new way of reading will be just as triumphant.

Quite frankly, I spend a great deal of time finding out whether people believe in their own magic. Most have stopped believing in themselves. They have lost or never discovered their purpose – their magical reason for being here. And thus they turn to divination for answers, confirmation or assurance. They believe their magic has failed them or never been given to them and so resort to cards and numbers and signs for guidance.

I think it is one of our primary roles, as readers, to bring that magical self-belief and self-confidence back. To attain this, I make sure the preframe for a reading is as effective as possible. In other words, I let people know ahead of time what is going to happen. Coming back to your original question, then, there are times when I do expressly talk about magic – the magic of the cards, the magic of symbols . . . and the magic of believing in yourself.

Of course, there are times when I simply allow the magic to speak for itself.

Now, when we talk about "magic" we may be talking about two different things. One is what people like to think magic is: a certain knowledge about the elements of nature, or about the language of these elements, so you can harness them for your own benefit. That's what the general audience for magic, the general 'occult' market, thinks magic is. On the other hand we have what magic actually seems to be: a purposeful use of symbols to engage the mind in a process of transformation. I make the distinction because I believe you are talking about this second notion. A magician knows how to speak to the human mind so he can shift the person's sense of what is possible. In that, I don't even think we are talking about the rational mind, but about something more profound that I connect with our emotions. Something I have learned by doing readings is that understanding something means nothing in terms of overcoming it. By this I mean that an intellectual understanding of our options, our talents, or as you define it, our "own magic" doesn't prompt anybody to action. It is only when we touch an emotional cord that the person reacts. That is, I think, the most important effect chance has in a reading. The fact that a person randomly chooses some cards that can speak to her directly, is an emotional experience, not an intellectual one. In a way, all magical experiences exist in a realm beyond reason.

I tend to believe that suggestion is the most powerful force in the realm of human affairs. Magic makes use of the suggestive power of substances, actions and elements to affect a person's sense of reality. Interestingly, the tarot carries a powerful suggestion that, I believe, it borrowed from its origin as a game: "the cards you got define your fate". This premise applies both to a poker hand and to a tarot reading. In a reading, a lot of the magic starts with the presence of the object in itself and the associations it brings about. To be honest, no mater how much I train myself, no matter how much I study the cards and the images, I feel that most of my work consists in getting out of the way, so the implicit suggestions carried by the tarot as an object, and the suggestions each one of the images carry, can operate as an effect on the person's emotional state. I tend to think of myself as a mood enhancer, which I guess goes along the lines of what you define as bringing "that magical self-belief and self-confidence back".

Now, in a way, any magical operator understands "beliefs" as another material: beliefs can be used to shape a certain kind of communication or to talk about cer-

tain ideas. Beliefs can be a vehicle. I wonder, how do you manage the dialogue between your own beliefs and your client's beliefs?

You are exactly right when you say, "a magician knows how to speak to the human mind so he can shift the person's, or his own, sense of what is possible." That is one of the reasons I use the tagline for my appearances: "No One's Mind is Safe." It sets the stage, so to speak, for what we will be accomplishing together. Once I have consent to work my "magic," that agreement – in and of itself – creates anticipation to be amazed, assumptions that miracles are possible, and eagerness for our time together to be phenomenally successful.

Before I expand on "managing expectations" (which is a phrase I prefer rather than "managing beliefs"), I must point out that I don't draw distinctions between an illusionist, an oracle, or an elemental adept. While the devices they use vary, their creative means are all the same to me. In each situation, if you are serving yourself and others well, you are intentionally constructing a change in consciousness. If you want to be congruent and authentic, then, as a magician you are steadfast in that role no matter what task or tool might be holding your attention at the moment.

For me, there is a contrast between what I call the "dabbler" or "puzzler" and someone who seeks "artistry" or "elegance." Anyone can buy a book from the store, learn a few secrets and half-heartedly fumble through a magic trick – but few have the *finesse* to impart a sense of true surprise and wonder with the performance. Anyone can buy a pack of Tarot cards, shuffle the deck, lay them out in the spread, and blindly regurgitate memorized meanings – but few have the flair to draw out life-changing lessons from the images. Anyone can recite the time-honored stories of a shaman – but few have skill to fill those tales with spirit, energy and passion.

This brings me to your question about the dialogue I use to manage expectations (presumably for a reading). This occurs on both verbal and non-verbal levels and an understanding of the two is important if you are going to masterfully guide, control, and lead the session. The conversation is certainly verbal when I tell someone that I will be using the symbols to trigger, enhance and project otherwise hidden and masked messages. I explain that the Major Arcana provide archetypal representations of our essence while the Minor Arcana reflect the way our fundamental qualities act out in the material world. I also stress, by the way, that the Future is not fixed. That last comment, alone, undeniably sets in motion the empowering quality I want the reading to have for the people listening.

There are also non-verbal aspects to any reading – some of which precede the reading itself – but which certainly have as much, if not more, to do with the expectations people bring with them to a reading session. If someone is seeking a reading, there is usually a deeply felt belief that magic exists or is possible. The cards and their symbols also spark a connection that is imbued with equal parts of curiosity, faith, and hope. I make certain that the verbal aspects of my exchange are in harmony with these more powerful, non-verbal aspects.

Above all else, I want a reading to be an experience; an event that is unforgettable and passionate. In my lectures and workshops I often equate a reading to a kiss. They both can convey love, desire, friendship, a promise, a goodbye, and respect, among many other sentiments. My dialogue before, during and after a reading is meant to accentuate the time we share together.

I want to give some attention to one thing you just said: the Future is not fixed. I take this statement as a suggestion, not only of the fact that the client can take charge of her future, but also underlying that there is the assumption of the future being somehow addressed in your reading. I find this important in that I never offer or intend to predict the future in my readings (and I know you don't predict the future), but even so, our cultural understanding of the tarot has the prediction aspect so embedded that I know half of the time people are assuming I am foretelling something. Sometimes they come back to report that "everything happened as you said". From our point of view as operators, this is useful in that it sets the client's expectations in such a way that may facilitate certain attitudes, and these attitudes may facilitate certain actions or changes. I take any prediction to be a suggestion, and I have no qualms at using them just as I have no qualms using any other narrative element to craft a message. But I always find this is a slippery slope. There is always something infantile in the idea of predicting the future. What are your thoughts about this?

I don't know that I would use the word "infantile" to describe a portion of what happens during and after a reading. There are a lot of professions driven by the ability of people to predict what will likely happen based on information, intuition, and, in some cases, pure chutzpah. Doctors do this. Lawyers, too. And Stockbrokers, just for starters. You see, predicting the Future is not the sole domain of an Oracle. Indeed, I openly tell people that I am paid to have dreams and nightmares for them – and I envision lots of things. So you see, I do speak of the Future when I give readings.

However, I always emphasize that the Future is not fixed. In fact, I discuss Fate and Free Will by comparing them to the old board game of "Life." There is the board, the tokens, the dice, the cards, and the rules. In fact, someone else even created all those things for us to play with. These things are fixed and cannot be changed without changing the nature of the game, itself. This is just one way of describing Fate.

Then there are the players. Each one is unique and each one has an expectation of doing the best he or she can do during the time they are together to play the game. The players get to choose the cars that are moved on the board. The players get to make decisions about how to throw the dice and the cards affect the ultimate outcome of the game. In some cases, the players can even decide how quickly the game will be played and if it should end early. This is one way of describing Free Will.

And then there is the finality we call the "end of the game;" a perfect combination of Fate and Free Will.

I always tell people that they, on some level, have the power to choose their own Futures or, at the very least, how they react and respond to the events in their lives. I urge them not to listen to me or anyone else who might try to tell them how the Future must be. I would never suggest that I know, without fail, what is going to happen. Indeed, the fact that people have some self-determination and can make different choices and decisions underscores the limitations of someone infallibly predicting anything all the time.

That being said, I also believe that suggestions can easily shape the Future and mold things yet to come. For that reason, I am very careful to discuss two things with people; namely, where they have come from and where they are now. Once those two things are known, I also believe that the Future for that person becomes tellable. So you see, I am using predictions to look backwards as much as the people coming to me might want me to look forward.

In the end, I want to help people develop, recognize, and tune in to the tools and skills that will allow them to manipulate and control their lives. I want to know what the person coming for a reading truly wants. If a reading can assist someone by focusing them on both a Future they might want and a Future they might not want, at least they start discerning changes that need to be made to gain pleasure and avoid pain.

I would be remiss if I didn't , in the end, discuss a fundamental thought of mine. In my public appearances I have openly said that divination and fortune telling are what we turn to when our own magic fails us. As such, I spend a great deal of my time working with people to help them discover their own magic and learning to believe in themselves again. That necessarily entails talking about and anticipating the Future.

You are quite right – most people seeking readings want to know about the Future. But this is no surprise. We live in a world that rewards the forward thinkers and those who can anticipate and plan accordingly. In fact, how can anyone make prudent and farsighted choices without foreseeing an expected Future? It is interesting, however, that those who generally seek readings of the Future have either forgotten or not learned how they can make their own precise and reliable foretellings.

It is my plan, during readings, to help the people who come to see me to sort out what has already happened and what is presently happening with them and to provide them tools to improve their Futures. What I do seems mystical to many people. I, on the other hand, believe we are all equipped for anticipating and telling things in advance . . . if we just take the time to listen, watch, and learn.

These days I have been remembering that what I expect from the tarot is the same thing I expect from poetry: to give me new words to talk about old things. When someone asks me what the tarot can do for them, I tell them that the tarot can help us think about something, and maybe, by chance or by surprise, it may show us a certain sense of truth. This conception of "truth" interests me a lot: the idea of something that is truthful simply because it happened by chance, without intrusion of our consciousness or will. More often than not, the answers we get in a reading are ephemeral forms. The specifics of these answers disappear, and what stays in us is the feeling of having been stirred up, shaken, even challenged. What I like about the tarot, in opposition to any other system, is precisely how arresting the images are. They stir us up. But they do so because, as they seem to be speaking about us with absolute precision, they happened by chance. In this context chance can be seen as another powerful convincer, of course.

Personal experience is the best tool we have to map the future. I am not talking only about our personal experience, but about our understanding of human experience or human condition. Each stage in a person's life comes with certain longings, with certain compulsions and with certain fears. We can map the causes of these longings, compulsions and fears, and we have seen how these longings, compulsions and fears play out in other people's lives. We know the most likely scenarios, given any specific situation. When any of these scenarios get validated by the poetics of chance, we experience something quite powerful. In truth, I suspect that the tarot is a great suggestive tool to validate common sense. The same common sense a person would dismiss if chance weren't involved.

You are pointing out something that is crucial: a person's future depends on where that person came from and where the person stands, now. That is one fascinating notion I learned from Milton Erickson: he wasn't really interested in knowing if a person was schizophrenic, depressed, bipolar, etc, but in knowing what the person can do. To me, "predicting" something is nothing more than assuring someone of how, when the time comes, he or she will remember what he can do. I call childish the notion of a future that will play out in this or that way despite what a person can actually do, or what the person can actually achieve. Luck is an important thing we all associate with fate. But in order to get lucky you need to be ready, and in order to be ready you need to know what you can do.

I suspect that there is a difference between projecting a future by applying our understanding of human experience to the specific potential of a person, and "seeing" the future. That second idea is the one I call infantile. Obviously, the other side of such infantility, in my view, is the idea of the reader having a special gift. I have no reason to believe that the creative impulse behind a reading is of a different nature than the creative impulse behind a painting, a song, or a poem. But even so, there is a tendency towards alienation in people who think of themselves as "sensitive" or "psychic" that one rarely sees in the world of artists and poets. I tend to be very reactive against "sensitive" people in that I find such sensibility disempowering. When people start telling me they are "special" because they get the pain others *get, or that they cannot live in a certain home or a certain room because of the vibrations in them, I often ask them: "O.K. but, can you cook?" Again, to me life seems to be about doing. The realm of doing is horizontal: it reaches out and touches others.*

I find very hard the idea of being a good operator out of pure faith, being this faith in a gift or mere good faith. I recently had a very frustrating experience while researching on homiletics. In a way, a tarot reading is a homily. We aren't only reminding someone of what he can do, but reminding him of what he can aspire at. In a way, that is not too different from what a priest does when he says a homily at church. So, I decided to look into homiletics, into the technique of it, to see if I could improve my way of doing readings.

I started asking around and got to talk to a couple of priests who basically told me: "the basic technique is to have faith". I read a couple of books on the subject, and again, they felt like sermons about the importance of faith. Now, I am the first one who thinks you have to believe in whatever you are doing, but let's be clear: no writer, poet, painter or composer will tell you that their craft consists in having faith. In some cases faith may be their doormat, but once you cross the threshold you find yourself in a workshop where you join generations and generations of technicians. The craft of poetry is what gives poets the backbone for their talent. The craft of painting is what turns you into an image-maker. The craft of music is what paves the road for the fingers of a guitar player to achieve mastery. Inside the workshop there is no talk about 'talent' or 'gifts', but pure technical struggle. And I wonder, what do we find in the workshop of readers? What do you think are the technical pillars of our craft?

You bring up some fascinating observations; some opinions, this time, where we diverge. Let me explain:

I employ old words to speak of new things. For me, the common sense and wisdom of our forefathers usually provides a clarifying and needed perspective for the Future and the plans we, as magicians, make for the time ahead.

I have neither confidence nor conviction in the concept of Chance and the role it might play in people's lives; those accidental, unintentional, and inadvertent happenings to which one might attribute an otherworldly message or import. I suggest to the people for whom I do readings that perhaps all things truly do happen for a reason and a purpose even though we might not be aware on a conscious level of the mechanisms that bring them about.

I believe that all artists (anyone who has mastery or perhaps innate genius in a particular area) have some faith; a trust, a confidence, and a belief in their own skills and techniques (even though there is still some room for doubt – in fact, I don't think it would surprise you to find that some of the most talented people I know suffer from a lack of confidence in their abilities to perform for others – as opposed to their conviction that they must create if they are to even exist). This is not to suggest that those who create rely upon blind faith. Rather, I submit that most people who bring things into existence as a painter, poet, dancer, writer, or reader adopt their beliefs and techniques when their opinions are ultimately born out by their reality.

Above all else – and this might sound foolhardy – I choose to believe in these things because they are a pleasure to believe! Richard Bach once wrote, ""We are game-playing, fun-having creatures, we are the otters of the universe. We cannot die, we cannot hurt ourselves any more than illusions on a screen can be hurt. But we can believe we're hurt, in whatever agonizing detail we want. We can believe we're victims, killed and killing, shuddered around by good luck and bad luck."

You bring up the concept of the "workshop." If I am going to use that term in a traditional sense, I need us to have the common understanding that we are speaking about a place that was constructed for the larger scale production and repair of "things." The workshop concept evolved for the artist and became essentially a studio wherein the skills and knowledge of the master, together with the philosophical tips and practical activities of the elders, were dispensed to and carried out by apprentices.

While I know you want to narrow our discussion down to the technical skills of reading, I am doubtful you can truly divorce the indifferent technique of turning a card over from the delightful play of ideas upon that flip of the wrist. As such, I ultimately developed something I fondly call the "Principles of Divination and Elegant Prophecy." These are general rules that I use for myself and which regulate, for the moment, my behavior and thoughts in giving readings.

Know what you have.

Know what you want and desire.

Know how to be aroused and inspired.

Know how to play.

Know how to embrace unexpected and fortunate discoveries.

Know that misadventures have their lessons, too.

Know that you are always right.

Know that you can always start over.

I find these eight principles the most important part of a reader's workshop or tool chest. The cards certainly are not. I have often said that, if you can read Tarot cards, you can read anything (light fixtures, street signs, nail polish cracks, etc.). In fact, as you know, much of the time I am not using physical cards at all. The reading space is not; I have read in the middle of an international airport and in the midst of a busy store.

Perhaps, then, the essential tools for the reader are actually the transcendental and internal symbols and signs that have a plainly personal meaning for that reader, combined with the successful ability to express the wonder that those symbols and signs impart. Unlike the painter or poet who needs a physical medium of paint and pen and paper to materialize a creation, or the dancer who needs an expressive body and limbs to move, the reader needs nothing more than a playful curiosity, a willingness to receive answers, and the special ability to share, convey, and exchange what is in one's mind to the ears of another person. I person hearing the reading will do the rest.

Of course, I don't mean to make the physical cards and their symbols less important than they really are. For the novice reader in our workshop, these pieces of paper and their images serve an important function; serving as visual devices to supplement and enhance and reinforce what is being taught by the master. Further, apprenticeship in our reader's workshop does not have any fixed period of time. Rather, much like the line from the old TV series, Kung Fu ("When you snatch the pebble from my hand, it will be time for you to leave."), our apprentice reader (our beginner) will eventually mature into a journeyman reader (someone who is reliable, but not outstanding). Some will develop into a master and start their own workshops and the cycle renews.

Finally, you ask about "technical pillars." There are four components to reading that I can express.

First, we have the cards, themselves. Traditionally, these can be as few as 22 (just the Major Arcana) or as many as 78 (a combination of Major and Minor Arcana). The use of cards distinguishes Tarot from other forms of divination like palmistry, runes, and numerology.

Second, we have the symbolism and images. Tarot, as you have so aptly and gracefully written about before, is a visual art. The Tarot is made up of suits, people, and archetypes that, for the most part, are fungible between decks but uniquely compartmentalized and grouped within traditional constraints. For example, there are the Major Arcana archetypes, the suits of Wands, Cups, Pentacles and Swords, the Court cards, etc.

Third, we have interpretation and common meanings. There are universal symbols that speak to all of us on both conscious and spiritual levels. These familiar concepts serve as the means of communicating between the person reading the cards and the individual receiving the reading.

Lastly, we have what I call "The Agreement." By this I mean that impregnated and expectant meeting place between the reader and the person receiving the reading where there is a consent – a seeing of eye-to-eye so to speak – that the details of the reading will be sought on the one hand, and truthfully exposed on the other. As readers, we are way-showers. The people for whom we read must agree to be shown or entertain that way or the reading is without a point and a waste of time. Without this moral concurrence between the reader and listener, we become nothing more than uninvited voyeurs.

Now some may ask about specific decks – new versus old, traditional versus unconventional, large versus small. For me, the choice of deck and size is truly just ornamental and may add to the tone and setting of the reading.

I think you are raising a crucial point: all beliefs are aesthetic preferences. I know most people find that idea problematic, but we do believe in whatever we find beautiful or pleasurable to believe in. Faith is, after all, that reliance on the idea of a certain kind of beauty that must be waiting for us elsewhere. What I consider important, or sober, especially given the kind of work we do, is the ability to take one step back and say: "I believe in this because it gives me pleasure" and not "I believe in this because it is true". Any operator, any person dealing with any type or form of magic, must be able to take that step back. That is what gives the operator the possibility of getting rid of a certain fiction as soon as it loses its power. To me, being a magician consists precisely on walking the landscape, with its deserts and mountains, right to the end, where we can see it was just a blanket. We peek underneath the blanket and see there is nothing – which is precisely what makes the blanket more precious.

I actually don't believe we have opposite views. I think we put an emphasis on different aspects of our practice, but that is almost a cosmetic instance, since the final end, as I understand it, is the same for you and for me: we are seeking to empower a person, so the person can face the future by making empowered choices. I find your approach to readings quite therapeutic. I don't think readings are therapy, but still, readings can have a therapeutic effect. By reading your work I get the impression that your readings aim at making people aware of their choices, within their reality, which is pretty much what I also hope to achieve with my readings. What I am trying to reinforce is the fact that such view runs opposite to the idea of telling people that life is going to happen to them by magic, as if magic were external to the individual. Life is always happening to us, but that is not living. To live is to have a dialogue with what happens.

Now, I have learned to give importance to chance for one reason: it brings the reading into that emotional realm where a person can actually be affected. Chance is magic waiting to be harnessed. In most cases, the fact that we rationally understand something doesn't mean we are going to do anything about it. It is only when we are emotionally moved that we change. I guess that, in a way, it is only when we are emotionally involved that we care about something. It is not that I believe everything happens for a reason. I don't. But we believe it does, and I can use that. Chance takes me, of course, into the visual aspect of the tarot. Many times my work simply consists in getting out of the way of what happens on the table, if this is clear enough for a person to be moved; or to build up on that just a bit to make it more clear to that person. But in any instance in which the images are working as images, I shut up.

This doesn't means I limit the idea of the workshop to dealing with a deck of cards. My main criticism of most people wanting to do readings is precisely that one can't limit the craft to learning what means what. We are working with people, so, if I were to pursue that workshop metaphor I would say that the cards aren't our material – people are. A person is our marble and the cards are our chisel, so to speak. I find the fact that there is no way to understand a chisel without marble very telling. The metaphor of the sculpture takes me back to Joseph Beuys and his idea of speech being a sculptural process. The throat muscles imprint shape into the air, so air can be experienced as meaning. Giving meaning to the air that comes out of our lungs takes me to storytelling, singing, suggestion, and of course, poetry. Hence my insistence on seeing the tarot as a poetic devise. The cards I place on the table form a poem I will read aloud, knowing that by reading it aloud I will misread it. But that misreading is, itself, what makes the poem relevant to one specific person. From the perspective of the poetic act, I know I cannot force epiphanies into people. The poem offers a hint, and it is up to the person to take it. Poems are fascinating to me in that they aren't fiction or non-fiction.

I think the main difficulty in understanding the craft of the diviner in our times is precisely that the role of the diviner seems to have been taken over by other practices. Divination occupies a marginal role in contemporary society because our culture seems to feel more comfortable with finding the same thing in other realms. It feels more safe, or respectable, to go see a therapist, or a priest, or a life coach. I would like to ask you: what do you think a reader offers that is unique and which differs from all those other practices?

I'm not certain that readers have something unparalleled to offer (when compared with other professions) as much as they have the noteworthy potency to capture the fascination and dreams of others. Anyone who pursues divination for the benefit of others invokes the world of imagination and evokes the promise of self-determination.

The challenge with many medical and mental health care providers that I see arrives when they dabble with or forget the great abilities they actually have; the power to transform the medical and psychological realities of their patients. I don't want this to be taken as a sweeping indictment of all professionals because it is certainly not meant that way. However, many doctors and therapists are simply inadequate magicians, witch doctors and medicine men. They may be spectacular technicians, clinicians, and diagnosticians, but they have forgotten, ignore or never skillfully learned how to dramatically identify and significantly change something much more powerful than a disease – someone's beliefs.

On the other hand, our spiritual advisers – the clergy and the life coaches you mention – obviously have the knowledge of how to elegantly and potently help restore a person's way of thinking. Unfortunately, many, themselves, don't demonstrate lives that are congruent with the secrets they seek to instill in their patrons. Because they don't give off an appearance – a show – that is faithful to their message, the force and might of their words is lost within and devoured by the disbelief of the person seeing and hearing them.

A pattern can be seen, then. Perhaps it is the ineffectual use of suggestions and the failure to appear authentic that causes many doctors, therapists, and life coaches to fail. For I think you'll agree that, as magicians, you and I often intentionally bend and willfully reshape what someone else might have once seen as their unshakable truth in order to give wonder, gift awe, and thus bestow them back with their faithful power; a belief in themselves as the creators of their worlds.

I am not discounting a doctor's, therapist's, priest's, or life coach's ability to cure and mend. I am merely pointing out that many of these same people disbelieve in the magic that you and I want to consider as a primary moving force in Life.

I do agree that many people want "good things" to happen "to" them rather than those individuals taking whatever action or deciding on a way of thinking that puts them in a place where they can magically say, "I choose." I endeavor to help people find their limiting beliefs and reshape those self-imposed restrictions to reduce, if not eliminate, unwanted and negative consequences. In other words, we remind people of their own magic – not some outside force that drives them to success or failure.

Ultimately, I desire people to take responsibility for their own lives!

New York / Los Angeles, March 2010

"Look at the image presented; study it in all its aspects; reflect upon it; allow its own multifaceted richness to guide insight and meaning."

A conversation with JEAN-MICHEL DAVID, tarot scholar, educator

Is there any of the tarot images you have never recovered from?

Interestingly, yes!

It's really the single card that has cost me thousands of dollars (literally), and had me hunting down a number of false leads. It's also the single card that initiated my deeper interest in tarot's history and the meaningful connections within each image...

...let me tell you a little (true) story:

In the 1980s, a single caption to an image in Fred Gettings's 1973 *The Book of Tarot* managed to make two incorrect references: the caption reads "Illustration to the *Golden Legend:* Reims Cathedral". The image is fantastic – and I have since referenced it many times. At the time, the internet did not exist, and even in the first few years of the 21st century, not that much was really available.

In 2000, my wife and I were in France on the way to a pedagogical conference, so we detoured and spent a couple of days in Reims, searching all around the exterior and interior of the building for this image. The Siberian frosty winds had just started, and we were whipped with fine particles of rain – something I remembered and 'enjoyed' as a young child growing up not far from Chartres. This time, however, it made the wild goose chase rather tedious... and after having spoken to all the guides I could find, and looked through the numerous books in the various shops, I finally had to admit defeat.

Before admitting total defeat, however, we looked around the city in case there was perhaps another Cathedral (a rarity, but it does happen). To no avail. I thought that perhaps the image was rather small – perhaps no more than a hand's breadth – and in some nook or cranny of that Cathedral, and that even the locals I had access to were simply ignorant of the same.

Similarly for the *Golden Legend*. I had gone through a copy of it in English translation, to no avail. So I also bought myself a 'complete edition' in French whilst in Paris, and again, after going through it, wondered what I had missed! It wasn't until my return to Melbourne that I happened to come across similar quadrefoils surrounding other images in a totally unrelated book. The reference therein was not to Reims, but rather to Amiens Cathedral! Now Amiens is North of Paris, Reims East!

By this stage, I assumed that the Reims reference was incorrect, and with the new reference, was indeed able to locate the image from art books and the slowly emerging internet. Having located the image, it wasn't difficult to also reference the image as stemming not from the *Golden Legend*, but rather from what are called *Infancy Gospels* depicting, in this case, the flight to Egypt. And from this was also able to find another similar image, this time in the South of France on the Moissac Abbey Church.

So the 'Maison Dieu' – so often translated as the 'Tower' – has made a rather deep impression! … and in 2005, we spent a number of days in sweltering heat in Amiens, took hundreds of photos, and realised how large the petroglyph in fact is. How Gettings was able to make those two major errors in such a short caption I still find incredible!

That is a great story! First, I am fascinated by the idea behind the "cost" of an image. I love that idea of acknowledging the amount of time, effort and money that knowing an image may take. The act of getting to know an image equals owning the image. Why is important to pursue an image until you can own it?

In my local courses, I usually bring along an accurately weighed replica of a mediæval sword. Similarly, in both my online and local courses, I suggest going to a zoo (or, better if you have the opportunity, a safari) to actually observe and behold a lion. To visit, when opportunity arises, European museums and come as close as possible to an actual Imperial crown – and to wear a replica, or even a real one, and be seated wearing such. To engage in *Lectio Divina*.

There's no way that the suit of swords, or, in order of those cards I just mentioned, Fortitude, the Empress or Emperor, or the Papesse, remain imagery of something remote. Seeing the card image anew becomes a living experience, in the same way that looking at a familiar photo taken during a highly memorable occasion or trip retains a quality, for that person, that remains otherwise detached and relatively meaningless for others.

See? That is exactly what I mean when I say that meaning is experiential. Those emotional, and psycho-physiological hangers that compose the actual experiece of a thing end up embedded in our brain, so we can hook back on them any image, word, or notion that is brought up. But I tend to feel that people dismiss that experiential quality of meaning. It seems easier, or safer, to think that meaning, and memory, are a matter of reason, as if the body's own mnemonic system, that of the senses, were as trustworthy as our intellectual recalling of some words or ideas. Why do you think that is?

It is, I think, often very difficult to talk about or describe experiential knowledge or even, for that matter, emotions: in these areas, our language has simply not developed sufficient subtleties – or perhaps it's more that most of us (myself included) have not paid sufficient attention to these subtleties as they may be expressed in language. Try describing the subtleties of an Inuit's experience of a particular type of snowstorm around the time of the winter solstice in broad mid-day darkness within the Arctic circle to someone who has lived all their life on the tropical Australian eastern coast. Or the taste and texture of a witchetty grub or a steak tartare to a tibetan monk coming from a strict vegetarian Buddhist family. Or indeed what it's like to ride a bicycle. In each case, what we're actually asking is for the person to enter imaginatively an experience vicariously, and in the process fill in so much that's missing not only of their own personal life experience, but also overcoming biases. It is, of course, possible – at least to quite an extent – to develop the imaginative-contemplative faculty to 'experience' these.

I suspect that it's not only that the 'body's mnemonic system' is here at stake – though I take your point – but also that entering these *experiencially* makes them far more living within one's conceptual life and, importantly, insight-enriched and meaning-filled.

But then, there is the quest for meaning in that precise image: 'La Maison Dieu.' I guess that there are images that question us, and images that don't. If I look at the image of a dog, or a boat, I will probably take them as that: a dog, a boat. But I feel that the images in the tarot are always questioning us. Do you think that the meaning of an image existed prior to the image itself?

That's a deep question – or perhaps I'm understanding it with all its philosophical ramifications.

Let me address the example first, and then move on to the question proper. If I see a dog or a boat, its 'meaning' will itself have developed for each of us in different ways, even if speaking the same language. Let me give you an example taken (and modified) from Quine's philosophical classic *Word and Object* – though I realize that I am changing the example a little from one of language to something a little broader: imagine being in a foreign land and the native speaker points to a running hare and calls 'gavagai!' What may this actually mean, and how does its meaning even influence the manner in which we view the event? For example, it could 'mean' (and thus be seen as) 'tonight's dinner', or 'look how gracefully it runs', or 'animal-hare'. So what it even 'means' to take the image of a dog or a boat as 'just that' is not at all obvious, but is rather informed by our own usually unconscious personal biography located within a specific language in a particular socio-cultural location and epoch.

To take the image of a boat again as example, its very imaging will have been selected by the artist: it's even quite a different 'meaning' to have the boat as depicted in Pierre Puvis de Chavannes's *Le Pauvre Pêcheur* to a photograph of a boat lying on a beach following a tsunami. In neither case, I would suggest, is the boat simply taken 'as just that', but is rather filled with meaning that invites to be reflected upon and discovered. Most of the time, we simply do NOT reflect and seek to further understand: our world remains as 'the currently unquestioned', or assumed, reality.

This whole question is really a wonderful opening to get into two of my favourite philosophers and philosophical areas: Rudolf Steiner's epistemology and John Deely's semiotics... but that may digress too much, so better hold back!

So, you mentioned that you feel that in the tarot the images are always questioning us: I agree – at least when we allow ourselves to question and seek insight and understanding. If anything, what social convention has done is to assume that with tarot imagery, one *should* question and seek meaning. This was not always the case, as Dummett and others have quite clearly made known by presuming the opposite when tarot is used for gaming. But let me also return to your actual question: do I think that the meaning of an image existed prior to the image itself? Yes and no:

The selection and creation of an image – especially, but not only, in the case of tarot – already had 'meaning' in the sense that the image-makers sought to illustrate some individual, allegory, or capture part of a story. Once created, however, the image's meaning becomes created anew with each viewer. In the case where the 'source' of the image is not known by the viewer, alternative 'explanations' and meanings arise, which in turn alter later depictions of both image and further understanding. A case in point here includes how the Papesse has been explained; how the World has been altered; how the Wheel of Fortune has been radically changed in many recent decks to something that is increasingly removed from Boethius's concept of the same.

If nothing else, reading De Gebelin (or De Mellet) as an example, his 'recognition' that tarot depicts Ancient Egyptian concepts and Gods and Goddesses shows how 'meaning-making' radically alters the 'selected meaning' the card image-makers would have had, instructed by *their* sources.

I think you are tapping into something important there: the meaning of the tarot as an artifact could be seen as separated from the waning of the images that compose the tarot, and that meaning is consistent with its usage: both as a game, and as a divination tool, a deck of cards include the idea of chance, and therefore, the expectation on chance being somehow relevant to us.

From a neurological point of view, some authors talk about the idea of afordabilities: a thing means whatever it can afford us. A dog can afford us protection, a sense of companion, loyalty, but also a good scare or even a bite. It is easy to see why a dog means what it means to us. 'Dog' is a concept that includes a set of experiences, both personal and collective, we have had with dogs. I guess that setting the boundaries of our experiences about the images we see in the tarot may be more challenging. But I am asking you about all these issues for two reasons. First, while talking to a friend of mine who is an art history professor, he pointed out how most medieval images were made by draftsmen working in the service of someone else. He suggested that there must be a tarot in book, or literary form hiding somewhere in some old library. What do you think about that? The other reason I have to ask you these things has to do with something I have been noticing in the current discourse of many contemporary artists and even poets: there is this aim, even a sense of pride, on talking about not having any representational intention in their work. I have problems with that idea. If one keeps an eye on what neuroscience is suggesting nowadays about the way we process meaning, I fail to see how there can be images without representation, either of one main idea fostered by the artist, or of the particular ideas that our subjective reading of a piece may elicit in us. What do you think about that? Do you think it is possible to make non-representational images?

There's a lot to unravel and comment on here, Enrique!

The first point I'll make is not directly related to tarot as such, but rather to meaning-making. Personally, I see neurological research as seeking to explain what we already observe when we carefully reflect on our own engagement in the world. So some may indeed tend to have a bit of a reductionist view of meaning as somehow being epiphenomenal on something like 'affordability' or suchlike. This point has similarities, in some ways, to the last point in your questions about 'non-representational images' – to which I'll return in a while.

Let me first briefly address your question arising from your historian friend. Could it be that tarot's imagery, at least as it presents itself in the trumps, is somehow first illustrations to a document or a literary sequence? I think that many of us would like to find such a document, and many amongst us who are interested in tarot's history have probably at one stage or another thought this as a strong possibility – myself included. Personally, I now doubt that this is the case. And even when an early document *is* found, such as with the very early Boiardo poem, it's clear that the reference is to cards and not to another work.

And so I now think it more likely that the earliest tarot-like deck, or rather, decks, arose out of a desire to have an additional and exclusive trump set to what was an already existing 'base' set of four suits (themselves being something like the Mamluk decks). This additional *trumping* suit, instead of being represented by an implement such as a baton, cup, coin, or sword, was painted with imagery and developed to be what we now know as the trump sequence. Why those particular images were selected is, I suspect, in part 'accidental'. What I mean by that is that the painter was very likely constrained to a specified number of cards (whether it be 14, 16, 20 or 22 makes no difference at this stage). Given this constraint, he or she – but very likely 'he' given the times we're talking about – selected some from images of worldly positions (the early part of the sequence), some popular allegories and virtues, some celestial concepts, and some theological ones. How he made them all 'fit' was likely more fixed by trying to reflect a breadth of considerations within the limited set than trying to produce an overall sequential 'trump story'.

If what I'm suggesting is correct, than I would suggest that books that mirror the trump sequence, if they exist, are likely to *refer* to an existing deck of cards rather than the deck reflecting a book. Again, a good example of this is the Boiardo poem. In mentioning all this, I've also probably at least *partially* answered some of the other questions you raised. I'll try and add a little more here, however… you've opened such a pandora's box!

Let me just touch on the comment that draftsmen worked in the service of others. This is of course generally correct. The problem comes, when we talk about tarot, as to what period we are discussing and what decks are at issue. In the earliest tarot-like decks to which we have evidence, they were hand-painted (I am thinking here of the Visconti-type decks). Once we get to woodblocks and what is effectively mass-manufacturing of tarot, then the craftsmen *already* had models to more or less base their own pattern upon.

What's interesting here, by the way, is that even with the various patterns that do emerge, there appears such consistency: even with, for example, card XVI in such disparate decks as the TdM-types and the Viéville, we have two different images very likely stemming from the *same* story. In the TdM, we have what has come to be the canonical version of the lightning-struck Maison-Dieu, whereas in the Viéville what emerges as a more northern 'pattern' with the shepherd near a tree under a 'storm'. These two images, by the way, are also carved together as illustrating part of the same infancy gospel on, again, Amiens Cathedral – in case someone else is interested, I have placed all these images on my *fourhares* website.

So returning to your historian friend's suggestion that perhaps all these images are in a 'book', the closest answer in the affirmative is that indeed they are, but not in the way this would normally be understood. Rather, the images are there to be discovered as statues and as petroglyphs within and upon the largest and most well known *Lumiere* (or 'Gothic') Cathedrals of the 12-14th centuries. Even there, however, they are not presented as a *set*, but rather some are within the building as perhaps woodcarvings and effigies, others as images on the outside of the buildings. With regards to these, it's a shame that what was undoubtedly the most important of these buildings or group of buildings has long gone: the Cluny Abbey.

Now as to the most difficult part of your question about 'representational images'. In terms of what I'll call 'classical' tarot – which includes, for this part of my reply, *most* decks calling themselves 'tarot' – then the imagery used is 'representational' in all its commonsensical meaning: it 'represents' or seeks to be a *simulacrum* or *mimesis* of the allegory or office or celestial category it depicts. In some decks, which I would personally hesitate to call 'tarot' (though I'd be quite happy to call them 'inspired by tarot') what appears are not *simulacra* but rather closer to an expressionist rendering. Of course, even there I'd agree with what you seem to be implying: there is in the product a 'representation' of the feeling or emotion expressed.

If we look at meaning-making, then I would suggest that any given image, through its mere participation in thought (whether of the artist or the viewer), becomes a 'representational image'. There's an aspect of this that can be found in Peirce's rather difficult letters to Lady Victoria Welby. But I've probably started to veer again towards a generalised discussion, rather than tarot-focussed.

I think there is something I find important, even sobering, about neuroscience, and it is the fact that it gives us tools to tackle the dynamic of perception and meaning-making. Obviously, by focusing on perception alone one may be reducing a whole range of spiritual experiences into mere chemistry, but still, I think it is important to acknowledge how it is that we are all equipped to construct, or detect, meaning in the world. It is important to acknowledge how naturally predisposed we are to 'trick ourselves into meaning'. Perhaps, because underneath our poetical ability to find patterns and make sense of what we see, we find a survival mechanism that renders meaning-making way more fundamental than we usually think it is. I think I will always privilege any set of tools that will allow me to own my fictions, instead of me being owned by them, without ever loosing sight of the importance of such fictions.

Within that context, I recall an interview given by poet Louise Glück, where she was talking about a certain poem of hers. In the poem, she had mapped a metaphor from a pile of snow over a table into a ceramic bowl. In the poem, the pile of snow, resembling an upside-down bowl, had fallen on the ground, breaking into pieces. In the interview, she said that a broken bowl never ceases to be a bowl, it just transcends its original purpose. A broken object is free from its original intention and it now can become anything else. This expansive gesture lies at the basis of all our contemporary art. But by now you may be suspecting where am I going with this: in the tarot, we have this trump-taking game that evolved into a divination device, and like Glück's broken bowl, the tarot went beyond its original purpose to becoming something else. This is not an unlikely happenstance since, after all, both gaming and divination are ruled by chance. The suggestion implicit in a tarot reading is the same suggestion that is implicit in a card game: the cards you get define your fate. Even so, some people have problems with this. They prefer a story where the tarot's original purpose included divination. You have been in the tarot's 'scene' for quite a while. As a matter of fact you have been one of the oldest proponents of the importance of focusing on historical decks. You have told me before how you have seen changes in the way people deal with the Marseille tarot. More people seem to be interested in those decks now than 20 years ago. The Marseille tradition seems to be gaining terrain in the English speaking world. But what has happened to the tarot's origins? Do you perceive any evolution in the way people deal, relate to, or accept the tarot's history?

Hmmmm... whether in the English speaking world or elsewhere, people that have had a deeper interest in tarot have generally also had an interest in its history. So for example, even if we go back 100 to 150 years, we have the likes, within the Golden Dawn, of not only Waite, but before him amongst the founders of the GD Mathers and Wescott, and after him people like Crowley, all referencing and seeking to have an appreciation for tarot's history. Where it has been a little more difficult for many people during most of the 20th century is that much of tarot's history was, until recently, mainly written in either French or German, and most early documents are in Latin, Italian, French or German – or even dialects of these! Unlike the times of Waite or Mathers, in which part and parcel of education included learning French, Latin and Greek – which meant that these people could access books in those languages – most of us living in English speaking nations during the 20th century do not tend to be bi- or tri-lingual by general education (though many are by 'choiced' education or by ancestral connections).

The other aspect is that tarot, despite its late 19th century inclusion by the GD, was really something 'new' to the English speaking world from roughly the 1960s. Even then, it was nearly impossible to obtain a deck. And here is where some credit is due to Stuart Kaplan: if it wasn't for his business activities, tarot may not have gained the prominence it has. Of course the deck also had to be supplemented by interpretation aides. First there was Eden Gray's book that influenced the hippy generation. But it wasn't really until the 1980s, with the neo-pagan revival — which can itself be viewed as a metamorphosis of the hippy movement — that tarot became rather popular. Of course by then, the deck that gained dominance was the one for which a handbook was easily available: and this was the Waite-Smith deck.

At the very same time, or just before, in 1978, the first volume of Kaplan's *Encyclopedia* came out. So here was an opportunity for an appreciation of both the variety of decks and a little of its history. Even if Dummett's *Game of Tarot* did not become popular, here was another really important work that came out at around the same time. And not long after that, in the mid 80s, was O'Neill's *Tarot Symbolism*. So already, contemporaneously with tarot's increased popularity were a number of admittedly difficult to find but important books. Then with the advent of the internet and at first bulletin boards (especially *TarotL*) and forums (especially *Aeclectic*), it became far easier for the content of those books, especially the more historically oriented ones, to be disseminated and the all too numerous faulty stories floating around to be seriously exposed or at least questioned. Again, it's not so much that many had access to the original material, but rather that these books, and those that later followed, especially by, again, Dummett and Co's with their two historical books (*Wicked Pack* and *History of Occult Tarot*) as well as, for example, Christine Payne-Towler's *Underground Stream*, that most tarot enthusiasts were inevitably exposed to their research and ideas.

That I may have had a part in this dissemination is more a reflection of my interest in pursuing an understanding of tarot's imagery *grounded* on what is actually presented.

In terms of tarot history, fortunes have now rather changed from generations past: most of the important historical works are now in English... and I have already mentioned them. This inevitably makes the English-speaking world more open to tarot's historical dimension. What emerges from this is that even if an author appears to be more interested in tarot as psychological tool, as I sense, for example, in Mary Greer's works, she still grounds it in historical research and, in her case with regards the Waite-Smith court cards or the founding women in the GD, furthers original research.

But let me get back, then, to this concept of 'grounding' with regards to tarot's imagery, and from this also address two important points you make with the example of Louise Gluck's poetry and tarot history's central importance.

This goes back also to some things I've said and written about before. It's not just a matter of looking at the image as given to us, but also seeking to understand the cultural context in which it emerged. Let me give you a brief example coming from both Kabbalistic tradition and Mediæval Biblical exegesis: a fourfold reading of the text. In this, the first is the literal text and this, from my perspective, cannot but include its historical context and setting; the second level is still grounded in the first, or takes it as a given *from* which to emerge, is its allegorical or typological level, in other words, what specifically marks this text or, in our case, image, and how does it meaningfully relate to other texts or parts of the text or image. In many ways, this is often the level at which readers wish to remain, but without grounding it by prior study on its more literal foundation. The third level is its tropological-moral dimension, basically seeking to ascertain how the current narrative assists one in meeting and engaging with the world as it meets us; whilst the fourth level seeks to ascertain its anagogical or 'secret' level – how does the reader transcend or ascend to its mystical intent, or how is he or she liberated by the insights brought to bear on the situation at hand?

So like Louise Glück's snow pile that resembles a bowl that fragments and is thus liberated from its original form, there is first a need to understand what this original form is and its historical or socio-cultural context. After all, even calling it a 'bowl', rather than, for example, a spittoon or potty, says something of the 'intent' that *grounds* the poem. Similarly in tarot: it's the grounding of the image within its historical setting that provides a depth going far beyond even the artist's knowledge or intent.

I would like to ask you an unfair question. Why do you think the tarot is so attractive to people? Where does its appeal reside?

I don't think we can go past how popularity breeds popularity as one of the ingredients. However, to remain in a long-term popular category, the item in question must have very special qualities of complexity, economy of design, intrigue, and relative ease of use. Not many things fit this criteria: chess and books fit, but not much else. Of books, its *content* will be of primary importance, and similarly with cards. Most decks do not have the inner tension that manifests with tarot's trumps, for example.

Unlike chess, however, tarot has something that is quite profound, and this is where its appeal, I would suggest, in part resides: its imagery encapsulates thousands of years of western philosophical striving expressed in archetypical western imagery. Even if this is not consciously held by the viewer, it reflects what permeates western culture.

Or at least, there's my brief answer to your err... unfair question...

"Inner tension". I like that notion. How would you define the tarot's inner tension?

There are a number of ways in which I see this manifest in tarot. Given that I've mentioned a fourfold exegesis, let me also take the opportunity to try and answer this question in that manner.

On a literal level, the sequence of images does not appear to give us a nice and easy continuous, coherent and complete narrative. For example, even if the fourth cardinal virtue of Wisdom is 'assigned' to one or another card, it is, from a literal perspective, missing. Also, in terms of looking for sets that are self explanatory, and again considering the cardinal virtues, they are scattered through the sequence rather than held in a nice and easy sub-group. There appears no rhyme or reason why, for example, the Wheel of Fortune follows the Hermit, or why Death *precedes* Temperance. These are some of the difficulties that especially face the person first coming to tarot, and reflects the deck's apparent incompleteness.

At the allegorical level, the deck as a whole presents itself as a movement within a symphony, each card like a bar with its own internal chords, keys and overtones, which somehow works by drawing from the great traditions. It's as if, to use the metaphor of a symphony again, someone wrote a movement in which each bar called to mind – at least to the musically savvy – existing important musical works, some from Schubert, some from Mozart, some from Albinoni, etc. And yet managed to somehow make the whole not sound cacophonous or discordant. In this case, to appreciate the musical piece, one could, of course, simply sit back and enjoy the experience. To allow its meaning to be enriched with a depth of understanding, however, not only would an appreciation of the source of each bar need to be studied, but also the context and full musical piece each part but echoes. The inner tension here is that the parts and the whole need to be reconciled and enriched beyond the limited presentation taken out of any context.

At the moral level or tropological level, one can begin to reflect on how each part gives us insights into not only human nature and the world around us, but appropriate and inappropriate reactions and engagements with it. How is *this* (whatever it is) situation presenting itself in this specific context instructed by, for example, reflecting on this particular card? The 'inner tension' here allows not only the 'meaning-making faculties' to be at play, but also applied with a sense of inner freedom and valuing of the human engagement or activity for its own sake – something that, in my view, reflects genuine ethics. Incidentally, an aspect of what I'm trying to present here is what Steiner calls *ethical individualism* in his *Philosophy of Freedom* – with the 'individualism' referring to an appreciation of the specifics of the individual situation at hand. In order to sense into the situation-at-hand, there is inevitably inner tension as insights begin to slowly emerge.

At the anagogical level, tarot's inner tensions manifest from two orientations: the horizontal and the vertical. On the *horizontal* axis, there is what I'll closely paraphrase from Bachelard's *Poetics of Space* – though there he speaks not of imagery, but of poetry: 'the image is not an echo of the past; on the contrary, through the brilliance of an image, the distant past resounds with echoes, and it is hard to know at what depth these echoes will reverberate and die away; because of its novelty and its action, the image has an entity and a dynamism of its own'. Here we see also the importance of seeking to appreciate tarot's history as well as each image's *pre*-history as, in part, a need to understand what the 'echoes' are. On the *vertical* axis, not only each image, but also the whole, can be seen as an archetypal pattern that takes form anew in each instantiation of a genuine tarot deck. This is a little like Goethe's description of the archetypal plant that manifests or unfurls out of a constant impulse – this sense of 'archetype' is somewhat different from the way in which it has come to be used in modern Jungian-type psychology, but rather harkens back to Plato's concept of eternal forms. At this level, the artist does not seek to understand how or why an image is placed therein, but rather leaves himself or herself open to the work manifesting through them. It is in part out of consideration of this aspect that I do not think that it is necessary the very early tarot 'need' to have been 'understood' or be viewed as 'coherent' by their artists.

I tend to find that fourfold exegesis very useful when it comes to tackle the tarot images, but somehow I feel that your answer was addressing the trumps alone. Am I right? In other words, I would like to know what role you assign to the pips. This is a tricky topic, I think, since it may seem that, when it comes to earlier decks, it is the graphic simplicity of the pips what turns most people off. I have seen the importance of the pips addressed by people like Paul Marteau, or in current times, by Alejandro Jodorowsky; but when it practice, those authors tend to disregard the pips. Other authors, like Jean-Claude Flornoy, would openly dismiss the pips. Obviously I am only talking of authors within the Marseille tradition, but I would love to know your thoughts on the pips.

I personally don't dismiss the pips, and I consider that a fourfold exegesis can actually deepen an understanding of these as well – and not just for the pips, but the court cards as well. Yet I also acknowledge that the pip and court cards have both a different 'quality' as well as a different history to them. But see, even here I'm beginning with that first of the fourfold division: I talk, right from the word go, of a different, and in many ways far simpler, history!

There's two aspects to this different history: in the first place, it's clear that the four suits – sometimes referred to as 'colours' – arise either directly or with only minor indirectness from the Mamluk decks of centuries earlier. Therein we have batons (or perhaps what some have considered to be polo sticks), cups, coins, and scimitars. In the second, we need to consider the implements depicted themselves. After all, the scimitar or sword isn't a two centimetre obsidian scalpel.

Looking at the four implements used in the suits, we can again begin to appreciate what they first 'literally' represent by first investigating and reflecting the purpose to which these were put or used, and *who* or what class of people had access or control of the same. For example, unlike Roman times, by late mediæval European times, swords were solely the province of the nobility. As another example, cups, as depicted, are not those used for everyday drinking, but rather Church chalices – and the Ace of the series certainly accentuates this even more. So again here we begin to gain a deeper *grounding* in the implement's 'literal' meaning grounded in its historical context. A related aspect that is often overlooked is whether cards depicting a single straight sword amidst curved ones – and I am here of course talking of those decks that are similar to the TdM – are to be considered upright when the sword's point is downwards or upwards: on this, being no longer in a society in which swords are common nor commonly depicted, a diminished sense of convention has set in... along with the implied meaning.

Another *historical* consideration that can illuminate the pips is whether or not a greater number is superior or inferior to a lesser number. For example, there are early rule books of card games that clearly show that some suits increase in power with number, others diminish their power with number – does a card with two cups win or lose against one with three? what of two and three batons? This very step in understanding also brings to reflection considerations that have to do with number.

So here we can now begin to take the next interpretative step, the allegorical-typological level, grounded within an augmented literal-historical understanding: each of the suits relates to classes of people – these classes, by the way, goes at least as far back as Zoroastrianism as they are mentioned in the *Pahlavi Dînkard* – 'priesthood, warriorship, husbandry, and artisanship'. It becomes quite clear, in this context, that 'swords' marks what may be considered the political-judicial sphere; 'cups' marks not only religion but also education and much of the arts; 'batons' marks farming and husbandry; and coins marks not only artisanship, but its modern various manufacturing equivalents.

When considering the number of implements depicted, considerations as to whether or not an increase of visual implements shows a dissipation of focussed 'energy', an increase in strength, or something else entirely, also becomes possible. For example, in considering eight rather than three cups, something of the notion of the tinctures of homeopathy may provide a sense as to alternatives to what is all too often considered as 'more'.

I'll leave the other two levels of interpretation for now, but I think we can begin to see how the topological-moral will instruct the specific context, itself arising out of the previous level of understanding and, similarly, the anagogical level will allow for a transcendence given the context and depth previously achieved. What this shows, it seems to me, is that seeking to understand the suits by reading them solely as though they were four elements, with these further viewed as thinking or intellect, emotion and feelings, sexual urges or will, and states or factual situations, tends to place eye-wear on the viewer that partially blinds one to looking at what's actually depicted.

So allow me to briefly put all this against Marteau, Flornoy, and Jodorowsky – acknowledging that I shall be doing justice to none given the brevity in which I'll caricature their respective views: Marteau wants to give too much credence to colour, despite the fact that this is amongst the most variant detail across decks; Flornoy, as you mentioned, tends to not place much importance on the pips, probably in part due to his focus on word-play – an important consideration, but perhaps diminishing the centrality of the implement as implement; and Jodorowsky tends to want to reduce the pips to somehow reflect what the trumps are saying by trump numbering-to-number of implements type correlation. Of course, each of these authors say many other things, and do not want in any way to diminish their respective important contributions and insights!

I see you and I have both a similar take on the pips. I also start at the literal level, by acknowledging the way in which these objects are commonly used: two objects function as extensions of the arm, keeping others at a distance. These are, of course, Swords and Wands. The other two objects are held inside the hand, suggesting the need for closeness. Those are Coins and Cups. In others words, each object can be placed within a certain kind of relationship, and the presence of these cards place the characters we see in the trumps within a certain kind of relationship as well. Any object crafted by men is the metonymy of a person's presence. Any one of those elements in the cards will therefore stand for a person. From there, we can map analogies between groups of objects and groups of people, and have each card showing a scene, or telling a story. This way, you can look at the Three of Cups and see a couple being interrupted by the arrival of a third party, or you can look at the

Ten of Swords and see a battle winding down, perhaps by the exhaustion of the armies. I find pips very useful to anchor the trumps, almost like consonants that, by opposing some resistance to the more primary, vowel-like, sound of the trumps, can help us 'pronounce' them. The literal level, in my view, is consistent with the level of our experience: how do we experience these objects in the world? We also have an experiential understanding of numbers that starts with us using our ten fingers to count, and manifest in both a comprehension of time and space: things move forward, things go backwards, things move slowly or suddenly. The only thing I would add to your approach is that the increase or decrease of numbers can be interpreted as positive or negative depending on the context in which we are looking at these images. That third cup could be the unwanted presence of a secret lover, or a welcomed guest. The reason why we look at the cards, that is, the questions we are asking ourselves through them, redefines the meaning of what we are seeing.

But I have to admit that I don't always use the pips. There is a point when, if I haven't seen them for a while, using them again feels great. But the same thing happens with the trumps after using the pips for a while. When you take only the trumps you feel as if the tarot went on steroids. The messages are so sharp and powerful! I guess it has to do with the need we have to look at things again, the need we have to refresh our glances by encountering things anew. So, sometimes I hide the pips for a while, to really look at then when I take them out again; just as working with the full deck equals hiding the trumps, burying them in a garden of pips. Now, you have put together what I consider the most comprehensive course on the Marseille tarot. What was in your mind while you were designing it? What would you say is the main point you wanted to come across, or the most important thing a person wanting to learn the tarot must know?

Thanks Enrique – relooking through the course materials I can see so much more I would like to say, but at the same time adding those things would somewhat muddy the focus. I had been asked by various people for some years to write a course that could be taken online. To be quite frank, however, I'm not sure exactly what was on my mind as I was designing or writing the course: like a reading, I allowed myself to be guided by its own unfolding. The main point that emerged, however, is probably clearer than I anticipated, and it is this: *look* at the image presented; study it in all its aspects; reflect upon it; allow its own multifaceted richness to guide insight and meaning.

In many ways, you have shown an aspect of this with your example of three cups – the third can be allowed to speak in a multifaceted way: as welcome or as detrimental; as literal or as metaphorical; as meaning-enriched or as depraved. Here is also where metonymy, since you mention it, becomes also a liberating force for the imaginative faculty to allow for meaning-making. It's as if, allowing ourselves to so be poetic, creativity is permitted to instruct deeper meaning... but here I'm going far beyond the course as it stands, though elements of this are also mentioned therein.

As to the most important thing a person wanting to learn tarot must know... so many of the things we've already covered, but also a deck's *structure* and its *canon*, without which what is produced may be wonderfully pretty and useful, but *tarot* it ain't.

In your view, when does a deck stops being tarot?

I understand that nowadays 'tarot' is basically an umbrella brand for all sort of decks that may, or may not have 78 cards, may, or may not have 22 majors and 56 minors; decks which draw their imagery and inspiration from anywhere: elves, cowboys, cats, Marilyn Monroe, Marc Chagall, vitamins or vampires. What is your opinion of all that?

I might begin, in attempting to justify my answer to that, by getting back to your example of the crown taken as metonymic, and consider – again – the Maison Dieu card, which, as I have already mentioned, historically very likely derives or depicts part of the infancy gospel story of the flight to Egypt. Atop the tower is a stylized crown which, read metonymically, can be seen as representing a whole realm: so here the 'crown', also representative of the whole people, tumbles, and the building or the state is shattered. Modern recent historical, though only partial, equivalents may include an image of Hiroshima or Nagasaki or even the signing of surrender, though these also differ in much of that which the infancy gospel speaks. Another metonymic reading of the same card image is in its kabbalistic sense, where the Crown – *Keter* – here is read as representative of the whole Tree, being shattered by not being able to contain the Divine Light, causing the shattered vessels to bring or to allow evil into the world.

Now, if a person was to reflect in a manner in which I just have, and then produce a deck imaging these reflections, I would personally consider the deck as not quite tarot, but nonetheless inspired by it. The deck, to my view, *would maintain its 'tarot-ness' to the extent that it can be explained against a 'rigidly designated' tarot deck* – to use Kripke's concept, which, having now used this term, I'll also have to explain a little later!

Conversely, there are decks that more or less re-present an existing image by artistic means: whether, in the extreme and obvious case, as Dali has done by collage; or, really, by any means that *begins* by seeking to somehow visually mimic an approximation of the image. Again, for myself at any rate, these are only tarot to the extent that each deck can be 'explained' by reference and comparison to a canon that has been 'rigidly designated'.

Kripke introduced this concept of 'rigid designation' in the philosophical literature in, if I recall, the mid-1970s in a small book entitled *Naming and Necessity*. In a nutshell, he gives the example of two possible worlds in which everything is the same save that what is here water is there another substance (but nonetheless *called* by the same name in both worlds). It is only by *pointing* or *designating* what we call 'water' that some kind of 'fixity of designation' clarifies what is or is not water. So with tarot – and indeed in many other areas – there can be real value is striving to point to something that is clearly tarot and seeing how other decks fare.

I suppose that in my own early investigation into tarot, that was one thing that I strove to do. Different people were pointing to different decks and saying 'this is tarot'. When looking at all that, one thing was clear: whether as gaming decks or more esoterically oriented ones, they all pointed to the TdM as a foundation or a core. In many instances, they pointed to a TdM type-II – well exemplified by the Marseille-based Conver of 1760. It isn't, of course, that the TdM is the first deck – far from it. And there are the various Visconti-type decks, as well as the Minchiate, the Sola Busca, the Mantegna – to name a few quite radically different styles of very early decks. The question can be asked of each of those whether they are 'tarot'.

This is where, of course, it gets quite interesting and also somewhat controversial. The Sola Busca, in many ways, stands a little like the gaming tarot of post-Revolutionary France: clearly connected to but allowed, within simply a base structure, to differ in significant ways from tarot. The Minchiate is clearly a deck that, taking tarot as its base, seeks to augment it to 'complete' its trumps with images of the zodiac, of the 'missing' virtues, etc... And the Mantegna seems to be related only to the extent that there are overlaps and similarities between its fifty images and the trumps.

The reason I mentioned these early decks is in large part to show that variety and various influence occurs in decks right from earliest of days. With the Visconti decks, we are faced with another 'problem'. They may indeed be the very first tarot-like decks. I would, however, consider those *proto*-tarot: even assuming that they consisted of four base suits and 22 trumps – the latter of which is far from clear – their image content appears too personally related to the Visconti and the Sforza families for these being considered a generic deck.

So personally, and given the apparent sourcing of tarot imagery, the TdM-type I (on which the type II is based), especially examplified in its Noblet version, seems like a deck to which we can point and say: '*THIS is a tarot deck*'. And from this deck trace deviations across space and time right down to our contemporary decks seeking their rank as 'tarot'. Could there be another more likely candidate for this central examplar? Absolutely! I personally suspect, as of course others have too, that the deck from which the World card found in the well of a Sforza castle, possibly dating from the late 15th or early 16th century, would best deserve that nomenclature.

This of course raises problems, for if we talk of a 'rigid designator', then we can't at the same time allow shifts and changes to the *designated* or 'pointed-to' deck. The difficulty here lies in that from a variety of decks we know what the canons more or less are, yet the clear deck of what 'ought' to be considered as examplar eludes us, perhaps forever destroyed. So, to return to your question, decks that take as their base either a tarot or a tarot derivative and allow images to be slotted reflecting, for example, Marilyn Monroe's life, are just that: allowing the artist to wear tarot-frames with, in this example, Marilyn's-life-coloured lenses. Is it *tarot*? No, but it certainly would not be able to be accurately described without reference to tarot!

Most of what passes for tarot today seems to come from draftsmen operating under the same frame as those architects who specialize on renovating apartments: people who feel entitled to 'improve' something they couldn't actually create in the first place. In a way, that lack of consistency seems the aesthetic parallel to the conceptual blandness of the whole New Age movement. There is a lack of standard in everything that is 'New Age' that seems to come from a marketing need: if you give yourself enough wiggle room you can package and repackage any set of ideas in several different ways, to sell. A market that will sell you Mayan prophecies only after it ran out of Native American myths, or more precisely, a market that will package the same tales as Egyptian, Native American, or Mayan to keep the buyers hooked, is simply eroding any chance of respectability in front of the society at large.

Here in the States there is something called 'Poet Laureate', which is basically a poet appointed by the Library of Congress as the nation's official poet. Some of these poet laureates simply assume the job as any other academic gig, but some of them have done a significant job at promoting poetry's presence in people's life. I am one of those who thinks that poetry is some sort of essential craft anybody must learn early in school, since it provides the most fundamental approach to understanding forms and metaphors as engines for thought. I guess that is why it is fascinating for me to think of the possibilities that such an official position may bring, both to poetry and to the country itself. Poet Marilyn Hacker said that, often, people read poets who share their own concerns, because they want to see how these poets are able to impose some order, "at least verbal, musical order" in those preoccupations. Poet Louise Glück also wrote: "the dream of art is not to assert what is already known but to illuminate what has been hidden, and the path to the hidden world is not inscribed by will". I see the tarot as a form of poetry. I see it consistent, both with Hacker's idea of being approached by those who hope to impose some order in the rhythm of their concerns, and with Glück's hint at how Chance often feeds our hunger for meaning by uncovering unexpected things. The tarot's poetry is the poetry of Chance. But it is clear that this is not the kind of discussion fostered by the tarot's market, and therefore, it is not the image the mainstream has of the tarot. If we take, for example, those books you mentioned above as fundamental for an understanding of the tarot's history, we see that they are out of print because they weren't popular. They don't tell the tale people want to hear. It is a sad fact that Dummet's research, for example, doesn't stand a chance – marketing wise – compared to a book that proposes to show the trump series as an ancient system designed to measure the size of unicorn horns. I would like to end this fascinating conversation with another unfair question: What do you think needs to happen within the tarot world so that we, one day, can have a 'Tarot Laureate' too?

Louise Glück's description, paraphrased, as bringing to light what has been unintentionally hidden, is something that certainly is one important aspect of art. Poetry also allows an encapsulation of an insight brought, as so often happens, in non-literal ways – so figures of speech such as metonymy, or synecdoche or metaphor or even allegory are all important tools that really allow for an ease of waking to polysemic value: in other words, these things can help us to consider that with-which-we-are-faced to be seen from a variety of perspectives. I do consider that imagery – especially imagery that in the first instance seeks to depict not a local landscape, but rather an allegory or a symbolic office, has similar abilities to that of poetry to wake us to a wide range of insights.

Here, I've got to be also a little careful as to what I say of poetry – I share an office with a poet whose dissertation was on Blake and who shares with me an interest in tarot. The difference between a 'Poet Laureate' (as I understand the position in the USA) and a potential 'Tarot Laureate' is that the former is not restricted to certain forms of poetry, whether in structural form or content. Perhaps a 'Tarot Laureate' would be the equivalent of an 'Iliad' or an 'Odyssey Laureate': wonderful to have, but also very focussed. What perhaps would be wonderful is if an 'artist in residence' (or 'artist laureate') included the possibility of someone, such as J-C. Flornoy, whose focus happened to be tarot.

Now, with the learning of poetry at school... I agree, but we need to be careful to not kill the very artistry, for it is a playful yet rigorous art... and perhaps I shall leave that aspect at that before I head too far into my professional life, which is in education.

In describing the renovation of apartments, I suspect you've also well captured something of the misgiving many of us have with many decks that seem to just package the latest trend into a packet of 78 cards. The *Lord of the Rings* 'tarot' is one of the worst amongst those. Yet, I can also see the real artistry in having a true architect craftsman re-design an existing apartment: to bring it to new light in all its glory. In cases of both the tarot and a renovated apartment, what needs to occur is for the touches of the renovator to allow for the user to discover what the apartment or tarot actually offers, rather than impose his or her (i.e., the renovator's) own views. It's especially obvious in a small apartment or house in which the architect has pre-determined where everything is to go, and the design forces one particular way of living. This is the analogy, from my perspective, with all too many modern decks that do something of the type – and which your example brings to light.

I feel there is something I need to add now that we are comparing tarot to poetry. I believe anybody can study poetry, read poetry, and enjoy poetry, just as anybody can look at the tarot and enjoy the tarot, but something that we see hammered once and again within the tarot world is this idea of how learning the tarot, or reading the tarot, has to be made easy. If we were to apply such idea to poetry, that is, the idea of how writing poetry should be made easy, we will see how absurd it is. No one should expect to be proficient as a poet, or respected as a poet, by using rhymezone.com. Lots of times I feel that people who want to learn how to read the tarot are hoping for a formula to make that poetic leap that one has eventually to make if one wants to find living meaning in he cards. I would submit that reading the cards requires a certain talent that is no different from the talent required to write poetry, to paint, to craft stories or to design objects. I do believe the tarot has the unique quality of being visual, and therefore, able to 'speak' to anybody who uses her eyes to listen, just as a painting or drawing will speak to whomever is willing to engage with it. But not everybody can, nor should, read the tarot for others. What are your views on this? What are the attributes a person needs have in order to become a tarot reader?

Here we come to one of those issues that can have quite unexpected ramifications if we're not careful... I'll try and explain what I mean in a short while. Firstly, let's pursue this analogy between reading tarot and poetry for a while: even a great poet has not, I would suggest, the muse at his or her beckoning. Of course, however, the more experience the poet has, the more there is from which to draw and, if somehow called upon to provide a literary piece 'on the spot', will generally be able to access this wealth of resources should the voice of the muse remain silent.

I've always very much liked your synesthetic metaphor: the reader as keenly listening with their eyes. It also very much reminds me of the stage in *Lectio Divina* where the reader-meditator 'listens within the chambers of one's heart'. Here is where text, image, sound, and even smell not so much blend, but rather reveal that which until then was sealed and concealed. The reader has to be open to this unfolding narrative, awake to dream-like realities and subtleties of the developing gifts. So here I am placing a very high demand on the reader – a demand that, as for the poet-in-the-act-of-poetry-making, the reader is aware of the sacred trust placed placed in her or him. At the same time it's often to the reader who remains open to its voice yet who inwardly lacks the *resolute* confidence that the muse *will* speak.

So I agree with your comment, Enrique, that reading the cards requires particular talent that is also developed with practice as well as careful study and reflection. We very likely would agree that we wouldn't want anybody to work on a public painting; nor would we read a very poorly written story. This, however, does not prevent the encouragement that each can be given to painting, or crafting stories. It may be that he or she develops to become both inspired by their muse as well as sufficiently developed in their skill to be able to present the insights in a most wonderful of ways. In that sense, there is 'reading for others' and 'reading for others' – in the same way that there is painting and there is painting, and the latter arises with a development of the former. In the art of reading, speaking with the ears of the open-eyed heart – if you allow a mild expansion of your wonderful expression – is something that can only occur with situations that allow its expression.

...Now who was it, Horace, who wrote *Ut pictura poesis*!? In some ways, the reader is allowing these to be combined: to the given tarot imagery a poetry unfurls in order for the listener to enter the spoken narrative and make meaning out of its newly worded image. Where the risk lies, in seeking to ensure or guarantee readings, is something akin to the disastrous Stalinist view of art: poetry, not less than the visual art, was bureaucratically state controlled. Those that seek for reader certification are not only basically doing the same, but also totally dismissing and not recognising the poetic in reading tarot. Perhaps here, again, the analogy with poetry is best: not everybody should read their poetry to others, but neither should they be prevented from so doing.

So what are the attributes I personally look for in a reader? An inner trust *they* have in their narrative; ideally an ongoing engagement in tarot studies; a lack of rigid dogma; an appreciation for the details their eyes detect in the moment of reading; a rich inner life.

Perhaps it would be important for me to make a precision here. Everybody who wants to write, or paint, or read the tarot, should pursue that urge. What I don't believe is that such a person should expect this pursuit to be easy. There are no shortcuts to any form of artistic production. Every person should be willing to put the work that learning a craft requires. Then of course, if we are talking about reading for others, I am reminded of something poet C.K. Williams said. I am paraphrasing here, but he said that the aim of the writer is to keep human values alive. I can see how one big component of what these tarot images show is that: how to live a beautiful life. But a person has to be very clear about his own motivations to become a tarot reader. Reading for others means spinning other people's tales. Tales that, for them, aren't just tales, but life itself. We may not be able, nor intent to change a person's life, but we can certainly affect the way a person talks, and thinks, about his or her own life. Would you mind sharing a little bit of what your personal motivations to become a reader were?

I entirely agree with what you raise here – and I don't think we can understate the impact that weaving a tale has on others: it alters, in either subtle or not so subtle manner, the way in which the person permits herself to engage with the world, and thus the narrative can even be a seed, for good or bad, that entirely sets a person to revision her world.

Now for myself, I rarely do readings for others these days. Apart from any other consideration, between work, other courses I teach, and other engagements, I am occupied every day and all too many evenings. I still regularly demonstrate how a particular spread *may* be read – mainly in the context of a course. I also regularly use the cards in assisting my reflections on various situational issues.

There was, however, a time in which I, far more regularly, engaged in reading for others. Now what were my personal motivations to become a reader? It's probably not a clearcut motive, but rather something that emerges as a response to situations – in the case of becoming a professionally advertised reader, the 'situation' includes the autobiographical element: a deepening engagement in working with tarot. Probably the single most important motive is that I strive to engage in an action for its own sake – for the love of it. In terms of reading tarot – which involves entering a particular creative state in the context of engagement with others – the value of the engagement in itself makes it worthwhile.

I'm not sure I've done full justice to your question, but here's an aspect I personally find difficult to answer to the satisfaction of others, probably in part due to various people having quite radically different motivations... so I'll leave it at this for now.

And finally, what would you like to see happening in the tarot world in the next ten years?

...now that's a difficult question!

What I *suspect* will happen in the next ten years is a real uptake of tarot in far eastern nations such as China, with the deck's inevitable re-design as part of its appropriation. So I suspect that we can expect to see a new tarot-based deck with imagery and concepts taken from the vast literary and cultural impulse from the region. In the west and in the Americas, I suspect a greater appreciation for Marseille-styled decks, as well as also a definite push towards imposing a more formal psychological or psycho-therapeutic reading of spreads. In general, there also already appears to be a move away from tarot's printed format to, in some cases solely, electronic versions. I cannot but see this trend continue – which may also be a blessing in disguise for canonical decks, which inevitably will also remain in print.

What I would *like* to see happen is a different question:

Firstly, in terms of availability of tarot decks, I'd like to see Flornoy work with people like Karen Mahony and Alex Ukolov (of Prague) as well as Osvaldo Menegazzi (Italy) on a new deck that captures tarot's essential characteristics – that allows the '*Ur-tarot*' as purely as possible to be expressed. The deck would have to take as its material basis on the Noblet, Dodal, Bolognese, and that single World card from the Sforza castle well, and as its non-material basis the research and insights that have already been presented in various places, including, I would hope, my own work. And then for that deck to also be worked into an electronic format with the skills of someone like Kat Black.

This concept of 'Ur-tarot', by the way, is something I started talking about some twelve or thirteen years ago and has at times been rather mis-understood (and mis-represented): though it's from the German, it does not refer to what 'ür' often means in popular language, but rather stems from Goethe's usage in his *Metamorphosis of Plants* – the *Ürplanzt* is there more like the unmanifest spiritual archetype that provides the impetus and blueprint for manifestion and incarnation. The *Ür-tarot*, in this sense, will forever take on shades and aspects of the ground out of which it manifests, but one can see, with study, approximately how it would look with the attrition of non-essential characteristics.

Secondly, in terms of *tarot books*, I'd like to see something that extends or reconfigures my own book – basically the course to which you referred, now also in bookform – and combines the likes of Dummett and Co's research with those of Andrea Vitali and Ross Caldwell, edited with Sophie Nusslé's and Robert Mealing's touches.

Thirdly, *online*, it would be fantastic to have the resources of *Tarotpedia*, *Andy's Playing Cards* and of *Trionfi* merged (without those horrid frames the latter still currently uses!), presented in a form somewhere between wiki-based and dupral-based content management.

And finally, and perhaps most importantly, I'd like to continue to see the growth of opportunities for *discussion* about tarot and studies of tarot in the wider community, amongst specialists and enthusiasts, and in formal educational settings. Can these things be achieved within the next ten years? I very much think it can, though the specific details as to the 'who' and 'how' remain to be seen!

One final question: a man is walking on the street and finds a card on the sidewalk. He stops, picks the card, turns it around... which card is it?

Wonderful to have had this opportunity to have this discussion with you, Enrique.

Now, with regards to your question... I'll finish off where I started, with another experienced event, walking, this time, in the *South* of France: the Page of...

New York / Melbourne, 2010

"We seek to share with others an interaction with the symbols that is beautiful and alive."

A conversation with MARY GREER, tarot historian and reader

I would like to start by sharing with you a quote from poet Li Young-Lee:

> We're living in a time when the word "sincere", and I didn't know this, is suddenly a bad thing. I don't get it. I heard a poet say to me, "Oh, I hate sincerity." And I thought, oh, what do you like? Insincerity? I don't get it. ... What do they mean by that? And then I was talking to a poet and I said to her, "Well, for me, poetry is a form of disillusionment, right? It frees you of your illusions in order to uncover the condition of all which we are constantly in the midst of." And she said, "Well, I don't like to be disillusioned." "Why? You want to be illusioned?" ... I mean, Hollywood gives us illusions. *People Magazine* gives us illusions. TV gives us illusions. But I think art gives us reality. And the reality that's uncovered is so rich. Maybe that's what it is – it's not only rich and beautiful but it's terrifying, too. So maybe we can't stand abundance. We can't stand abundance and so we keep making models of scarcity. ... I want to be disillusioned. When I first read the poets that I love, I thought, wow, you mean, this is real existence, this is somebody speaking truthfully about my own experience of all. And I just don't want to live in illusion.

I wonder what your thoughts are on this quote. Do we need illusions? And then, how do you see the role of the tarot in the making of illusions?

Enrique, I love your questions, even if I'm not sure what they mean! They generate a dozen thoughts and responses. The dictionary gives two meanings to sincerity: 1) free from pretense or deceit and 2) proceeding from genuine feelings. As a moral principle sincerity suggests being good or right rather than bad or wrong. I don't think we humans are ever totally free from pretense or deceit – it's part of what makes living creatures interesting and the reason for a lifetime's work of getting to "Know Thyself." In social situations pretense may be necessary for protection or even to convince ourselves that we have abilities that we doubt. So, on one hand, sincerity is always somewhat false or conflicted. On the other hand, I think that we always proceed from genuine feelings. However, these feelings are more-or-less hidden to ourselves and others, and so we don't always communicate those genuine feelings. Sincerity is a belief and most beliefs are based on subjective opinions, not objective reality, that in turn are based on feelings. The task is to see through sincerity to what is genuine behind it, which may totally contradict what we thought was sincere. Therefore, I understand what is meant about wanting to be "disillusioned." I love the thrill of having the blinders taken off. But, it's risky business and, as you say, often terrifying.

I also sometimes enjoy illusions in the form of Coleridge's "willing suspension of disbelief," which is based on accepting, at least temporarily, a "semblance of truth." This is the core idea behind a myth – which Joseph Campbell referred to as an outer lie expressing an inner truth. By giving myself over to the myth of tarot's creation by the god Thoth in Egypt, for instance, I access a truth of what tarot touches on in me. This occult "lie" about the tarot creates the illusion that we can predict the future and/or follow a "royal road" to self-knowledge and to the Divine through the cards. Yet it is this illusion that can set us firmly on such a path long enough to become more dis-illusioned than we ever thought possible and thus come closer to who we really are and what the tarot really is.

So, do we need illusions? Yes, I believe we do. I love the movies and TV and fiction and I want, to some extent, to be carried away by the illusion. But, I also love being dis-illusioned. I like learning the truth of things, while yet knowing that all truths contain a lie (the drop of black in a gallon of white paint). Literary critic Lionel Trilling contrasted sincerity with authenticity but refused to define either of them. As mentioned, I see the first as a moral principle that is more often false than absolutely true. Authenticity, to me, has room to include falseness and paradox. It rests on our genuine feelings – bad or good, right or wrong. For instance, I used to teach "Women's Biography and Autobiography" at a college. In reading both, I discovered that people always lie about themselves in their autobiographies, and yet most autobiographies are, to me, far more true than biographies (written by others) that expose the lies and supposedly reveal the truth about the person. Some of the so-called lies are deliberately told by the autobiographer and some are instances where the autobiographer is lying to him or herself – yet both proceed from something genuine within the person. Both are "authentic" in that they do more to reveal the real person than all the facts discovered by others about that person's life. Still, sometimes we need the disillusionment that results from discovering the facts in order to perceive the real authenticity. For instance, in the case of the Irish revolutionary Maud Gonne, in her autobiography she claimed to have adopted a boy and a girl, although they were, in fact, her own illegitimate children, yet she left instructions to be buried with the booties, carried with her always, of the "adopted" baby who died while she was absent fighting for the Irish cause. All of that is who she authentically was.

I see the role of tarot as a making of illusions – the telling a story, a fiction, about who we are, what we are doing, why we are doing it and where we are going with it. Yet, we are always both more and less that story. I examine the illusions in order to see myself better through them. Then I welcome the dis-illusion in order to see more. I willingly suspend a disbelief that cardboard pictures are mirrors or windows into my past, present and future. This illusion becomes an opening into a potential dis-illusionment of what I may have thought was sincerity of action and purpose, to get in touch with the authenticity, the genuine feelings and desires, behind the outer display. For example, I often suggest that my students try a yes-no tarot spread about a choice they have to make where they sincerely believe either choice will be fine. Then I ask them to carefully observe their response to the answer they get. Were they ecstatic, were they disappointed, did they want to try again? Their response is usually where their authentic answer lies. However, that doesn't mean that they should or shouldn't follow the option offered by the cards. The choice is up to them; it's just that they are now more aware.

I may sincerely want to see through my illusions while fighting true insight every step of the way. That is authentically who I am, and that is the part of me I want and need to know. The tarot helps me both know the illusions and see through them. Aren't you involved in the world of magic, mentalism and prestidigitation? Isn't that all about creating illusions? Would you say these illusions are sincerely done? Where does the dis-illusionment come in if everyone already knows they are tricks? How are such illusions similar or different than tarot?

Lets start with something I heard painter Anselm Kiefer saying: "even the phrase 'it is a nice day' is an illusion". I love the phrase because I think it is a very hard pill to swallow. It is one thing to go see a magician performing magic, and to suspend our disbelief, for a moment, so we can enjoy his tricks, and a very different thing to accept that we are always, to some extent, suspending our disbelief just to survive a world that is too random and chaotic. You are pointing our something crucial: sincerity, or our preference for it, demands a suspension of disbelief. I am asking you this question because I have been thinking about these things myself, for a long time now, and I am not quite sure I have a definitive answer. Once I understood that I was interested in readings as an expressive medium, I decided to study cold reading. That is, I decided to contrast the actual methodology to read the tarot or any other kind of oracle to the deceptive ways professionals use to fake psychic powers. I started looking at the tarot in 1987. I started studying cold reading around 2000. I have a very conflicting view of cold reading, since I suspect it is no different from any other divination system, or more precisely, since the brain processes it involves aren't different from any other kind of divination: we feed the brain with information, the brain detects certain patterns, and by matching those patterns with the person's life experience, it creates meaning. That very act of meaning-making is what I equate with a poetic response, or that 'opening' you are talking about. That moment in which Chance overlaps with our subjective experience in a way that doesn't feels consciously manipulated by anybody, can inspire people to do great things. But the moment in itself is an illusion, just as the response to any work of art is illusory. I am having a hard time understanding if that should be called 'beauty' or 'truth'. I rather call it 'beauty' but, who knows?

The important difference is the context in which these illusions are presented. I would say that most mentalists and magicians – at least the ones working under these denominations – are pretty honest. As a matter of fact, they are almost fastidious in their need to convince you that they have no real powers. I often see them as the extreme right of the supernatural world! But then again, the term 'magician' or 'mentalist' is in itself a disclaimer. I would say that someone operating under the 'mentalist' label is openly acknowledging the fictitious nature of his craft. It is easy for a person to accept whatever a magician says or does as an illusion, because a magician operates within a context in which believing in illusions is permissible. But the same person would have a hard time accepting that real life is composed by countless illusions. It is very hard to accept that we bet our life on stories that are of a more or less fictitious nature. The dangerous thing about the tarot is that, for most people, it doesn't inhabit a space where believing in illusions is permissible. In my experience, it is impossible for the average human mind to find meaning in illusions. The vast majority of people who come for a reading will reject the idea of being told a story. They want to be told 'facts'. Tell them you are going to tell them a story, a piece of fiction, and they will go elsewhere. But we are telling stories. We are weaving fictions into the fabric of reality. I reclaim the sacredness of that role. But I reject any pretense.

For a few months, I have been thinking of Bas Jan Ader. His entire work was about making room for the unavoidable. He would stand on a rooftop, or hold onto the branch of a tree, until gravity would take him down. He disappeared in the ocean, trying to cross it in the smallest boat ever. He made room for the ocean to behave like the ocean, and the ocean swallowed him. I have no greater aspiration for my work than making room for Chance. Chance possess beautiful poetry. That moment in which a few images reflect whatever mindset you brought with you, contains a powerful truth, a powerful beauty. I cannot make it happen. The main difference between the tarot, and divination in general, and magic or mentalism, is that the tarot is a self-working illusion. The reader is there to create the space so a person can experience the poetry of chance on her own. So it is alwyas the client's brain the one that creates meaning, and makes magic.

This is, of course, my disillusioning take on readings! We cannot resist the illusion of seeing ourselves in the tarot because our brains are hungry for meaning. But that is not a wise way of going around selling readings! People prefer more colorful explanations. I am fascinated by the work of artists like Olafur Eliasson, or Peter Fischl & David Weiss, whose pieces tend to create an illusion while giving themselves away. I am interested in working with clients who can play that game with me: to look at reality from where we stand, and then, pull back, opening up the shot to show the wires, the fat guy holding the microphone, and the big reflectors faking stars. I wish I could work all my readings at these two levels: crafting an illusion and enjoying it along with my client as an illusion.

Now, when I think about illusions I am thinking of foundational ideas, like 'justice', or 'courage'; notions we need to believe in, so we can function in society, but these are fictitious insofar as there is no guarantee that the faith we put in them will ever pay off. You are mentioning a different kind of illusion: historical illusions, like the tarot coming from Egypt. Do you think it is easier, or less harmful, to be disillusioned coming from historical fictions?

I agree that even the phrase 'it's a nice day' is an illusion. One person's nice day can be another person's nightmare. It can also be a trap. I'm reminded of *The Book of Die* by Luke Rhinehart (aka George Cockcroft), a philosophical work based on Rhinehart's first book, *The Dice Man*, a cult classic from the early 1970s (soon to be a movie). Essentially, Rhinehart, a psychologist, was looking for alternatives to traditional therapy. He became intrigued by the idea that 'all beliefs are illusion,' so, to find happiness, he decided to liberate himself from the illusion of a separate and controlling identity. He took a huge risk and surrendered his 'self' to the whims of chance, living and traveling according the throws of a die – each of the six sides representing different options. For instance, at a train station he would identify six different destinations and role a die. He would then role a die for what he'd do when he got there or for what to eat. He felt that giving oneself over to the God of Chance resulted in a greater enjoyment of the things of this world. *The Dice Man* is a novel based on this theory.

In some ways, tarot can be like this. We willingly surrender ourselves to the results of random draws out of a deck of seventy-eight cards. If nothing else, a previously unexplored option, as depicted in the cards, can break us out of a rut and send us in new directions, supported by a belief that we can succeed by doing so. Research has shown that both exploring new areas and an optimistic attitude can increase our chances of survival and success and enhance our sense of well-being.

I wrote about mentalism and cold reading in a couple of posts on my blog.[1] Frankly I was shocked by the exploitive attitude found in some of the tarot and pseudo-psychic training manuals that demonstrate how to work psychic fairs and telephone lines using canned spiels. However, as a former graduate student studying linguistics I had already become familiar with most cold reading techniques as they are part of the complex, but very ordinary, bundle of behaviors that human beings consciously and unconsciously use all the time when communicating with others. We cannot *not* do them. Some people naturally develop refined sensitivity to non-verbal and verbally-nuanced interactions, aided by empathy (or highly functioning mirror-neurons in the brain). Others, mentalists among them, consciously train to 'read' the signs. The fact that 72% of the over 300 respondents to a Myers-Briggs Type Indicator poll on Aeclectic's tarotforum claim to be 'Introvert Intuitives,' with nearly 50% labeling themselves as 'Introvert Intuitive Feeling,' is an indication to me that tarot readers naturally tend toward being empathic. (By contrast, only 1% identified themselves as 'Extrovert Sensates.')[2]

---

1   http://marygreer.wordpress.com/2008/12/01/cold-reading-and-tarot-part-1/
2   http://www.tarotforum.net/showthread.php?t=12143

What I find disturbing in the tarot world is the number of people who seem to feel that to be effective you have to remain ignorant – that there is some kind of danger in knowing anything about cold reading or psychology or meditation or history or scientific research. Rather you should rely only on what 'naturally' comes up when you look at the cards. In part, I think it is an unconscious fear of dis-illusionment about their tarot reading skills and effectiveness that leads to the relatively low number of people who attend workshops and conferences (especially as compared to astrologers). Thankfully, this is changing, but many readers are still afraid of looking too closely at what they are doing for fear it might go away.

Switching direction: I had never heard of Bas Jan Ader until I saw a reference you made to him a couple of months ago. I was amazed by his total commitment to pushing the boundaries of art. I couldn't help admiring his work, while at the same time I felt overwhelmed by the intensity of purpose, perhaps by the raw authentic-ness of his self (in which he gave himself completely over to a kind of inevitably of Chance). If his art is Beauty, it is a Terrible Beauty – and I don't mean anything pejorative about that. (I am not familiar with the other artists you mentioned, although I briefly looked them up on the web.)

I wonder what would change if there was an assumption that we look for Beauty in a tarot reading rather than Truth (despite Keats' claim that they are the same)? That appeals to me. Beauty respects and appreciates illusion but is also there to greet us once we've moved all the way through dis-illusion.

I agree with your description of how tarot works: "Tarot is a self-working illusion. The reader is there to create the space so a person can experience the poetry of chance on her own. So it is alwyas the client's brain the one that creates meaning, and makes magic." I describe my own readings as interactive, transformational and empowering. But, the fact is that the transformation and empowerment have to be the client's. And I also agree with your explanation of divination: *"We feed the brain with information, the brain detects certain patterns, and by matching those patterns with the person's life experience, it creates meaning."* Chosing meaning-making as a major life value is a kind of existential choice in the face of an otherwise meaningless universe, but it's the kind of choice that poets, shamans, explorers and 'cultural creatives' make, and it seems, as you say, to inspire great things.

Even if that was all that is going on in a tarot reading, it is enough. I define meaning as 'symbol + emotion,' that is, a projective identification of our orientation to the world that moves us. Meaning, when it breaks through boundaries, is magic. But, despite this elegantly simple and so-true explanation, I have had far too many experiences with the cards that go beyond it. They strain the belief that we are only making meaning out of totally random cards. I can't explain these happenings, so I always treat the appearance of "the perfect cards" and the numinous moment as welcome gifts that defy explanation. But it's part of why I am so drawn to tarot. Nothing else for me has quite this same power.

When you talk about 'foundational ideas' like justice or courage I think of fundamental beliefs. The bedrock of any belief is a fundament that is so hidden that we don't even recognize it as being anything but an absolute. Everyone has their own fundamentalism somewhere! Which is all the more dangerous for not being recognized since it is perceived as identical to reality. Fundaments are a limit beyond which we never even think of going, and that we expect to be true for others. The Golden Dawn magician, Florence Farr, defined magic as "taking the limits off what we experience." I think that speaks to everything I've said so far.

So, to answer your question: We can be more easily dis-illusioned from historical fictions the further they are from our personal fundaments. Being dis-illusioned from a personal fundament can be devastating, like the mathematicians who committed suicide when it was proved that mathematics was not an objective description of reality but a self-referential system. Personally, I am always looking to discover another fundament within myself because, by becoming conscious of it, I assume the potential to move through and beyond it, and that is magic! Since I use decks with pictorial scenes on all the cards, people's reactions to and stories about the cards illustrate their beliefs and sometimes fundaments. I try to support them in gently pulling the curtain aside for themselves, rather than my tearing it asunder. Furthermore, to me, naming and honoring one's illusions (becoming conscious of how they have served us) is an important step in truly accepting and even welcoming necessary disillusionment. I like what you say about pulling back and showing the wires. It reminds me of the Wizard of Oz.

So what do you think is true magic?

My working definition for magic is the purposeful use of symbols to engage the mind in a process of transformation. Magic relies heavily on metaphor. "As above, so below" is in itself a good definition for metaphor, since it talks about mapping the likeness of those things we cannot control into those things we can. Sympathetic magic is in itself an exercise on metaphorical thinking. Magic by contact functions through metonymy and synecdoche. I am not talking about a problem of mere verbal language, but about understanding and using the suggestive power of objects, substances, gestures and materials. The brain accepts metaphors as real, and by taking symbols for reality, it could elicit all kinds of psychophysiologic reactions under the influence of these symbols. I think that the greatest book on Western magic is the Wizard of Oz. What the wizard accomplishes, by giving, for example, a diploma to the scarecrow, is to use a symbol for intelligence to transfer these qualities into the person herself. A clock shares some of the qualities of a heart. With a clock on your chest your experience the constant ticking on a pulsating heart. A medal is a symbol for courage. A good magician has to be proficient at making and using metaphors. Magic is a creative act. It is the language of how some shapes resemble other ones. That is the language of the tarot itself. We hope that the shapes in the trait will mirror the shapes in the world, and by understanding the images on the table, we will understand life.

In my view, the only thing magic can really do for us is to give us strength. That is also what I think the tarot accomplishes. Within that frame, fashion would be as effective as voodoo. But I would love to know, what, if anything, do you expect from magic?

My favorite statement of the purpose of tarot is: "Tarot helps you meet whatever comes in the best possible way." To do this often requires a transformation from our old way of being (or awareness) to a new one. That could be described as magic. I expect magic to take me out of my normal experience and perception of things. Dion Fortune modified Aleister Crowley's definition of magic as creating change in accord with will, to add "a change of consciousness." Magic is usually seen as a "willed" activity – like the "purposeful" use of your definition. I like what Evelyn Underhill wrote in *Mysticism*, "Magic is a system whereby the self tries to assuage its transcendental curiosity by extending the activities of the will beyond their usual limits." This gets at Florence Farr's description of magic as unlimiting of our experience. At Greek airports a luggage carrier is a metaphor. It's a Greek word for carrying something from one place to another – that's why magic is a change in consciousness – like metaphor it moves us from one inner place, feeling or attitude to another. It literally helps us transport our baggage!

For me, a magical ritual involves transformation, and the most important thing that is transformed is something in the self. For instance, I was once teaching a workshop on "Tarot and Magic," at a place with a beautiful outdoor deck for classes. Everyone wanted our sessions to be held on the deck, but there were predictions of rain, as we were in the middle of a drought, it was desperately needed. When I asked what the purpose of our evening's ritual should be, the majority wanted no rain the following day so we could be outdoors. Others protested this because of the drought. I suggested that we begin that night's ritual with "no rain" (as we could then test the efficacy of our work), but I told everyone that something could change that purpose within the ritual itself and we should be open to that. The heart of the ritual involved laying out cards from multiple tarot decks to create a magical mirror of our purpose and then telling what we saw the cards as depicting.

It was fascinating to hear how the cards and descriptions started with no rain (from some) and rain (from others) and slowly changed until we were all describing a harmony and attunement with Nature and with "What Is." We got to the point where we were no longer feel ourselves as separate but experience a kind of unity or oneness with everything around us. By the end, we all realized that it didn't matter whether it rained or not; we were at peace with whatever was to happen. For me, that was the real magic! Others would say it was what happened the next day. It rained a little early in the morning and then the sun came out and quickly dried the deck just in time for class. It rained again the minute we broke for lunch and had dried out by the time we came back out. Then it rained a little more in the evening just as the mosquitos arrived and we were starting to go in.

When people ask the tarot for advice, they want to know what is the "right" thing to do. But "right" and even "best" are not really the ideal words. You say tarot/magic gives us strength. I like to think of it as being in a relatively conscious harmonious alignment with "What Is," knowing that "What Is" is really so much more than we can normally imagine. That is why I love the tarot symbols; because, to me, their meanings are not fixed but infinite and alive and so much more than we think they are.

I'm curious. You use the Marseille-style tarot decks, I believe. So you are in the position of telling people, especially in the case of the Minor Arcana, what the cards mean, interpreting their symbols and saying what the cards advise, aren't you? How do you keep clients from simply being passive recipients of what you tell them? How do you bring the tarot's metaphors to life so that they can work their magic?

If I show you the Two of Cups, and I tell you it is about a couple celebrating, you will see it. If I show you the Eight of Cups and tell you it shows a party at which two people have finally found each other, and now they are chatting in the middle of the room, or that it shows two ambassadors greeting each other while a crow observes them, you will see it. You will see these things because any object produced by men is a metonymy of a person. Our objects hunt at our presence. You have seen couples raising their cups to toast, and the cups themselves stand for that action. So, the pips in the Marseille tarots are as illustrated as the trumps. If we take any one of these four symbols, and we understand in which context we experience them, we can see meaning in them. But the limit of such meaning, like the meaning of any metaphor, has to do with the limit of those experiences we associate with the symbol we are looking at. I cannot show you the Two of Swords, tell you that it shows a couple cheering up, and expect that you will see it, because that isn't actually represented in the card. Swords inhabit a whole different semantic field from the idea of 'celebration'. Even so, we could still be talking about a couple while looking at the suit of swords, but we would be looking at an argument, not a celebration. That you will see.

When a client can follow the mapping of these analogies, she becomes an active participant. When she can't follow them, she sits back and becomes a passive receptor of whatever you are telling her. The great thing is that we are the ones controlling that process. To me, using the cards visually is very important. Otherwise there is no point in choosing the tarot as your media. Using the cards visually implies finding that visual common ground with the client. It is not about what I see, but about what we both see.

All metaphors are limited. You can only stretch them so far. If you keep your interpretation of the cards within the semantic field of its symbols, it will make visual sense to the client. We tend to disengage when we cannot figure something out. That is why I won't be so sure that a tarot card can represent anything. The metaphor of the Hermit, for example, won't cover a virgin girl wanting to give herself to a quarterback. Can you imagine yourself talking about a young woman who is discovering her body, while you are pointing at the Hermit? It would be a stretch that will take your client to that point where the fabric of fiction starts tearing apart.

You once mentioned some research you did, showing people cards and having them sorting them out in 'good' or 'bad'. Can you tell me more about that? Which cards are more consistently perceived as negative? What have you discovered?

What drew me to tarot, too, was the visual metaphors. But, it took me almost forty years to start seeing the images in the Marseille Minors anything like the way you do. Admittedly, I didn't try very hard since I was happy with my Rider-Waite-Smith and other pictorial decks. Then, a couple of years ago, I got Major Tom's re-vision of a Marseille deck and used it for a reading for someone. Suddenly, it was like those Minors with their crossing batons and swords and the curling florals were telling me a story in pictures. I tried to explain what I was seeing but I'm not sure the querent got it in quite the same way I did. It was very exciting for me, but I felt she was far more engaged with my words than with the pictures, even though she easily identified the situation described. Personally, I like to turn as much control of what's perceived in the cards over to the querent as possible. Thus, I characterize myself as a 'midwife of the soul' assisting another to bring their own wisdom to birth.

I agree that swords bring connotations of a certain type to almost everyone. It is not that difficult for people to associate them with mental processes (if linked with Air) or to will and courage (if associated with Fire). The Marseille Seven of Swords, for instance seems to show someone standing up against the odds and winning through, whereas in the similar Nine of Swords the opposition to the central sword appears overwhelming. I can understand helping someone see that and then working with them to see how that's functioning in their life right now.

However, I'm far more intrigued with what the querent sees in the cards and what happens when that precipitates a breakthrough in themselves. I earlier defined meaning as "symbol + emotion." When someone describes a card there is often a moment when they suddenly see themselves in the words or picture, and the emotion connected with that self-image floods them. They experience it in their body (somatically) as well as mind, which opens them and makes that moment malleable. Other cards form a pattern showing its connection with other things in their life that they may have thought were unconnected. Now they can feel how a choice in one direction can affect all the others. Or they can see that if they value one piece of the pattern strongly what that implies for the other pieces. I'm sorry to be so abstract, so let me give you an example that I've used before.

A couple who were close friends of mine wanted a reading before finalizing their breakup, which was desired by Noah but resisted by Beth. I used a relationship spread by Angie Arrien and, the Ace of Wands appeared in the position of "What Beth gives Noah." Since Beth had just come into some money I could see she felt she was offering him adventure, excitement and new beginnings. First I asked Noah to describe the card, just as he'd been doing perfectly up to that point. He said he couldn't. I tried prompting him to just begin with "there's a hand reaching out of a cloud holding . . ." He couldn't even say that. After a long struggle, he suddenly broke out in an explosion: "It's a carrot on a stick and I don't want it!" The shock of that statement reverberated through the room, and all of us "got it." In that moment Beth accepted the inevitable, and Noah knew there was no going back. I've never seen that card the same since. Talk about a word or simple image that stands in for something huge in a person (would you call that metonymy?).

I've found that often when a person disengages with a card it's because it touches on something they are resisting or are in denial about. Sometimes another card will provide a gentler way in, so I try not to push anything. (Plus it may not be appropriate to push into some areas in a tarot reading.) I also find it is very important when someone sees something in a card that is strikingly different than the usual. So if a person were to describe the Hermit as "a youth disguised for an erotic assignation" (not that I've ever had this happen), then I'd figure it was pretty darn significant. In my own mind I'd be juxtaposing their response with the traditional meanings – circumspection, a search for wisdom, etc. – looking for the key in the paradox. Plus, I'd ask what specific details in the card led to the description. I try not to assume anything. Part of what I'm getting at when I ask students in my classes to sort cards into piles based on "good" and "bad" (or any other topic, like "prosperity" and "scarcity") is for them to see where there are areas of general consensus and where others in the class see something far different (now we're back to the fundaments these perceptions are based on). I want people to understand the power of diversity and to not make assumptions about the reactions or needs of another. So, while most people see the Devil or the Nine of Swords as "bad," there are individuals who see the Devil as Socrates' "gadfly" who makes us question our assumptions, and the Nine of Swords as awaking from a nightmare and being comforted – good things.

I also did a research project in which 85 people (who were involved in tarot at varying levels) matched each card of the Rider-Waite-Smith deck with what they perceived as its most relevant emotion from a list of 97 emotion-words. Quite a few of the cards had nearly unanimous agreement, if not of the exact word, then of the sentiment. Only a couple of cards showed practically no agreement. So the Rider-Waite deck has a very strong emotional component that is experienced similarly among mostly native English speakers. I want to be clear that, while I've developed my own approach and relationship to the cards, I don't think that it is necessarily right for everyone else. I emphasize it in my teaching because it's the best I have to offer. What would you say is the best of yourself that you have to offer?

I think that what you are describing is what I call a poetic response. The making of meaning, that is felt, as you said, in the whole body. Again, I would say that is akin to experiencing beauty. It shakes us, and it lifts us too. What I can offer is the experience of tarot. I hope to help someone experience it in the most unadulterated way. Most people I know are either dismissive, or contemptuous, about the tarot. I can create a clean, and sober, space where they can look at the images with me, and I am always hoping for that moment when the images click in them, and I am not needed anymore. I rather share a moment of beauty with people than appear as the center of attention. The only thing I have is my enthusiasm for these images. That is what I have to offer. Not a very promising sales pitch! I have a final question for you: what is your earliest memory of flowers?

"The only thing I have is my enthusiasm for these images." I think that's what most people in the tarot world share – whether they are historians or collectors or readers. But it's the second part, "That is what I have to offer [others]," that is, perhaps, what distinguishes readers. We seek to share with others an interaction with the symbols that is beautiful and alive. One of my tasks during a reading is to keep what I perceive as a kind of continuous 'rubber-band of energy' taut as it stretches from the cards in a spread to the querent and myself. Distractions make the band flabby. Total engagement makes both the energy band and the cards shimmer and vibrate. It awakens something marvelous.

My earliest memory of flowers? No one has ever asked me that. The first thing that comes to mind and the only thing that emerges, even when I look further, is being four or five years old in Tokyo, Japan. I had a kimono that was white with flowers all over it that were primarily pink and orange. I feel cheerful whenever I think of it. I also remember visiting one of the temples during the cherry blossom festival and feeling like I was a part of it in my beautiful kimono. I so wanted to look just like the Japanese girls with their long silky black hair rather than my short red curls but at least my hair went perfectly with my bright flowers.

New York, 2011

"Co-creation of an outcome is much more satisfying intellectually and emotionally."

A conversation with TODD LANDMAN, professor, magician

Would you say that the experience of the tarot starts where words end?

Language has always been an inadequate means of communication, capturing and expressing but a fragment of our overall sense of meaning. Early communication between humans was much more dependent on pictures and symbols. While visual images are still very much part of our daily lives, written and spoken language has transcended our use of symbols and pictures in some degree. Tarot draws on this more traditional form of communication and the experience it evokes for both the reader and the querent is one that taps into a different part of our subjective understanding of the human condition. The forms, shapes, colours, actions, symbols, icons, and layout of each card as well as the array of cards that feature in any reading unveil a different level of consciousness and experience that cannot be expressed through words. The turning of the cards for each querent creates a personal microcosm of subjectivity that is only partially accessible through the language and the words shared with the reader.

I like what you are saying about the cards on the table being a 'microcosm'. I have always felt that there is an "as above, so below" kind of feeling in our hopes to understand, or even control, reality, by making sense of our small cards on the table. The whole proposition is fundamentally magical in that it operates through a series of metaphorical mappings between our microcosm and real life, whose main intention is to affect reality (or our perception of it). But before we continue, let me ask you something: why do you think it is that grown ups like you and me are still playing with magic in this time and age?

Magic has been a part of my life since the age of 8, so at one level it is a fundamental part of my identity. I then spent the last 30 years studying science, philosophy, politics, and travelled to over 35 countries... all of which reintroduced the notion of the 'magical' or that special something that simply goes beyond the material and empirical experiences, call it 'spirit' if you will. I have returned to deep reading across the magical spectrum from tricks to mentalism to the occult and have found so many parallels and pathways of interest. My magic is now all relational in that I want to develop material that relates to people's fundamental questions in life at a deep level. But to be totally honest, I want (and if I really am pushed believe) magic to be real.

Yes, but, what is real, or needs to be real, in magic? The experience or the result?

The experience and the result.

Talking to Mary Greer about cold reading, she mentioned there was something "exploitative" in the tone in which most books on the subject are written. Technically speaking, I tend to think that cold reading is just another divination technique, as valid as any oracle, but I think she has a point. Most cold reading books seem to want to pass along some techniques heavily wrapped in a repetitious "you can get away with it!" tone whose aim is to give encouragement to the reader but definitively borders the exploitative. At least, there seems to be something misguided on thinking that the main reason for doing readings is that you can get away with them. Especially because the craft of cold reading seems to be less about technique and more about artistry, from the ability the reader has to convey conviction in his own words, to his ability to spin a tale and tailor it to a person. Cold reading is a profoundly creative process. It is also a process that has direct impact on people's lives. At the same time, it seems to be a craft in which the magician gives away the reality of his own magical experience in the hope to create a real effect in the client's mind. Is that the magician's curse, to know that there is always a man behind the curtain?

Yes the magician's (or at least a particular kind of magician) curse is a need to expose the Wizard of Oz... cold reading has been narrowly interpreted by magicians who want easy to learn 'systems' to get away with it, as you put it. But the 'cold' means to me that you know very little about a person when a reading starts, but you do have initial intuitive glimpses, and as the reading unfolds you co-create an outcome that neither of you expected. I learn as much from giving a reading as the sitter does in 'receving' it. I put the word 'receving' in quotes since we often depict the relationship between reader and sitter as one of a hiearchy, which in my view is wrong. Co-creation of an outcome is much more satisfying intellectually and emotionally. The curse of which you speak was in high relief in London during your lecture when a large proportion of the gathered group simply could not comprehend why you do what you do. That reading is an end in itself, not some instrument to promote the ego of the performer/reader.

Would you say that, in a way, all readings are a performance piece?

Yes, both the sitter and the reader are performing, since they are playing in some degree to role expectations. It may be that after many iterations, both the sitter and reader learn about their true nature and drop some of the pretence of performance, but there is a lot of role play in reading in my view.

Could you tell me more about the sitter as performer? I find that to be a fascinating notion!

The sitter comes to the reader with preconceptions about what is going to happen. They also have a set of questions they want answered and doubts about the process itself, so it seems a safe proposition to suggest that a sitter peforms as much as the reader. The less they know the reader the more inclined they are to perform, since they will play to type, at least initially. They might give part answers to questions and even think they know what the Tarot cards mean. If they know the reader they might be less inclined to perform, but then again, they may want to 'please' the reader in ways that compromise the authenticity of the reading. As in narrative analysis, the reader must decipher what the sitter is saying and interpret the meaning. There are significant questions of veracity and authenticity surrounding the account a sitter will give, and it seems to me that these questions are a function of the degree to which the sitter is performing.

Would you say then that, to some extent, a good reading is the one where either the reader, the sitter, or both, break out of character?

Depends on what you mean by a 'good' reading, since such a judgment is down to the sitter who is after all the client. If by good we mean 'authentic' then we are faced with a continuum akin to that which exists for film: documentary (high authenticity), historical fiction (medium authenticity), and fictional drama (low authenticity). If both the sitter and reader break from character, the script is abandoned but the revelations are very authentic. Ultimately the goodness of the reading is highly subjective and depends on what the sitter desires from the reading. It may be that a sitter is falsely conscious about his or her role playing and character, in which case the reading will be authentic for them, but may mask their real concerns. If the goal is really to help the sitter, then there should not be character issues, but I think that would be rare... how many therapist-client relationships are not imbued with role play and character?

Well, I doubt there is any relationship that isn't imbued with role-playing, but I doubt most clients would think they are 'performing' a role. I think it is a great way of putting it, nonetheless. I would guess that the client who is playing his role to the letter is the one who sits passively and expects to be told some things. One finds these clients all the time, people who will tell you "Oh, I know. I am not supposed to tell you anything" or things like that. They are certainly complying with what is expected from a client, within the frame of what is expected from a reader, and from a reading. I personally try to have these clients breaking from character, because I am after what I would call 'the experience of tarot', in which the client actually has to engage, visually, with the images. That dialogue created outside the boundaries of language is what I am after. But language is always there, and with it, the performative aspect of the reading.

Now, you have published a revisited version of the inkblot test. Artist Anthony Gormley said in an interview that we live in a culture of 'expanded symbols' in which an iconographic approach to images is insufficient, since all images are open to receive our subjective input. In that regard ink blots are interesting, since in a concrete way they don't represent anything. Yet they always become representational. I would guess that, for a client, it would be easier to map analogies between herself and a tarot card, but I would like to know your thoughts on the differences between doing readings with tarot cards versus doing them with inkblots. What are the advantages and disadvantages on both cases?

I would argue that the client who engages in a dialogue is nonetheless playing a role and performing, but perhaps I did noy make myself clear. The inkblot cards are great precisely because of their permanent ambiguity and their transcultural nature. The iconography of Tarot is primarily Western medieval which gives them a relatively fixed cultural grounding. But they are also associated with esotericism which for many makes them something to be feared. The inkblot cards, while grounded in a 19th Century parlour game, do not have the same cultural referent nor do they evoke fear. Rather they are seen as more scientific and 'rational', making them more acceptable. I have used them in China in Shanghai with a group of young people from China and Europe. The cards transcended cultural boundaries and prompted intense discussion.

Since the images are 'of nothing' the sitter and reader are left with a tremendous amount of freedom and flexibility to interpret the meanings and how they relate to the issue at hand. But a good reader friend of mine simply cannot relate to the images and does not use them for readings. The other drawback of course is that there are only ten images which for some readers is too constrained. For me, each card still has so many variables that there are literally millions of combinations possible from any ten card spread.

I think it would be nice to have the sitter producing the inkblot and literally 'pouring' herself on the blank page. One image can be enough to prompt a powerful reading. The fact that there are only ten inkblots doesn't bothers me as much as the fact that they don't seem to leave a strong visual imprint in the client, whether with the tarot they can always go back to the memory of the images and, if you did your job properly, that memory will have anchored certain suggestions. But notice that when I talk about giving people the experience of the tarot, I am actually talking about having them engaging with the images in the same way you would engage with a work of art. I feel that this is the experience that has been adulterated by the occultists. I believe we can restore that experience back to something more sober, more along the lines of 'tarocchi appropriati,' where there can be amusement, but the experience can also be edifying.

Changing topics a little bit, do you find that the concerns of people in a country like China, for example, differ from our concerns in any significant way? With people from Japan, for example, there are two questions they usually hope a reading will answer: "when?" and "where?" I don't necessarily think those are the best questions to ask oneself while looking at the tarot, that is, unless you accept that the answer will never be literal, as in "on May 15th, 10:23 a.m. at Crosby Street and Prince". How is that interaction in other countries you have visited, like China, Mongolia, etc?

China and Mongolia have strong collectivist traditions which change the sense of individuality and therefore the expectation for a reading. There is a more holistic appreciation for life and a greater attention to balance. Although they have embraced capitalism, there is still a very strong sense of collectivism. Moreover,

Mongolia has a strong cultural identification with Shamanism and China the I-Ching, so the metaphysical pursuits are alive and well. In my own experience the Chinese are more openly curious about all things 'magical' than their neighbours from the North.

In Korea, for example, they have 'Philosophical Offices', places where people go to a specialist to consult the I Ching. Eastern cultures also rely more on receiver-oriented communication. Many things are hinted at, and it is up to the listener to fill in the blanks. Wold you say that Chinese people, for example, are a better audience for readings?

They certainly could be but the language barriers are too much for me to provide a more detailed answer. They are exceedingly curious and open to a range of alternative ways of knowing.

I would like to draw this conversation to an end by getting back to the beginning. A couple of years ago I was looking at artists Olafur Eliasson's waterfalls, here in New York. He built several waterfalls both at the East and the Hudson rivers. From afar these looked like natural waterfalls, but as soon as you approached them you noticed that they were totally fake: the water would come down from a totally visibly scaffold. He did something similar in London, at the Turbine Hall, where he recreated a sun sphere. People would go there to sunbathe, just as if it were the real sun, but further inspection would show you it was again an illusion. In other words, you could get a real tan from a fake sun!

Secular magic works is a similar way via suspension of disbelief. There is always a point where the audience can 'zoom-out' and see the wires, or remember that all is an illusion. I wonder, what are your thoughts in terms of how that process applies to readings? It seems that the client that comes for a reading finds that 'zooming-out' more troublesome. What do you think? Can we still benefit from illusions once we discover they are illusory?

Of course we can still benefit from illusions once we discover they are illusory. If the event itself (the waterfall, the sun, the levitation, and the array of major and minor arcana) brings joy, comfort, or closure in some way, the method or route to that result does not matter as much as the result itself. Many people are fully conscious of the illusory nature of many things in which they engage and yet it does not discourage participation. Moreover there is a fair bit of anecdotal evidence that when people discover an illusion they nonetheless ignore it and continue to draw value from the experience. A good reader need not engage in outright deception but recognize that much of what we do is illusory even though in the end it does not matter.

New York / East Bergholt, England, 2010

"The need for magic in the modern world comes from a hardwired precondition in human consciousness that seeks release and self-expression."

A conversation with ERIC K. LERNER, artist, writer, priest

Coming from Venezuela, I have a certain sense of familiarity with the African-diaspora religions, and some first hand experiences. That is why, when I received the Association for Tarot Studies's newsletter with your article in it, I was a little bit cautious at first. It seems to me that one of the main gestures of the new age movement, something that perhaps started with Blavatsky's Theosophy, is an attempt to equalize all belief systems while arguing that, underneath, they are all the same. I suspect the real effect of such idea in today's world is to preclude people from compromising any specific belief system. Instead of that, people now hover over the whole spiritual spectrum, burning a candle for a saint, praying with beads, going to mass on Sunday and to an ashram on Tuesday... Within this context, I have always had a problem with all the tarot decks that feature a Santeria theme. Not only because, as you pointed out in your text, both systems aren't really compatible, or at least, you can't really overlap them, but most importantly because I understand the significant amount of time and dedication a true practitioner must invest in order to have the license to work with the Diloggun. I don't believe in shortcuts. If someone is really interested in such practices, there is some work to be done and some commitment to be accepted. But while I was fearing to find in your article just more of the "we are all the same" nonsense we find everywhere, it was an extraordinary surprise to read a well informed and sober comparison between the tarot and the diloggun. So, let me start by thanking you for that!

I have many things I want to ask you, but I think it would be good to start at the beginning. Could you tell me, how did you first get in contact with Santeria?

About eleven years ago I published the following article in an ethnography journal called *Shaman's Drum*. It seems to pretty thoroughly answer your question as to how I became involved with Santeria. Here is the first paragraph:

In 1994 a fellow writer approached me to write a screenplay with her. The story would follow the lines of a B slasher flick. She recommended that we give it a twist based on her Cuban ancestry and incorporate Santeria. My co-author, an affluent Cuban Jewess, had no contact with Afro-Cubans, the core of the Cuban populace and rank and file followers of "La Regla de Ocha." After a brief period of book research, I decided that Santeria could not be the subject of a horror movie. Scant investigation revealed a religion that had maintained its integrity as a source of spiritual empowerment and comfort for the West Africans who endured the middle passage. Personal living deities – orisha – whose mythology evinced great poetry and profundity charged it. The altars and objects used in worship were beautiful. As an artist and writer, I was intrigued and continued my research. Today, I am a novitiate priest of Obatala, the great orisha of creativity whose brilliance is exuded by the sun itself. My service to orisha is the defining characteristic of my life and has enabled me to live with HIV-disease.

I believe it was Malidoma Patrice Some the one who wrote that 'magic' is that moment when one connects with the land that gave you birth. There is something profoundly powerful in that sentence, in that it describes magic as something that is both physically grounding and emotionally uplifting. The sentence also uncovers a problem I have with western esoteric magic: to me it feels extremely intellectual, by the book, full of "it is said that this will...", instead of "this is this", and ritualized to an extreme in which the metaphors that compose it have lost touch with their referents. All that feels quite contrary to that maxim, I believe from the Congos, that says "Somo o no somo", you are or you aren't, there is no theory, no pretense. One of the reasons I have always been so interested in African magic is precisely because of its practicality. 'Magic' may now be a silly word, in that it has been widely trivialized, but although the word itself may not be so useful anymore, I would still like to know: what is magic to you, and why do you think it is important in today's world?

I think being simple and direct works best to answer your question.

I think that I was a little taken back by your question since 'magic' has become such a ballyhooed word. I agree with much of what you write about the difference between Western esoteric and African beliefs, but the straightforward question is: what does it mean to me personally? After spending a lot of time spinning my wheels delineating the differences between the West and Africa in the sterile language of anthropology (I can be quite academic in spinning words), I realized that it is best just to be straightforward. To me 'magic' is embodied by any act in which I am completely integrated in realizing. In the occult realm this applies to telekinesis, psychotelemetry, precognition and the verge of trance-possession. In the conventionally mundane aspects of existence it applies to making love, creating a work of art, or speaking one's mind. I do not perceive any sort of gulf between those two areas, and my own expression in both comes from the same reflexes. The need for magic in the modern world comes from a hardwired precondition in human consciousness that seeks release and self-expression.

Yes, that is why I apologized beforehand at using the term 'magic', since the term has become some sort of caricature of itself. I think you provided an extremely useful, and clear answer. Thanks for that!

Now, it seems to me that most of African divination has a two-part structure. I know that the kind of reading that is done in Santeria is a highly ritualized ceremony, but allow me to oversimplify: there is a diagnosis, which is done with the oracle and which amounts to what we could equate to the classical idea of a reading that comes to most people's minds, in which a person is told a series of things about herself. But then, there is a second part of the reading, which is basically a prescription: once the diagnosis has been made, and the person's problem has been 'outed', the reader proceeds to outline a set of actions to help solve that problem. Those actions could take the form of a ritual, an offering, a cleanse, etc. In a sense, and perhaps because at one time the diviners functioned as holistic doctors, healing both, the person's body and the person's relationship with society (and therefore, healing society's body) was commonsense. A reading like that seems to accomplish two things: to elucidate a person's problem and its causes, and to give the person some tools to fix it. Would you say this is correct?

I mention this because it seems to me that the classical tarot reading doesn't follow that pattern, and seems to stop at the first half of the process. The reading mainly consists of bringing forward a person's situation, and in the case of predictive readings, it would suggest some outcomes. But the prescriptive aspect doesn't seem to be as clearly present as with the reading of the Obi, or the Diloggun. What are your thoughts on this?

As usual, your question has made me think something through that otherwise I would simply do.

From my perspective, I believe a Diloggun reading does follow at least a two-part structure, but not necessarily along the lines you describe. For me, the first part of the reading is the ritualized prayer, an opening of the door. This is profoundly important for a number of reasons:

1. It puts the client on notice that she is about to enter a sacred dialogue.

2. The prayers, the relationship between the diviner, the client, and spiritual forces governing the reading, established during the recitation may have a profoundly healing effect on both the client and diviner regardless of the diagnostic reading that follows.

3. The client is motivated through the ritual structure of the prayers to face her own life issues and to contemplate where she stands in the greater scheme of existence.

In practice the actual reading does not always follow a linear statement of the issues then rectified by the prescription of a spiritual or practical remedy. Often readings raise multiple situations, and many readers, including myself, are inclined to address remedial steps as one situation is described, and then move on to the next issue. Let me give an example. A client comes for a reading, and the reading opens in a letter sacred to Obatala. Frequently, divinatory verses that involve Obatala relate to someone's head. Depending on the orientation of the letter, it can be very appropriate to ask the client whether she suffers from frequent or migraine headaches. If the answer is yes, I would probably immediately mark some type of remedy to that situation before moving on to the next issue revealed in the reading. She may have come to talk about her career, marriage or education. The client is likely to face multiple issues. These include interpersonal relationships, spiritual relationships, as well as economic, romantic and health complications. I often cite proverbs and mythic stories that pertain to the letter revealed and which seem to relate to the circumstances at hand. In some cases, there will be multiple letters thrown in a reading. I try to recapitulate the remedies prescribed in a reading at its conclusion, and always address the question as to whether all the relevant issues have been discussed before marking the reading's closure. Also, what happens to me personally during a Diloggun reading is that, frequently, I enter a somewhat altered state of perception. Often, I speak from a place that seems other than my own intellect. I do not always remember everything that I say. I find other readers experience this too, and often they have an assistant present to make written notes of a reading or permit the client to make some type of recording. It is not the same as a trance-possession but a kind of an intoxicated state between normal intellectual perception and the surrender of all perception to another driving consciousness.

In sum, I feel that a Diloggun reading always has two significant parts: the ritualized opening prayers and the reading itself. However, the reading portion does not always follow a consistent structure because it is subject to the proclivity of the spirits called forth by the opening prayers.

What you describe is consistent with my own experience about the importance of setting the right context for a reading. What you define as 'sacred' is both an internal and external space, a situation and a mindset. This mindset is fundamental for the reading in order to have its full effect on the client.

How do you determine if a client needs a tarot reading, or a Diloggun reading? Is the client's belief in Santeria a factor?

Now, something that I also really want to know about is your thoughts on the use of metaphors. The way I see it, African spirituality is full of examples of the practical use of metaphor. I am thinking of metaphor as the mapping of a connection between two things that share similar characteristics. If there is an external event we cannot control, we look for its metaphorical representation, and we affect this representation in the hope of affecting the external event. A piece of someone's clothing, his body fluids, his hair, etc, stand for that person, and therefore, we will affect that part of the person as a means to affect the person himself. That would be consistent with the classic esoteric idea of "as above, so below". I understand that we cannot really comprehend Santeria without acknowledging its spiritual component, but still, I would like to know if you ever received any training in how to create treatments based on the metaphorical properties of substances, if you make any conscious emphasis on this idea, or if all the remedies, prescriptions or advice you give have been passed down as part of a tradition. Is there any room for creativity in your practice?

Obviously whether or not someone practices Santeria is very much a determining factor in whether or not she will benefit from a Diloggun reading as opposed to a tarot reading. Recommending a Diloggun reading to someone who does not practice Santeria is fraught with problems, primarily because you ask her to participate in a religious system in which she is not invested. The one exception I make here is when someone faces a life threatening condition and there appears to be no viable recourse through traditional medical remedies, legal strategies, etc. I know that Santeria offers effective remedies to problems that otherwise seem unsolvable. Of course, an important part of a Santeria reading occurs when you have the client state that she wishes to join with the orisha of her own free will. (This is done during the opening prayers.) The reading cannot proceed if she does not make such a statement.

As for the use of metaphor in African magical practices, most do employ what is termed sympathetic magic. For instance in Santeria, an image or personal object from a person is frequently substituted for the individual if she cannot be present. A simple example of this follows. Say you wish to engender someone's good favor or bring sweetness into someone's life. You can take a photo of that person, place it on a white plate and cover it with honey, and place it before the orisha Oshun along with a yellow candle or other appropriate offerings for Oshun and thus petition her to manifest her bounty for that person.

There is a great deal of room for creativity in my practice as a Santero. Even the way I orate prayers for someone involves a lot of creative decision making. Let me give you an example. A couple years back I had to give Warriors to a young lady who was extremely nervous about it. In order to change her perception that this was indeed something positive and life affirming I decided to inject a lot of humor into how I presented this to her. I made jokes. I even did a little improvisational dancing. (Believe me the sight of a white guy, unless he's Russian and got a six pack set of abs, borders on absurdist theatre.) She loosened up. It became an enjoyable celebration for her. Now, with someone who approaches receiving Warriors with a very cavalier attitude I might decide to put her in penance for a couple hours, brusquely press the sacrificial birds into her face etc. and make it clear that this is serious business. My attitude here is not unique among santeros. Most pride themselves on how they perform ritual acts and bring an element of theatre to them.

Also the orisha Oba teaches us that we need to be open to learning from other cultures and religious practices. Most santeros I know are open to employing healing methods they have learned from other cultures. The governing rule is that YOU DO NOT MIX SANTERIA RITUALS WITH THOSE FROM OTHER RELIGIONS. However, a santero may decide to employ a healing technique he learned from a North Amerian Indian for a client if it seems applicable to a predicament. One thing making the saint (becoming a Santeria priest) teaches you is that you have a divine spark of orisha within you that you can trust in making decisions. I have learned effective healing practices from curanderos, Roma, South German hexworkers, Italian folk magic practitioners and others that I employ. I believe that the orisha and ancestors who guide me put these healers in my life path so that I could learn things from them.

I have had the opportunity to read the sayings associated with the 'letras' for the Diloggun and find them very beautiful. I remember things like "an arrow between brothers" or "no one knows what lies at the bottom of the sea". I wish I could come up with things like that! Those phrases have a strong poetic power, in that the response they elicit can be very profound when they tap into a person's particular situation. There is something important, I believe, about a religion like Santeria, in the fact that the practitioner still rely strongly on oral tradition. Because of this, the cowry shells become an index for a repository of knowledge stored in the mind of the priest. Each number of open mouths in any given throw of the oracle is associated to a saying, and that saying is also associated to a story, or stories. The cowry shells function like a mnemonic device. Obviously, there is no engagement between the client and the oracle itself, but between the client and the sayings and stories the reader recalls when prompted by the oracle. In the tarot, an engagement between the client and the oracle is possible. That is what I call the "experience of tarot", a moment when the person experiences the image by focusing his or her attention on it, and the image 'speaks'. That form of speaking is what Jean-Claude Flornoy calls the 'operativity' of the image: the image works us by eliciting all kinds of personal associations so we can arrive to a certain truth. I have seen people crying, laughing, freezing or sighting with relief, at the sole sight of a tarot image. Even when, at one level, the tarot can function as a mnemonic device, if we recite a set of predefined meanings to describe each card, there is always this other level, a completely visual experience we can have access to. But I feel that a sentence like: "scooping water with a basket" can have the same poetic impact an image has. As a matter of fact, those phrases tend to be very visual. Are they metaphors for real actions or events? How do people relate to those seemingly cryptic, koan-like, sentences?

I find intellectual stimulation and personal enjoyment in the metaphors provided by Diloggun proverbs, divination verses, and narratives. I find that they provide a valid basis for understanding real life events a client, or myself when I am the client, faces. However, not everyone responds in the same way. Some people do not think metaphorically or associatively. Practically, it is hard to make a predetermination as to what sort of client is likely to appreciate the poetic discourse that unfolds in a Diloggun reading. I have seen clients with PhDs utterly unable to process proverbs and narratives when I relate them as part of a divination, and I have encountered functionally illiterate clients who embrace such language enthusiastically. Being able to process poetic language is not something that is ethnically, culturally, or educationally predetermined. As a diviner, one must be willing to tailor a reading according to a client's mindset. Since I very much appreciate word-play and the framework engendered by poetic discourse, I usually incorporate them into a reading. Practically, I must be prepared to move away from using such language promptly and get into the nuts and bolts of pragmatic language if I see that the poetic language is not offering value to a client. Sometimes I'll feel out a client's intellectual processes by reciting a proverb or narrative and asking her how she would apply it to her own situation. However, in accepting one's job as a diviner, you must realize that your job is to make the substance of what is revealed by an oracle useful to a client, and you must accept that part the job at hand is to provide guidance and counsel as needed.

I have a final question: How potent do you think a symbol can be on its own? Let's say, I take a bottle of water, clean, clear, pure mineral water. Then let's say that I peel the label off and draw a skull and crossbones on the bottle. Do you think that water could kill someone?

Symbols can be very powerful foci for pscyo-kinetic projection. I know that an adept shaman can use such a methodology to destroy someone else. However, in this particular example I believe that if someone dies from drinking this 'fake' water, it would be more due to the manifestation of the shaman's will and ability to achieve such a result than it would be a result of the specific symbol he employs as a conduit.

New York / Baltimore, 2010

"Still, those two authors were much closer to the origin of tarot than we are, and they were deeply fascinated by the cards, so their explanations deserve our attention."

A brief conversation with MARCO PONZI and ROSS S. CALDWELL, tarot scholars

First, I am very interested in your choice for the title of your book: Explaining the Tarot *(2010). I guess that every single book on the tarot out there seeks to explain the tarot. What is different about this explanation?*

ROSS: We discussed the title over the course of a few days, through email, but before looking up why we chose it I'll give my impressions without those references.

I think it's a bold title, despite seeming commonplace. That's because once you read the subtitle "Two Italian Renaissance Essays on the Meaning of the Tarot Pack", the main title, *Explaining the Tarot,* takes on an added gravitas, a distance from any modern books with contemporary readings or explanations of the images and their sequence. So it is kind of a surprise – these "explanations" are from the 16th century! They are only a little more than a century removed from the invention of the game itself.

I have just looked up the discussion among us – it seems there were seven suggestions before we chose the final one:

"Tarot Interpretation in the XVIth Century: Two Discourses"

"Explaining the Tarot: Two Italian Renaissance Readings of the Tarot"

"Interpreting the Tarot in the Renaissance: Two Italian Essays on the Tarot"

"Two XVIth Century Italian Essays on Tarot"

"The Meaning of the Tarot: Two Italian Renaissance Readings"

"Explaining the Tarot in Renaissance Italy: Two Essays"

"Explaining the Tarot in Renaissance Italy: Two Discourses"

We wanted to avoid the redundancy of having "the Tarot" twice in the title, so making it "Tarot Pack" at the very end of the subtitle seemed to take the pressure off of the force of "the Tarot" in the main title, and changed the emphasis slightly. I think the chosen title is quite elegant.

MARCO: I want to add that, at first glance, the title may seem bold, but actually our work has been quite humble: we have tried to make the ideas of our two authors accessible to contemporary people. You will not find much of our opinions in the book. Of course, the fact that those explanations of the meaning of tarot are ancient does not make them "true". XVI Century people were as subject to anachronistically projecting their ideas as we are. Still those two authors were much closer to the origin of tarot than we are, and they were deeply fascinated by the cards, so their explanations deserve our attention.

Are there any earlier explanations to the tarot you are aware of?

ROSS: No, these are unique, and easily the first attempts to explain both the symbolism of the cards and their sequence, or to moralize the game. It's quite remarkable that there are two of them, actually, done at almost exactly the same time – but without knowledge of one another. Other kinds of card decks had been moralized, since as early as 1377, but these two essays are the first moralization for any kind of regular Tarot cards. Another one would not be attempted until Antoine Court de Gébelin's occult moralization, over two centuries later.

MARCO: The fact that there are no other ancient explanations of the meaning of tarot makes these two documents very important to those interested in the subject.

Ross, could you amplify on your use of the term 'moralizing'? In which sense are all explanations of the tarot a way of moralizing it?

ROSS: Sure. A morality is when a game is explained as reflecting the human condition, human customs and society, or some aspect of them (like war). It can be both diagnostic (describing society or the particular part the morality is concerned with) and prescriptive (how to live in society, or behave in war, and the purpose of life). Since the world was seen as the center of the universe, and man was the center of the world, and everything was united in a chain of being from God through the stars and planets down to the elements and living things, then a morality can sometimes include both cosmogony and human society. Both the play and the objects used in the game can be moralized.

Not all explanations would be moralities. If the explanation were that it was an alchemical formula, or a verbal riddle, that wouldn't be a morality.

In the sense we use it here, it is a technical term that refers to a category of literature for which the epitome and reference-point is the Dominican monk Jacob of Cessolis' morality of Chess, *Liber de moribus hominum et officiis nobilium ac popularium super ludo scachorum*, written around 1300. The earliest morality of cards, *De moribus et disciplina humanae conversacionis* (also called *Ludus cartularum moralisatus*) written by John of Rheinfelden in 1377, appeals explicitly to Cessolis' example. Note that both authors use the word 'morals', and John explicitly uses the adjective 'moralized.'

Our Anonymous author cites two such moralities as his inspiration, Marco Girolamo Vida on Chess, first published in 1510, and Claudius Galen's ancient one on playing ball.

Are those two essays consistent between themselves? Can we say that they share a similar explanation of the tarot?

ROSS: I wouldn't say the essays are consistent between themselves at all – first, each is using a different kind of standard Tarot – and their specific methods are very different as well. But, in the end, their purpose is moral and their conclusion is broadly similar. We tried to sum up this similarity by descibing the ultimate purpose of Tarot's moral teaching as "how to seek God". However, in detail, each author is quite different. Piscina considers his Tarot to be explicitly Catholic. He moralizes the four suits, but not the court cards. His examples are few, his morality quotidian, his method conversational, sometimes polemical, and even humorous. We have to remember he was only about 25 when he wrote it – and his inspiration for writing came as a "sudden caprice" when he saw a lady playing the game during a feast day. The Anonymous, by contrast, explains that he is trying to fill in the gap in the moralizing literature on games – Chess and Ball playing have moralities, but Tarot, the noblest game of all, has none. Like Piscina, he moralizes the suits, but he also gives detailed examples for his moralities of the Kings. His approach is more abstract and philosophical. He uses many more examples than Piscina, mostly drawn from classical history. Yet despite their differences, each considers their Tarots to be a very full and complete description of Man's condition, and how to rise above worldly concerns to the realm of God.

Marco created a comparative chart that summarizes the authors side-by-side, which everyone who has the texts will find very helpful I believe. I refer to it constantly.

MARCO: There is a specific point on which the two authors agree and that was unexpected to me: both of them explicitly link "the Tower" (Piscina calls it "Fire", while the Anonymous calls it "the Skies") to the cosmological sequence formed by the Star, the Moon, and the Sun. I would have expected the Tower to be related to the some kind of divine punishment, but this is not the case. I agree with the differences in mood underlined by Ross: the Anonymous is more grave and serious and sees in the game also a depiction of the dramatic struggle against the Devil, while all Piscina sees in that card is the representation of some innocuous elemental daemons. I also like the fact that the Anonymous begins his essay with a complete allegorical explanation of the suits and the court cards; he says that the inventor decided to add the trumps to the game in order to complete his allegory of human life with a set of sacred images that would lead to the contemplation of God. He almost seems to have intuited that the trumps had to be a later addition to the standard playing-card deck. In general, my personal feeling is that the Anonymous gets closer to what could have been the original meaning of the sequence of the trumps.

Do you know if Piscina's discorso was available in any shape or form around 1969, when Calvino wrote his Castle Of Crossed Destinies? *Piscina's discourse starts with the motif of the Inn, which is exactly the motif Calvino chose for his book, both as a castle turned into an inn, and as a tavern in the middle of the woods. It may be a coincidence, of course, but still, I wonder if Calvino could have read Piscina. There is even something in the voice of both authors I find similar.*

ROSS: I wouldn't think so. Although Piscina's *Discorso* is listed in Alfredo Lensi, *Bibliografia italiana di giuochi di carte*, 1892, and a few inventories and catalogues over the centuries, we found no evidence that anybody sought out a copy and read it before Franco Pratesi in the late 1980s (he published an article about it in *The Playing Card* in 1987). There are only two copies known, one in the small town of Borgomanero, where it resides in the public library, and there is also a copy in private hands. It is obviously not impossible that people involved in Calvino's study of the Tarot, like Sergio Samek Ludovici, had found and read it, but I don't know of any evidence that they did.

It is an interesting coincidence, whether you take it as indirect evidence for the late 60s circle of Italian tarot researchers having read it or not. Also coincidentally, Andrea Alciato called the Bagatto, an innkeeper or publican (the Latin word *caupo*) in his list of trumps in 1547. He is writing from Milan, and uses the C order (the first to list it in fact), so perhaps in Lombardy and Piedmonte there was a popular design where the Bagatto looked more like an innkeeper than it does in any surviving pack we know.

MARCO: I agree that the fact that both Piscina and Calvino used the image of the inn suggests something about the message conveyed by the cards. After all, card games have always been played in inns. Also the anti-gambling preachers quoted by Ross in his recent paper about "The Proto-Historiography of Playing Cards" used the rhetoric expedient of the "diabolic liturgy", in which playing cards replaced the sacred icons and inns and taverns replaced the churches.

Finally, what do you think are the advantages of working with other two authors? Did you decide beforehand that you wanted to work together, or did it happen after each one of you had some research done?

ROSS: Well the advantages are obvious – three people passionate about the subject are better than one! For competences, all of our skills differed but complemented one another – Marco is Italian, and is fluent in English, and finds no trouble translating the written word from his mother-tongue into English. He was also tireless in his analysis and comparison of the two main manuscripts we used for the Anonymous Discourse. Do I need to introduce Thierry Depaulis' talents and qualifications for this work? He is an expert historical researcher and a first-class scholar, in my opinion the foremost historian of playing cards today – and for Tarot history there is no one nearly his equal. He also reads Italian fluently (and I suspect speaks it too). He is a pre-press manager and graphic designer, and he designed and set the book. The main talent I brought to the project was my enthusiasm, and my most important skill is a native ability in English. I am familiar enough with Italian to navigate the sources, but my research contributions were modest, as were my translation suggestions. My main job was to get the English right.

As for the sequence of events, Marco and I had already collaborated on translating Piscina, and I had given him the Bologna copy of the Anonymous Discourse, which was a copy of a copy (given to me by Giordano Berti about three years ago), so very hard to read in places. He had begun translating it, and I knew that Thierry had also found a manuscript in the Arsenal library in Paris, so I wanted to share the transcription with him and ask what he could add from his own manuscript. This was in August of last year, I believe. Thierry quickly became interested in getting a perfect copy of the Arsenal manuscript, which he had up to then only partially transcribed. It proved to be superior in almost every respect to the Bologna copy. The idea for a publication of the two discourses, text and translation, germinated in a series of emails, and in September Thierry found a publisher associated with the *International Playing Card Society* who was interested in the project. I introduced Thierry and Marco, and we began working together comparing the manuscripts, translating the text, and researching the references. For Piscina the main thing was to improve the translation and comment on the people, places and things in the text, as we did also for the Anonymous.

MARCO: I must say that, without the other two authors, I would never have attempted to translate and publish these two texts. I am very grateful to both of them. The translation itself has been difficult, since ancient Italian often is convoluted. Moreover, the references, sometimes just allusions, to game rules, would have been lost, without the deep knowledge of Thierry and Ross. Also, most of the linguistic analysis of the Anonymous manuscript has been performed by them. Thierry has filled the wide gap between writing something and publishing a book: a huge amount of work. I must say that working via email is very convenient, but it is not as being with other people and talking to them. Here I feel that Ross has been great, keeping the communication and the collaboration going. Also, when he was in Milan a couple of years ago, he was so kind to propose to me to meet him and his wife. Without the experience of that conversation, when we actually met, I don't think I would have undertaken the task of contributing to the book.

June 2010, New York / Béziers / Milan

"My job is to lift them up and make them feel positive and sure about themselves after my reading."

A conversation with RONI SHACHNAEY, mystic

Let's start at the beginning: what got you interested in doing readings?

Since very early age I was interested in the unknown and the unexplained. In my country of Israel I met people that introduced me to the Cabbala and I felt drawn to the ancient mysteries and the thoughts behind those deep mysteries. I learnt that the ancient Hebrews believed that the creator created the universe with the holly Hebrew letters. I learnt that each letter has numerological value from the first Hebrew letter, number one, to the last Hebrew letter, number four hundred, and that the using of the letters as numbers is called *Gematria*. I also learnt that every Hebrew letter has a meaning, so a person's name that is made out of certain letters can be translated into a number; plus it could also be "Deciphered" and have a meaning using the "Hidden" name and meaning of each and every letter of any given name. I started using those two principles on my friends and relatives, taking their names and telling them the numerological value of it and the meaning of that number. I called it: Name Number. Then with the meaning of each and every letter I told them more about their Character and the total meaning of their name. I found it fascinating that, for every name, the use of Cabbalistic explanations and meanings to decode it in relation to the person bearing it was very accurate. When I went to visit friends or go to parties people approached me and asked me to give them a Reading using their name. This developed to ladies asking me if their name was compatible with their partners' name, then their children's names, and later it developed into the type of questions, 'what name should I give my child?' or 'will that name protect my child?'

Those where the early days and in my book *Roni on Reading* I teach the individual how to use these systems. I myself still use those early days systems with great success and when I do a reading I still start with the Name Number and The Letters of your name.

Of course, I find that fascinating! Not only from the perspective of how poetry and magic are linked in the faith in language they both share, but because I am quite fascinated by names and letters myself. I learned to look at the letters in a name and find meaning in it through the tarot. At some point, it became evident to me that, just as The Magician can be seen as an invitation to stand up, the letter A is in itself a man standing with his legs spread to gain stability. Then I read somewhere that Milton Erickson used a similar technique to teach his grandmother to read: a letter M would be a horse grassing, and a letter E would be a horse standing on its rear legs. But in truth, it was only after I was confronted with the English language that I was able to see these things. Spanish is my native language, and English has allowed me to look at words as foreign objects, with an emphasis on 'objects'. I look at words, and I look at letters, and I can almost feel their sharp edges on the tip of my tongue. Sometimes, in a reading, I will be working with the tarot and I will have the person writing her name on a piece of paper, so I can look at the letters and see which actions and which attitudes are being suggested there. Sometimes it is nice how those things I see in the letters relate to the cards the person got.

So, if I were to look at the name RONI, for example, I would make a distinction between the vowels as the soul of the word, and the consonants as the body of the word. The soul of your name is OI, which is kind if nice because we start with a low sound: "OOOOOOO" and we end with a high one: "IIIIIII". The sound itself is like a plane taking off! Most importantly, it has an uplifting quality, as of something that could give us a very serious first impression, almost grave or even intimidating, to turn into something friendly, almost amusing. I like that twist. Just as I like the transition from the letter O, whose wholeness reminds us of The World card and which looks the way one hopes a strong Self would look to the letter I, which looks like The Magician, or like a man standing. A man standing outside the circle of himself. That is quite nice!

(At this point, you would realize I am not talking about letters anymore, but about qualities you can map onto yourself).

I like how that idea of someone who can look intimidating and 'private' at first glance and then reveals himself as sociable and uplifting, resonates what I see happening with the consonants in your name: RN. The letter R is like The Fool, in that we can almost see it walking, with a leg outstretched, ready to take the next step. But the letter N is like a bumper. Two letters I united by a diagonal line that gives them flexibility. While the letter R pushes forward, the letter N moderates its impulses by acting like a cushion. The Fool meets Temperance. Any youthful impulse *can be moderated by experience. Even the sound, the harsh "RRRRR" turns into a soothing "NNNNNN". Growling becomes lullabying. See? Your whole name gives that sense of someone seemingly tough that reveals himself as friendly, or someone strong but willing to bend, a tower turned into a bridge.*

I also love how organically your relationship with readings evolved. It all started with understanding your heritage, and transforming it into something useful. I am not too interested in the idea of 'profit' but I am very interested in the idea of 'usefulness'. I think that there is a distinction there, and I wonder: what use do you think people have of the kind of readings you do?

First I would like to thank you for the way you have described how my name feels to you. It is truly fascinating and thought provoking, and yes, it makes much sense to me. Back to your question of usefulness.

When a sitter enters my space (the place I do my readings in I call 'my space' as they enter my domain. If I am invited to their house to do private readings there, I enter 'their space.') Just a quick explanation about "My Space" and "Their Space": In "My Space" they have to cross the threshold, and walk a few steps towards me, and then usually wait until I invite them to seat down. In this sentence, to me there is a complete hidden knowledge. Crossing the threshold equals BIRTH in my mind. So, their birth (the way their body language speaks what are they wearing) is very important to me. Next, they are in. The few steps they take as they come closer to where I seat signifies their first steps after being re-born, so to speak. This speaks volumes to me because I learn how the "child" progresses. Is the child hesitant? Confident? Walking with dignity? Then I invite them to have a sit. The way they take the sit, their preparations in getting comfortable, their facial expressions tell me more about this child now as a grown up (invited to seat with the adults). I gain quite a lot of knowledge about the individual through that short experience and the way my brain processes the new born to adulthood.

"Their Space" is very different. Now I am the one who has to be a re-born child so just like a child I am very inquisitive. I look around to see what is around me, process that information, and draw conclusions. I am always very interested in seeing where they decide I should sit during the reading. What room? What chair? Is their a cushion on the chair, water on the table? What are they wearing? And, of course, the sound of their voices (this is something I pay attention to in both spaces, mine and theirs.) Hence, a lot of information is being processed by me and I arrive at a few conclusions that I may use during the reading. So far, all this is useful to me. But, what about the sitter?

As I said previously I start with "Name Number". I explain that just like on a bottle of a rich wine they see a label that tells them what's inside the bottle so it is true of their names. The name is a sort of a label that was put on our foreheads by our loving parents. I tell the sitters that what we are going to do is learn what their names holds within their inner worlds by looking at the name through Cabbalistic eyes and ancient knowledge. So, I ask for the name (this step removes the potential question, 'why are you asking me what my name is, you are the Psychic you tell me'), as the sitter is now interested in learning about her name and its hidden values. After I have done the summing and reducing the figures into one single digit I explain to the sitter what the name holds in Numerology. I then give them my card on whose back it is printed: Your name number is: _____ Please keep this for your protection.

So, the usefulness of such steps is twofold: The sitters have learned about the numerical meaning of their names and hopefully they will keep my business card for future use. By this time I broke the ice with the sitter. We have a casual but interesting chat, and they don't feel they have to be on guard. This makes the second phase easier.

The second phase is getting to the letters of their name. Here again I explain to them what the ancient Hebrew says about the letters in their names, and what they are made of, and then we both decide if their personality is in fact close to what the name of each and every letter means. On the basis of this can we create a sentence. I emphasise "we decide" as now we are more like friends chatting about this and that with the attention pointing all the time toward them. There is so much more I can say about all of this but I believe you get gist of what I find meaningful and useful in all this. It is only after the Name Number and the Letters of the Name have been established that I start the reading, as by then I will have proved to them that I know what I am talking about and they will have received a number exercise on paper (like with you and the blindfold drawing) and which they can take with them as a memento.

I understand what you are saying. It never fails to amaze me how many things you can tell about how a person handles life by seeing that person handling a deck of tarots. The way the person chooses her cards is telling you if she is confident, or careless, firm or hesitant, etc. But what I especially like about your work is the symbolic layer you overlap onto the physical space. The BIRTH-CHILDHOOD metaphor is beautiful! It is of course also very useful. Do you openly share these impressions with your sitter, or do you use them without saying where you got them from?

Now, talking about usefulness, the most memorable thing that happened to me through reading names involved a man who wanted to change sex. I asked him what his name was. He has a very masculine name full of 'R' sounds. When I asked what name he wanted to have as a woman, he mentioned a name he had made up, with several letter G in it, and no R whatsoever. The name wasn't a real name, more of a stage name. It became evident to me that this man didn't want to become a woman, but a sex toy. The letter G is always pointing towards itself. I figured this man wanted to become some sort of a pin-up girl. And of course, severing all the letters R seemed to mirror the idea of severing his penis. I mentioned all of this to him and asked if he really wanted to become a woman, or a sex-object. Only then the story emerged: he had been raped as a child, and the only image he had of himself was of a passive sex object. With the sex-change operation he was aiming at formalizing that image by becoming some sort of bimbo. Not a real woman, but a sex-toy. Do you recall any experience in which a reading of yours uncovered an unexpected find?

Thank you very much for your kind words. It means a lot to me coming from you. Reading is a wonderful world. People open themselves to you in many different ways. They have never met you before but they are willing to share with you details and secrets they may not share with their families, friends or doctors. We are indeed privileged to be given that position of trust and therefore when I do my reading I am very much aware of the privilege given, and never take advantage of their vulnerabilities. The point is that people come to me for a reading because they may be troubled. The way I see myself is as an elevator. My job is to lift them up and make them feel positive and sure about themselves after my reading. There are no "Warnings" in my readings, as I firmly believe that any sentence can be delivered sweetly and warmly. Hence, even when I see in my mind's eye something "Dark" I can use words that will not alarm the sitter but rather hand the sitter a task of sorts. For instance, if I see illness, my words may be:

"make sure to give your wife the attention she is seeking" rather than: "You need to take your wife to the Doctor". But, back to your question of sharing impressions with my sitter. I usually do, and especially when asked "How do you know this?" To a question of this nature I would answer: "Having you in front of me creates pictures in my mind, rather than words. The interpretation of these pictures is what I give you as spoken words. Every word translates into a picture in my mind, so, if I say to you 'day' you may see some brightness. If I say 'street' you may see people walking. 'Yes' you may imagine as a smile, perhaps, and 'No' as severe action." As far as I am concerned, when you stop seeing images as a result of a spoken word or a sentence, you enter what we call "The Twilight Zone". I will not go further into that.

As to my experience of the unexpected, I can recall two that will remain with me forever. I was booked by Mitsubishi when they have launched a brand new very large car dealership. I was given the manager's office in which to do readings for their invited guests. My wife Laraine came with me that night as I did not feel very good. I took my chair behind the desk and Laraine set to my right. A very nice looking lady came into the room and as I said before I was watching as she opened the door, took a few steps toward me, and sat down. Just as the lady sat down Laraine said to me: "Aren't you warm? It's quite hot in here" to which I have replied "take your coat off and put it on the back of the chair". Suddenly the lady said: "Sorry, but I have got nothing underneath". Although it was very funny at the time, it proved beyond doubt that this lady in particular thought that the world revolves around her! My reading was made very easy with her that night.

The next experience I remember well was in a Harley Davidson outlet. It was their Christmas party and I was part of the entertainment. I worked fast and hard that night amongst all the macho men, their butch girlfriends/wives, and the Tattooed shaved heads. A real Hell's Angels type of crowd.

I finished my reading and was about to leave when I was approached by a huge man that said "A word please". I was worried but went with him to the side of the room when he said: "We believe that you have special powers. We spoke about your reading and we feel we need you to do something for us. He pointed to where a good few of them where standing next to their Harley Davidsons and said: All these people want you to go over to their Bikes and bless the Bikes so the riders will be protected. We will pay you well for that. Well, that night I blessed over twenty Bikes and was handsomely rewarded.

This is how strong a reading can be. It is therefore that when I do a reading I consider people's feelings and make sure that they go home high, thinking that the world is their oyster.

How do you deal with people who come wanting predictions? I understand that working with their names doesn't lend itself to that, but still, there is a strong link in people's minds between readings and futurology. I have found that what works best for me is to accept their question without entering into any major metaphysical debate, but I never give them predictions. Every time a person asks me "what is going to happen with…?" I answer by telling them "this is the best you can do about it".

How do you manage these questions?

When I was working on Cruise ships people used to approach me with pictures of their loved ones either for me to try and make spiritual contact with the one in the picture or to ask me how their loved one feels. To me, asking me how a loved one feels is very close to a asking for a prediction. I thought at the time that I needed an answer that they will appreciate and respect and I came up with this: "Looking at this picture, what I see is this wonderful person looking at me and what I get from him/her is how he/she felt at the time when this picture was taken, which I am sure was a wonderful time. I am sure you will agree with me that in here (meaning, in the picture) he/she feels very good and peaceful. The words "in here" are the key words in this sentence. Whereas to them the words 'in here' means 'at *this* very time', to me, 'in here' mens 'at the time the picture was taken.'

When people ask me about their future as I do the reading I usually tell them that "this will come a little later", and then I move on. If the question persists I ask them to pick one more card. It does not matter what card they pick, as I say: "All is very clear now, I have a very strong feeling that in the next few months nothing will take an unwanted turn. All that we talked about indicates that you should proceed with confidence. Your future is as good as we are seating here now."

Sometimes I nod my head and say: "With a person like you, how do you think things can't be good? If I was you I will be absolutely confident in what I am planning to do". Predictions are not for me to give, but, to reassure people of a good future and positive outcome is very important to me. I agree that this is where the teller/ tarot reader must walk a very fine line, but we can't make predictions, simply because we are entertainers and not the man upstairs. I do hope that readers, wherever they are, will understand the importance of keeping away from predicting the future and find words that may sound as if it was a prediction but in fact is not even near it.

There is something brilliant about what you do while reading these photos, in that you are resetting the time of the image. A photo is, by definition, a vestige of the past. It shows what once was. But by focusing in the moment depicted in the photograph you are shifting the language of the reading, from the past, to the present. I guess that is something that can be even easier to accomplish with the tarot, since the tarot's images exist in an eternal present. Roni, I want to thank you very much for what has been a pleasant conversation full of sound advice and great insights. I have, still, one final question: would you say that, in the current state of affairs, readings do more harm than good?

Giving psychological readings will not do harm. Of course, this is very much depending upon the person that does the reading. I believe that if times are hard you will find that fashion labels will start using bright, cheerful colours and all adverts will be cheery and accompanied by warm reassuring colours. Now we are facing a downward path in the economy and many are losing their jobs, their businesses, and families break up as a result. Usually this is the time when people feel they should consult the oracles or some higher authority that they believe have an insight to their future and may be therefore able to give them the reassurance they are seeking.

Like any one that is a professional in whatever they do, there are also those that are out to get you. There are sincere and insincere people. I therefore believe that readings can help in many ways providing they are given by a professional reader who is sincere and honest. Perhaps the time has come to launch a professional body/board that will be able to regulate the divinatory profession and even issue certificates to those who can do a professional job. If you think this is possible and should happen, I will be very willing to be part of such an organisation.

New York / Scarborough, England

"As readers, we have to accept that the myth stream about tarot exists and we have to accept that people will come to us ready to surrender. We do not, however, have to accept that surrender."

A conversation with MAJOR TOM SCHICK, tarot reader and creator

What is the first thing that comes to mind when you think of the tarot?

When I think of tarot I think of a book. A book that I consult daily. I think it was Jean-Michel David writing on the Aeclectic Tarot Forum that said something like, "Tarot is a book of 78 separate symbolic pages that may be imaginatively read in any order".

I'm also reminded of Paul Foster Case in his book *The Tarot – A Key to the Wisdom of the Ages* quoting Eliphas Levi as saying, "As an erudite Kabalistic book, all combinations of which reveal the harmonies preexisting between signs, letters and numbers, the practical value of the Tarot is truly and above all marvelous. A prisoner devoid of books, had he only a Tarot of which he knew how to make use, could in a few years acquire a universal science, and converse with an unequalled doctrine and inexhaustible eloquence."

For myself, I like to think of the tarot as an operating manual for a human being. Reading this manual is learning about oneself – who one really is.

There is something peculiar that happens with tarot images: they are at once old friends and new acquaintances. I guess it is because of its unbounded quality that we can see the tarot as a book that is always new. Or perhaps we are always a new book.

In which sense would you say that what that 'book' tells you is 'true'?

You touch on something I truly love about tarot, that it is at once an old friend and a new acquaintance. I am initmately acquainted with all 78 images yet I am constantly surprised by the new. I love tarot because there is always more to learn about it.

Truth is such a slippery concept because what is true for me may well be false for another. I think most people accept what they believe to be true as truth whether or not they have any factual evidence to back it up. We especially see evidence of this in politics.

I remember a series of conversations several years ago on the *Aeclectic Tarot Forum*. A lovely woman who had the most wonderful fantasy storytelling style of reading tarot asked if it was necessary to believe tarot worked in order to receive any value from the reading. She said she did not believe that any sort of divine agency interferred in the laying of the cards nor did she believe in sycnchronicity bringing meaning to a random selection of cards. She's seen enough evidence on the forums of readings that were 'totally off' that she'd come to worry about getting the 'right' cards in her own readings. So she started a number of threads to explore these ideas and as is the nature of public forums received replies across the spectrum of belief to disbelief. Meanwhile she continued to offer readings to forum members using her wonderfully imaginative storytelling style. As time went on demand for her readings became so high that she had to put limits on her offers. "I'm offering tarot readings using the Margret Petersen Tarot for the first five people to respond". Finally, she came around to accepting that something wonderful happens when we read the book that is tarot. "I propose the 'suspension of disbelief' — suspend disbelief surrounding whether tarot works, how it works etc, whether supernatural intervention is required, etc … just long enough to see see for yourself what you get out of it. To suspend disbelief, in my head, was not a search for belief but a choice to privilege *experience* over judgement."

In my Learn Tarot course I only give my students one piece of homework. I ask them to randomly pick one card and to record their selection and reflections upon that selection daily in their notebooks. Most of my students find this practice so useful that they continue with it long after the course has finished. So, to answer your question, I know what the book tells me is true through experience.

I think that such line of questioning, like that lady was doing, is healthy as long as it rids us from paralyzing superstitions. But I often wonder why it is that poets don't have that problem, or why the painters don't need to invoke the supernatural to paint, yet a reading is a creative act very similar in nature to writing or painting. Perhaps it is more obvious how we, readers, are always ridding Chance, but still, it takes the same leap to make meaning from some cards or to make meaning from some words. You mentioned you have a "reader tent". Could you describe it to me? What happens in there?

I'm not certain I agree that poets and painters don't share at least some of the problems experienced by tarot readers. Dan Pelletier came to Framlingham back in 2004 when I had organized a Tarot Get-together. He gave us a talk featuring Native American myths and demonstrated the seed of truth in those myths regarding geological formations in the Pacific Northwest. He went on to talk about the tarot myth stream and how as tarot readers we ignore that stream at our peril.

Poets and painters each have their own myth stream that operates differently from the readers' myth stream. Poets get writers' block and have superstitions regarding getting in touch with their muse. Painters have similar superstitions regarding their source of inspiration. And of course, the general public, the source of the myth stream, have their own superstitions regarding poets and painters. Everyone knows poets are moody and painters are eccentric.

My tarot reading tent is the vehicle I use to immerse myself in the tarot myth stream. I dearly love to get out in my tent at a country fair, music festival, village *fete* or any event really and offer tarot readings for people. In my part of the world people aren't used to seeing such offerings and it gives me a chance to see their reactions and begin to challenge some of their beliefs. The variety of reactions gives me the opportunity to judge for myself the depth and flow of the myth stream.

Here's some of the things I see and hear:

Some people will walk right past my tent not daring to look inside. I've questioned some of these people and they generally fall into three categories. Those who are genuinely not interested and just don't care to look. (Although I've also noticed that many of these aren't interested in much and don't look at much). Those that have a religious objection to tarot reading, and some of these actually fear the workings of the devil or demons. And those that fear that if they look me in the eye I will know everything there is to know about them.

I often hear the same conversation between parent and child.

> Child: What's that daddy?
>
> Dad: That's a tarrot (rhymes with carrot) card reader.
>
> Child: Yes, but what does he do?
>
> Dad: He tells your fortune.
>
> Child: What's my fortune?
>
> Dad: It's what fate holds in store for you in your life.

I also often hear this conversation between friends.

> Friend 1: Oh look – a tarot card reader! Are you going to get your tarot cards read?
>
> Friend 2: (nervous laugh) No! I don't want to know.
>
> Friend 1 & 2: (nervous laughter)

The current in the myth stream that says tarot card reading is fortune telling is deep and strong in eastern rural England but I suspect the same is true in many urban areas around the world as well.

I am not a fortune teller. I want to empower the people I read for. I try to help the people I read for see and understand their options. I try to help them see how their thoughts, words and actions shape their futures from moment to moment. I use *Major Tom's Tarot of Marseilles* and work with them to formulate and clarify their questions. By being there and offering this service, I do my small part in redirecting the course of the myth stream. Despite my intent I very occasionally get people who insist on having their fortunes told. Even when I explain that fortune telling robs them of their personal power, they still insist. One can only redirect the flow as best one can. The combined efforts of most of the world's tarot readers over the past 30 or more years cannot stop it.

You are tapping into a notion that interests me a lot: art as superstition. It starts with the a-causal idea of the representation of a thing being more 'valuable' than the thing itself: the price of Van Gogh's painting of a chair exceeds what a carpenter makes in a year. But art-as-superstition extends itself through all strata of the art world, to the point when art has become an aesthetically acceptable outlet for our need of transcendence. But art is the only belief system that encourages skepti-

cism. Art criticism is an exercise in which we are asked, once and again, to give into the art experience with one eye shut and the other wide open. It is interesting how the whole Modernist enterprise seemed to have had as one of its premises the secularization of art. So, in art, believing is not about 'surrendering' but about 'engaging'.

I wish that distance between surrendering and engaging could be easier to bridge for most clients. I don't think your experience differs in much to what I have found in a city like New York. Most people don't care about the tarot, some people find it beneath them, some others laugh nervously, and some might argue that it goes against their faith. Where I may not agree with you is in that I think we are in a minority. By 'we' I mean those readers who seek to create a space for empowerment. The idea of giving people inspiration, or strength, to go on with their lives can be seen as one of art's true aims. But that is not what comes to most people's minds when they think of tarot, or when they come for a reading. Most people come to a reading expecting, or even demanding, fortunetelling, because the public image of the tarot is constructed by fortunetellers. They are the majority. I recently had a friend visiting and he was amazed as how, in New York, there are as many psychic parlors as bakeries. Whenever you look, you see fortunetelling being offered as the 'real thing'. How do you defuse that in your work? I will also like to know: what do you think are your responsibilities as a reader? What should people expect from you? What do you expect from yourself?

Yes, I think we as readers can learn quite a bit from the modernist/post-modernist movements in art in terms of 'engaging' our audience. It may be that secularization for reading holds the key. Certainly I have my own spiritual beliefs, but I do not impose them on anyone else, especially in my work. I do wonder if those readers making their beliefs an integral part of their practice aren't contributing to the depth and flow of the myth stream – inadvertently encouraging surrender.

I visited New York City last year and was also struck by the number of psychic parlors in Manhattan. I was even handed a flyer for a 'tarot reader' being passed out on the street. I do wonder if New York isn't unique for that. Certainly here in rural Suffolk, of the dozen or so readers I know of, there is only one 'fortune teller' who works out of a booth on the sea side in Felixstowe. The rest all attempt to engage.

I really like what you say about the idea of giving people inspiration, or strength to go on with their lives being seen as one of art's true aims. I do like to consider myself an artist even within my work as a reader. For me, it often boils down to helping people accept responsibility for their lives. Granted that circumstance can and does intervene in people's lives, but it is still their responsibility how to deal with circumstance. As readers, we have to accept that the myth stream about tarot exists and we have to accept that people will come to us ready to surrender. We do not however have to accept that surrender. We are uniquely placed to give people the inspiration and strength to live the kind of lives they most desire.

I see it as my responsibility to be honest, confidential, and non-judgemental, and everyone who comes to me for a reading can expect that from me. I seek to encourage my clients to think through their options and don't feel I've done my job unless they come away from their reading with things to think about. I seek to create a space where connections between thoughts, words, actions and their consequences can be made. This is why I love my tarot reading tent. I use the myth stream to create the space where people can see their options from an objective perspective in order to make informed choices. They step into the tent thinking they'll hear about what the future holds for them and leave realizing that the future is in their own hands with clear ideas about how to get there. Of course, there will always be those who demand to have their fortunes told, but they remain a small minority, and I keep learning in order to try to reach them too. For me it's all good fun and satisfying work.

In a conversation with Karen Mahony, from Baba Studio, she mentioned she was a fortuneteller. I confess I don't have a problem with that. In fact, I was telling her that the difficulty I have with explaining what I do comes from the fact that I take fortunetelling out of the equation. If you offer to predict futures, your offering becomes extremely clear and understandable, even unique, especially given the expectation people have about tarot. When we take that element out, we end up with a pile of concepts defining all these subprocesses we enact in a reading that are somehow secondary to the telling of fortunesn namely, making people think, giving them attention, encouraging them to take responsibility of their lives. I feel I haven't found good labels to describe what I do in a way that could be as clear, or attractive as 'telling the future'.

Now, in my experience, rather than contradicting a client's expectation about being told her future, one has to utilize that. I mean this in the same sense Milton Erickson utilized whatever worldview his patients brought to a session. One thing that interests me deeply in Erickson's work is the way he did his patients' assessment. He wasn't too interested in defining them as 'depressed' or 'schizophrenic', but he was interested in what that person could actually do. He often spoke of "prescribing the symptom". If the only thing a person could do was to wet his bed, Erickson would prescribe him to wet his bed. As long as you realize that you have control over your bed-wetting, you also understand that it takes the same control to withhold your pee than it takes to release it. This was never overtly stated. It was suggested by the very act of prescribing it. When a person comes to a reading expecting to be told her future, whatever you say is taken as a prediction. I often have clients coming back to tell me "everything happened as you said", when the fact of the matter is that I didn't predict anything! What I did, what I do, is to suggest a certain attitude they might find useful to enact when the time comes and they find themselves facing that conundrum they fear. In other words, what they take as a prediction is my suggestion of them being able to use their own strengths whenever they need it.

What are these things you have learned to reach out to those who only want fortunetelling? I also want to know more about your deck. What made you feel you needed to create your own deck of tarot?

I don't have any problems with fortunetellers either. In another conversation I recently called fortune telling possibly the third oldest profession. Certainly fortune telling has been with us since the very beginnings of civilisation and is likely to be with us forever. It only turns into a problem when it's used as a front for a con. Do let me know if you discover a label as clear or attractive as 'telling the future' for what we do. And thanks for introducing me to Milton Erickson. I'd not previously heard of him so looked him up. What a fascinating character!

Like you, I also have clients come back to say "everything happened as you said" when I didn't actually predict anything. One thing I have learned is that it is pointless to challenge these sorts of statements because they often form the bedrock of the client's world view. Instead, I'll accept the statement and respond with something like, "I'm glad the ideas you got from your reading paid dividends".

Almost everyone who steps into my tarot reading tent is expecting to have their fortune told. I satisfy this expectation by working out the client's birth number and introducing them to their birth card. Following that I ask them to shuffle the cards and think of a question. When they're finished shuffling I ask them to tell me their question and then engage in dialogue. Here's a sample:

Client: Will I move house this year?

Me: Your question begs a question. Do you want to move house this year?

Client: Yes, yes I do.

Me: I want this to be useful for you and if I tell you, 'yes you will' or 'no you won't', there's nothing you can do about it. Would it be more useful if you asked "What can I do to move house this year?"

Client: Yes, I can see that would be more useful.

Then I lay out the cards and together we brainstorm things the client can do to move house. I've yet to discover a strategy that works for the rare client who says, "No, I just want you to tell me if I'm going to move house this year". So I'd appreciate any ideas you might have, Enrique.

I first encountered tarot cards as a child of 10 at my grandparents house. I was visiting and searching through their cupboards looking for playing cards and found a tarot deck – what I later learned was the 1JJ Swiss. The cards fascinated me and I spent a couple of hours looking through them and laying them out discovering patterns. I was especially drawn to the swords because of the pattern of circles they made. Even then I had thoughts of being an artist and thought how cool it would be to make my own deck of cards like that. So at age 10 I conceived the ambition to create my own deck.

I didn't begin studying tarot until my twenties. It was before the internet and there was very little information readily available – one or two books in the local bookstore and nothing in the library. The only deck readily available was the Rider Waite Smith. I had no idea there were lots of tarot decks even then being created. In 2001 I found *Aeclectic Tarot Forum* on the internet and discovered the vast array of tarot decks available and a community of people interested in tarot deck creation. I also rediscovered the Marseille pattern at Aeclectic.

In 2003 Jean-Michel David proposed a 78 week study, that is, to study one card per week in the 78 weeks leading up to the Melbourne International Tarot Conference. I decided this was the perfect opportunity to realise my old ambition. I decided to use the Tarot of Marseille for the study and create my own deck as part of that study. I had already discovered Nancy Garen's book *Creating Your Own Tarot Cards* and had been promoting the idea of creating your own deck as a means of learning tarot. It seemed a natural fit and *Major Tom's Tarot of Marseille* is the result.

When a client puts me on the spot, and wants a definitive answer about the future, I remind him or her of the metaphorical quality of the tarot by answering the question in a metaphorical way. A Japanese man asked me once: "When would be the right time for me to marry?" I told him "when you are done making room". He understood. Even when he was expecting an answer like "next February", he understood what I meant.

But I can tell you of an extreme case in which this girl asked me: "I want to know if I am going to have to work too hard to get that job, because in that case, I won't do it!" I simply told her: "I think you just answered your own question!"

The ritual of a reading is a very well designed, time-tested, procedure. Everything in it is aimed at creating the conditions in which the client will accept whatever the reader says. When you tell a person to mix the cards while thinking of a question, you are at once narrowing down the frame of reference the person will use to contrast any information you will give her (therefore facilitating the mapping of analogies between the cards and her personal experience), you are creating an emotional link between the client and the final arrangement of the cards, and you are linking that emotional connection to that final arrangement. By making the experience meaningful in that way the chances of being wrong that a reader faces are minimal.

Jean-Claude Flornoy talks at length about how, by redrawing the trumps, he came to understanding them in an experiential way. Is that your experience too? What insights have you gained from reflecting on the Marseille Tarot's images by making your own version of it?

Ah yes, the metaphorical answer. Thanks for reminding me. I told the last person wanting a definitive answer about a house move, "You'll move house when you let go of your attachment to your current home". I have had a very few who were dissatisfied with the metaphorical answer. But as you say, the ritual of a reading keeps these instances to a minimum.

I'm not at all surprised Jean-Claude came to understanding the trumps in an experiential way. Both, in my work putting together the *Tarot Lovers' Calendars* and in discussions on the *Aeclectic Tarot Forum* I am in contact with a good number of people involved in drawing/painting/creating tarot decks. Many (but certainly not all) of these people report that the very act of drawing a tarot card can bring the energy of that card into their lives. For some this effect is so strong that they feel anxiety over drawing some cards – such as The Tower, for example – that they seek ways to minimise the effect. Interestingly enough, and this is only based on anecdotal evidence, those who create their decks in no particular order, or in an 'inspired' order seem to have stronger experiences of the cards they are creating. Whereas those who follow an order while creating their decks, for example, starting with the trumps in number order, followed by the aces, twos, threes, etc. still have experiences but don't seem as strongly affected. Similarly, speed of work seems another contributing factor. Those working more slowly, spending days or weeks creating a card feel the effects more strongly while those who produce several cards in a single day might not feel any effects at all. I think it's related to what happens within the ritual of reading. The greater the emotional investment in creating the card, the greater the likelihood of feeling that card in an experiential way.

I created *Major Tom's Tarot of Marseille* in order, starting with the trumps then moving to the batons, cups, coins, and finishing with the swords. I spent one week with each card. Right from the very first card, Le Bateleur, which I renamed The Conjuror, I started understanding the cards in an experiential way. My intent and will became focused. I intended to finish the deck, get it published and travel to Australia for the Melbourne International Tarot Conference. I felt that if I focused my will and intent, these things would come to pass, and so they did. I had similar experiences with all the cards to a greater or lesser degree but for some reason it's my experience with The Conjuror that remains with me most strongly. I suspect that was the card into which I made the strongest emotional investment.

New York / Suffolk, England, 2010

"To be honest, I wish there were fewer readers."

A conversation with TONY EYE, psychic entertainer, palm reader, tarot reader, mind reader

Would you say that a fake tarot reader can be as effective as a 'real' one?

When I first read this question, my impulse was to say "NO". But as I thought about it, I began to consider two key terms in the sentence, "fake tarot reader" and "effective", and depending upon how these terms are defined, the answer can be different. I've come up with several different types of "fake tarot readers".

The first type is what I call "script readers". These are those how have learned a small group of scripted statements, such as the "Barnum statements", "one size fits all" statements that can apply to anyone in some manner or another. These lines are recited regardless of the cards that are drawn. The cards are there as a visual prop.

The second type is what I call "key worders". These are the people who have learned a key word or two for each card, and recite these words to describe the sitter and or her situation. Advanced "key worders" move beyond mentioning just the meaning of each lone card and combine the key words of the cards together to form some sort of story or theme. This can also be described as the beginning stage of becoming a "tarot reader". They have started to build a basic vocabulary of the tarot.

The third type of "fake tarot reader" is a true reader, (intuitive and psychological are two examples), a counselor who reads the person (or something else) and uses the tarot as a visual prop either as eye candy for the sitter, as a way of drawing the focus off themselves to fit the elements of an event, or some other reason or combinations of reasons.

As for what constitutes a "real tarot reader", for this question I'll define him or her as a reader and or counselor with understanding of the tarot beyond a basic keyword (knowledge of the symbols, colors, various meanings, and interactive affects of the cards in conjunction with one another) and for whom this constitutes "a core element" of the readings given.

I'm sure I could break out this even further, but for the sake of brevity and clarity, I'll stick with the above mentioned categories.

Effectiveness would depend on the purpose of the reading. For simplicity's sake, I'll define 3 categories, "personal gratification readings", "entertainment readings", and "personal readings". The "personal gratification" or "ego" readings are quick statements/readings given by performers to build themselves up in the eyes of the public, as they do not really constitute readings in my mind. "Effectiveness" is measured in the amazement or "wow factor" of the person being spoken to and those who witness the "stunt". This is an area where the script readers shine. These are very quick, lasting less than 3 minutes (usually averaging much less) and the sitter is bombarded with statements. No real insight or counseling takes place, it is not about the client but about the person making the statements. These are usually a "one off" reading and not repeated. This is ideal for the "script reader". "Key worders" can be moderately successful as they have a limited vocabulary, and if are quick on their feet, they can construct a few quick statements using the key words of the cards selected. Readers will be least effective in this format as their interest is in that of the person being read for, and the format does not allow for a connection to be made, nor does the time criteria allow for meaningful conversation to take place.

"Entertainment readings" are readings usually lasting between 3 and 7 minutes. These reading usually consist of "telling the sitter about herself", answering a single question or doing a short forecast of the sitter's life anywhere from a week to a year, or a combination of the previous mentioned elements. These readings are "light" and "upbeat" and are meant to be taken as entertainment, although many do come into them with serious concerns they are looking for guidance on. Attendees to these functions also compare readings, and often times overhear each other's readings.

In this type of function, the "script readers" will fail. As they have a limited amount of "lines", they will end up repeating the same key things to most all the sitters, and they do not provide anything meaningful to the sitter. Very quickly they will be identified for what they are, and any and all interest in them will be lost. I've witnessed several trying to work this type of venue. Not one has been rehired, and most do not complete the event.

"Key worders" can be effective in this type of venue, especially if the "reader" is personable and or entertaining. Knowing keywords for each card allows for differing readings for each sitter, eliminating the issues that the "script readers" have. Moreover, the limited knowledge fits well within the short time period and limited scope inherent in "entertainment readings". This is based on the assumption that the "reader" is well rehearsed and does more than just list the keywords. I've witnessed several in this category working in this type of venue. Most do not get rehired (several have been fired during the event). There are also complaints from the sitters and other readers that they do not provide meaningful answers, and that some provide incoherent nonsense. In order for this type to succeed, he must learn to apply his limited knowledge to the client.

"Readers" will range in effectiveness from moderately effective to highly effective, based on their experience in this type of venue. Many readers are used to longer time periods, and limiting/condensing what they say and do to such a short period of time is not something all can adapt to. Those who can, provide meaningful advice and insight that the others cannot.

"Personal readings": these are private or semi-private readings where the focus is on questions or concerns of the sitter. The time period can range from 10 minutes to as long as it takes. The effectiveness of anyone other than a skilled counselor ranges from nonexistent to negative (and dangerous).

In short, the effectiveness of a reading given by a "fake reader" varies inversely to the length of time and the involvement of the client, and the effectiveness of a reader/counselor varies directly with these variables.

What are your thoughts about those who suggest working with an incomplete deck, a deck of tarots in which 'harsh' cards like Death, The Hanged Man, or The Devil have been eliminated? In which category would you place them?

As you know, I've been involved in a debate on this topic over the past week on an "Entertainer's" forum. Key points that I made and stand by are as follows:

I feel removing cards from the deck is a personal decision based on the venue, the guests, the deck being used, and the experience and personal preference of the reader.

My preference is to use a complete deck for my readings. If someone chooses not to, that is his/her choice. Although I don't remove cards, I do sometimes move to a different deck (based upon the venue). There are a lot of decks out there, and many have different names for the cards. In some the Death card is call Reincarnation, Rebirth, Change, Transformation, and the imagery reflects the different title.

The deck I use for colleges (Rohrig) is a modern deck and does depict a bit of nudity. That particular deck would not be the best choice for the Rotary Club. There is a different deck that I use for high tech groups, the imagery is more relatable. Different decks can have 'themes' that fit certain groups better than others. I understand why some do remove cards, and I do not feel this has anything to do with whether behind the reading is a "real" reader or not. As professionals, the welfare and care of the client is more important than our own egos. And if the reader feels this necessitates removing cards, or finding a deck that is a closer fit to where he/she will be reading, I also feel that this is what should be done. "Know your audience" was the first rule of speaking that I've learned, back in a former life. I find that it holds true for most everything. The other rule is "know thyself."

As to whether or not removing cards applies more to the "fakes" than the "real" readers, I'm not sure. What I do know is that some fakes advocate removing certain cards from the deck permanently. To me this indicates a lack of understanding of the cards, a lack of confidence in their own abilities, and a lack of trust in the intellect and understanding of the clients. But I also know several well informed and educated readers who advise removing certain cards from their decks when doing public entertainment readings (upbeat quick readings in an open setting) and tableside readings. As I said earlier, I do understand the reasoning behind it, but I feel that in this day and age, given the huge selection of decks to choose from, one can find a deck that fits a certain type of venue and client. Moreover, having the right tool (deck) is better than bastardizing the tool we have and trying to make it fit.

I am very interested in what I call "the experience of tarot". That is what I "sell". These days, I keep repeating that what we get from a tarot reading depends on what we expect from images in general and from the tarot's images in particular.

But if I were to remove some cards from the deck, the experience of tarot would be incomplete.

Now, Tony, I work under the premise that a tarot reading is an illusion. It may not imply deception from the part of the reader, but it is still an illusion based in our ability to detect familiar patterns in any kind from the input we receive. In a sense, it is a self working illusion.

I would like to share with you a quote from the Jesuit scholar Baltasar Gracian, who in 1647 wrote:

> KEEP MATTERS FOR A TIME IN SUSPENSE. Admiration at their novelty heightens the value of your achievements. It is both useless and insipid to play with your cards on the table. If you do not declare yourself immediately, you arouse expectation, especially when the importance of your position makes you the object of general attention. Mix a little mystery with everything, and the very mystery arouses veneration. And when you explain, do not be too explicit, just as you do not expose your inmost thoughts in ordinary conversation. Cautious silence is the sacred sanctuary of wordily wisdom. A resolution declared is never highly thought of – it only leaves room for criticism. And if it happens to fail, you are doubly unfortunate. Besides, you imitate the divine way when you inspire people to wonder and watch.

In Gracian's view prudence seems to inhabit the threshold between what we disclose and what we withhold. As a reader, where would you place that boundary? To what extent should a reader who understands the cognitive illusions at play in a reading conceal the true nature of what he is doing, to what extent should he reveal it?

My mind works, perhaps, differently than most. When I see, hear, read, or experience something, some part of my mind looks for patterns, relationships, and connections with other things or experiences. This is not a conscious process and I'm not sure that it ever was (something I'll discuss in just a bit). For example, when I saw the quote you provided, William Shakespeare and his play, *As You Like It*, popped into mind. My favorite quote from this play begins with "All the world is a stage". What follows, the "Seven Stages of Man", forms what I consider to be the precursor of the modern "Cradle to Grave" reading (relating back to your first question on "fake readers". (*As You Like It*, Act II, Scene VII, lines 139-166). Shakespeare's play was written in about about 1600 and was published in 1623, 24 years before the quote you cited. In my thinking, this would have been known by Gracian and may have influenced him. His comments on the handling of the cards and not revealing everything in order to keep the mystery, this to me speaks of "theater". One of the ways I relate to reading comes from reading.

As children we learn to read by first learning the letters, the sounds they make and their associations with each other. After we learn the "meanings" of the "symbols" we learn how to combine them to symbolize the names of actions, objects, concepts, and ideas. We call these words. We learn these words by sounding out each of the letters in the word to create a group of sounds that represents the words. Later we learn punctuation, which provides pauses, emphases, and clarification on the group of words that helps define the intent. We consciously direct our eyes from left to right, from the top of the page to down, focusing on each mark on the page. By using the rules that we've learned, we translate these into sounds that provide meaning.

Very quickly the rules become ingrained in our minds, and we no longer consciously apply them. We see a page of a text and look at it, and see groups of letters (symbols) as patterns we recognize (words) representing other symbols. Eventually we get to the point where reading becomes a completely unconscious act. We see the text and look at it, and ideas, concepts, and images pop up and play out in our heads. A right-brained, conscious activity has become an unconscious activity feeding the visual and creative left brain.

We see scenes play out, we may picture ourselves in them, our minds may jump to situations or experiences we have and relate them to what we are reading. We may question what we are reading and try to fit it into context, analyze it, question what has happened prior to this, project where this is leading, perhaps to a combination of right and left brain activities that occur simultaneously, sparked by the cryptic little symbols on the page. These symbols provide a gateway into what the author "may" be trying to tell, but also into ourselves, our experiences, and a universe of other things and concepts.

If asked to explain what we read, the right-brain kicks in again, reviews what the mind had seen, heard, and experienced, and it performs an edit so we can relate what we perceive to be of interest to the other party and summarize the experience in what we believe fits the context of the reason for the explanation. These explanations will be colored by our own bias based on what we believe is being asked, and what we understand at the time of what we are experiencing. There is, of course, the possibility that we are not getting the true meaning of what we are reading. This occurs in reading a text as well as oracles or anything else. But as we grow (as in reading text) through practical experience and continued work, our vocabulary grows, and we learn to subconsciously absorb what is contextual to the situation. We then relate an abbreviated version of that to the sitter.

So, as Gracian states, that we should not say everything that we 'see' and apply it to a conscious action, I also believe that this is already being done in a subconscious manner. What pops into my mind is what I feel are applicable concepts for the reading. I do hold back on what I experience at times, depending on the state of the sitter and what I have to say. There is still a bit of editing I consciously do (whether the readings are better of worse for this, I cannot say), but I am working on trying to get this process remain an unconscious activity.

The theatricality or illusion of the reading is essential for the acceptance of the reading. Walk into a doctor's office. You will see diplomas on the wall, the tools of the trade, the doctor himself, and how he/she is dressed, handles himself/herself. Then note how the doctor makes his/her entrance. Consider the waiting to see the doctor, the questions asked, the responses, how the doctor reacts and acts. Everything about the experience either adds to acceptance of this person as an authority and acceptance of what is said, or not. It is theater. The same holds true for most all professions.

People draw opinions and assumptions of one another almost instantly upon meeting. How we dress, our speech, our actions, mannerisms, how we greet each other, our smell, facial expressions, the setting, and many other things are processed and form the basis for these opinions. As professionals, if we are to be taken as we wish to, we must consider all of these things that express our persona. Mixed messages create confusion, and confusion creates doubt. Our dress, appearance, speech, attitude, rituals, and tools must all be consistent with what we are trying to portray. Otherwise, the "illusion" is broken. As tarot readers, the main items for producing theatricality are ourselves and our tools. Gracian spoke of both in your quote. The holding back of information and the handling of the cards are two of his points. The question we should ask ourselves is, are they consistent with who I present myself as?

For your final question: "To what extent should a reader who understands the cognitive illusions at play in a reading conceal the true nature of what he is doing; to what extent should he reveal it?" In my opinion, revealing the process, or what one recognizes of the process, should be done if and only if it helps in relating or understanding the information being provided and if it aids in the theatricality of the situation. There is an exception though, namely, when the sitter reacts in a way that requires explaining *the* or a mundane rationale for obtaining the information or guidance provided and which aids in their well being. For a reader, the sitter is more importance than anything else, and their well being overrides the theatricality of the reading or our own egos.

I don't remember who said that getting people into poetry was a good thing, because for every person turned into a poet there is one less idiot in the world. Would you say the same thing applies to readers? Can people improve themselves by becoming readers, and by extension improve reality?

Absolutely not, but I'll get back to this shortly. About 10 years ago, I had a conversation with Bob Neale and the topic of pastoral counseling came up. (Dr. Neale is a retired Professor of psychology from Union Theological Seminary, and one of the preeminent authors in the field of pastoral psychology.) His words on the topic were, "It scares the Hell out of me." We were discussing counseling done by ministers, highly educated people who have devoted their lives to helping others, people who had at least some training in counseling, and a support network. These people are doing God's work, they are authority figures, and their word is accepted by many without question. The thing is, though, that there are many areas in which they are not qualified to give advice. Let's just say that some are not aware of their limitations, and some coming for guidance are unaware of these limitations, as they belive that the minister is a conduit for God. Areas that should not be discussed, and which, instead, should be referred to the appropriate agency, are discussed, mishandled, and things become worse for all involved. "The road to Hell is paved with good intentions."

As with all of my conversations with Bob, this one made me think. If there are concerns about counseling provided by people who have gone through a system of education, assessment, a vetting process (weeding out of people who are not committed, and those who discontinue the process or do not succeed academically), people who have a full support network and have received at least some training (although the amount of training and continuing education is an issue), then what about the regular 'reader'?

Who is a reader? The fact is, anyone can call himself/herself a reader. There is no regulation and or required training. I've known some people who woke up one day and said they were readers, and who then began calling themselves a reader and working as one, giving readings, guidance, and advice. Some of these people may read a book or several, or buy a deck of tarot cards. Some may attend a workshop or see a video; some may come from a tradition (family tradition, cultural tradition, or religious tradition). What level of training in counseling do these people have? What are their qualifications? Why are they in this field? Thinking about this and what effects some may have on clients is scary!

To be honest, I wish there were fewer readers. I've been involved with reading for most of my life and have met and known hundreds of 'readers'. Some are fantastic, others not so good. Some are well trained and continue their education. Some are amazingly natural counselors and stay within their boundaries. Some recognize issues that are outside their purview, and as a consequence they refer the client to soemone else. Some feel that something outside of them speaks through them and provides answers and there are no real boundaries. Some were less honest, but I won't go into that here. One can look at this and say, "I perform readings for entertainment, and say that on my card and when I meet the client." In the mind of someone looking for guidance, one who comes to a reader for advice, such a disclosure may not even register. As a matter of fact, even when reading at an entertainment venue, people come to you with issues even though you are there for "entertainment" only.

A few years ago I was reading at a post-graduation event at a high school. There were 4 of us there doing entertainment reading for the graduates. About an hour into the event, a young lady came to my area and asked me if I could speak with the dead. She then said that her father had passed away the week before, and there were tears in her eyes. This poor girl was at her graduation party. She had suffered a loss. When she saw 'psychics' at the event she came looking for something, something we were not there to give. I pushed my cards out of the way, turned off the clock, and we just sat and talked for a while. My only focus was her; she stayed until she said she was OK. After she left I found the woman running the event and asked her to keep an eye on this girl. I thank God that she came to me that night, as I have no idea what would have happened if she had seen one of the other psychics.

I've had other experiences like the one above, and I've witnessed the aftermath of bad advice and ego related guidance. (You never hear of situations that are handled correctly, just the ones that are not.) As Harry Callahan said in *Magnum Force*: "A man's got to know his limitations."

Getting back to the original question: When a poet explores one's own feelings and experiences and creates an artistic and thought-provoking narrative that others may read, and then consider art. The reader, in contrast, is taken as an authority figure. Many who go for readings are seeking advice and guidance for a situation, and take what is said in a reading as such. There is a world of difference.

I am very attracted to some of the things you are saying, because I suspect that tarot readings are, by their very nature, very close to homilies. You and I know that most readers base their learning on getting acquainted with the 'craft' of the reading, that is, the whole conjunct of processes and techniques that happen when you are in relationship with a client. There is an important amount of comprehensible stress that comes with dealing with an actual person in real time. Learning about the tool of choice is just a part of that. I agree in that becoming proficient at this kind of communication is very important. Even so, given that the tarot has an almost unique visual quality, I have founded my practice on understanding how images work, what can we expect from them, and how can they be used to affect a person. A departure point, for me, has been to understand the tarot's history: when these cards created, with what purpose, how they were understood, etc. Until very recently, the most sober approach to the meaning of the tarot I had seen came from Michael Hurst. I won't go into its details here, but let me say that the recent publication of both Francesco Piscina and Anonymous discourses on the tarot, both written nearly a hundred years after the tarot's invention, both written when the tarot was still being used for gaming, seem to confirm Hurst's thesis of the tarot being a visual sermon – Michael won't necessarily say it like that – about the need to live a virtuous life, in contempt for worldly matters. The 'text' we read through this hierarchy of images is consistent with a Western world-view which is pretty much informed by Christian stoicism. 'Virtue', we are told, is our best bet at trumping Death.

Given that in today's world the tarot as a political space has been taken by feminism and paganism, the thesis I just summarized generates lots of antipathy. Still, it give us a very useful way to understand what to expect from these images. There is a technical reason why I cannot expect the tarot to predict my future: images don't work like that. But there is a very specific form of advise I can expect from these images, as they illustrate notions that are fundamental to acknowledge if we want to live a beautiful life: the immanence of Death, the inconstancy of Fortune, the need for fairness, the importance of courage, the reassurance of moderation... By reading these images we are given the possibility to re-create ourselves by re-membering these things we are entitled to aspire to. It does sound like a homily, doesn't it? I have found that facing the tarot in this way helps us operate a 'mise-en-perspective' for any concern a client may bring.

Last week I saw this girl who kept asking if she could 'get' help from this or that person. She asked the same question about eight or ten people. Soon enough it became evident that she had wronged all these persons in one way or another. A basic theme emerged: "make amends". When I told her so, she acknowledged she had wronged all of them, yet she was hoping to profit from them without having to acknowledge what she had done. I think this is a great example of what 'giving perspective' means, and also a great example of the kind of work that is reasonable, feasible, and ethically safe to do with tarot. I can't tell her what this or that person is thinking about her. I can't tell her what to say to each one of these persons, or what to do to them. But I can help her understand there is an underlying pattern there, and within that perspective suggest that she won't go far by turning wrongdoing into her policy. Still, dealing with people in this way isn't always easy. Most clients don't come to a tarot reading to be reasonable, but to get something beyond what is reasonable.

Just as with this girl, you and I can put together an encyclopedia of cases in which what the person expected to hear and what the person needed to hear weren't the same thing. Do you remember any specific instance when you understood that there was an underlying pattern that was more important than the specific concern the person brought to the table?

I really enjoy reading your thoughts. They are so full of information and insight, and inspire me to think deeper into what I do and how I think.

'Homilies' is the faintest word to use. Prior to Waite's restructuring of the tarot to conform to his "magical" tradition, the tarot had moved to a "Christian friendly" oracle. (The wealthy were the only ones with means to commission or purchase hand painted decks of tarot, and the "wealthy" in Europe consisted of the Church, Royalty, and merchants. All (at least publicly) followed the ideals of the Church. So, the cards, at least overtly, express Christian values and lessons as well as Christian iconography.

Waite, who I consider a librarian because his work is essentially a systematic representation of the work of others, commissioned Pamela Coleman Smith to redraw the tarot. How much influence he had over her work is not known to me, but the new cards had not only added images to the minor arcana (making them easier to interpret) but also reversed numerically two cards in the major arcana. These were their main contributions to the tarot, at least the publicly acknowledged contributions (in addition to Waite's, *Key to the Tarot,* a systematic collection of meanings for each card). The not so public contribution was in the imagery of the cards themselves. Embedded amongst the Christian iconography and motifs were the iconography and motifs of the Golden Dawn magic system (both Smith and Waite were members of the Golden Dawn). There is also a bit of Freemason iconography in the cards. Waite was a Freemason at the time, but some of that iconography had been absorbed by the Golden Dawn, so it is difficult to tell whether that was came from Waite or Smith. But what this added to the traditional tarot cards was an additional set of vocabulary for the meanings of the cards.

Sorry for this digression, but your words on history got me thinking. I agree with you in your thoughts of studying writings over 100 years old, in this case here, mostly written after 1910 (with a few notable exceptions) and which are mostly based on Smith and Waite's work and classification.

A few weeks ago while reading at a graduation event, a young lady came in for a reading. I don't recall the entire spread, but two of the cards stand out in my mind because of what happened, the 7 of Wands and the 4 of Wands. The 7 in my deck depicts a scene with two opposing cliffs with a chasm between. There is a figure, covered in light, leaping from one cliff to the other. This card is entitled Victory. The 4 shows a large glossing spree hovering above the land, and in the background one can make out the two cliffs. This card is labeled Completion. Together they create the simple message that there are obstacles in the way but you have the ability to overcome them, leap over them and reach completion. The cards are Wands and deal with knowledge. The young lady listened to the reading and was drawn to the two wand cards. She asked a question about the color. It turns out that she had applied to a school and had not been accepted. She enrolled in another with hopes to reapply to the one that had not accepted her after she had proven herself. The color in the two wand cards was the color of the school she wanted to attend. She took the message as working hard to overcome her academic obstacles and prove herself to the school and the completion as being accepted by the "choice" school. Although that is not how I read the Completion card (I see it as hovering over that obstacle and many others), she took it as explaining her "current" concern. To me this brings home two points, that sometimes we are drawn to a specific element and not necessarily the entire metaphor, and that we see what we want to, or expect to see in the cards.

As for your question, the most significant part, I can tell you about an event that took place about 10 years ago. I was reading for a woman who was in her early 50s. She came to me and was very upset. She told me that she wanted to know if she would see her grandchild again, who had been kidnapped. She sat down and we began to talk. It turned out that her adult son had fathered a child with a teenage girl. The girl moved in with her and her son for a short time period and the child was born. The girl and her child then moved back to her parents, who then relocated the whole family. There were so many things wrong with this situation (one of which was that I was at a college hired to perform entertainment readings for the students; this woman was part of the kitchen staff, and there was nothing entertaining about her story). Plus I was limited by time, but here I was with this troubled person.

It was more than evident that she saw this as a crime against her. She did not see that the underage mother and child living with her family was a legal and natural thing, nor did she see that her son was in the wrong and was lucky not to be in jail. All she saw was that HER grandchild had been taken away from her. I thought to offer her the alternative view that a mother and child (just like her and her son) are a sacred union that should not be broken unless there are serious issues. And that the girl and her child should remain together, and that the girl and her mother had the same type of bond. She did not really accept this and kept going on about how she was wronged. My advice to her was to seek out professional council on this (yet she took it as legal council).

Personally, I hope that the girl's new situation provides healthy support for her and her child, and that she got the opportunity to go back to school and complete her education. I credit her parents with removing her and the baby from the situation they were in.

In this situation, I did not use the cards, but if I had, the woman would have taken whatever they were – as she did my suggestions – into her own context to re-enforce her delusional view of her situation.

After she left I spread the top 5 cards. I don't recall all of them, but the first card was the Moon, and the last card was the Devil. I'm not sure if those cards were meant for me or the woman who had just left, but they did fit the situation. The Moon indicating that things are not as they seem, and ending in the Devil, being pulled in several different directions, a great trial, test, and deception. And just as her situation fit those cards, so did the situation she brought to me at my table.

As to your question, this woman clearly wanted to hear that "she would get her grandchild back in her home". What she needed to hear was that she was not seeing the situation correctly, but that was something she could not accept. Instead, she took the advice to get help as re-enforcement of her situation. As the cards showed, illusion and deception (especially self deception) are hard to overcome, and maybe that is why they are part of the Major Arcana series.

Your story reminded me of the time I saw an old lady, who wanted to know if she could make a business from being a foster mom. She had renovated her house to host as many kids as possible, and she wanted to know if Child Services would find everything right. I remember the first card she got was The Devil. I still think the woman was, herself, a depiction of the devil.

I have a final question for you: after being a reader for more than two decades, in which way would you say the tarot has changed you?

First, let me thank you for a fun and thought-provoking experience. I really love the way you think and your questions, which, like the tarot, seem rather simple at first glance but contain layers and layers of subtext and meaning when examined. This has been a wonderful experience and has had me examining myself and what I do in ways I could not have thought of, and your own insights are leading me off in new directions. For this, I thank you.

Your other question is much more difficult to answer, "how has tarot changed me?" I've gone back and forth on this question, and it is one that I cannot answer.

I received my first tarot deck in 1972, but by that time I had already been exposed to and working with dreams, images, colors, and numbers (as well as a deck my grandmother had that was similar to tarot). So, tarot has been part of my life for close to 40 years, and the elements that go into doing tarot go even further back. I don't feel the cards have changed me; they are part of me and essentially always have been.

What I can say is that being a reader and counselor has allowed me to meet many people, which has enriched my life. I've also made some great friendships: Richard Webster has been an idol of mine for many years. I love his writing style and he is just so brilliant. He is also very kind and a good friend. Jon Saint Germaine he has become a friend over the past few years and I credit him with giving me permission to come out of the 'reader's closet. Another influence on me from the 90s is Ron Martin. It was because I'm a reader that I met my brother from another mother, now also my friend, bouncing board, and inspiration, Scott Grossberg. It was Tarot that brought me to Susan Deren, a very gifted medium and animal communicator (soon to have a program on the *Animal Planet*); she is the one who got me out doing public readings and teaching Tarot. It was readings that led me to my friend, the gifted reader and eloquent writer, Dean Montalbano. And it was reading that connected the two of us. You too inspire me and get me to look at things in a new light. These are just a few of the wonderful friendships and relationships that being a reader has made possible.

New York / Boston, July 2010

"We like to work with warm, emotive images, not cool ones."

A conversation with KAREN MAHONY, designer, writer, publisher

I think it is safe to say that you and Alex Ukolov are the most interesting publishers of contemporary tarots in today's tarot world, so, my question is: Why? What got you started? What did you feel the tarot was missing?

Oh, I was somehow expecting a much more oblique first question – but down-to-earth is good too.

I don't think we are the most interesting publishers of contemporary tarot today. I think others are more interesting than us and are changing tarot more. However, I don't think "interesting" is necessarily all good. I have a feeling I shouldn't say any more. So, what got us started? Meeting one another. Alex was literally revealed to me from behind a curtain by a friend who is a living manifestation of the Magician. After that everything changed, and all the creative work that I wanted to do but had previously supressed as either "impossible" or "not proper" or even "not cool" started to happen.

What did we feel tarot was missing? A Tarot of Prague. Quite simply, we were amazed that no-one had made a tarot based on this incredible city and we decided that we should do it because we were arrogant enough to think we'd do it right, and someone else might do it wrong. We didn't think beyond that one deck and never planned to do more.

I have a 'stranger' question for you. What is the time-frame of a tarot image? I tend to suspect that the images in the tarot exist in some sort of eternal present state, in opposition to a photograph, for example, which always show us an event from the past, but I wonder what your thoughts on this are.

I don't think an image becomes timeless – or acquires some unusual relationship to time – just because it's on a tarot card. Many tarot decks are very much of their time and reflect the obsessions, ideas or fashions of the culture around them. In a reading, sure, any card can speak of things happening now – or in the past or the future. But does that mean that the image "exist[s] in some sort of eternal present state"? Not in my experience. The images on tarots show when they were made – they carry their provenance in their style, content and technique. They may become a powerful and lasting historical record (like, for example, a Goya or a Picasso image). But far more often they will lose much of their relevance and reference and become outdated, quaint or simply faded and nostalgic – as do most images. I think, though, that you may be asking something that's intended to be taken in a more arcane way. If so, please elaborate.

Actually, I was talking about the experience of an image, from the point of view of how artwork exists in a qualitative time, different from the quantitative time we exist in. We cannot say of an image: "this drawing is two minutes quicker than my previous drawing". Something happened to me last week, as I was doing a reading for a woman whose mother-in-law has alzheimer. She wanted to know what to do about it, and from all cards she could get, she got the Queen of Coins, which in the Dodal shows a woman holding a coin up to her face. I told her that alzheimer turns us into mirrors. When you look at yourself in a mirror you don't see the person you were a minute ago, nor an hour ago, nor a decade ago. Facing the mirror you can only speak to, or about, that person who is right there, 'now' in front of you. It would be absurd to describe yourself by recalling memories of who you were five years ago. So, that connection you create with an alzheimer patient, the 'now', is all you got, just as that person in front of the mirror, now, is all you got.

But you brought up something important: style as a way to measure time. I agree with you that some tarot images look as if you were looking at yourself in the mirror today, while wearing your prom dress. Style, or an excessive attachment to any aesthetic, could limit the life of an image. Thanks for that!

How do you fight that? What strategies do you follow in your work to make your images as timeless as possible? Is that a concern of yours?

Yes, I thought that that's probably what you meant. Though I also wondered you might be asking in some more metaphysical sense that I hadn't understood. So why then would a tarot card picture be any more timeless than any other image? You can look at a painting and also see yourself in it – people look at films and see themselves or situations they recognize. This applies to many images whether or not they're on cards. I don't see why any of this is exclusive to tarot cards. So I'll send the question back to you. Why should an image on a tarot card be any more timeless than any other image? Qualitatively or otherwise? Is the answer because you use it for divination? But many things are used for divination. Is an icon or a statue of a saint more timeless than another image? It's also used to speak to the divine. But we look at a Baroque image of a saint and we see "Baroque" as well as the saint. We can use the statue to envisage the saint as we pray – but the image in and of itself is dated. To talk in semiotic terms (which can be useful I think) the signified may arguably be timeless, but the signifier is not.

No, the timelessness of images does not concern me. Alex may feel differently. Mostly we work to produce an image that is the best we can do. Here and now. We want to work in our own style of course, not in the style of what's currently fashionable. But we are locked in time as everyone is. In the future I've no doubt our images will look very "period" and "Noughties". Of course, like all things, the "Noughties" will come back into fashion. That's inescapable. So I realize I now have another question for you. Why do you want tarot card images to be exceptionally timeless? What would be the benefit of that? I believe very much in what John Berger taught – that you can only ever see and interpret an image within the experience of the see-er – images do not exist outside time, context, and the way in which they're seen by each individual. Any idea that they do is illusory.

I wasn't implying that tarot images are somehow different than any other images. Sorry if I somehow mislead you to think I did. I like your example of the saint. It is curious because I feel that a saint isn't dated, but timeless. It may have to do with how hard it is to represent contemporary clothing and artifacts in traditional sculpting media, like bronze or marble. It usually feels weird. But I would guess that an aesthetic becomes timeless when it adds something to the ongoing art discourse, so it becomes a signpost in the history of visual representation. Yesterday I went to see an exhibition of late Monet paintings. These were mainly paintings of ponds showing reflections of the sky. What made these paintings look 'old' wasn't the technique or the style, but the golden frames they had. Isn't that interesting? The paintings themselves looked fresh, even when they were actually old. It was exciting to see how many of these Monets were pushing the boundaries of painting by the time they were created. Painting a little pond today in the same way wouldn't be as exciting.

I am not sure the experience of a tarot reading would benefit from images that are timeless. It is interesting you are making me think of that. I think the world becomes less interesting when we pollute it with irrelevant images. By extension, any experience centered around bland images would be less rewarding, to me at least. I used to think you can't make any kind of artistic production while thinking: "this has to be timeless. This has to be relevant". You can only be honest about what you do. Lately I haven't been so sure about the first half of this statement. It is very hard to think now in terms of new styles. All aesthetics are communicational strategies: if you want to appeal to a certain audience, you work with a hip-hop aesthetic. If you want to appeal to another audience, you work with a minimalistic aesthetic, and so on. So, you have to be honest about why you do what you do, but you cannot be naive in terms of what you are communicating in aesthetic terms.

A couple of years ago someone showed me a deck you had just published. I can't remember the name. This person was complaining about how dark – as in, very black – the images where. The person wondered if it was a printing error. I thought that the blackness made the images perfect. That darkness made the images challenging. The whole episode reminded me of some people's reactions to Clint Eastwood's The Unforgiven, *which is also a very black movie. Such darkness made some people mad, since they felt that they went to watch a movie in which most of the time you couldn't distinguish anything. I though that that was a 'good darkness', since it kept you alert, just as these images you printed do.*

So – I actually didn't mean that the saints were dated. I meant that all images of saints are dated one way or another. But in fact, you're right, the saints themselves ARE dated. I think about Saint Wilgefortis – who I first saw depicted in the Loreta Chapel here. In its time, her story was seemingly a tragic one. But to us nowadays, it's hard not to find it tragi-comic – and to relate it to feminist commentaries about why women are expected to be devoid of body hair, and to be very alienated by the whole tale. Her miracle – growing a beard overnight to avoid marriage to a muslim – would be impossible now. She would simply be given depilatory cream and told to get down the altar. Or she would have already run away and would now be in sessions with a therapist to come to terms with her despotic parents. I visit her statue occasionally, but it's mostly for the sheer bizarre spectacle, I'm afraid, and not out of piety. Yes, saints and martyrs also date.

So – back to readings. I find that readings are totally anchored in time. When I read I'm very aware that given a particular spread I might interpret it differently yesterday or tomorrow. But that doesn't matter, because the reading is happening today. Today it's the right reading.

The deck you're talking about is the *Bohemian Gothic Tarot*[1], and yes, it's printed very dark. That was Alex's decision more than mine, but I supported it. There was a lot of protest about this when it came out – although the deck was wildly popular so in the end it didn't affect anything, it was still bought and used. But you're right, people wanted to be able to see everything in the image easily and immediately, and they couldn't. Alex would have more to say about this, but I'll just ask – if you read a story by Edgar Allen Poe do you "see" it all, right away? I had to read some of his stories two or three times to see the connections and connotations.

We're reprinting a new version of the *Bohemian Gothic* this summer and it will be less dark. I'll be interested to see what reaction there is to that. My guess is that some of the same people who complained about the first cards being dark will now have become accustomed to that and will dislike the lighter images. It reminds me of the way in which ancient buildings that have been cleaned often offend people – once they are used to seeing the building black with grime and dirt they come to prefer it that way.

The problem is that we aren't used to giving too much time to an image anymore. In that regard, tarot cards may be a privileged format, since tarots are images we experience first hand, in close quarters, over and over again. How do you feel about that? You seem to put lots of detail, and effort, in the image you make. Do you think it is 'safer' to put all these details in tarot cards than in any other kind of illustration? How challenging do you want your images to be?

Yes, it's true that tarot images are looked at and *used* in a very different way from most images. For the person who makes those images, this is both demanding and very satisfying. Effort? Well, anyone who makes images to be used by others should put lots of effort in, shouldn't they? We like decoration and detail and it's very much our studio style – so yes, we put a tremendous amount of time into each image we make. But safer? I don't understand that. Please can you explain what you mean by that question? Do you mean that it's safer because in another

---

[1] http://www.bohemiangothic.com

type of image the viewer might not look properly? Why would an inattentive viewer be a danger to us? I think I'm missing part of your meaning here.

As for how challenging we want our images to be, well, that's hard to answer exactly as we don't think of it that way, so I'll answer another way. We make the images as good as they can be in our own judgement. We made the decision years ago not to work for clients (my background is in corporate design consulting and I've worked with just about all the UK "Blue Chips", and much as I loved some of my clients, client work has restrictions that I wanted to get away from). We also decided not to accept publishing offers for the decks – we've had offers from the "biggies" and felt we had to say no – again, because there would then be restrictions and we would lose editorial control. So we've ensured that we're in a position where we can do whatever we feel is right for an image, without having to listen to anyone telling us to make it cuter or more commercial or less complex or whatever. That gives our decks a certain flavour I think – the style and content is very uncompromisingly "Baba". Some people are turned off by the way that our decks have such a strong voice, others love it.

I believe it was Ernst H. Gombrich who said that art is a game with only one rule: as long as you think you can do better you must do it again. Even if it means you have to start over. But I wonder if reprinting the deck would really make it better. I like the idea of an image that doesn't show itself all at once.

If there is something I respect is the ability a person may have to design herself a beautiful life. What you describe about what you do, and how, feels very close to that. I also wanted to mention arrogance, picking up on something you referred to at the beginning of our conversation, in regards of doing your first deck because you were arrogant enough to think you could do it. I think that kind of arrogance, that feeling of the world being incomplete without that drawing, that poem, that deck of cards you want to make, is the basis for all artistic production. I often find that such arrogance is the primary response as to why I do readings.

I guess I am trying to get a sense of how you feel about images, and a sense of 'why' the tarot. By 'safe' I mean precisely what you intuited: the odds of someone actually paying attention to the details you put into an image are higher if your image is a tarot card than if your image is a billboard, or a magazine ad. This may sound odd but, at some point I found out that, when I did a drawing, certain details of it would get anchored to the thoughts or events I was experiencing while I was making it; so by looking at that section of the drawing, these memories would be elicited again, as in a pure act of anamnesis. This is, of course, a private event. Only I can experience that, since those are my memories I am retrieving from my own, silent, experiences. Does that ever happen to you?

Now, if I understood correctly, you do readings yourself. Is there any consideration you take, when you are designing a deck, in terms of how to make your decks 'reader friendly'? Do you design them with the reader, or the collector, in mind?

Hey, Gombrich is a name from the past! I should read him again, as I don't think I have since I was a teenager. But, anyway, I don't regard myself as an artist, I'm first and foremost a designer. Which brings me first to the last part of your question – what consideration do we take to make our decks "reader friendly"? For me, the job of making a deck is that of making a beautiful tool – it's a thing to be used, not a painting on the wall to be looked at. So the usability of a card image is a very high priority when we design it. If I can't imagine using that image to read, then we don't go with it. I have the great advantage of usually writing up the companion book for each of our decks as I'm designing the cards so if I find that I can't coherently describe what an image might mean in a reading, then it's also a signal that the image isn't right and I'll go back and alter it. So we make very readable decks, which is a large part of their success.

Do I read myself? I'm not sure if that was a question, but yes, of course I do. How else could I design a deck? But I am a very definite style of reader – "intuitive" (I put that word in inverted commas because I often think it's the ideologically sound way to describe something that's unmentionable these days), serious (I don't like "flip" readings) and very definitely a fortune-teller. I know it's not fashionable to say that. I ought to say that I use reading to help sitters explore their options or therapeutically to understand themselves or something like that. But to me, that's the job of a therapist. I don't do therapy, I foretell fortunes. But you're right – telling someone their fortune, or what you see as their fortune, perhaps does require a kind of arrogance. Or maybe – do you think this is true? – it requires just the opposite, a complete putting aside of the ego. When I read I try to leave myself out of it and just tell what I see. If I allow my own opinions to enter in, I often get things wrong.

"Designing a beautiful life" – what a striking idea. I love that. Yes, maybe that's what Alex and I both try to do. We're very uncompromising. We live the way we want, we do the work we want. We don't take very much account of conventions or other people's opinions. But we also live by "do no harm" and I don't think we're selfish, just hopeful – we hope and expect to be able to live in the way that best lets us do our work. The work is the heart of everything for both of us – that makes certain demands on the way we go about most aspects of our life together.

How do I feel about images? Goodness, I don't know how to answer that. I'm intensely visual and Alex even more so. In a way, I'm not sure if we care if anyone sees everything in our images – certainly there is a good deal of stuff in many of our decks that as far as we know no-one has ever noticed. I watch Alex sometimes putting detail into part of a picture that I am pretty sure no-one will ever see – except for me and him. But then, why not? If he feels that the image is better that way, then he should do it.

Anamnesis? Do you have photographic recall of events? I'm more likely to remember things visually than verbally or, say, by smell or touch. I am very poor at remembering people's names for instance, but I can spot a face I recognize even from years ago. When we are designing cards I will sometimes pull out an image that I've stored away to use – there's something about a style or the way something is placed that strikes me. I wish Alex would comment on this, because he has an amazing range of imagery in his head – he draws on many traditions that I'm not familiar with. I may ask him to comment just on this part. He is one of the most talented visual people I've ever worked with and part of my joy in making the studio functional – i.e. making it make us a living – is that it's meant he was able to leave behind corporate work (he was doing advertising brochures and logos etc. when I met him) and just do what he really wants to. Clearing the corporate clutter out of his way was one of my best "artistic" achievements.

Years ago I made a pact with my memory: it let me remember all the stories if I let her forget all the facts. So, I can't retain names or phone numbers, but I never forget a face, nor the context where I saw it in. I am eminently visual. Years ago I used to play a game with my wife: if we were traveling by plane and there was a movie, I would watch it without earphones. Now and then she wold be asking me, "so, what is he saying?" and most of the times I would be right in the sense of what was trans-

piring, just by paying attention to the way the actors moved, interacted, and reacted. I am consider myself a quite proficient mind reader, if we understand by 'mind reading' that moment in which the body follows the destination of the mind.

In a conversation with Robert M. Place he mentioned that, many times, it is while reading with his own decks that he really understands the meaning, or purpose, of some of the symbols he put there in the first place. Is that something that happens to you?

But before I forget, I want to know more about fortune-telling. As I read you paraphrasing the way most contemporary readers describe what they do, I can't help but flinch, as I flinch at any cliché. I agree with you in that readings aren't therapy. Sadly, most of the time not even therapy is therapeutic! But I would like to know what you think your responsibilities as a reader are. What should a client expect from you? I would also like to know if you have any thoughts as to why such things as fortune-telling have become unmentionable?

Remembering the stories and forgetting the facts – how fabulously Irish of you! I like that a lot and I think there is a real truth to it. Sometimes the stories are more true when the facts are not allowed to dominate. Have you read Flann O'Brien? If not, you should. Yes, I agree with Robert Place. Alex and I often only fully understand our decks (well, perhaps we never can fully understand them in fact?) when we read with them. AND – and this is important – it applies just as much when we see other people reading with our cards. We both enjoy and appreciate other people's readings of our imagery. It's every bit as valid as our own – even when we don't agree with it.

Fortune-telling? I may sleep on that one before answering because it's such a sensitive issue to many tarot people. I know that what I said about therapy was overstated – but sometimes it's a good way to provoke some discussion. But really, I do think the way in which fortune-telling has become something that's almost looked down upon among some readers is problematic. What do most querents want from a tarot reading? They want to know their fortune – they ask, "What will happen about…?" That needs to be respected; there are good reasons why people look to tarot readers for fortune-telling and to therapists for therapy. If you believe that all fortune telling is charlatanism then obviously you won't want tarot associated with that. But I believe in fortune-telling – I believe that time is nothing like linear. Which brings us back to Flann O'Brien. Oh, maybe I answered that question after all.

Ah! This is great. I appreciate your sincerity. One thing that interests me is the tarot's role in contemporary culture. I suspect that the description you were paraphrasing, about "helping sitters explore their options to understand themselves" emerged from that reaction against fortune-telling you are talking about. What you are describing about clients wanting to know "what is going to happen about..." is true. If we discard predicting the future, then, what? The answer becomes a convoluted concatenation of these events that are by-products of a reading, when a person may vent some issues, when a person may find some insights about her life, when a person may understand certain issues better, or even feel healed, all of it within the process of being told her future. Within a traditional mindset, when you take the prediction of the future out of the equation, the tarot seems pointless. The problem arises by the fact that we live in a culture that has outgrown such superstition. I am not saying that we don't have an interesting – marketing wise – number of people who seek fortune-telling. What I mean is that our culture at large rejects the possibility of being represented by things like magic or divination. I don't believe for a second we live in a superstition-free culture, but the way society at large relates to the tarot makes me suspect these superstitions surrounding it are dated. By the same token, I do think that the 'readings as therapy for the poor man' label is ineffective.

Here I would have to confess that I have an agenda: my own design for a beautiful life includes sitting with intelligent, and interesting people, to share with them my enthusiasm for the tarot, and my faith in those images. This is not religious faith, but the faith any artistically oriented person has in the fact that images can affect us, inspire us, and lift us up. An integral part of my design for a beautiful life is to reach out of the tarot's traditional market, simply because otherwise I get bored listening to people who believe Sylvia Browne is be an intellectual, or that Dan Brown is a historian. I seek another kind of beauty. But let me also confess that I suspect I am the one who is mistaken. Tarot readings probably are about fortune-telling. It is just that I need to find another way of understanding, and using, the tarot as my expressive media.

The problem I have is that I suspect that readings are an illusion, a magic trick. I say it in the most provocative, yet proud, way. I mean, I find beauty in that thought.

This illusion is irresistible, as it relies on our brain's thirst for patterns and meaning. If I were to observe the only three verifiable factors taking place in a tarot reading, I would have a set of images on the table, a person describing at them, and a person listening. Notice I am saying 'verifiable' factors. (I am leaving any supernatural happenstance, or even faith, out of the equation because I don't know how to learn craftsmanship from faith. Besides, I am pretty convinced that beliefs are just aesthetic preferences, and I don't find beauty in the paranormal). An image on the table suggests certain things. In the case of the tarot, there is a primary suggestion: "these are tarot cards. They tell you things about you". When a proficient reader describes these images, he or she counts on a powerful confederate: the client's brain, which is trying hard to make everything fit. It is really hard to give a bad reading, yet, one can achieve greatness in the telling of these tales. To me, the challenge isn't to be accurate, but to be inspiring. I was just reading some excerpts from the Russian poet Anna Kamienska's journal. There was a quote that interested me: "Poetry is a foretaste of truth. It is the vestibule of faith. It is contemporary poets who have turned it into smoke and mirrors". I was thinking on my own work, my own ideas about the tarot, against the background of that quote, and I thought: "hooray for smoke and mirrors!" I would happily take the blame of reducing tarot readings to smoke and mirrors if that makes it useful and relevant to people in a way that fits my own thirst for beauty. Talk about arrogance!

An image-maker like you knows that we can enjoy an image even after we are let into the secrets of its making. But knowing how a trick works kills the magic. It is hard to share with people the beauty of the tarot's illusion. We run on fictions, even when we consciously reject this fact.

So, I would ask you: is there really a place for fortune-tellers in today's world?

But of course – a huge place. People want to know the future. Don't you?

What does "knowing the future" means?

Ask your future self the answer to that. He will tell you.

I take the 'future self' to be an imaginary exercise. Do you mean something else?

There is a precision I want to make about my use of the term 'illusion'. I don't think that a prediction you give is an illusion. A prediction is just an unverified statement with 50% chances of being right and an even higher probability of being forgotten if it ends up being wrong. The illusion resides in the very act of making meaning. All meaning is illusory, as we are the ones who assign meaning, not to Life, which in itself is an illusory narrative, but to Nature. Since the illusion of meaning seems to be fundamental to our survival, I believe it to be 'sacred'.

Now, in your view, what is the role of the cards within fortune-telling?

I have a question also though. Have you ever used any of our decks? If so, how did they work for you? I'm curious.

I have never used a non-Marseille deck. Back in Venezuela, where I come from, the Marseille was the default deck. It is only recently, through the proliferation of a chain of New Age shops, that some other decks are becoming available over there. I never felt the need to look at one of those decks.

So, if you don't use our decks, what made you interested in interviewing us?

I don't listen to music. Don't ask me why. I am weird like that. But I love to talk to musicians about what they do. On one hand, I am interested in people's creative processes. On the other hand, I am interested in a broader – broader than my own – understanding of the tarot. You are great at what you do. Why wouldn't I want to talk to you?

I found this made me think a lot – "If we discard predicting the future, then, what? The answer becomes a convoluted concatenation of these events that are by-products of a reading, where a person may vent some issues, when a person may find some insights about her life, when a person may understand certain issues better, or even feel healed, all of it within the process of being told her future. Within a traditional mindset, when you take the prediction of the future out of the equation, the tarot seems pointless." I agree – although I'm not sure I would use the phrase "traditional mindset". I mean, I am a real believer in good therapists, and in the therapeutic value of uncovering, questioning and discussing personal issues. I fully accept that the tarot can be used for that – of course it can. But I also think you're essentially right when you say that these things are by-products of a reading and are not, to most querents, the central point or purpose.

Is it traditional to want fortune-telling from a reading? If so, it's a tradition followed by most querents. They come to us to be told what's going to happen.

But for you, the tarot is about beauty? Is that what you are saying? Yes, that seems valid and one reason we put so much energy into our card imagery is that we both (I can speak for Alex here, I think) feel that tarot should be beautiful and meaningful – not just one or the other, but both. But is just looking at the images enough? Don't they come to life only in readings?

I'm perhaps jumping from one point to another, but there is a whole potential conversation here about the differences between cultures. In Prague there's magic in the stones – it's interesting how many people here accept that and take it for granted. One sensible young Czech woman told me last year that she found ghosts boring because she sees them every day and they are "so what?" I have a hunch that if you did "therapeutic" readings here, that might be considered a kind of charlatanism. Tarot readings here are expected to be about predictions and, based on those predictions, advice. So it's all illusion, smoke and mirrors? Maybe. But can't magic be real? Is it too dangerous, in the 21st century, to ask that? Maybe so.

Somehow, this conversation got very diverted into fortune-telling and I feel I ought to be talking more about our visual work, as that's what people mostly are interested in. Still, this question brings it back – somewhat – to that.

The role of cards within fortune-telling is – for me (I'm not generalizing to others) – to act as a visual basis for the story I am telling. By story, I don't mean a fiction. I mean something that I see, make into a narrative and that I believe, at least while I'll telling it, is true. I'm very visual, so the pictures on the card start off all sorts of associations (including associations to the "standard" meanings) from which I can pull a coherent tale. (I just quickly looked at the latest conversation on your site. How very interesting. Your interviewee said something like, "It's not up to us to make predictions because we aren't the man upstairs." So I ought to add perhaps that the way I see it is that I don't make predictions, I read them, the way you might read a passage from novel (I don't write novels either). Sometimes it's as clear as reading a book, sometimes not. But I read what I see – this is what a "reading" is. I don't channel, I don't go into a trance, I don't speak to spirits. I just read what I see. Just like you are doing now).

So – anything you'd like to ask now about our visual design? (insert big grin smiley here). When I'm asked what I do, I say that I'm first and foremost a visual designer. Tarot reading is one of the other things I do. Deeply interesting and satisfying as it is, it's not my main occupation.

I meant to say that people traditionally think of readings as fortune-telling. That is what readings have been. In the minds of a vast majority of people, that is what readings are. But what can reading can be that depends on the imagination of those who give them? The development of a craft, any craft, is only limited by the imagination of it's practitioners.

Yes, and no. I'd say that a craft is developed by its practitioners and by its users (I don't like the word "consumers"). A reading is a two-way event.

To me, the term 'practitioners' includes both consumers and providers.

But then, my background is in interactive media (I'm trained as a human-computer interface designer not a graphic designer – though my training is somewhat odd and diverse) and so thinking about users – those who use, not those who just look – is fundamental to my approach. A querent does use a reading – unless they decide to ignore it – and in using it, they help to create what it eventually comes to mean.

I don't see magic as a supernatural event. My only faith goes to the images. So, yes, let's get back to the images!

Yes, magic is natural, not supernatural. Or is it? Here – I'll send some magic your way. Did you see it?

What does it means to have 'faith' in images? It has to do with what we expect from them. I don't expect from an image to tell me what is going to happen, since nothing in the nature of image-making gives images that property. But images are made so we can be reminded of certain things. Images are memorable forms we create to contain ideas. What I expect from images, personally, is for them to provide me with beauty. There is a kind of beauty that comes from what these images are: composition, shape, color, rhythms, and patterns… There is another kind of beauty that comes from what these images remind us of. An image can remind us of what has happened to us, and it can also tell us about the event from a past we all share. If we accept that History likes to swallow its own tail, and all that happened once could happen again, perhaps we could see our future in an image, and if we were able to compile all these life experiences into a set of images, we would have an Ars

Memoria. More importantly, to me, is the fact that images can remind us what we are, or they can remind us what we can be. Either way, they inspire us. I hope I can share these two kinds of beauty with others. I hope the beauty of these images can lift them up too.

What do you, as a graphic designer, expect from images?

I'm not really a graphic designer – I'm just a "designer" these days. Actually, traditional commercial graphic design often makes me shudder, but that's another story. Alex would probably describe himself as an illustrator – when he isn't describing himself as a "crazy Russian", that is.

What do I expect from images? It's hard to say. I can't live without making them. I've made stuff since I was three, when I used to have to hide my drawings and my home-made paper toys because they were considered rubbish. The thing that makes me happiest is making things that are useful and beautiful. It's simple really. When I see something wonderful I nearly always want to make it, not buy it. Buying is second best, though sometimes it's the only way.

Something else I would like to know has to do with your process. How do you decide the theme for a new deck?

Hah, a conventional question at last Enrique – and now that you've kindly asked the kind of question I demanded, I miss the other type. I've enjoyed this conversation very much.

So – themes. I don't quite know. I decide on the themes, that's my job. Alex okays them or not. I made *The Fairytale Tarot* because without fairytales I would never have found Alex. That's another long story, but he was the only man I'd ever had a relationship with who understood fairytales – really understood them. I wanted to do the *Baroque Bohemian Cats* partly because we needed to do something very unlike what people expected of us after *Tarot of Prague* (it would have been oh so easy and a terrible trap to do *Tarot of London, Tarot of Ireland, Tarot of Russia*...) and because I used to be equally fascinated and repulsed by the cats-in-clothes paintings of Louis Wain. Oh – and there are lots of other reasons, the *Bohemian Cats* are a story in themselves. I can't live without cats – it's impossible for me.

Victorian Romantic? Because I wanted an excuse to spend months in the antiquarian bookshops here – before they all closed down (many have gone just in the last three years). *The Bohemian Gothic* because I needed to come to terms with certain things. Including death. I made it while my father was dying. But let's not say more about that. It was a very painful deck to do.

Alice is just because. You have to do Alice, don't you?

So, that's a set of answers that's mostly about personal motivation. There are different – and just as valid – answers about why we thought these decks would work in readings – and that was just as powerful a reason to make them. Plus, well, we both like to challenge concepts of what's "okay" or "cool" in art and design. We like to work with warm, emotive images, not cool ones. Pictures such as the ones we make are very much out of favour with the whole ubiquitous modernist thing (which, by the way, is over, but just hasn't realized it yet) and that's part of what makes them interesting. And they're subversive in an unexpected way – because the revolutionary aspects of modernism have long since hardened into a predictable conservatism. As Natalia Ilyin has said, real rebellion in graphic design lies, nowadays, in daring to draw a picture of a mouse in a bonnet. If we can make images that are powerful by using realism, humour, the fantastic and a beauty that isn't based on minimalism, then we're doing our job.

It seems that one of Modernity's main gestures was a secularization of the arts. When you speak of making images that aren't 'modernist', do you want to put god back into these images?

No, beauty and human emotion. It kind of depends if you think that's what god(ess) is.

I ought to say that I adore modernism – in its place, which was mid to late last century. Now I am just saddened by the way it's been appropriated as a cheap stylistic trick that sells stuff – it's not what it was about.

Once the theme has been defined, where do the images come from? You two work them from scratch?

The way we do the images varies. Maybe that's too complicated a question to answer quickly, but I'll try. We photographed everything for *Tarot of Prague* then assembled the images in collage style (I would say it's our only collage deck).

Likewise for *Bohemian Cats* – though because we worked with small dressed puppets the style evolved into digital composition rather than classic collage. We based *Victorian Romantic* completely on old Victorian engravings – much re-worked – and *Bohemian Gothic* on 19th century photographs, although we did many, many photographs and bits of photographs ourselves. People think the *Bohemian Gothic* illustrations are old pictures, but mostly, they aren't, they're new – but don't tell anyone! *Alice* is done in the way that most digital illustrations are done now – based on photographs which are then re-painted and re-drawn. The way we do most of our decks is madly and wildly time-consuming and this is particularly true of *Alice* so it'll be one of the last decks we do. We think we only have two or three more in us at the most. Then we will retire from deck designing.

I'd love to say more about *Alice* – it will be a powerful reading deck I think – but I'll leave that for another time. Or another time the "crazy Russian" can do the talking!

New York / Prague, 2010

"That's the beauty of the Tarot: it never ceases to amaze if learned properly."

A conversation with BRIAN HALLIDAY, therapist, hypnotist, mentalist

Let me share with you this quote from Baltazar Gracián:

> HAVE NOTHING TO DO WITH DISREPUTABLE OCCUPATIONS. And have still less to do with fads that bring more notoriety than good reputation. There are many fanciful sects, and the prudent person flees from them all. There are people with bizarre tastes that always take to heart everything that wise people repudiate. They live in love with eccentricity, and this may make them well known indeed but more as an object of ridicule than of good reputation. A cautious person does not make public his pursuit of wisdom, still less those matters that make him or his followers seem ridiculous. These need not be specified – common contempt has sufficiently singled them out.

Gracián wrote that in 1647. As I read it, a comment you made in a discussion among magicians came to mind: readings are the "lowest form of our art". I take as my departure point tha idea that readings are indeed an illusion, albeit of a cognitive nature. So, even when the client's own brain is the true 'man behind the curtain', readings are a form of trickery, for the making of meaning is in itself an illusion. But do you really think readings are the lowest thing a magician can aspire to? I am asking you this because your comment taps into something I perceive daily, and this is a generalized contempt for readings in the vast majority of the population. This is a contempt that people from the tarot world seem to either ignore or overlook.

I think readings can be empowering and extremely useful as a vehicle to get clients out of stuck ways of thinking. I respect Oracles. Unfortunately it's the way readings are done "commercially", and especially magicians, that really bother me. And also how easy it is to dupe "believers" out of money. Which is the main purpose of magicians, psychics etc. I think readings as part of the magicians' art is the lowest form when used as another way to deceive or trick. I've not come from a magician's background. I was a hypnotist and therapist for many years, then a mentalist. I was never a magician. Magicians are always trying to trick you. From that point of view tricking someone with tarot is the lowest form of that art. Especially if it's to make you look good or scam money. For pure entertainment, that's a different thing.

I think reality is illusion. Problems are illusion. In fact we think in stuck patterns that create reality for us. I believe tarot and other oracles are great tools for breaking those patterns and freeing up our thinking. The randomness of the cards and their symbology makes us look at other aspects of our life from a different perspective. The contempt you mention stems from the popular assumption that all readers are the same tricksters I would think. I love playing around with the tarot, although I haven't not done it in ages now.

Baltasar Gracian also wrote: "While vulgar folly wonders, wisdom watches for the deception". I do find that the gap between the average magician's mind and what readings are about is hard to close. Sadly, the end result of that is that we have more and more magicians taking up on doing readings, and therefore fostering that low image of the reader as a conman. But you have done some other, very interesting, things using tarots. Why don't you tell me about the use of tarot to aid recovery addicts you developed?

The tarot was part of a complete strategy. I was asked by a local community project if I would help them develop a programme for ex alcohol and drug users. They had got the funding from government but had no clue as to what to do with it. It was a political flavour of the month helping drug addicts. It was a lot of money, they rented nice offices, bought new equipment, and filled the fridge with nice food. However one of the things we discovered was that agencies had self interest in keeping the drug addicts stuck. They wouldn't refer them to us to start with since that's how they got their funding. We were supposed to be the last stage of support and help them get into education or back to work. The usual things that happened would be that the community projects would spend money taking them on holidays, etc.

I saw it differently. I wanted to create an environment that was a massive interrupt of their current thought patterns from the minute they came to see us till the minute they left. It was a 12 week programme. It was very successful in a number of ways. First of all the ALL stayed the 12 weeks. And if they couldn't come in they would phone and tell us. That was a huge breakthrough for this client group, apparently. I set it up then left, and I heard later that it had been more successful than anything before and was going to be the subject of a study.

Basically we didn't allow the drug addicts to think like drug addicts. I trained the staff to interrupt their patterns any time they tried to tell us their problems. We made them accountable for everything. Even made them compete for places and grilled them at an interview. The opposite of everything that was happening in their lives before. The room was set up in a particular way to facilitate this. For example, we had a large table at the front door with chairs around. So anyone coming in would sit here first. It was full of funny books. Some made farting noises when you opened them others were full of ridiculous jokes, etc. The idea was, first thing in the morning or at ant time, whoever came in would sit there, pick up the books and their states would be changed etc. Inside we had all kinds of stimulation. We had a relaxation room and a training room. In the training room we had loads of "toys", including oracles, tarot decks, and creativity decks.

It was easy to deliver positive messages and get them to think outside of their stuck patterns in order to break free from all the external pressure to stay where they were. Every one of the agencies seemed to have a personal investment on keeping them stuck. If you were to lecture them you would get resistance. If you were to engage them with tarot and other tools you could get them to think differently. If you constantly interrupted their patterns of telling you their problems, they would stop focusing on them so they would become less important. That was the basic plan which seemed to work to a degree, to the point where it was regarded successful. Although I think most of the clients were beyond complete rehabilitation.

I usually think in terms on 'inertia'. By repeating or reinforcing a set of actions we end up developing an inertia that has us stuck in that pattern. I often suspect we can only exist within a state of inertia, but some inertia is better than other. Breaking from a state of inertia is hard, and we need another state of inertia to move into before we can really say "I am done with this". You have a background in hypnotherapy. I tend to suspect that a tarot reading – and readings in general – function through hypnotic patterns, with the cards functioning as convincers for certain suggestions we may give. But each card also elicits a bodily experience expressed through certain associations, memories and feelings that are suggestions in themselves, to the point that we can anchor certain reactions to specific images, so the client, by remembering the image, could reenact these feelings or attitudes hours, days, or months after a reading. That is why I tend to believe that what we call 'predictions' are just post-session suggestions.

In her book, Can't Remember What I Forgot, Sue Halpern says that "memory is how we know the world". I often wonder if memories get erased or eroded, or if they just aren't recorded properly in the first place. Remembering is always misremembering. What would you say is the role of memory in a reading?

Memories are recorded through the senses. How we perceive and respond in the world is largely due to how our memories are coded and what they mean to us. If you are like most people, you will have a predominant sense, either visual, kino, or auditory, plus two others, taste and smell. Because you are dominant in one you will tend to record your memories like data on a hard drive with that configuration. In order to have a more fully enriched life you need to develop the other senses so your memories have more data. Memories are living documents and they constantly change. As you grow older you have more experiences which adjust and change. Memories can also be charged with emotional gestalts that haven't been processed or released, which is why, sometimes, a few words can trigger strong emotions from a reading. You are taking someone back into a memory that hasn't been processed.

Another thing about readings is that they stimulate a search for meaning, TDS (Transderivational Search), which means that it looks for ways to match the meanings in a reading. This also involves digging up and examining memories in ways that can facilitate change. Predictions of the future create memories of the future which could be why self prophecy is possible with readings. It creates a memory of the future with which people respond to. That response might only be that they pay attention to certain things which they otherwise wouldn't. So, now, when the prediction comes true, it's obvious the reading was accurate. The thing about the tarot is that it seems to be an encyclopedia for universal experience. And if you stop and pay attention we will find those experiences all around us now or buried in our past memories or alerted due to our future memories.

Painter Francesco Clemente said once that part of his work consisted on helping images recover their memory. In a sense, a reading is a process where we lend our memories to an image, therefore filling it with meaning. Transderivational Search *seems to be a main component in the illusion of meaning. In my view, what makes a reading such a powerful illusion is precisely how much a reading relies on cognitive processes that are more or less automatic, processes which thread the fabric of what we understand as reality.*

To what extent it is the duty of a reader who doesn't believe in psychic powers to disclose these illusions to a client?

I don't think Tarot is necessarily an illusion. I used to frame a reading by telling the sitter that "the cards will reveal the underlying trends and influences in your life but nothing is set in stone. You have all the answers inside and you have influence over your destiny". The thing about memories is that that's all we are really, in a sense. Without memories we don't exist. It's the "random" access to memories and constructs that the Tarot facilitates that make it a useful and powerful tool (or is it random? it seems to be really accurate most of the time. That's the beauty of the Tarot. It never ceases to amaze if learned properly.) If you are stuck in a way of thinking and a reading frees up your mind to look at what's happening in other aspects, or whatever, then the process of freeing up your mind (or programming it) to my mind is real.

Shut eyes and believers, I leave that up to them. Unlike many smart ass magicians/mentalists, I don't see it as my responsibility to save them. Magicians out to deceive and make themselves look good miss the whole point of readings. I don't know about duty, but I do think it's a shame some "performers" don't learn how to do readings properly and how to adopt the way of thinking which revolves around the desire to create a useful and powerful experience for the sitter, instead of trying to fool the world into believing that they have special powers.

I understand what you are saying about how powerful, and seemingly accurate, the tarot's magic is. It seems we always get the cards we need. It also saddens me to see how many professional magicians, mentalists and mystery entertainers get into readings without even having a clear idea as to why they are doing it. The usual result is a reader who dismisses both the technique and the outcome, while embracing strategies that have nothing to do with honoring their craft: removing 'bad' cards from the deck, using the tool as a prop, answering all questions with the same formula, and therefore avoiding any possible engagement with their clients…

The result of that is a yearly hatching of readers who will go out there and contribute to the already poor image readings have in our world.

I have a final question for you. You stopped doing readings, so you won't be confused with all these charlatans. Is that the only dignified way?

I stopped doing readings because it didn't fit in with my other work. I was a "persuasion consultant" working with companies in sales and marketing. I was a full time stage hypnotist most of the 90s. After it went out of fashion I started going down the psychic route purely as a means to make money. However, I quickly came to repel the magician's attitude and studied the tarot and a few oracles in more depth. After doing a few psychic fares over here I realized I didn't like the shut eyes and some of the bad advice they were giving out. So I stopped, realizing I didn't belong to either camp.

New York / Edinburgh, May 2010

"Maybe silence would be that uncorrupted initial state of being."

A conversation with LENA RUTH STEFANOVIC, PhD cand. in methodics, writer, tarot reader

Is the tarot a work of fiction or non-fiction?

Great question, though I believe it escapes an easy and brief answer.

Most of my work is written in a genre commonly called 'magical realism' – think of an ending of Emir Kustirica's movie – when the going gets really tough, the sky opens and characters fly into it, or the cows break out on an island and drift away to the greener pastures (or something like that). I come from the Balkans, and I think our reality would be impossible to digest without leaving that tiny opening, never mind whether in the sky or somewhere else – equally unreachable, where one can eventually escape from the grim reality of what can be perceived with the five senses as our 'shared reality'. So, I take the so-called objective reality (is there such a thing?) with a grain of salt, and if non-fiction is defined as accounts of facts... I think we need to define what's a fact too.

In one of the ontological discussions at *Aeclectic Tarot Forum* on the topic it has been pointed out that even scientists and historians operate according to sets of beliefs shared among themselves about reality. Mary Greer also says that: "even an historian 'believes' that using rules of logic and an assemblage of facts will result in a story that resembles truth more closely than other methods". That would be the definition (of a fact) that resonates the most with my perception.

I come from a culture where storytelling is big and where the border between historical truth and myth is quite blurred and sometimes even invisible; thus, for me, it's natural to accept Tarot as a blend of magickal elements with realistic surroundings in such as a way so that a deeper perception and understanding of reality is born.

What do we get from fiction? What does a person from the Balkans get from storytelling? I mean, what kind of profit derives both from writing stories and from listening to them?

Oral epic has developed in these parts over a period of a thousand years. Generally, in Montenegrin (oral) epic poetry is history that's in the foreground – it deals with the struggle for the liberation of Montenegrin people from the enemy and thus had preserved the memory of the resistance to the Ottoman empire. Oftentimes, real historical personages are described in the language of myth, and the narrattion itself constantly shifts back and forth from the fantastic to the concrete historical world. *Guslari,* the poet-singers composing to the accompaniment of the traditional intrument with strings, *gusle*, were simultaneolsy the performers of the oral tradition and the trasmitters and interpretors of the historical events.

Montenegrin prince-bishop Petar II Petrović-Njegoš, who happens to be the most famous poet and author of the works *The Mountain Wreth* and *The Light of Microcosm* – in his former work, through his character Vuk Mićunović says: "In a house where the *gusle* is not heard, both the house and the people there are dead". So vital was traditionally considered the role of storytelling.

Recently I have been considering the idea of the alphabet as a paupers's boneyard. Anybody, anything, can be buried in it. Anybody can find a bone in there! While considering this promise hinted at us by our beloved letters, I realized that your name: Lena Stefanovic, is an anagram for 'fascinate novel'. It is precisely through the apparent relevance of the anagram – after all, Lena Stefanovic seems to be, indeed, fascinated by novels – that I can see reading the tarot as a form of anagramming.

Nomen est omen... I realize that your name, Enrique Enriquez, is an anagram for 'enquire ere en quiz'!

Writing consists of making infinite permutations of the same few letters, or more precisely, it consists on anagramming the same few images. 'Abcdefghijklmnopqrstuvwxyz' is a landscape, and 'qwertyuiopasdfghjklzxcvbnm' is another landscape. Any of those landscapes, by shape alone, suggests a different place. 'ABCDE...' take us to our early days, to school, and to colorful plates with animals and figures standing for each letter, while 'QWERTY...' remind us of our typewriters, our keyboards, and of our hands traveling blind across them. The contours of any word, like the contours of any city, or the contours of any sequence of cards, carry specific promises. I bet you don't feel the same while approaching your "White City" than while approaching Lisbon or New York. We don't feel the same while looking at The Fool walking towards Death than while looking at The Fool parting ways with Death.

I believe that a thought initiates the emotion which eventually results in the word that could burry anybody or anything or... could be "in the beginning".

In the same way that 'justice' is 'just ice', the story the tarot's trumps tell if we deal them in perfect order promise something quite different to the many other stories we can create by anagramming these trumps, by will or by chance. Still, what makes all these permutations 'true' is not their facts or their fictions, but the flaring clarity of the symmetries they show. A person that encounters herself in a few cards experiences a little Aha! moment, similar to the one I experienced by finding out that 'Lena Stefanovic' contains 'fascinate novel'. I suspect that moment is often mute, wordless.

I have mixed feelings towards words. In a way, they are tools for creation, for betterment, for healing, but the fact that we need to alter something, anything, for the better indicates that, indeed, the initial condition was in some way spoiled and deteriorated. Maybe the silence would be that uncorrupted initial state of being?

I mention this because something I have learned by reading the tarot to others is that no amount of 'reason' will heal a person. The fact that we understand something doesn't means we are going to do anything about it. We can talk until our teeth get dry and still, these words may not prompt any action in a client, unless, they touch a nerve. It is only when something impacts our emotions that we do something about it.

The healing, in my view, originates in the place beyond reasoning, where faith resides...

Very often I have experienced how what 'heals' – bear in mind that for me, to heal is just to change direction – a person isn't the meaning of my words, not even the meaning of the images on the table, but the coincidence between these images and what the person is experiencing: seeing herself in that landscape, finding it familiar and therefore, 'true'. What makes 'fascinate novel' an emotionally relevant – albeit grammatically awkward – anagram for me, is that you, Lena Stefanovic, are a writer. That is the magic in the game.

You are a person 'of the word'. What does the tarot give you that words can't?

Such (meaningful) coincidences C.G. Jung named synchronicity. Take, for instace, sir William Herschell, the astronomer who discovered Uranus in 1781. Uranus' distance from the Sun is said to be exactly 1.781 millon miles away. Sir Herschell died when he was 84 years and 1 day old, which is believed to be the exact number of Earth years that make one Uranus year – it's so far away that it takes that long to go around the Sun.

Recently I read an article, "Introduction to Psychological Astrology – Uranus", by Clare Martin, on synchronicity in terms of astrology where it's linked to planet Uranus. The term 'metalog' is used to describe a phenomenon occurring when working with astrology, meaning 'that which is being discussed is also arising', as an expression of the magical world which begins to come alive as we are thinking and living with an awareness of its existence.

To illustrate the principle of the example of Uranus, J.M. Roberts, non-astrologer historian is quoted (*from A History of the World*):

> After 1789 there began to be the beginning of a new sort of revolution, a rupture with the past, characterised by violence, by limitless possibilities for fundamental change, social, political and economic. Men began to think, too, that this new phenomenon might transcend national boundaries and have something universal and general about it.

In the same vein, to me Tarot cards are such, let's say, triggers of the future, seventy-eight tools or keys for spiritual invocation.

Take the card The Tower. In Tarot, it's ruled by Uranus (by the way, the etymology of the name Enrique is "ruler") – and it brings to mind another Tower, that of Babel – prior to its erection, as we are told, "the whole earth was of one language, and of one speech" (Genesis 11: 1, King James Version). (As a side note, my frst name comes from Magdalena – the etymology leads us to 'migdal', which happens to be the Hebrew word for the Tower.) What was so wrong with the Tower of Babel seems to be the intent: behind the construction was vanity, pure and simple, and it all had lead to the utter confusion with words that lasts to this day. I think that we are daily given bricks in the shape of words and the opportunities to either build another, personal Tower of Babel, or as you put it – pauper's boneyard; or we can use those bricks to pave the way with good and constructive intentions, void of vanity, that eventually leads to ultimate creativity and the creator himself/herself. What I am trying to say, and to answer your question, is that I don't really think of Tarot and words in terms of separation, but rather more like in terms of mystical union, when dancing and whirling becomes oneness.

I guess faith can make stronger our emotional response, or perhaps it helps by suspending critical judgement, which is what a healer will accomplish by cleansing you with an egg that is assumed to be fresh, but when cracked afterwards it shows a rotten, blackened creature inside. A sleight can crack an egg, and more importantly, it can crack our own perception of reality. But there can be healing without faith. Or perhaps we could define 'faith' as any kind of engagement with what we have in front if us. Perhaps, acknowledging that something is there is a way of acknowledging the possibilities of that very thing. But then of course, that won't be blind faith.

You know the story of that relic, Buddha's tooth, kept in Singaporese Chinatown? Long time ago, a tooth was found and it was believed to have belonged to the historical Buddha. A beautiful temple was built to store the relic whose power was such that it was shown to the worshippers on very special occasions only – twice a year, on Buddha's birthday and the first day of the Chinese New Year. Eventually, doctors of some kind found out that the tooth wasn't even human, but probably of a water buffalo! So, what did the Singaporeans do? They kept on worshipping it anyway and the tooth allegedly kept on invoking the energy of miracles! "To me, it has always been real, and I have never questioned its authenticity," the venerable Shi Fazhao, the curator of the temple, told the newspapers; as for the opinion of the dental experts, he said: "I don't care what they say. If you believe it's real, then it's real."

The word 'believe' has 'lie' at its core. What I find self-defeating about the story of Buddha's tooth, what I find self-defeating about most organized religion, is the fixation with 'truth'. Things don't have to be true to be meaningful, yet we insist on 'proving' the veracity of myth. To give you an example, the amount of time and attention that has been wasted in something that irrelevant as the reality of immacu-

late conception is just ridiculous. Mary's virginity neither adds nor subtracts from Jesus's practice.

In defence of the worshipers of the tooth, I must add that to the best of my knowledge they've never asked for some external verification. As usual it was a non-believer who asked for proofs. I believe that all of us have somewhere, even if deep down, even if dismissed – that energy, that potential to create what seems unexpected and unrealistic to the rational mind. Miracles, if you wish. For some it's a tooth, for some it's the virgin's birth, for some it's the parting of the Red Sea. To me, all is well as long as it doesn't create a separation that enhances the mentality of 'us versus them'. You know, I doubt that God/ Godess /Universal Love/ – insert whichever you like – really cares what we call this energy. It is interesting though that the first war in the history of the civilization was a religious one and that this ongoing chaos is carried through by various (presumably) men of faith.

Whenever such topics are discussed, I recall Dostoevsky's *The Brothers Karamazov* and in particular *The Grand Inquisitor* – probably one of the best-written passages in the history of literature. Jesus comes back to earth, in Spain, during the inquisition; he performs miracles and people recognize him, and just when you think the lamb will, as expected, lie down with the lion and that would be it, with the history of the world getting its long expected happy ending in the style of the Hollywood blockbusters, the Grand Inquisitor says: "thank you, but no, thank you". You see, the Church doesn't need Jesus anymore and his return interferes with the mission of the institution itself. Would he kindly disappear and go back wherever it is that he came from, without making anymore fuss?

There are two things I personally dislike organized: faith and travel. But then, I think there is no need to juxtapose organized religion and the so-called new religious movements either, the difference there, to quote the eminent Kabbalist Shaul Youdkevitch, is sometimes only a question of a hundred years.

If a fake tooth can move us to create miracles, then we should have more appreciation for our own magic. That is why I tend to have more respect for the kind of faith most artists profess. Making a living at crafting metaphors without losing sight of the fact they aren't real – only it's effects are real – seems more elegant to me.

I think that true art is a form of legitimate magic.

Artist Thomas Hirschhorn said that thinking is "the most important activity an artwork can provoke". I am not sure I agree with that. Do you?

No, not really and I do find that thinking as a process and its final product or end result are higly overrated in (already) thinking beings, that is. I believe there are more important 'states' art can awaken – those of having hope, being compassionate, and, sometimes, even being remorseful.

What is the most important thing you hope to provoke through your writings, and how does it compare with these things you hope to provoke through the tarot?

What do I hope for? I believe that the choosing goes both ways – as much as we choose writing and Tarot, they choose us as well. Sometimes the intent and the whole idea behind it is not so clear from the beginning. It polishes itself with time and hard work until that magical 'aha' moment that you were mentioning earlier occurs.

I hope, at best, to bring in some light, some kind of order beneath the apparent chaos, meaning if you like, or certainty, in kabbablist understanding. The first book I've written, *Archetype of Miracles*, is heavily imbued with Kabbalistic thought, and the second book – both collections of short stories – is Tarot based fiction. Neither Kabbalah nor Tarot are really common in our parts, so, among much else, as I was gaining knowledge during a decade or so of studying and practicing, and I wanted in a way to spread the word too. You know, during the wars here (in former Yugoslavia) there was a flood of nationalist literature that didn't come from the place of love, that is, to use a euphemism. This whole ugly, nationalist monster-politics was initiatied by some writers with creepy, aggrandizing ideas and carried on by power-greedy politicans. For quite some time we were spoon-fed the cheapest demagogy disguised as belletristic, which led to four wars in ten years. Those ugly ideas that turned into novels and poems were sold not for cash but for blood.

In Montenegro, our greatest living men of word of the older generation – such as Sreten Asanovic – a world known master of the short story, great novelist Zuvdija Hodzic, brilliant poet Jevrem Brkovic – were opposed to this hatred for no reason and wars. Back than they suffered harshly for the choices they made. Some of them ended in exile, some stayed at home but isolated. Their work was unpublished and their lives threatened. The price that is paid in the Balkans for choosing the right side is sometimes very high.

I myself belong to the new generation of writers, among them, most prominent being Montenegrin contemporary classic Balsa Brkovic and award-winning Ognjen Spahic, Andrej Nikolaidis, Dragan Radulovic, to mention just a few. There is no nationalist pathos anymore, and most of the writers I mentioned consider themselves postmodernist. Again, I don't see Tarot as being separate from the whole story – it goes hand in hand with my writing, and even more so, it became an integral (and probably the best) part of my being.

My second book, *Io Triumpe*, was published with Tarot of Black Mountains created by magnificent Emily Carding for that purpose; my third book, *The Devil: An Unauthorized Biography*, is again inspired by Kabbalistic thought and Tarot (this time the form is different, though, surprisingly even for me, as it's a collection of poems). It also features illustrations by Spanish artist Francisco J. Campos.

Robert Frost used to advise not to get too caught up in our own metaphors. We can only stretch a metaphor so much. Beyond that point it breaks, it becomes useless. When was the last time you understood you had outgrow one of your metaphors?

Honestly, it was a long time ago, so long ago that I don't even remember. Maybe before I coined my own metaphors and was, in a way, borrowing from others without really understanding them. I think that life itself is an absolute metaphor that's endless. It can't be worn out or broken, only re-told again with some matyphoric variations. We define metaphor as an analogy between two objects or ideas – knowing that all is interconnected and ultimately one. If someone finds a way for themselves to carry on (as you say) The Story – not to forget that in Greek *metaphora* means 'carrying over'– it can sometimes be a burden, insofar as at the end of the day, the carrier himself/herself can (metaphorically speaking) get carried away with influencing their own personal, meaningful, and fulfilling end destination.

Tell me more about your use of the tarot to write stories. I have mentioned elsewhere that my earliest interest in the tarot was informed by Italo Calvino's Castle of Crossed Destinies. *But soon I realized I didn't want to use the tarot to tell 'a story'. I wanted to tell 'the Story'. 'The Story' is that story only you care about, be-*

cause it is yours. That is why I became a tarot reader. Do you use the cards to prompt associations? You develop plots card by card? How does it works?

Oh, no! I don't use the cards to develop a plot – it's more likely that the cards use me to revive their characters and plots once again through storytelling and to send them out into the big world! I like to link the archetypes I see in Tarot cards to our contemporaries and engage together with them into some kind of role-playing that enables me to tell my part of The Story. I do believe that all of us are part of the same story and each and everyone is adding someting – some, like you, Enrique, add whole chapters, some add a paragraph, some a sentence, and some ephemeral storytellers just put a comma. But we all do add something.

How can we make the tarot contemporary? Is that even relevant to you?

Yes, very much so!

Of course, one of the ways, in my opinion, is the expansion of the three main traditions, *Tarot de Marseille (TdM), Raider Waite Smith (RWS) and Thoth Tarot,* Then we must create decks which artwork that suits individual orientations, lifestyles, and belief systems. On a personal level, it's important to comprehend and grasp every card and its story separately. What is the Emperor's message for me? Does his power intimidate or empower me? Is he a creature of circumstances – or does he create the circumstances? Does the light of the Moon frighten me or awakenes and inspires the creative in me, or both? How much of the Sun is too much and will eventually cause a burn out? How to implement the energy of the Temperance without compomising? Does the Devil, Satan, actually mean only the gap in time between the (good) deeds and the desired result, when it's all just a test? These are just some of my questions, for which I want to find the answers myself by reading Tarot. For me, such personal internalization makes Tarot living and contemporary, relevant to the present moment and its power.

I guess a fundamental issue here would be to understand what kind of promise tarot can hold for a contemporary audience. In my conversation with Karen Mahony she suggested that contemporary audiences seek fortunetelling just like any other audience from the past. My own experience differs a little bit from hers, in that it is only after I have made it clear that I have no interest in predicting the future that most people I socially meet accept the possibility of any conversation about the tarot. Before that precision is made, they either shudder in contempt, or look at my with a "but you look so normal!" expression on their faces.

Karen is one of my favorite contemporary Tarot authors. I admire her and Alex's work. The topic you are bringing up is one of the most controversial, I think, in Tarot circles. I have to digress. I graduated from Diplomatic Academy and I remember a lecture by professor Radovan Vukadinovic, when we learned that just before the collapse of the former Soviet Union there were over a hundred institutions in the US that were analyzing foreign policies of the USSR and its possible future developments. What do you call it, political analysis? By the way, none of them foresaw the collapse, so it seems that they did quite a lousy job too. One of the methods that was used to distinguish rising and falling stars at the Central Committee of the Communist Party-orbit was the following: the observers were following at what distance was a given politician standing from the General Secretary at various pictures taken during official meetings and parades. That's a reading to me, but such a so-called 'analysis' based on elusive sources is nothing but fortune-telling – of course it's not what it's called officially. Weather forecasts? Financial analysis? Sports betting? It all includes a big deal of trying to predict the future, no? I believe that 'fortune-telling' as a term became somehow politically incorrect, and when it's used nowadays, many think of the situation when the reader predicts that a "tall dark stranger" comes to you.

Fortune-telling is understood with the pejorative connotations. These carry the implication that readers list some future facts to the querent as if they were written in stone and there is nothing the sitter can do about it. But that is not my reading style. Such reading protocols are opposed to the belief system I adhere to. It's all together another story when querents can and sometimes do fall into the victim mentality when they feel they can't exert control over what's happening in the outer reality – many don't even think in terms of 'mind over matter', so what do you do, then? I personally prefer reading for folks who know that they do have all the power within, and if their vibration has, in a way, fallen, I think it's up to the reader to help it rise again. Still, what to do with the sitters who are not (yet) there?

I don't want to say that I, or someone else, am more spiritually advanced, but as I am into Kabbalah many things that seem normal to me would seem science fiction to others. As far as I'm concerned, a magical way of thinking is the norm.

On the other hand, what I am supposed to do when someone asks whether their lover or lost cat will return? Give them an introduction to Kabbalah? "The Secret"? Mahayana Buddhism? Or perhaps I can give them a 'teaser', like any good (metaphorically speaking) merchant would do and hope it will lead to the understanding that "there are more things in heaven and earth, Horatio, than are dreamt of in your philosophy".

My late maternal grandmother, Vezilja, was a reader. She read Gypsy Fortunes, an oracle from the family of Lenormand cards (that's how I grew fond of cards in the first place) and coffee cups too; she never charged, but she was a practicing and respected reader after WWII. What I know from her is that people would come with very concrete questions – whether their dearest survived the battles and camps. Will they see their children again? Will the crop be good so there will be enough food during the winter? I doubt that under such circumstances many were interested in some kind of applied psychology.

I did postgrad studies in China, (Language and Culture in Beijing) and while living there I could get an idea of the way the *Yi Jing, The Book of Changes,* that well of wisdom, is read. You'd expect the questions to be about Dao, the way about the universe or at least about the superior's man cultivation of virtue. Well, mostly it would still be about a lover or a pet gone missing. Of course, I do know what you are talking about and it did take me a lot of studying and hard work, self improvement too, to take myself seriously and to come out of the Tarot closet; I think that in the moment we learn to respect what we do, and let others follow. You see, those (challenging) others might be there only to push our buttons so we can grow.

What promise does the tarot hold for you? What unique promises do you think it holds for the people of our times? At the same time, when you talk about "expanding" from the RWS and the TdM traditions, I wonder, what do you think the true nature of the tarot is? The idea about having images that trump other images? The idea of a cosmology? What do you think?

I can speak only of my own understanding, and to me it's the same, as in Kabbalah as in Tarot. As the story goes, when a student approached a respected Kabbalist and asked him to be thought Kabbalah while standing on one leg, the wise man replied "Love thy neighbor as yourself, the rest is simply an explanation. Now go and learn!" To me, again, it's very personal, and I don't expect others to agree in the first place, that Tarot is Kabbalah in pictures, that the cards themselves are like memo cards of that ancient wisdom.

That is a great story about your grandmother. A few years ago I was sitting at my usual coffee shop, where I give reading for free, when a very elegant black man – too elegant for my coffee shop – wearing an impeccable blue suit, approached me and asked: "who was the old lady?" I didn't understand what he was talking about. He kept asking, "who was the old lady" until I asked him "which old lady" and he told me, "the one who passed on the gift to you". Since I wasn't aware of any old lady, I told him there was none. He kept insisting, I kept denying the existence of any old lady, and he left. In retrospective I would have liked to talk more with him, but we never got pass that first question. The guy actually pissed me off.

I don't know why, more often than not, people who have some important message for us, do get on our nerves. Maybe it has to do with what the Kabbalists call 'surrounding light', and the pressure we feel to fulfill our potential.

Artist Thomas Hirschhorn, who I already mentioned, said something fantastic in an interview: "The decision to be an artist is the decision to be free. Freedom is the condition of responsibility... The decision to be an artist is a decision for the absolute and for the eternity. That has nothing to do with romanticism or idealism, it is a question of courage". It was a certain desire for freedom, and the courage to accept the responsibility that came with that freedom that turned me into a tarot reader. No old lady did that. I felt that that man, with his question, was disrespecting that.

I couldn't agree more with Thomas Hirschhorn and with you. Indeed, art is always a question of personal courage; Grapus is close to my heart not because all of them were members of the Communist Party, but because they were promoting political and social engagement of the artist – I personally don't get 'l'art pour l'art' thing, excuse me, but where I am from it would be immoral not to get engaged.

The thing is that, two years ago when my brother died I told that story to my father, who told me that the old lady was his maternal grandmother, who was a spiritualist and used to read the cards. Usually, when I tell this story to people, this is the part where they all go "Ahhhhhhhh!"

Your story reminds me of late baba Vanga, (baba means grandmother), a clairvoyant from Bulgaria, whom I had the honor of meeting in person a couple of times. She was amazing, extraordinary, a pure soul like a righteous or a saint, and she spoke to you as if it went without saying that she saw everything. Her accuracy was unbelievable. The fun part was that she didn't mystify what she did, she would address you as your own grandma would. She was – in a good way – very simple and very direct.

She used to communicate with departed souls and I think that the elegant man in the impeccable suit who initially got on your nerves had some kind of a similar gift, because it seems that he recognized your grandmother beside you.

Grandmother stories always get good ratings!

Yes, indeed. I know that these stories might seem too unusual and twisted for some, but then, as a Kabbalist I do believe that there is much more to reality than what we get through our five senses.

Your grandmother didn't charge. I have heard countless times, especially in South America, that only those who doesn't charge are the real deal. What do you think?

It's another controversial topic and I really don't have an answer. Baba Vanga didn't charge either. In the Balkans, it's like in South America, but I do know readers from North America who are the real deal and charging for readings. I don't charge. For me personally it's a kind of sharing when I can give back something in return for all the Blessings that I have in my life – but indeed it seems to be a regional thing.

If you were to give one tarot card to Baba Vanga, which one would it be?

It would be the Wheel of Fortune, as I relate the tenth Arcanum to Divine Providence.

I have a final question for you. You say you don't get the "l'art pour l'art thing". I have been pleasantly surprised by the strength and vividness of some Balkan poets' imagery. I wonder, as a writer, what do you think is the role of writers in a political landscape that is as unstable as the one you live in?

Not speaking of commercial stuff here, I regret trees being cut off to print the petty results of hyperproduction caused by greed. Big literature isn't inspired by profit. It doesn't exist. I hear often people mentioning the 'writer's block'; for goodness sake – what is that? I don't know of a single anthological, extraordinary local writer whose work exceeds a couple of thousand pages – and these are people who've been writing for decades, some of them for half a century. It's about quality not quantity, and in my view one has to write only when one absolutely has to, when one tries to suppress that urge and one can't. So strong is the desire to share one's thoughts, and so strong is the conviction that this mental sharing will actually give something to the reader, and not only deprive them of their money and time. The rest, in my opinion, is scribomania.

When it comes to social engagement, more often than not, writing is nothing more than similar to the act of that naive child in Hans Christian Andersen's fairytale. The one who didn't care about being considered 'hopelessly stupid' and who first called out from the crowd that the Emperor was naked...

New York / Montenegro, June 2010

"The true encounter with an image begins, and perhaps ends, with silence."

A conversation with RACHEL POLLACK, tarot scholar, writer

We often talk about the fact that the tarot's images "speak". There is that moment when an image taps into a certain string of memories and we feel as if it is talking to us. Lots of attention has been paid to the image's voice, and I wonder: what is the role that silence plays in the experience of tarot? Can images be silent and still be useful?

Silence is essential to the true contemplation of an image. Ultimately, the tarot is made of pictures, not words. I know there are many people, almost the main line of the occult tradition, that consider the pictures a sort of stand-in for doctrines, and information, such as the correspondences on the Tree of Life. So in effect, they are seeing the images as cues, or flash cards, for words, and will judge a deck on the accuracy of the words it conveys. To me, the image is the ground, the words a structure built around it. The true encounter with an image begins, and perhaps ends, with silence.

This is hard to remember, harder to do. The reader, and even more the querent, want an immediate translation into words, information – what's going to happen, or on a deeper level, aspects of those complicated doctrines. We are fearful of silence, fearful that if we enter it, or allow it to enter us, we will never emerge into proper information. There's a slight moment of panic before each card is turned over. What if I have nothing to say? What if I can't get anything at all from this card? When we discover we can, we are grateful and leap right to it.

Silence allows us to look, and to feel, to let the card wash over us. But even this is a jump into information. As anyone who's ever been on a silent retreat can attest, it's actually a very difficult quality, or experience, to enter and maintain. I suspect it's easier with a deck for which we already feel some deep affinity. I know I can experience at least glimmerings of silence with my own *Shining Tribe* deck more than I might with, say, the *Rider Waite Smith*. Or perhaps we need decks that are a little bit strange, and beautiful. I can be silent with the *Golden Tarot of the Renaissance*, because the pictures are lovely and surreal. Similarly with an odd and obscure deck called the Minotarot, an art deck that contains four characters in endless variation – Theseus, Ariadne, the Minotaur, and the Minotauress.

There is a card that I see as the emblem of silence – the High Priestess. Often we see cards 1 and 2, Magician and High Priestess, as reason and intuition, but it might be more accurate to describe them as communication and silence. What happens if you don't unroll the scroll, don't open the book?

Here is a short poem of mine, based on a verse from the Tao Te Ching, as transferred to the Fool and cards 1-3 of the Major Arcana:

> Out of Nothing comes Magic.
>
> Out of Magic comes Silence.
>
> Out of Silence comes Passion.
>
> Out of Passion comes the flow of earth
>
> between heaven and birth.

Recently somebody told me that the difference between psychology and poetry is that psychology is all about remembering and poetry is all about creating meaning. I am not sure I agree. Not only because making meaning can be a form of remembrance, but because I think the tarot includes both 'movements': there is anamnesis in the act of looking at an image, and let it take us back to our own experiences, and then there is poiesis in the act of revelation that comes from contemplation. I agree with you that La Papesse, or High Priestess, is a great representation of this. I am very interested in the notion of embodiment, and within that frame La Papesse can be mirrored by enacting that silent stare into 'nothing'. I read once an argument about how La Papesse could be the Virgin Mary. I won't necessarily vouch for the veracity of such a claim, but thanks to that comment, and by pairing La Papesse with Judgement, I understood the contemplative nature of that image. If La Papesse were the Virgin, as in the annunciation, then she would be waiting for an angel. In truth, she may not be waiting for Gabriel, but she is in that state we all have been at some point, when we have been reading for a while, and we suddenly stop, we lower the book and we stare at the empty space in front of us. Just then, something that wasn't totally in us, nor was totally in the book, becomes clear. That is anagogy where 1+1 equals 3.

Some days I secretly wish to become an automaton: I would simply slide a card towards my client without uttering a word, and she, or he, will leave with a complete understanding of what was 'said'.

But as you said, this is hard. Silence is hard. We can only manage to be silent in the company of those we really feel comfortable with. Besides, the client has expectations. I find myself repeating quite often that I don't seek the tarot by the pound. Many clients think that the more cards you use and the more words you say, the more they are getting for their money. I feel that has to do with some sort of a cartoonish idea the general public has of readers and diviners in general. I would like to know if there is anything you consciously do to counter that cartoonish image.

Interesting observations, Enrique. Is anamnesis the return of personal memories? In esoteric traditions, it seems to be the awakening to the true self, uncreated and eternal. At one level the Tarot always triggers memories and life lessons, which is one reason to ask the querent what she sees, so it is not simply the reader's life that is displayed. But there has to be that deeper level, the almost impersonal truth. The goal, really, is to make those one, the sense of self and history with the sense of true being. When you say you are very interested in embodiment what is it that calls to you? I wonder if we might say that even though the Major Arcana deals with this theme – the Fool as soul taking on a body, the Empress as nature and our own mothers, as well as bodily passion – the Minor Arcana might be the realm of embodiment. Even the suits that seem to be least physical, notably the Swords in most decks, nevertheless take place in the world of the body.

If the Papesse, card 2, is Mary listening to Gabriel, then she does not really get her answer until card 20, Judgement (20=2). Thus, all the cards between are the waiting: 1, before the Papesse, is the promise, and 21, the fulfillment, that is, the giving birth. So what is interesting here is that while we might think the progress is one of disembodiment – anamnesis, restoration of the primordial being in the World, Adam Kadmon – in this view the whole movement is to the moment of God's embodiment as human. And the Fool? I would think both before and after. That is, before the whole story it's the divine being ready for embodiment, and after the birth of the World it's the divine being in the world. Notice I do not actually say Christ here, so I don't want to confuse this interpretation with a specific myth/religion (even though it began with the idea of a female pope who symbolizes the Virgin Mary!).

I began to be interested in embodiment through the "language of the birds". The "language of the birds" is a notion that I approach very cautiously (as cautiously as calling La Papesse the Virgin Mary), as there is no single work from a reputable source I can refer to that actually knows what it is. Most of what contemporary authors, such Luc Bige or Yves Monin, claim to be the "language if the birds" is either solely related to playing with homophonies in French, or to things they made up along the way. But we can rescue that notion of homophony, of things that resonate between each other, as a basis for a "language of the birds" that is fact the language of shape. Jean-Claude Flornoy defines it as a language of "direct comprehension", akin to the language of the cathedrals, in which things are explained to us through images and we can tell what they mean by resonating with these images from a bodily perspective.

Another way to understand this would be street signs. A sign that shows a man using a shovel actually means: "men working", and by extension, "construction ahead". The notion of embodiment helps me to see each tarot card as a street sign that is actually saying: "sit", "move on", "drop it" and so on, and therefore providing direct, visual advise. Then there is the notion of embodiment from a neurological perspective, in which we know that by recalling the body posture expressed by a card, we are activating neural networks in which several neural chains associated with different actions, feelings or memories, fire together. The very act of embodiment includes the idea of anamnesis as that recalling of past experiences.

But I guess that, to answer your question, I would have to go further back, or at least, I need to provide more context. I have come to realize that I have faith in images. I truly believe images can operate wonders in us. Faced with the tarot, I wasn't really interested in the occult traditions associated with it, but in the images in themselves. For that reason, I went back to the late medieval context where the images seem to belong and asked myself: "how were images used then?" The answer is, of course, that they were used to communicate ideas and doctrines when the written word wasn't an option. Within that usage, symmetry was an important notion, since it was by mapping visual symmetries, this is, visual likeness between different elements in a work, that some ideas were linked or reinforced. It turns out that those medieval draftsmen were quite proficient at fostering analogical think-

ing as a teaching tool! Those old tarots are indeed filled with visual symmetries. They are still clear in all the Marseille tarots. But at some point it became obvious to me that not only the symmetries between the cards were important, but also the way one card would mirror another as part of a chain of associations that exceeds the cards themselves as soon as the person looking at the cards enter the game of symmetries by finding herself in the mirror of the cards. This was in fact the principle behind 'tarocchi appropriati,' a game that seems to be as old as the tarot itself, in which a person would give a trump to another player, and then, he would describe why the person was like the chosen card. Again, it seemed to have been – albeit unconsciously – a game of embodiments.

Something that interests me from the idea of embodiment is precisely that it bridges the most classical usage of the tarot, one step beyond gaming, with our current understanding of the brain and the processes of cognition. This is very exciting, since it helps one to understand why, when you tell to someone to "sit like La Papesse and wait for inspiration" this statement is actually tapping into a whole body of experiential knowledge that person already has.

Now, I would like to thank you for taking that detour with me! What attracted you to tarot in the first place?

Enrique, for a long time I've taken 'the language of the birds' to mean prophecy. This is because I look to myths as the primary source to understand something, and there are so many stories of someone who commits a magical act – often tasting the blood of a serpent or a dragon – and suddenly can understand the language of the birds. Serpent venom, if not blood, can induce visions; for example, cobra venom is dried and smoked in India. Birds are the divinatory animals *par excellence,* because they fly, and thus can travel to the heavens and return, and they make beautiful sounds, sounds that most of us cannot comprehend.

Can shape and sound be experienced as one? (There's a term for one thing laid perfectly on top of another, but I can't remember what it is.) I'm not sure. I can think of four distinct forms, or categories, of language. These would be visual forms, sounds without direct reference, at least for us (birds, animals, etc.), spoken reference (the sound "tree" to indicate the concept of tall plants with branches, etc.), and writing. They overlap in various ways but they are not the same.

To what extent is the Tarot, especially the *Tarot de Marseille*, an outgrowth of medieval non-literate symbol awareness? For one thing, the people in the Middle Ages who would have had the complex knowledge of symbolism were literate. For another, the *Tarot de Marseille* dates from about 1650 (Noblet, though Bob Place has found woodcut fragments from a much earlier time that seem to be a bridge from the very earliest cards and Noblet), so a significantly later time than Medieval.

I just did a very interesting short reading with the Noblet Tarot, and using my own method for pip cards, which is to link them to planets, as in the Golden Dawn Tree, but without the entire astrological system. The spread was from Zoe Matoff, a spread that is my standard.

2	1	3
don't do	issue	do

1. (card in the middle, chosen first) 10 of Swords, Earth-embodiment, the very issue, of mind. Isn't the tarot wonderful? Goes right to the question. What will embody mind, give it concrete form.

2. (card on the left) 9 of Cups. Moon of Water. These two influences together stress psychic or intutive ways of embodiment, and the position indicates we cannot bridge the gap between mind and body in this way, however much we might want to.

3. (card on the right) 10 of Cups. So, a clear alternative to the 9, and closely related to the center card of the issue. Earth of water, embodiment of mind through emotions. The way to embodying the mind is through embodying the emotions. Put another way, we might say that Cups is sort of halfway embodiment between the pure mind and physicality.

As to what first "attracted" me to Tarot, the really interesting question is what attracted Tarot to me. I became fascinated with the cards when a friend gave me a reading in 1970. I saw them as an art form, a mix of images and text, since like so many of us she read with a book (Eden Gray, godmother of the *Tarot Renaissance*).

I got a deck and began to play with the images (*Rider*, that's all there was, though *Thoth* was just out for a specialized audience, and *Aquarian* shortly after). Now, that reading was in one sense a random event that had consequences, but suppose we play with the idea that I "needed" to know about the Tarot? To the extent that my work has made a contribution to people who love the cards, that contribution was made possible by this woman. She was the agent for the cards to come into my hands at that particular moment (I suspect my whole response would have been different if I did not hear about Tarot until it was already an established subject). This sounds terribly conceited, but I do not mean to suggest I am particularly important, just that cause and effect are not necessarily linear, and attraction is not always from mind to subject. Here is an historical example. Paul Foster Case, founder of the *Builders of the Adytum* (BOTA) is certainly one of the pillars of 20th century Tarot, as indispensable to the way we understand the cards as someone can be. Mr. Case was a vaudeville performer, a stage magician apparently, when one day he was waiting backstage and another performer said idly to him, "Say, Case, where do you suppose playing cards come from?" That man probably never thought twice about that question, it was just something that popped into his head. And maybe it was a lucky chance that he asked it and set all of BOTA into motion. But suppose he was the agent for the Tarot to attract itself to someone who would advance its meaning and presence?

Those three cards you got are very suggestive. We have ten swords in the middle, nine cups on the left and ten cups on the right. There is a nice sense of expansion there. As objects we use for celebration and sharing, cups bring us close; but swords are extensions of the arm designed to hurt at a distance. One could cool off a sword inside a cup, but of course, nine cups aren't enough to cool off ten swords. Fortunately, ten cups are. If I were to look at these cards in the context of your statement: "isn't the tarot wonderful?", I would see these three cards as a suggestion about how we always get the cards we need to get. If we have a "ten of swords kind of problem", nine cups would be meaningless. But ten cups are the perfect answer for ten swords. That would be an attractive pattern for our brain to find meaning in it!

For the naked eye, a cathedral is a concert of street signs. Now that I think of it, you are making me realize how overlooked has been the disregard that contemporary church has for image-makers. They used to have the best people for the job. Now we don't even know who they have! As you said, the Marseille tarot is far from being medieval. But its imagery is medieval. At least in terms of what is iconographically verifiable. I wish things about the language of the birds were as easy! I am aware of what you're saying about birds being the divinatory animal par excellence, and I have always found that approach to the language of the birds to be the predominant one in the English-speaking world. There is even an attractive theory, suggesting that the oracle at Delphi was fed information via pigeons sent out from all parts of the known world. It is always so hard to separate fact from fable! Within the French language, 'la langue des oiseaux' is a form of word playing which, it is believed, had a visual counterpart at some point. One explanation (there are many) as of why it is called "of the birds" has to do with the fact that, being a sound event, it existed only "on the air", without ever landing on the page. That is why it is so hard to map, even when it is still somehow alive. The French language is wonderful for that kind of thing. Spanish is not so good. But I think English is also full of wonderful homophonies.

I am lured by that kind of approach to the tarot because it makes it into a poetic experience. Verbal homophony translates into visual symmetry, or visual rhymes. It is fascinating to find that the eagle on the Empress's shield rhymes with the black bird in The Star, or that these two rows of stars in The Star card rhyme with the two poles in the Hanged Man, which also rhyme with The Pope's throne; or that the tip of the Ace Of Swords rhymes with the tip of the Ace of Cups... One card is always winking at another one!

Are you talking about synesthesia? Synesthesia is the condition when a person would hear colors, taste shapes, feel flavors, etc. It was believed to be a myth until Ryan Cytowic gave it credibility, just a couple of decades ago. Now it is almost in fashion. In itself, we can say synesthesia is a 'condition', like color blindness; but V.S. Ramachandran has a very interesting theory about how synesthesia could explain how metaphors emerge in the brain, when two neural centers that are too close fire at once.

I promised I wouldn't take too much of your time. I have only two more questions. Here is the next one: recently, around the city, someone has been drawing circles with chalk, on the sidewalk. Some circles are marked as "good luck spots" and some circles are marked as "bad luck spots". I have been paying attention to people's response to this, and it seems most people work harder at avoiding the bad luck spots than at gearing closer to the good luck spots. I tend to suspect that negative predictions, or negative suggestions, are easier to implant than the positive ones. Is that *your experience? Would you say that it is easier to be suggestioned into believing that something bad is going to happen, than to believe something good could happen?*

Enrique, I like your idea, so literal, that nine cups are not enough for a ten swords problem. As for getting the cards we need, a friend says that my special power is to draw the perfect card to answer a question.

Your comment about modern churches having lost the language of symbolism reminded me of an observation I made some time ago. Temples and churches at one time were built on specific places, that had certain characteristics of landscape and/or energy. They might be aligned with particular mountain formations that were symbolically suggestive, or over a place of ley line power, or a spring rich in iron so that it looked red, like the goddess's blood. There is a cathedral in Europe (I cannot remember which one, I'm sorry) that was built on the site of a Pagan temple. The temple was built on the site of a stone circle, and the circle was erected there because it was the place an underground stream broke into the surface. Today, a church or a synagogue puts up a building wherever the building committee can find some property they can afford.

I like your idea of visual rhymes and winks. The Marseille Tarot has many of these kinds of visual connections. One of my favorites in the Rider comes if we arrange them in three rows of seven, then we have:

Hierophant

Hanged Man

Sun

The Hanged Man's face is filled with light. This is the light of the Sun. He turns the Hierophant's emphasis on doctrine, and the role of the intermediary, upside down and experiences the glory of the Sun directly. Or we might say he plants his feet in tradition and sees the light.

I confess I'm not sure how we got to synesthesia here. And I was surprised to read that many considered it a myth when there are so many accounts of it, including James Joyce and our own Pamela Colman Smith.

How interesting about the luck places, and the propensity of people to give more energy to the ones marked bad. This is something I noticed long ago, people's inherent pessimism. You can do a reading with a great number of positive cards and people will say "Well, I'll believe it when I see it." But if you turn over a fearsome card people will say, "Oh god, I knew it." But as I think about this, it seems this was an observation more from my early days as a reader. I find now that many people have a hunger for good news, and are likely to take away any "happy predictions," in particular about future romance.

And now I have a question. I find that some of my readings take the form of a kind of spiritual sermon, teaching people about the nature of possibility and hope, with the cards that come up as the spark to guide us. Do you find you do readings like this? What place do you think this should have in the world of readings?

Have you seen a movie titled Cléo From 5 to 7? *It is a French movie from 1962 by Agnés Varda, showing two hours in the life of a quite self-centered singer who is in agony, awaiting the results of a biopsy. The movie opens with a tarot reading. We see a table from above, and the hands of a woman who spreads a deck of cards. Although the reader asks the client, Cléo, if she knows the tarot, the deck in question is actually 'Le grand jeu de mademoiselle Lenormand'. As Cléo is instructed to pick some cards – three for the past, three for the present, three for the future – and these are turned over, the reader, who we don't see yet, is saying things like: "You have a close friend who is a widow, and she is a negative influence" or "I see a new acquaintance. A talkative young man who will amuse you." The reading follows the classic schema of describing past events to build up credibility, so the predictions about the future can be accepted under the premise: "if she was right abut my past, she will be right about my future".*

About the future, the reader says: "I see evil forces... A doctor... His task is hazardous..." and as an afterthought she puts those cards aside and says: "These cards are difficult to read. We must try again". Here, she produces a tarot pack, the Marseille tarot, by Grimaud. Then the reader turns the Hanged Man, and then The Empress. "A change, but for the worse!" Now the camera shows us her face, an old lady with white hair who looks like a character from Wes Anderson's 'Fantastic Mr. Fox' and asks Cléo: "are you ill?" "The illness is upon you". As Cléo cries, the reader asks he to cheer up: "you don't want people to think I am a bearer of bad news!"

The scene shows exactly what people expect from a tarot reading and, of course, what most tarot readers do. We want to be told what is going to happen, and although we hope to be told "everything is going to be fine" we are really attentive to whatever we are told that could confirm our fears. I have wondered for a while about people's inclination to validate, or to respond more promptly, to negative suggestions than to positive ones, and I now suspect it is a survival mechanism. Avoiding a whole in the ground is more urgent than enjoying the breeze. We tend to overlook the positive things that may be said in a reading because we think we will always know how to manage wellness and prosperity. What we fear is misfortune, and we would like to now beforehand so we can avoid it.

Then, sadly, I disagree with all that!

By this I mean that I understand such line of thoughts, but I don't think it is realistic or useful. I don't believe we are better suited for prosperity than for misfortune. As proof of it I offer the shenanigans of our celebrities and athletes! If there is something to learn from them is that good fortune can crush us as badly as bad fortune does. To me, one of the most interesting cards in the tarot is The Wheel of Fortune. I started really liking it after I understood its connection with the motif of the Circulus Vicissitudinis Rerum Humanarum, in which we are told that life is a constant cycle that takes us from wealth to poverty, from war to peace, from pride to humility, or in other words, from expansion to contraction, and then to expansion again. To me, The Wheel carries a fundamental message, because it is talking about how our moral fiber is our only defense against Fate. The only thing I can confidently predict to someone who gets The Wheel is this: "you will be tested by Fate". One doesn't need superpowers to see that, as being tested by Fate is a daily feature of our human condition. So, my work as a reader would be incomplete if I simply told someone: "change is coming". Change is coming every day! What The Wheel reminds us is to remain true to ourselves in the face if change. That is what I have to tell to a person who gets The Wheel: "don't get cocky if you pull it off, and don't crumble if you don't. Don't abandon yourself just because things change, for better or worse".

I had one of such reading yesterday, with a woman who drew Justice, The Wheel, and The Hermit. I looked at these three cards and thought: "what a moralizing sequence!" To me, the underlining question behind any card a person draws is: "why does this person need to reflect upon this image?" That is the question I hope we can both answer. I did a reading once that was like the one in the movie I am telling you about. A bald girl wearing a bandana to cover the effects of her cancer treatment came to see me, and from all the cards she could get, she got Death. Where I would disagree with the reader in the movie is the point when I wouldn't tell someone "I see a change, for the worse!" What I would assume is that we need to take about Death. The girl I saw, she died a couple of months after that reading. I know this because her mother came to thank me. I didn't understand why she was so thankful to me, until she explained that, for her daughter, getting the Death card was the beginning of her reconciliation with the idea of Death.

So, yesterday, I was looking at Justice, The Wheel, and The Hermit, and I thought of Piscina again. In his Discourse, he is actually describing a sequence of trumps that goes in that order: Justice, which is "now governed by one, and now by someone else", followed by Fortune, which is "not firm, now it steals and now it gives" followed by the Hermit who "represents a prudent counsel, with which you can win any Fortune, because in prosperous things he does not make us proud or superb, in adversities and unfavourable things it does not make us despair". I thought that getting a reading mirroring Piscina's discourse was beautiful, and I made the whole reading about fairness. I asked myself, "why does this person need to think about Justice, Fate, and the Hermit?" And I spoke to her about how a person's ability to be fair, to act with justice, is her only defense against the challenges Fate can bring. That tension between success and failure we all think life is about, that is not the big picture. In the big picture, we are all shamans traveling to the underworld, and every action we take has us retrieving a piece of our soul. I don't think our soul is a given. There are souless people out there! I think it is our duty to build a soul for ourselves. Sometimes, we retrieve crooked pieces, and the soul we build starts looking like that tower at Pisa. Some other times, we retrieve a good piece. It is up to us. Those are the choices that define us. That is what "living up to your full potential" means to me. I think the tarot is useful to remind us of that, and that is what I hope to achieve with my readings. So, yes, I think readings are, at some level, homilies.

I have been wanting to look into homilies again. Thanks for reminding me! I mean, the actual craft of composing homilies. I think my work would benefit greatly from it. My previous attempts haven't been too successful. I had the fortune of contacting some priests, but the only thing they had to offer, in terms of technique, was to have faith. I think that is cute, but that is not it. That is why I like talking to poets so much. A poet can talk about the most abstract notions, but he or she can also talk *about adjectives, or nouns; just as a carpenter can tell you about which kind of nail is better for a certain kind of wood.*

Speaking of craft, I would like to go back to something you said, in regard of consulting books during a reading, or "reading from books". What does that means? How does it works?

Today I bought a lottery ticket. This was after a discussion at Omega in which someone said she'd read some research that everyone who wins the lottery –every single one, apparently – finds it a horrible experience. Everyone at the table seemed to think this was quite funny and agreed we'd all like the chance to give it a shot. So did I, apparently, since I bought a ticket. I used the numbers from two fortune cookies, one that read "You will have a comfortable old age, and one that said "You have at your command the wisdom of the ages." So why do I think I will be different? Why do all of us think that, about so many things?

The Wheel of Fortune has many interesting resonances, and yet it has many frustrating qualities for a reader. Its essence, it seems to me, is that the wheel turns, and we cannot know how it will end or what it will bring us. To tell someone that is to risk them thinking they've thrown away their money coming to a Tarot reader. Talking about reaching for the still center of the wheel, or any other moral lessons to be learned, does not seem like much of a boost. I suppose one can choose to consider the turn either good or bad, and thus predict unpredictable but good (or bad) developments. Not much help there.

I like the idea of Justice challenging us to act with justice. I would go further, saying it calls on us, at least in the context of the reading, to be a force for justice. "Justice, justice shall you pursue, that you may live and inhabit the world the Infinite, your God, is giving you." Such repetition is very rare in the Torah, and as you might imagine has given rise to much discussion. Some see it as really emphasizing justice. Others see it saying that as we pursue justice we must do so in a just way, no end justifies the means. To me it means pursuing worldly justice alongside spiritual justice.

In one practical way the reading you did, with Justice, the Wheel, and the Hermit, seems to imply just that the person did not shuffle the cards very much. But so what? Shuffling them at length would have given a greater sense of randomness, but the three cards would be what they were.

It's hard to say just what qualities a reader needs. Empathy, the ability to see, in a deep sense, both images and people. We need to gauge the level of the person, so that the interpretation is useful. The desire to be of use seems crucial, along with a lively interest in the odd quirks of humans. I always enjoy it in Dr. Who when the Doctor says "Humans!" and goes on to mention some odd endearing quality of the one species in the universe that somehow looks exactly like a Timelord. These are the human qualities. Then there are the divine, which is to say, a fascination with symbols, ancient wisdom, and the intrusion of the divine into our transitory consciousness.

Here is a prayer for Friday night: *"Brucha ath Yah, Shekhinah Ruach ha-olam."* Blessed are You, Presence, Breath of the world. On Friday nights the Shekhinah brings a spiritual soul to accompany the animal and mental souls that we experience during the week. Ever since the days of the Lion, Holy Rabbi Isaac Luria, Jews have actively welcomed the Shekhinah, either in fields or by opening a door, preferably towards the east.

Readers should be attuned to such things, even if they judge the client would have as little interest in such levels as in a reader saying "this card means that fate will turn for you in some unpredictable way you cannot control."

Shalom, salaam, pax, shantih. It probably does a reader good to know a few invocations accepting peace.

Poet Aleksandar Ristović has a wonderful phrase:

    I've every reason to believe that I'll experience what others have experienced.

I think readers ought to remember that at all times. Somehow, that line puts the whole business of prediction in perspective. We may not be able to choose not to fall for a mermaid song, but we can choose to be tied to the mast of our ship. That is why The Wheel is so interesting to me. I have heard some other readers complaining about the Wheel. The wheel brings a message many people need to hear: "no matter what you have done, no matter what you have achieved, everything can change".

At least, they usually seem thankful to hear it!

About that reading I did, actually none of my clients shuffle my deck. I do. Then I spread the deck face down on the table and they pick cards. I often work with the hand-stenciled decks Jean-Claude Flornoy makes, and I can't afford having people treating them as if they were playing Uno. One thing that, at some point, became important to me was to assess the usefulness of all the superstitions associated with the tarot: cutting the deck with the left hand, wrapping the cards in silk, giving them moon baths... Bear in mind that I believe superstitions are very useful mental techniques. The only one of all those superstitions that seemed consistent with the cognitive process behind a reading was the need for randomness. Choosing cards the way I ask my clients to do it seems to satisfy the need for randomness they have. It is interesting how much you can learn from the way a person approaches a task, any task. Some are very direct. Some are hesitant. Some of them feel the cards with their hands. Some others like the cards that are underneath others, some like to pick from both extremes of the deck, or some take three cards that are together. This is the essence of what a character reading is: throwing a person a poetic object to see how he catches it is already present in that choice.

How do you improve in what you do? Is there any formal pursuit you are engaged in? I am now working hard at getting rid of certain terms we use to talk about people and their problems, like 'comfort zone', 'inner self', 'empowerment', and anything that sounds as if it came from a self-help manual. I find that when people feel these words coming, their attention diminishes. After all, clichés are useful communication tools, but they have no healing power. I guess I could say that my aesthetic pursuit, at the moment, is to find better words to talk to the people who come to see me. As a tarot reader, do you have any aesthetic pursuit?

Enrique, latest delay – I'm now at Goddard College (right after the *Omega* tarot conference) where I teach creative writing for the Master of Fine Arts degree. This may seem very different from Tarot, and indeed when I first came I thought how maybe I should play down the divinatory work. Hah. The program director is a medium and has just published a channeled book, several of the faculty do Tarot every day, others see ghosts (of which there are many here), and others are healers. And at the same time everyone is a dedicated and a highly developed writer. In the spectrum between skeptic and true believer I probably fall somewhere on the skeptic end, only because I think I have somewhat more knowledge about these issues, and am less gee whiz.

The faculty all give short readings from their current work. I read a new project, a translation I've done, with David Vine, of Sophocles's play *Oedipus Rex* (though we go back to the original Greek, *Oidipous Tyrannos*, published with this very press here, EyeCorner Press). David is a scholar of Classical languages, so he does the heavy lifting of the literal translation, and gets to have the last word on whether something is correct. What's interesting for our purposes here is that David, like me, is a Tarotist, and so we're both very aware of how the story is just steeped in oracles, bird omens, soothsaying, prophecy. It's an exciting project.

So what would Oedipus – or Sophocles – say about the Wheel of Fortune? Quite a bit, actually. Oedipus has everything, wealth, honor, power, and is destroyed, just like those old Wheel of Fortune cards, where a king sits in state at the top but is seen crushed at the bottom. At the end the Choros (Greek spelling) says something like "count no man happy until he is dead." Not because being dead is good (not a Greek view) but because no matter how happy we are, that Wheel can turn at any moment. On the other hand, we have that famous medieval Anglo-Saxon poem about the bard cast out from court and miserable as he tries to make his way. "This too shall pass" he consoles himself. So, the meaning of the Wheel depends on where you are! Because where you are will change. And the predictive side of the card is to say that it will change, and maybe soon.

Alejandro Jodorowsky sees the Wheel as the end of a cycle or the beginning of another, and asks the useful question, What turns the Wheel? This is made clearer in the Marseille version, with the mysterious crank in the center, so that the wheel does not magically turn by itself but a hand must take hold and turn it. Which, actually, resembles the underlying reality? That is, do events and shifts and even reincarnation just happen, or does some active force turn the Wheel? And if so, what is that force? Newton, that grand alchemist, tired to God's divine order, the endless intimate connections between Above and Below. One result, perhaps unexpected by him, was to open the way to an impersonal machine universe, in which if a creator established the structure it was long ago, and everything just ticks along like a superb 18th century clock. We have struggled our way out of that, at least intellectually, but it's still hard for us, even with the insights of quantum physics and the uncertainty principle pointing the way, to really see the universe as vitally alive, to truly believe there is a hand that cranks the Wheel, and we can influence that hand, or even become it.

How do I improve my reading skills? Mostly by teaching. I cannot stand to do the same thing all the time when I teach, it bores me, and I consider it unethical, so I challenge myself to see and do new things. And all my teaching (writing as well as Tarot) is learner centered, which gives me a chance to find out what other people are seeing and doing.

And, finally, I must know: when was the last time that a pair of shoes made you happy?

I don't have all that great luck with shoes, I'm afraid. Fats Waller would say of me "Yo feets too big," plus I have some minor problems, so my main concern is that they be comfortable to walk in. I do have a pair of sandals I like a lot, that look nice enough to wear to a wedding, if not quite snazzy enough were the wedding to be my own.

New York / Rhinebeck, May/Jun 2010

"Although the insight took only seconds, it took me seven years of research, drawing, and writing to realize that vision in its physical form."

A conversation with ROBERT M. PLACE, tarot scholar, artist

There is a fascinating episode in the life of Henri de Toulouse-Lautrec, when he was taken into a psychiatric facility. Lautrec suffered from some delirium caused by drinking. As the story goes, after a few weeks of having him locked in there, a friend brought some paper and pencils. Lautrec spent his time drawing scenes and characters from the circus, by memory. His drawings were so masterful, so vivid and full of detail, that the doctors let him out. "No one" – they said – "who can draw with such precision can be crazy". I don't know if that story is true, but I like it anyway! I like the idea of memories that are recovered by drawing. You have a relationship with drawing. As a matter of fact, you have drawn several different tarot decks. Have you recovered any part of yourself in that process?

Plato said that all knowledge is "anamnesis," which is related to the word "amnesia" but has the opposite meaning. In other words, knowledge comes because we stop forgetting. Because Plato believed in reincarnation, he reasoned that we have knowledge from past lives that we can recover in this one, but this statement goes beyond that. Plato was talking about flashes of profound insight about the true archetypal nature of reality. He believed that we are capable of these revelations because in the beginning, before all of our reincarnations began, we were one with ultimate reality and we have memories of that state that we can call up into consciousness.

My drawing style began when I was a child. There was never a time when I did not consider myself an artist, which in itself suggests that I retained the skill from a past life. I learned to draw by observing the objects around me and drawing them continuously. I always had a pad and pencil with me and when my parents would visit a friend I would have my pad with me. I would look at all the objects in the room and make pictures of as many as I could: knickknacks, clocks, statues, and things like that. Besides drawing objects, I loved to look at the illustrations in books, like encyclopedias, dictionaries, history books, and even magazines. I was particularly in love with the type of line drawings or engravings that you find in dictionaries. So, I also began to copy these and absorb the style as my own. By letting myself be inspired by these works – many of which could be 100s of years old – I was engaging in a visual conversation with other artists, a conversation that was spread out over centuries.

In college in the 1960s I discovered the occult and began collecting occult books, particularly ones with illustrations. I absorbed these antique woodcuts and enigmatic surreal images into my style also. I even began to create a Tarot deck based on the *Tarot of Marseille* but gave up after creating four cards. These alchemical and occult images retain tremendous power. It is the power to awaken the imagination and I think this is the type of imagination that Plato was referring to as memory. In 1987 I was studying one of these alchemical images representing the Philosopher's Stone when it unleashed a flow of images from the recesses of my mind. In an instant I saw that the Tarot's trumps were telling the same story as alchemical images illustrating the Great Work, the work that creates the Philosopher's Stone. This was the inspiration that started me on the creation of *The Alchemical Tarot*. Although the insight took only seconds, it took me seven years of research, drawing, and writing to realize that vision in its physical form.

The drawings in *The Alchemical Tarot* are directly influenced by alchemical engravings but I redrew all of the symbols in a coherent style that is based on Albrecht Durer's woodcuts. I also made up new alchemical images from my imagination – sometimes directly from personal visions. At times I would add details to drawings and not be conscious of why. It was only later when the cards were printed and I was using them in readings that I was able to understand some of my own drawings. A profound philosophy emerged in the drawings that I had to learn from working with them, in spite of having created them. This is why I am not entirely satisfied with the book that I wrote to accompany the deck, because I had to write it before the cards existed as cards and I had time to work with them.

I was just talking to Rachel Pollack about anamnesis. It seems that, somehow, experiencing an image is always an act of remembrance. Joseph Beuys used to say that drawing was a thinking process. In a way, what you were doing as a child, by drawing all these objects in a room, was to reflect upon images. Drawing is a way of owning something by its form. I once did a reading for a man who worked for Anselm Kiefer. Kiefer used to visit Beuys, seeking advice. This person I met through the tarot confided the most important piece of advise Beuys gave to Kiefer: "find yourself a mythology". Judging by Kiefer's body of work, it is clear he followed Beuy's advice!

Why do you think these alchemical and occult images are more effective at exciting our imagination? Is this because of the images in themselves, or because of the context they inhabit?

I definitely feel that there is a power in the alchemical images because of how they were conceived and because they were intended to bring about the alchemical transmutation. These images came directly from the unconscious minds of alchemists who were working on the alchemical Opus, which in its most exalted from is the quest for enlightenment. Often, the most important messages communicated in alchemical texts were expressed in pictures or symbols.

The legendary 14th century alchemist, Nicolas Flamel, was said to have come across an alchemical text that contained the secret of creating the Philosopher's Stone. He worked with the book for years but was unsuccessful because the most important secrets of the process were contained in the center of the book in several pages filled with enigmatic illustrations but no text. It was not until he made the acquaintance of an old Jewish scholar in Spain, who knew how to read the pictures, that he was successful. According to the legend he created the Stone and he was able to turn lead into gold and also create the elixir of life that allowed him and his wife to live for centuries. I identify with the scholar in the story because I have always had a talent for reading pictures.

Poet Christian Bök defined his book Crystallography *as an "encyclopedia that misreads the language of poetry through the conceits of geology." His is a brilliant book that benefits from the crossing of metaphors, using geology to understand poetry. To me, the key word here us 'misreading'. Geology is not poetry, but geology can be used to understand poetry. We see this strategy of misreading employed over an over to understand the tarot: we approach it through all kinds of systems of symbols. Sometimes, this strategy renders useful insights. Do you think that it is important for those misreadings to be historically validated in order for those insights to be meaningful?*

I haven't read *Crystallography* but my understanding of the book is that it is a collection of poems, which makes use of correlations such as *gematria* (the correlation between letters and numbers), correlations between letters and rock formations, and correlations between words and geometric forms. As the aim of the book is to use words and letters in creative ways to bring the reader into a new lucidity about language, I applaud it. Lucidity in dreams is one of the most important goals of dream work and my method of working with the Tarot is totally based on dreams. The Tarot was introduced to me by a dream, many of my layouts have come to me in dreams, and my method of interpreting the cards is to look at them as a waking dream.

I think that if someone was to apply correlations to the Tarot in an open experimental way, like Bök, some of the results could be insightful and meaningful. I do not think, however, that this is what most 19th century occultists were doing. At their worst, they were ignoring the pictures on the cards and turning the whole deck into a nonsensical secret code. Their correlations were mostly arbitrary. Then they were claiming that the code was the real intent of the original creators of the Tarot and they used these false claims to gather followers. This practice was egotistical and, if it was an intentional lie, it was immoral.

My method of reading the cards is to read them in groups of three, all right-side-up. I look at the three cards as one message – as if it came from a dream and that is how I interpret it. When I interpret a dream, I first look at the actual plot or at the direction of the action. Then I pick out the key symbols. I want to know as much as I can about the history of these symbols and about their archetypal quality. When this ground work is complete, I look at how this dream applies to me personally, to what has been happening in my life or will be happening.

I think that people misunderstand my interest in history and many misunderstand history as well. History is simply the study of what has happened up until now. If I meet someone and I want to get to know them better I will talk to them about their experiences and their life. If I want to really know them well to understand their views, the way a therapist does, I will get them to talk about their childhood. To feel that you know someone, and to feel close to them it is important to know their personal history. Otherwise you will most likely fill in the unknown aspects of that person's life with your own misconceptions and projections. You will not really know them but a fantasy of them. I want to know the

Tarot in this way. I want to know what the artists who first created these decks were thinking and how that message was changed and added to over the centuries. My interest is primarily in the symbolism and philosophy of the Tarot. I feel that occultists and modern authors have made valuable contributions to the interpretation of the Tarot, but we have also lost sight of some of the profound mystical symbolism that was there in the beginning. I want to bridge this gap. I want to reclaim the original mysticism and draw attention to the broader archetypal insights of modern Tarot artists. This was the focus of the exhibition that I curated at the Craft and Folk Art Museum in LA. It looked at the Tarot as a visual conversation between artists, occultists, and mystics that has been going on for over 500 years.

I share the same understanding of the tarot being some sort of dream landscape we then interpret it, although, sometimes, I feel that describing it is in itself a form of interpretation. To me, a simple layout has the same advantage over a complex spread as poetry has over prose: a paragraph has too many words! This makes it harder for me to savor each one of them! But it is, of course, a matter of personal preference.

May I ask, what happens next? South African sangomas believe dreams to be instructions that must be carried-on the next day, like recipes. Many people I know see dreams as presages, messages about things that are going to happen. I am happy to understand them as a way of making sense of some random neuronal firing. How do you face that dream you see on the table? What are your clients supposed to expect to get from it?

I find that dreams respond to our expectations of them. If we think that a dream is just an illogical random series of images that rehashes our daily lives we tend to get that. If we think that dreams are therapeutic discussions of childhood traumas, we tend to get that. If we think dreams are spiritual messages from God we tend to get that. But dreams come from the Higher Self – Dream Maker, as shamans call him, or Hermes, in Classical mythology – and the Dream Maker has his own agenda.

Jung tells us that dreams are always balancing and compensating the conscious mind – letting us see the other side and driving us toward enlightenment or individuation, as Jung calls it. I believe this is true but my dreams also deal with practical concerns. I have had dreams that have told me how to fix my computer when it was broken. I have also had dreams that were an undeniable communication with my Higher Self, such as the dream that introduced me to the Tarot. My dreams have given me ideas for my Tarot decks. They help me deal with my past. But they also predict the future. At one time, for several months I consistently had a dream each night that predicted an event that would happen the next day. At other times, I have had dreams that made predictions about events months or even years in advance. These had to do with larger issues in my life and career and they included details that were startling in their accuracy.

I tend to leave predictions for actual dreamwork and use the Tarot to get advice. In a reading I am aiming for perspective and a better understanding of a current situation. Most of all I want advice from the Higher Self about how to proceed. It is like getting advice from a wise friend.

In which sense do you feel people misinterpret your interest in history? I remember reading your book a few years back and thinking 'this guy has the most sober understanding of the tarot's history I have seen in a book for the mass-market.' But then I was a little surprised when I saw your Buddhist deck. I understand what you are saying about the tarot's history being a 500 years-long "conversation" about image-makers. Art is in itself a centuries-long conversation about forms. Poetry is a conversation about language, or words, taking place from generation to generation, with each generation expanding the boundaries of that conversation by responding to previous poems, or adding new poems to the mix. I understand the tarot cannot remain static, but why a Buddhist deck? To test the boundaries of the tarot as a format? To contrast Eastern and Western thought? Given the level of misinformation about history that exists in the tarot world, and the huge amount of wishful thinking going on in the New Age market, weren't you concerned that having a person like you, with your knowledge about the tarot's history, making a deck with Buddhist motifs, could be misconstrued as a statement about the tarot's Buddhist origins?

Of the decks that I have designed, *The Buddha Tarot* is one my favorites. It is the epitome of what I am after. I don't think people totally understand it unless they read the book that I wrote to accompany it and unfortunately the publisher decided to sell the book separately. It is not just about Buddhism but it is a comparison between Buddhist philosophy and Western Mysticism, showing the similarities. I am using the Tarot as a window into Western Mysticism and that is where my understanding of history comes in. You have to know the history of the Tarot to be able to read the story told in pictures that is the series of trumps. When you do, it is obvious that it is the archetypal story of the hero striving for enlightenment and, although the Tarot's designers were not thinking about Siddhartha when they created it, his story closely follows the same pattern. I was able to find standard Buddhist icons that fit each of the trumps. I was also able to demonstrate that the Tarot, with its five suits, embodies an archetypal sacred structure – it is a mandala composed of cards.

I feel that the *Buddha Tarot,* like my other decks, was inspired by a dream, but I cannot actually recall the dream. The inspiration for this deck started on Christmas in 1996. I had been reading *The Illustrated World's Religions* by Huston Smith and went to bed after reading the section on Buddhism. When I woke on Christmas morning, a correlation between the life of Buddha and the Tarot was all worked out. I could clearly see how the details of the story of Buddha's life – how Siddhartha became the enlightened Buddha – fit together with the Tarot trumps.

There were the four sights that convinced Siddhartha to leave his life of pleasure and his lover and become an ascetic: an old man, suffering, death, and a hermit. There was the Chariot that he used to ride to town to see the sights. Before this, his farther had ruled his life like a Pope and had been guiding him toward the role of Emperor, another trump. Once he realized that the ascetic life was also a dead end, he embraced the virtue of Temperance and had to deal with the temptations of Mara, the Devil. Buddha remained undefeated and rose through various levels of enlightenment just as the Tarot depicted a hierarchy of celestial images leading to the mystical vision on the highest trump. The story even fit the three-part pattern that I have found in the Tarot: the first dealing with hope, the second with fear, and the third the middle path, beyond hope and fear that leads to mastery or enlightenment.

At first publishers were not ready for the idea. It seemed to be too much of a stretch for them. But in 1999, I delivered a lecture on Buddha and the Tarot at the World Tarot congress in Chicago and after that Llewellyn went for it. It was published in 2004.

When I study the history of the Tarot I find that in many ways there was more experimentation and variation in early decks than there is now. There was not one original Tarot. The Tarot evolved in the 15th century and there were variations in the number of cards, the order, and in what icons were included. To see what is similar about them I have to step back and find the connections. I have to step back from the details and perceive the pattern that is there behind the scenes. I feel that this is the highest wisdom, to see the patterns that are timeless, and connections between centuries, continents, and cultures. This is what happened to Siddhartha as he sat under the Bodhi Tree, he saw the pattern of all his incarnations like a great wheel. This wheel-like pattern is called a mandala in Buddhism. It is a sacred pattern of archetypal reality that emerges from the visions of enlightened masters, and is captured by artists.

The wheel of the mandala is a circle that surrounds a hub. The hub represents the most sacred spot, the sacred center. This center is the fifth location that is the source of the other four directions, north, south, east, and west, which define physical reality and form a square around the circle. The alchemists called the sacred center the *Quinta Essentia*, meaning the essential fifth. They pictured it as a goddess, the World Soul, who is the mother of the physical world. This is what is depicted on the mandala that we call the World trump – a goddess in the center of a circular wreath with the symbols of the four evangelists pointing to the four directions.

As Buddhism developed, Buddha himself was given this archetypal pattern, when he ascended to Nirvana. He became not just one Buddha but five, the five Jinas, one for the center and one for each of the four cardinal directions. This is the same pattern that runs through the entire Tarot deck with its five divisions, the four minor suits, representing the four directions and other four-fold associations, and the trumps, representing the sacred center and the hero's journey. For each of the minor suits I was able to use one of the Jinas as the King, his female partner or Sakti at the queen, his protector animal as the knight, and his Dakini servant as the Page. Also each Jina has a magic object that is his symbol. These became the suite symbols. The Buddha Tarot is not just another theme deck. It illustrates the deep archetypal connection between Eastern and Western symbolism and shows how that symbolism is expressed in the Tarot.

Lately, I have been thinking a lot of all those mappings of the other-world, as I have been reading The Invisible Gorilla, And Other Ways Our Intuitions Deceive Us, *by Christopher Chabris and Daniel Simons. They describe six every day illusions we all engage in, which determine our understanding of reality: illusions of attention, memory, confidence, knowledge, cause, and potential. Chabris and Simons became well known for the experiment they devised, in which they ask people to watch a video of a basketball game and count the number of passes in it. In the video, some basketball players are indeed passing the ball along, but suddenly, a gorilla enters the picture, looks at the camera and beats its chest. 50% of the people who watch the video miss the gorilla. They simply don't see it. This is an experiment that has been widely replicated, and quoted by the media. The book, which shows the continuation of their research on perception, talks about how our mind doesn't necessarily work the way we think it does, and therefore, many of the assumptions about what we are perceiving are flawed. I guess this shouldn't be news to us, yet we insist on a blind trust in our 'automatic pilot', which is what these two authors define as 'intuition'. I am quite comfortable with using these six illusions as a map for the other side. It occurs to me that the role of a magical person in the contemporary world may very well be to understand these six illusions. After all, whoever knows the limits of perception is indeed standing on the threshold between worlds.*

I find fascinating your comparative analysis on Buddhism and Western spirituality. Ah! I have to say, I read your book on the subject!

I have a very pragmatic view of the trump cycle. I don't see it as the depiction of a journey, but as a manual for traveling; like a little recipe on how to live a moral life, which is not so much directed to expand the 'self within the self' but to engage with the world out there without getting lost in our own folly. These days I have been enjoying a lot Baltasar Gracián's Oráculo manual y arte de prudencia, *(Manual Oracle and Art of Prudence). It seems embedded with the same practicality of the tarot's trumps. That is why I like what you are saying about using the tarot for advise. Life is what it is, but we always have the choice of reacting to it in one way or another. These choices define us. I even find intriguing that the three moral virtues we have in the tarot: Justice, Fortitude, and Temperance, can very well be applied to the making of art. All images need a sense of balance, a sense of strength, and very importantly, a sense of self-containment. Now, talking about images and image-making, there is some sort of a constant in these conversations I am having. Again and again I find readers who tell me that the images are 'just images' or 'just* symbols'. I am not quite sure what that means, since I can see how images are presences whose physicality is meaningful in itself. Many times, the effect of an image precedes our understanding of it. What do you think about that? What do you expect from images? Do the images, for and in themselves, play any role in the kind of readings you do?

Christopher Chabris and Daniel Simons's book provides valuable insight into how consciousness works in a selective manner. What they have uncovered is the same truth that mystics and magicians have professed over the centuries. As Buddha said, "our thoughts create the world." In other words, our consciousness is constantly editing what we perceive and these edits become our reality. Plato was addressing this same phenomena when he distinguished between common opinion and true ideas that come from philosophical insight.

The way the authors use the word intuition, however, has nothing in common with my use of the word or Jung's definition of the term. It seems to me, that they are using intuition to mean misconceptions or commonly held beliefs that stand in the way of perception. By intuition I mean material that is worked on by the unconscious mind instead of the conscious mind and then delivered to the conscious mind as an insight or as guidance.

Similarly, people who say that images are 'just images' or 'just symbols' are not working with the same definition as I am and they are not perceiving true symbols. Jung distinguishes between what he calls signs and true symbols. A sign is a pictorial communication that is created consciously by an artist. A symbol works the other way. It is a gift from the unconscious mind. It originates in the unconscious and is used to communicate with the conscious mind. Symbols happen spontaneously in dreams and visions and that is why they have the power to draw us into that world.

I do see the trumps as the archetypal myth of the Hero's Journey but the myth is also meant to be a guide, as you say, "a manual for traveling." This is the main focus of my *Tarot of the Sevenfold Mystery*, which was the highlight of the Tarot exhibition in LA.

My theory of the trumps is based on the concept of the triune soul found in the teaching of Pythagoras and Plato. Pythagoras was said to have theorized that there are three kinds of people characterized by their level of spiritual development: those who love profit, those who love fame, and those who love wisdom. Plato, continuing this idea, stated that each person has three souls or three soul levels: the Soul of Appetite, the Soul of Will, and the Soul of Reason, which he symbolized by a chariot with two winged horses and a driver. In *The Republic*, Plato made it clear that these three levels form a hierarchy, from Appetite to Reason, and as individuals developed and balanced each soul they would be able to move up to a higher position in his perfect society.

The keys to balance and development were the Cardinal Virtues. The three lower virtues were each designed to balance a soul center and the attainment of the fourth virtue coincided with enlightenment. The hero who achieved this state became the philosopher king or queen.

By the Renaissance, the Cardinal Virtues linked to each of these soul levels were the same three that are depicted in the Tarot: Temperance to the Soul of Appetite, Strength to the Soul of Will, and Justice to the Soul of Reason, and if we divide the twenty-one trumps into three groups of seven cards, we find that the theme of each group corresponds sequentially to one of these soul levels. The seven cards in each section also echo the mystical number of ascent associated with the seven ancient planets: Luna, Mercury, Venus, Sol, Mars, Jupiter, and Saturn. The planets were believed to form a ladder between Heaven and Earth that the soul would descend at birth. These seven planets were thought of as the soul centers of the cosmos, and corresponding soul centers could be found ascending the spine, from the sacrum to the crown of the head, in the microcosm of the human body. The three Christian virtues were added to the cardinal virtues to create seven virtues, each intended to balance a soul center. The culminating virtue was Prudence, which I believe is depicted on the World card.

New York City / Saugerties, New York, Jun-July 2010

"Yes, ancient poetry is (oh, how the Irish agree) curses and blessings, blessings and curses, wisdom and history."

A conversation with THOMAS HASTINGS, editor

What is the deal with poetry in this time and age? Is it almost as useless as magic?

Wonderful question, Enrique! I'll confer with my inner beings in the house of the ancestors and then respond, but let's abandon the useless midway proving ground of classic and modern poetry to scholars and advance/return to the ancient/contemporary imago/logo chase grand stand. How grim the grimoire when we do not learn from our emotions and get the spells wrong... yes the inner beings say poetry, like magic, is as useless or useful as the security guards of irony, superstition, and honor allow, and encourage through an individual's personality development.

Why do you think it is too hard for most of us to keep our respect for something after we have discovered it is an illusion?

The blue dominates the red of the hydrangeas in my neighbor's yard... We train body and mind but training the imagination seems to be valued less except in advertising and psychology.

Yes but, how much blue is too much red?

Yes, the sun's angle to the rods and cones determines how much blue and red is percieved in the hydrangeas...the albedo and rubedo manifests much much more at dusk! I saw this magic with my own eyes, Enrique!

Is there any antidote for language? Do we need one?

Words seem useful to reason things out and create imaginary order as well as pigment the multicolor universe... A useless antidote for language is activating dormant neanderthal telepathy gene but you must not lie to yourself or others to access its code.

Would you say that the tarot is a 'pataphysical machine?

Yes, fondly from rubedo, the halcyon kingfisher says tarot is pataphysical machine when it ignites the bride's love gasoline.

Isso says the tarot is a pataphysical machine when you wave sound around imago and logo hooray!

Do you think it is true that Hope has better memory than Gratitude?

I know now someone put aluminum in the hydrangeas to change their pinkness to blueness. For a long time, folks living around the equator couldn't see the color blue with their sunbent rods and cones. I do not know how the word and perception for blue came into being for them but I hope they are grateful.

In the 20s painter Armando Reverón used only white to pain Caribbean landscapes. Those weren't snow landscapes, but light landscapes. In the Caribbean, light burns everything. What should we expect from images?

Yes, what can we expect from the albedo? It has its nigredo and rubedo contents to protect when it isn't in the pure baptismal *ablutio* state... then it is remembered as silver then golden as well.

Thomas Hastings,

Shaman Ghost Its Asthmas, Hosting Aghast Shin Most

A Hansoms Tights? Satan Hog Smiths? Amassing Shh Tot?

Aha! Thongs Mists...

Merci, merci... I had the itch to post the theme song from *Caspar the Friendly Ghost* on my facebook performance wall all day.... Aha thongs mists... Just posted dramatic song (hot pants) before your message... Your questions are so much fun in our intraview... I'm curious to see what you'll send to place in the seventh cannister...it has become the tarology cannister!

Verbal overshadowinggniwodahsrevo labrev

It really worries me, you know?

Underlighting beige rage facebook data farmers sideways... i.e. Personality tests for all the inner beings! Sphygmomanometers for all my friends! Hooray!

A lenticular ceiling moves when we move and stops when we stop. How can we tell isn't all lenticular?

In May, we had to 8:00 PM rainbows to the east... My wife and I practiced lenticular peripheral gazing to make them appear and disappear... Have you tried this before?

The men in the gorilla suit* say there are six daily illusions:

Attention, Memory, Confidence, Knowledge, Cause and Potential.

If the average brain is constantly pulling rabbits from hats that weren't there in the first place, what do we need professional illusionists for?

* Actually, the one wearing the suit was a hired woman.

We need professional illusionists for their perceptual instructions like polyglots need childhood translators.

Is uncertainty the antonymous for 'beauty'?

Certainty is as well. Breton proposed a convulsive attribute as well.

If moments are not afraid to leave, why are we?

We only fear the moment... like a bad tooth. You had yours fixed because it still has a relationship with your other teeth. Mine was all by its lonesome in the back useless and hurting like an old abandoned delusional person. At $300, sleeping through its removal was not an option. Once a tooth goes hot...

What would be more omnivorous than Death?

Both the voracity and diversity of life are evolutionarily more omnivorous than death especially if we count data as dietary supplement.

André Bretón admired the Marseille tarot. He even wrote a book of poems whose title, 'Arcane 17', was inspired by that precise tarot card: Lestoille, or The Star. What is the tarot to you? Why is the tarot to you?

It is an omnidirectional channel changing cynosure.

As you know, my friend, why is because a hazelmouse fell through my mother-in-law's gazebo roof.

Sometimes, while I am looking at some tarots, on the table, for someone else who is in front of me, I feel like saying: "it is red, you idiot! The message is red!", or something like that. Has that ever happened to you?

Yes, Enrique... especially since I have been learning about the gender/fairy tale/alchemical progressions of rubedo-albedo-negredo personality development thresh-holds and edges... the first reading I entered with someone else ten years ago (who had asked me three times) was the most instructive ever because the cards were all the "negative" ones... every single one... I learned how the color-state and available channels do creatively emerge in a ceremony of their own devices maneuvering in the transgenerational wave of identified archetypal possession through projection, differentiation, reconciliation and cultivation.

Yes... you could say in transferable/countertransferable terms, our most stubborn and willful inner beings emerge through each card's doorway of pictures, numbers, sounds, emotions and gestures of older pre-literate omenic knowledge systems.

Enrique, I hope you will contribute by this emu some logo/imago to the seventh cannister (out of the ten) I am assembling for mischief sake and I would also be most grateful.

Maybe

wrapped in water wanting,

rolling exhausted

Dice

Down the world, up the sky

Marvelously portable balls

Mostly married,   naked

Not bananas nor carrot bells,

But the heart   cursing the land

Excellent! Thank you, Enrique! Am placing into solstice installation! Thunder-words! Old 3131 thanks you with gratitude for your 31 words of blessings and curses! Yes, ancient poetry is (oh, how the Irish agree) curses and blessings, blessings and curses, wisdom and history. You are a precious gem!

New York / "a town where my father was born in the great American Midwest", Jun 2010

"As an esotericist I was fascinated with the naked truth nude, not her lingerie."

A conversation with PAUL NAGY, esotericist, tarot scholar

What do you want from tarot? Has this changed from 1977, when you discovered it?

Well, I did not exactly discover Tarot in 1977, it was just then that I set time aside to formally study the system. Unfortunately this was for me pre-Rachel Pollack and her *78 Degrees of Wisdom*, so with a trusty Rider Waite Smith (RWS) deck in hand, I studied A. E. Waite's *Pictorial Key to the Tarot* (1911), Papus' *Tarot of the Bohemians*, Eliphas Levi's *Transcendental Magic: Its Doctrine and Ritual*, P. D. Ouspensky's *The Symbolism of the Tarot*, Mouni Sadhu's *The Tarot – A Contemporary Course on the Quintessence of Hermetic Occultism*, (1962) Paul Foster Case's *The Tarot: A Key to the Wisdom of the Ages* (1947), Mayanananda's *Tarot for Today* (1963). This is not a list I would suggest to anyone to learn tarot today!

The net result of this study was a feeling of disappointment. Tarot seemed arbitrary and falsely constructed, especially in the cabbala and tree of life analogs. The card meanings generally seemed contrived and capricious. With such an inauspicious beginning, it is amazing I stuck with tarot at all. At the same time I had plenty of success reading for friends and strangers, and I wondered how my intuition was interacting with these symbols to create plausible insight for others and myself?

I discovered tarot as a young teenager during the time I furtively haunted Fritzi Armstrong's quaint second story bookshop on Powell Street in downtown San Francisco. The Metaphysical Towne-Hall Book Shop was furnished like a Victorian pallor. Cluttered with books of the popularly arcane, a shrill and cranky Fritzi or her ubiquitous assistant, a chunky middle-aged waif, Mickey, would, in short bursts, tolerate my sneaky browsing in various corners, discovering books on yoga, astral projection, spiritualism, crystal-scrying, UFOs and yes, tarot. Here I met the RWS cards, though I have no particular memory of their hold on my attention. Here I had my first chance to hear a Hindu Swami tell us how to contract and relax rhythmically the sphincter muscles to stimulate the rise of Kundalini. My curiosity far out stripped any coin I might have been able to proffer. My purchases were carefully considered. The cards were not among them, though I did have uncanny success with an Ouija board.

About a decade later, I attended sporadically Jason Lotterhand's Thursday night class hosted by Fritzi for years before it moved to Fort Mason in the Marina district. At the time I was not receptive to Lotterhand's iconic reverence for the archetypes, so I never quite appreciated his dedication to the BOTA variant of tarot. Some of his students were careful to collect the essence of these classes in the book: *The Thursday Night Tarot* (1989). I read it a few years back and would now give a careful nod to it as a useful approach to tarot. At the time I dropped in on Lotterhand's classes, I was obsessed with a variety approaches to *samadhi*, non-dual enstatic trances. Working directly with consciousness like that made his orientation to cards seem too tame, awkwardly mediated and moralistic. So this is a summary of my misperceptions at the time and not what Jason was really about.

It's hard to say what I wanted from tarot in 1977. Probably curiosity about how the oracle worked. I emphasize how because I was pretty convinced why it worked: Reality is a seamless whole without a second, so that all parts reflect that whole at all times if we but pay attention. If we only pay attention to parts, we have little sense of the whole, and meaning may well seem piecemeal and escape us. If, by quieting the mind of distractions and becoming acutely aware of awareness as it is for itself and not as it seems as a servant for our whims and senses, the true simple wholeness of everything shines forth like a radiant jewel. Tarot cards are like business cards to transcendence. Tarot is an invitation to divine reality.

Coming to the realization that I still needed to understand first-hand aspects of esoteric philosophy to come to appreciate how tarot works, I continued to explore esoteric initiatory and contemplative cults mostly of non-Christian and eastern provenance through the 1970s and 80s.

Another way of approach to this question of long-range perspective on what I want from tarot is comparing my first and second Saturn return. 1978 was my first Saturn return and represented my full blooming of adult interests. By that time I was reasonably well-educated (if not degreed) in cultural anthropology as a research paradigm. I had had preliminary training in classical raja yoga, and a close initiatory training in a shamanic style Sino-Mongolian tantric Buddhism. I was reasonably well read in mystical literatures eastern and western and was pretty sure that I was at root a simple mystic who just happen to like to think! (Thinking is stinking! Bliss smells sweet!) I was more keenly concerned with the new eastern religions in America and less interested in the Western style esotericisms. I had been active in the local branch of the Theosophical Society as leader and librarian and was a mystic without religion or the necessity of God and with a drive to learn and understand. This orientation was a self-consistent development from my young adolescence. I knew where I was going and what I was about and I was pretty much doing it as my inner lights guided. Besides studying the tarot I also became initiated into Wicca that year. Aspects of my initiation can be read about in Starhawks' *The Spiral Dance* (1978).

One can say the first Saturn return is: Have I grown up yet? And am I ready to take on my adult tasks? Then the second Saturn return is a looking backward at my accomplishments. I am then around 58 years old.

During the interregnum I had some advanced esoteric study (1980) of Muhyiddin Ibn 'Arabi at the Chisholm Institute of the Beshara Foundation in the UK. This was especially gratifying as it was an unsought fellowship that confirmed some visionary experiences and inspired a lifelong gratitude for the teaching of the Sheikh al-Akbar. I advanced the cause of Wicca by helping orient people new to Goddess worship. I facilitated quite study groups (1986-1997) of select esoteric texts, settling after some years with some esoteric Buddhist texts and Kashmir Shaivite Siva Sutras within the framework of dream work, meditation and imaginative individuation (through arts and literature, creative writing). I also became aware that my person is counter-charismatic and people are not drawn to me. (Trust the teaching, not the teacher; trust the meaning and not the form of the teaching; trust the unmediated light of truth, and not the meaning: then discus that with the teacher.) My esoteric study companions brought in new people. Of course all these activities were without finance. No contributions were sought because what can be bought occults the essence. I avoided any ready identification with a particular religious tradition. As an esotericist I was fascinated with the naked truth nude, not her lingerie.

As my second Saturn return approached I rediscovered tarot as a possible vehicle to share key aspects of my esoteric interests. I am at the age of reaping the harvest of my life. I have lived a quiet and unconventional life: yet one remarkably consistent in a broad but single-minded pursuit of esoteric insight or salvific gnosis.

I did a quick read of *Meditations on the Tarot* when it first appeared in the mid-80s. I thought our anonymous author's superstructure of Christian Hermeticism, a doctrinaire construct, a rationale for casting a broad net (tarot trumps) into the ocean of metaphysical self-inquiry, in other words, a conceptual autohagiography where the hermeticist (the anonymous author) is idealized as a jack-of-all-metaphysical-trades. Theosophists had something of the same conceit in the 1890s. In fact, such universalizing is much like the French savant that innovated modern occult theories of the tarot divination and its Egyptian origin. Antoine Court de Gébelin's ideas about the Book of Thoth, where tarot cards encrypt symbols as keys to complete knowledge is such a universalizing vision, admittedly legendary, obviously now, not historic, perhaps impracticable, and after Gödel's theorem, indeterminately reflexive, fuels my own tarot hermeneutics project. To move in the direction of discovering how 78 cards may guide our understanding, not only of me but all and everything else too, is the unitative, universalistic vision of tarot as the keys to understanding all knowledge that I share with the Court de Gébelin.

Last year I concluded a 2 ½ year teleconference reading and discussing aloud the entire *Meditations on the Tarot*. It was developed in response to some tarotists who wanted to explore that rich and complex esoteric work. I have a background that could facilitate an informed reading of the text. We met weekly for about 2 hours to discuss his sense of the Major Arcana. We were mostly tarot readers attending and we noticed how his vision of Christian Hermeticism challenges some of the more pedestrian uses of tarot. Perhaps some variant of his hybrid vision of Hermeticism may seriously inform how we understand the larger scope of esoteric tarot. In my mind his servility to orthodoxy and dogma need not be a serious barrier to adaptations of the core of his views.

As an estotericist I am not generally interested in the cookbook-style, how-to informative pretense to gnosis that clutters the marketplace of tarot commodities. However, I would not ignore them entirely either, because this is where the popular center of tarot practice is. The community of tarot readers is where the future of tarot is. Any successful innovator in tarot needs to respect, to a degree, majority opinion. And if one wants to shift that opinion or practice, one will need to attract their attention respectfully and then offer persuasive, compelling reasons for a shift to occur.

Personally I am still in creative ferment as how to best proceed to some ideas that clarify tarot structure as prelude to card symbols, which means that I am now more promise than proof. For instance, I am perennially curious about the structure of tarot, especially the numbers and structure derivative from dice and knuckle bones gaming. John Opsopaus' *Guide to the Pythagorean Tarot* (2001) briefly touches this correlation. Jodorowsky in his recently translated *The Way of the Tarot* (2010) offers an additive only style of number theory that deserves close attention, because of its relative simplicity and elegance.

I believe a closer look at Platonic-Pythagorean number symbolism as archetypes still has not given forth all its secrets as relevant to tarot-structure and generative significance for tarot practice. The logic of experience and experiment as suggested by Gaston Bachelard's studies of traditional elements offers ways to expand tarot pip associations. The four elements as experience is still the way we poetically construct our everyday sense of the world, no matter the level of our scientific or technical training. So the fabric of experience shows we have not much moved beyond the elementary-quaternary structure of the pips. Realizing this helps us to both recognize our habitual limits and attempt to see beyond them.

I have always held a special affection for qualitative numbers; where the qualities of numbers themselves generate mathematical operations and analog qualities of consciousness. Dai Léon's recent work, *Origins of Tarot* (2009), as brilliant as it is in attempting to demonstrate a phenomenology of integral consciousness in the cards, arrogantly ignores contemporary tarot traditions of interpretation. Unfortunately this means that few have seemed willing to entertain, much less integrate his insights into the stream of contemporary tarot practice. His somewhat arbitrary historicizing of an ur-tarot, really seems unnecessary, as does his reliance on some of the conceits of perennial traditionalists, though I do plan to give him a closer reading in the near future. So these remarks are preliminary.

My instinct is that after serious nods to archetypal numerology, one must find the key to the living symbols of the tarot, not initially in the images on the cards but in the images from our dreams. If I knew serious tarot readers who wanted to awaken to the universal knowledge promise of tarot reading, I would begin any study of the tarot with serious and perpetual dream work. By dream work I mean a commitment to remembering and recording one's night dreams, struggling with self and others to learn how to understand and interpret them on any and all levels, and then inquiring of the tarot by random draw to comment on the dream and the process toward understanding. Such dream study is as potent as any esoteric initiation and so should not be undertaken without realizing that one will, in due course, change in ways unimaginably radical and fundamental to one's self. At the same time, it will unfold at the level most suitable to one's own self because it is the unconscious wholeness of one's own mind and heart that is guiding the process, not some teacher or teaching.

If dream work was a more widespread discipline for tarot readers, perhaps the promiscuous collecting of decks might diminish, at least as a rational for opening-up the meaning of the cards. Even relatively standardized symbol-sets, especially pictures and images that occur on tarot cards, offer entry to the multivariate meaning genitrix of natural symbols that unlike signs are not arbitrarily delimited by connotation or denotation.

Beside archetypal-numeric-structural-oneiric-imagistic levels of influence on tarot, some knowledge of the history and culture of tarot is useful as a check on anachronic fantasists, even ones of longstanding such as correspondences with cabbala and the Hebrew alphabet. Personally I am inclined to let stand some version of these overlays as they may very well offer useful ways of evolving deeper ways of inquiring with tarot. Since 1977 I have reconciled aspects of modern tarot innovation by taking the informed long view that tarot is an integral continuation of divination that has an unbroken pedigree to the ancient Sumerians.

It is the discriminate development of some aspects of these overlays that brings me full circle, or spiral round to what I want to do with tarot. I hope to encourage some tarot readers to use the tarot to understand the deeper meaning, or potential meanings that tarot has yet to reveal.

For me tarot is not a map to the spirit and psyche, but is rather the map's keys.

The map is the living mind and heart of the tarot reader as well as the querent.

I hope in due course to show how there are ways these keys can be read that show more than is now suspected about the self, the world and the tarot itself.

The predominate practice of tarot these days is some form of self-enquiry, usually about the conditions or challenges of adapting to lifespan stages of development and self understanding, unexpected or habitual behavior. This therapeutic model of recognizing that a random draw of cards may very well reframe how we see or do not see the situations before us, is a powerful tool and offers no end to fascination for many. Still as pervasive as this style of practice and use of tarot is I want to suggest to the community of tarot readers that they should set some time aside to explore the living mystery of the tarot in other ways. True, aspects of that mystery occur potentially in every reading situation, but we owe it to ourselves as readers to the unleashed latent significance of the oracle, to make time to read the cards in ways not dictated by the whims of our querents.

In this preliminary formulation, I suggest whatever you happen to be studying, bring the tarot to it to comment. However once you have your cards and a preliminary interpretation of how they might apply. Seriously consider both sides of the inquiry. How does the appearance of this card alter my appreciation of this subject? Write it down. Next how does this card's association with this subject affect my understanding of this card and its symbolism? Again write it down. Keep a log. The future of tarot meanings as a universal key to all knowledge will be revealed in the community of tarot readers to the degree we reflect upon and share with one another our variant experiences of card meanings, repetitive patterns of cards with diverse subjects and stories, and literary texts, works of art, historic moments.

Like all natural symbol systems, tarot significance, not just card meanings, is reflexive. It carries within itself an indistinct redundancy to reproduce itself in any and all contexts, however, the context, not the reflexivity, shapes the mirroring of significance. Some names for classic repetitive styles of this transformative mirroring are image, sign, representation, mark, icon, pictogram, emblem, badge, logo, indication, character, description, metaphor, analogy, allegory, figure, simile, comparison, parable, genre, story, fable, tale, substitution, transformation and symbol. This list assumes no system but aspects of the mirroring are characterized by these words to narrow or broaden the focus. Metaphor, for example, represents a focus upon the similarity or difference or one thing for another. It is this thing as another thing that creates the energy of transformation that gives sense (cognitivity) to significance. Even as it (this thing as another thing) both confuses by indentifying one thing and another thing in its image or name as itself, which is false and fictive, and simultaneously as another unlike thing or symbol which is true but falls short of the connectivity of significance. The old paradox is here recognized. If I speak I must lie to tell the truth. And if I remain silent, the truth is ever present but remains unidentified and so may not be known. Why does knowledge require falsehood to prove it? Is there a truth that is not caught in the net of our conjectures?

Linguists claim that word-meaning develops by the use of words in community to apply to variant situations and experiences. The meanings drift by application and context and may spread or narrow in significance depending upon the speaking community's use of the word. Tarot cards are much more richly endowed with prospective significance than any words of a speaking community. I hope to persuade some tarot readers to recognize aspects of this endowment; especially the reflexive nature of tarot and its images so that the open-ended, ever reaching, creativity of tarot may open more doors to a significant life lived in fuller consciousness and contextual, actually, experiential possibility.

Though my focus and emphasis are somewhat different, there is more than a family resemblance to work done by Rachel Pollack in her wisdom readings (See especially, *Tarot Wisdom,* and *Forest of Souls*); and by James Rickleff's *Tarot Tells the Tale,* that touches upon themes close to my own tarot hermeneutics, especially in adapting random draws to the analysis of stories. I thank Mary K. Greer for alerting me to James's work.

My first reaction to your very interesting response is: could someone expect anything from the tarot outside of occultism? In a conversation with Ross Caldwell he said something that I found useful: "occultism is just one way the game is played", which suggests, of course, that there were/are other ways. What do you think? I am asking because in one of your essays you wrote something like "to assess the true importance of occultism, the whole human history would need to be rewritten" (I am paraphrasing here). Won't it be more realistic to rewrite the tarot's history, by acknowledging the tarot's link to occultism as part of the broader context of the tarot as a game?

There are several things you touched there and I want you to expand on, but let's start with your comment on dreams, because this is something I have also discussed with Robert M. Place. In our conversation, he hinted at that relationship between the tarot and dreams. This is also something that intrigues me, although I often fail at making my point. Every time I have tried to explain to someone that we can experience the tarot as a dream, they look at me as if wanting to say "dreams are dreams and the tarot is the tarot". Still, from a qualitative point of view, both events seem somehow similar: we experience a scene of a more or less random nature that we read as meaningful by assigning an emotional value, meaning, to each one of its components. Often in a dream we see a character changing faces: "it was my aunt... well, it wasn't really my aunt but I know that it was my aunt" just as in a tarot reading we may be successively represented by several different characters. We may be The Emperor and then the Page of Coins, or even that solitary cup in the upper section of the Three of Cups. Both in a dream and in a tarot reading we experience the event as witness and participants at once. Both can, of course, elicit strong emotional responses. Both can be intriguing or useful.

The many strategies to tackle the origin of dreams we know of usually take two main forms: there are psychological explanations and there are physiological explanations. I guess it is safe to say that these psychological explanations are way more popular than the physiological ones. We really like them better! Since psychology is our contemporary branch of shamanism, its starting point is that dreams are meaningful in themselves: manifestations of unconscious urges, repressed content emerging into consciousness, inner wisdom breaching out, cognitive rehearsal in response to daily problems, etc. The physiology of dreaming often feels more 'mechanical', suggesting something we hate: a lack of agency; from the Activation Synthesis Model of dreaming suggested by Hobson and McCarley, in which dreams are mere neural firing the forebrain 'reads' in a meaningful way, to some research suggesting that the kind of dreams we have depend on the sleep stage we are at. In any case, the discussion about why we dream seems to mirror the discussion about why the tarot works. Both come down to some sort of match: Higher Wisdom vs. Chance. Obviously, I don't want to spend our time together arguing the pros and cons of each 'contender', but I wonder: is the tarot a doorway to our dreams, or it is a crutch for the dreamless?

I believe, as you note, Ross Caldwell's comment suggests a serious revamping (truly a dissertation-in-waiting) of how we understand tarot! Yes, it makes sense that we closely look at and evaluate tarot game practices. The historic connection is not in dispute. The unique characteristics of tarot games, their rules and the strategies implied in their play should be explored. Probabilistic scales should be worked out for the various ways one scores the game and the relative odds for winning hands. Most of the tarot games I know and play a hand is pretty much won or lost during the bidding phase of the game. The actual playing out of the hand merely confirms the skill of the bids.

(It is odd that there are no divination tarot studies I know of, to have explored the scales of randomness for the deck. For instance, what are the odds that one is to pull a major arcana card in a five-card spread? (if my math is right 22/78 = 0.28* for an initial selection, changing slightly with each additional selection and its outcome, to 5/78 = 0.064* comes to about 1. If one draws none it is against odds, if you draw 1 with-in odds, if you draw 2, somewhat against odds, 3 and above quite unusual.) After all with only 78 cards our random field of possibility is quite small and worthy of exposition. Any mathematicians wanting to help an innumerate tarotist get his odds tables right?)

Since the historical structure and images of the deck were developed as a gaming pass-time and that the use of tarot in divination is a relatively recent innovation, it seems obvious we should explore closely the nature of tarot games. Likewise we should open up to questions of gaming and gambling in general as a contiguous behavior to divining. Both deal with small random fields. Both deal with the mystery of change and stretching to control or know the outcome of change. Time calculated as small increments of randomness. Gaming is set up as a win/lose situation. Divining is a matter of nuance and fine distinctions of outcome. Both can be understood as a bet on the unknown and unknowable future. Yes there is much to notice in these yet perhaps underexplored relationships between gaming in general and the relations of games to divination. If we recognize the game qualities of tarot it may bring up the shadow-side of gaming, gambling-addictions, issue avoidances that obsessive play may generate in practitioners. I also suspect that much thought has already gone into this academically but has not been as yet tied into tarot divination practice.

When I wrote how a true history of the occult would completely rework and revalue the connections of our cultural histories, I had some work in mind. My acceptance of tarot as it is a community of readers today does not make me think that game theory is the overriding arch into which to next put occult tarot practice and innovation. Rather I think primordial divination is the greater arch in which occult and esoteric tarot is a modern innovation. (However I would not reject that gambling and divination may well inhabit the same primitive tent; their purposes seem to carry strong reasons to recognize their difference as well as resemblance.)

There is a nice précis of old world divination as strung upon the vine connection world civilizations continuity by the overland silk road. Brian Baumann translated a relatively common Mongolian textbook from around 1900. The book is relatively brief; it covers basic knowledge of astrology and divination. As a dissertation, translation alone of such a text does not cut it in academia without serious justification, which Baumann provided in a massive introduction, where he demonstrates an unbroken continuity from the earliest records of Sumerian Babylonian through Western classical, Indian, Buddhist, Central Asian and Tibetan-Chinese cultures of divination. The continuities far outweigh the variations in theory and practice. [See Brian Baumann: *Divine Knowledge: Buddhist Mathematics according to the Anonymous Manual of Mongolian Astrology and Divination* (Brill's Inner Asian Library, 20: Brill Academic, 2008)]

The question of divinatory tarot as a necessary adaption of playing cards to address the unknown, usually the future seems to address perennial human need to assuage stress of change and unpredictable developments. Let me note in passing that the majority, by far, of artistic depictions of cartomancy, found by Mary K. Greer, show playing cards and not tarot. That tarot as a modern innovation concerns me less now than when I first encountered the artificial correspondences of esoteric tarot in 1977. I believe other tarotists have touched upon tarot as modern. I also feel that the occult, to which divination is an aspect, represents in our modern science, secular and religious sectarian hegemonic culture, a leaven to dominate forces. As vibrant occultisms manifest in our global cultures, they subsist as parasites. For they need healthy or sickly hegemonic institutions, sciences, religions, ideologies, histories, stories, to which they attach their minority positions. The minority helps facilitate change and greases shifts in routine behavior to new options.

People have the capacity to see many behaviors and practices through the lens of the occult. It is like going around and focusing only on the shadows of things and ignoring the things that make the shadows. If we did this, we would see another world of interpenetrating presences phasing in and out of intensity with one another. A new view of causality would perhaps come to notice, and we might well realize, that colors act as distractions and distortions to luminous shadow play. This shadow world exists, but our exoteric, thing trained eyes are not sensitive to its layered patterning.

Tarot as a deck of cards with strange images on them is not occult or esoteric. What makes them occult is the way they are understood, approached, and used by people. Some thinkers us the terms, 'occult' and 'esoteric', to represent significantly different but related phenomena. Both terms relate to the intimation that the world has an inside like people have an inside with motives and purposes not plainly seen. The occult is this intimation as 'looking from the outside in'. The occult is interest in and experience of occult phenomena as, for example, telepathy, telekinesis, auditions, visionary experiences, synchronicities, prophet dreams, etc. The approach of people with this 'looking from the outside in' is to want to understand these as we understand the world. It is egotistic and dualistic. It is psyche and soma delimited. It is power and control driven.

The esoteric is this intimation as 'looking from the inside out.' The net effect is that for the esoteric, there is no inside or outside, just a world, whole, full, empty, complete and alive. Here the limit of soul-story and body-history is erased and enlivened in endless spirit. It is self as freedom and nondualistic. It is erotic and ludic (play) driven.

I see tarot reading as divination as straddling the divide between the occult and the esoteric, between recognizing the occult's refreshing news of the world and entering a genuine esoteric transvaluation of the self and world in freedom. My personal orientation is to encourage people to discover the esoteric sense of knowing themselves and not to suffer the occult too long as it may enervate.

I do not agree that the occult tarot is only another game unless we take something like James Carse's ideas seriously in his little book called *Finite and Infinite Games: A Vision of Life as Play and Possibility* (1987). Here I see Carse offering an orientation to the juncture of Tarot as gaming and as divinization. "The rules of the finite game may not change (during a game); the rules of an infinite game must change." "Finite players play within boundaries; infinite players play with boundaries." "A finite player plays to be powerful; an infinite player plays with strength." "Finite players are serious; infinite games are playful." Unlike Carse I see tarot practice as fitting into a threefold grid instead of his twofold one. Tarot is a finite game as is any other card game. It has rules and players play to win. "A finite player consumes time; an infinite player generates time."

Occult tarot divination is both a finite and an infinite game. It is finite as the cards are consulted with a question and there is sought an answer. This fits finite play. However as a student of tarot we may know that the cards also address deeper issues that are not delimited by any one reading or any set of questions. "The finite player aims for eternal life; the infinite player aims for eternal birth."

To the degree we realize to continue to play with strength as reading tarot, our divination becomes occult and esoteric infinite play. "There is but one infinite game." The choice is always ours: how we approach tarot or our own life. In my tarot parlor patter for newbie readees, I have a bit that explains how tarot works: The occult meaning of tarot is that everything is connected and the symbol-images on the cards speak to that ineffable connection that our consciousness perfectly mirrors the world and the world is a perfect mirror to our consciousness and intentions. A scientific explanation of how tarot works is that everything is connected, and by reading tarot, we construct a way of seeing significance in that acausal connectivity of everything, by associating it with whatever story we have in mind at the time we consult the tarot.

This tongue-in-cheek contrast between the occult or mystical explanation and a scientific rationalization for the efficacy of tarot readings is rarely challenged, and usually settles the querent down enough to select cards at random to commence a reading.

Personally I share some investment in both the 'occult' and the 'scientific' 'explanations' of how tarot works. (After all I am only a quasi-Trickster and a quasi-Fool in a Schrödinger's box of cards that combines a probabilistic interpretation with deterministic dynamics of competing plots.) I may very well posit an 'ineffable connection that our consciousness perfectly mirrors the world and the world is a perfect mirror to our consciousness and intentions.' However we are persistently running interference with this seamless whole of consciousness and world. We interfere by monologuing stories in our heads that are nonresponsive to the reality of our situation now. These quasi-formulated stories derive from daydreams, distractive desires without release, toxic worry about and incomplete imitation of semi-perceived others. We ignore our senses, distort perceptions, and warp our being in place, lack a way to settle in and listen to rather than direct our own awareness. We somnambulate through the day, while we wakewalk at night, addicted to an insomniac's sleep-cycle. In such a place of inauthenticity, it is easy to see how a set of cards might wake us up or set us straight to notice the flowers and pause to sniff.

The dream tarot section of your question evokes an easy response for me and betrays certain epistemological biases that the waking world of perceptions is real and the whimsical world of sleep and dreams, symbols and desires is less real and contingent upon the waking experience, the true measure of the world and the self as body. Let me be more allusive here. The loco classicist is the late *Mandukya Upanishad*[1] that describes four levels to consciousness: Waking, dreaming, deep or dreamless sleep, and the fourth. (To be fair beside my own yogic experience, insights from *The Spiritual Teaching of Ramana Maharshi*, a book that collects the sage's advice to visitors, and the *Siva Sutras*, a central text of Trika Shaivism, inform my understanding of this phenomenology.)

Everybody experiences waking, dreaming and deep sleep. It is useful as a phenomenology of awareness. Many of us experience them as discreet. Waking gets most of the attention as it seems more real than the others. This bias runs deep. Even the mapping of brain activity on dreams and dreamless sleep is marginalized by those who look for measurable energetic correlates to perceptions, conceptions, sensations, memory, and simulation. I think this work is interesting as far as it goes. Even the postulate that dream-images are a sort of randomness that our waking sense imposes structure and meaning upon as we move to arousal does not invalidate the revaluation of the 3-4 states. (I do not deal with the nature of the 4th (or 5th) here except in passing. I will offer a tease, however, that this 3-4 or 5 levels or aspects address deep archetypal enfoldments that speak to primal numbers and the nature of the 4 elements of the pips.)

---

1 http://www.anandway.com/blog/post/Mandukya-Upanishad-Sanskrit-text-and-English-translation.aspx

The practice of meditation may well awaken one to a fuller view of the nature of consciousness and oneself. Rather than being a servant to our waking sense perceptions and our commonsense, commingling of it in our inchoate sensations, emotions, images, words, and story, attention or awareness has qualities of its own that our exterior-oriented, waking culture has assiduously ignored and neglected. As we awaken to the qualities of awareness by paying attention to awareness (the royal road of meditation and contemplation, realization) we become more aware of what dreams are. We likewise become aware that the seeming blank of no-time, no-memory, no-self, no-experience of deep sleep opens to qualities of awareness that (among other possibilities) releases the seamless oneness of deep sleep. This unity ('activated' as the 4th, 'persistent' as the 5th) does nothing, but it appears in awareness to unify all parts of waking dreaming and deep sleep.

Even without this radical refocusing of experience released by realization, we can recognize all three states of awareness while awake. Being awake we are aware of the world. Close our eyes (senses generally), and we are more aware of our inner senses which is the sum and substance of daydreams and dreams. Open our eyes and we can see that we can locate our dreaming capacity, eclipsed by the loudness and our attending to our sensation. Likewise we can feel a blank back drop, a silence listening, an unmoved witness, of dreamless sleep as abysmal silence and nothingness. So we have in waking wonderful capacities that we do not know how to pay attention to because it is refocusing awareness to levels of experience we have been taught by our cultures to ignore. Dreaming and understanding dreams is the natural genetrix of symbols, images, the stuff of significance that may be the commentary, story of our self in the world. (Here I mean the world to be inclusive of waking, dreaming, deep sleep and the 4th).

The issue of meaning as dichotomy between 'Higher Wisdom vs. Chance' boils down to insisting that the analytic trumps the synthetic. The classic law of identity, as Aristotle put it, A=A, or logical identity axiom that asserts an object's uniqueness with itself, is so close to tautology as to appear unassailable. Of course, this initial axiom makes sense if we invest in the stuff of the world as timeless. However the world is never without time, change or process. Heraclitus of Ephesus observed 'you cannot step into the same river twice'. One Alexandrian wag noted in comment to this insight that 'you cannot step into the same river once!' Analytic subjects are often the results of previous synthetic processes and the assumption of static axiomatic analytic is swallowed in change. Even change changes change, perhaps a good definition of chance. Can you take a chance?

If I have been clear enough you can see that your dream questions do not arise as problematic because tarot reading is a sort of waking dream for any active reader. It is this possibility in the community of tarot readers that we can use the cards as prompts to real dreams and actual divining. My hope is to challenge some in this community to move beyond the occult and more toward the esoteric in their tarot contemplations. I see the esoteric as quickening not only the soulful symbols of individual experience and dreams and myths (group-dreams) but the spirit hearkening promise of abysmal deep dreamless sleep and its treasure trove of riches beyond number or speech or image, love divine.

I agree with you about the similarities between gaming and fortunetelling. I often think that even the suggestions a pack of tarot carries within itself come from the tarot's origin as a game of chance. After all, both on the card-shark and the diviner's table, "the cards you got define your fate".

But I often wonder about that relationship between cartomancy and what you define as 'primordial divination'. I agree in that there is a common primal impulse there. The cards lend themselves very well to divination. But I wonder if there is really a continuum, as in "I am done with goat's entrails, let me grab a pack of cards instead!," or if cartomancy can be seen as a lighter, tamed, manifestation of the same impulse that came to be in a non-religious context. By this I don't mean it appeared in non-religious cultures, but that it came to be in what can still be seen as a recreational setting. While helping Ross Caldwell with the translation of Fernando De La Torre's manual for cartomancy – the oldest manual we know, if I recall correctly – the amusing tone of the text soon became evident. When we compare this manual with other early texts on cartomancy, we notice a common denominator: most of them seem to deal with the problem of 'love'. In other words, most of these manuals are aimed at telling people – women, really – if and when they would find a man. There is also a whole "amuse your friends and be the light of the party" kind of feeling in these manuals that is contrary to the grave tone of divination. At the risk of sounding sacrilegous, I wonder if we could see cartomancy as something closer to a parlor game than to divination. For once, in all these countries where it is still relevant or socially accepted, divination is associated with a more complex body of religious practices. You don't toy with it, you don't do it yourself. In these settings, oracles are the voice of the gods. I wonder if we could see cartomancy as a more 'secular' practice. I also wonder: which god, gods, or goddesses do you think speak through the tarot?

Now, I would like to take this conversation in a different direction. You wrote a fascinating account of your experiences becoming a reader. In that account you mention an episode, early on, when this woman you knew read the cards for you, and kept 'seeing' your partner having an affair with another man. You were quite skeptical about the whole thing, and even so, the reader's insistency over several sessions ended up eroding your confidence a little bit. You actually started to look for the 'blond man' crossing paths with your woman. In which way would you say that this experience informed the work you did as a reader later on?

The gods and goddesses are always speaking. It is we who have forgotten how to listen. And we have also forgotten who to consult when we cannot hear them for ourselves. I would rather have people learn how to hear the gods for themselves than trust the word of someone who says they can consult the gods for us.

I agree that the modern world has cleaned up the act of divination. Official divination in the modern world has become the province of science. Religious divination is profoundly connected with sacrifice. The purpose of modernity is the hegemony of a secular understanding of the world. Part of that hegemonic entitlement is the trivialization of sacred practices and ideologies.

The need for divination and perhaps the need for gaming run deep in our human nature. There are no people who do not have various forms of both gambling and divination. I think that taking up cards as a form of divination was really adapting what was at hand. I think if I were a chicken farmer I might still be reading the entrails of chickens. But it is easier and neater to shuffle a pack of cards than to disembowel a living chicken over the kitchen sink. I do not think I would ingratiate myself to my clients with such bloody goings-on.

I believe early cartomancy, the use of playing cards for light divining, especially as concerned with the game of love, is a gender social class transformation of the gaming-room into the salon. I am not familiar with the various social customs that extend to gambling and the role of women in the gaming-room. But love is a kind of bet. I think that there are also important variants related to class and marriage. Most of these issues are handled differently at different historic times depending upon your social station. The degree that the sexes interacted was under public and formal scrutiny. Otherwise in the upper and middle classes women and men led the gender separated lives and activities. Of course this does not fully apply to the underclasses and serving classes, but our records are of the upper classes when it comes to the early history of cartomancy and the origins of tarot.

I am glad you have so thoroughly investigated my website, but I must confess that you misread the attribution of the piece on becoming a tarot reader. It is taken from one of the few dissertations on the nature of the occult tarot. The name of the book is *The Esoteric Scene, Cultic Milieu, And Occult Tarot* by Danny L. Jorgensen (Garland Publishing, 1992). This is Danny's account of becoming a tarot reader in the late 1970s. However, this does remind me of an antidote from the other night. I was at a party, and, as I often do, I offer to do short readings for people. One fellow told me that when he was in college his grandmother would write him long letters that were based on her tarot readings of what he was up to. He especially remembered how insistent his grandmother was about him dating a blonde woman. When he said that he wasn't dating anyone, she dismissed his denials saying that the tarot is not wrong! Needless to say this fellow wasn't interested in having his tarot read!

In the late 60s, when I was still active in the esoteric Buddhist shamanic cult, a professional tarot reader and trance medium from Columbus Ohio came out to visit to get an initiation into certain *sadhanas* of the cult. Elisabeth Valentine Bacon was a woman about the same age as my mother who had spent her life studying and practicing the occult, or as we said then, the 'metaphysical.' While she was visiting I took her out to visit my mother and she read her tarot cards. I also remember that she read mine, but what she said did not interest me much as it was about my particular *dharma* in the metaphysical arts and not about some fetching woman I was going to hook up with!

Some five years later I visited her in Columbus where I met some of her clients; many of them were lab technicians who had the rudiments of a technical scientific education. Her main way of working with them was to go into trance, and have her spirit guides consult about issues.

I did have an opportunity to see what her spirit guides looked like. What I saw were strange hybrid entities, not human nor any definite kind of animal. They were not so monstrous as weirdly configured. By paying attention to these strange apparitions that occurred in my mind's eye, I did realize that they carried with them some fascinating energies that awakened in me a kind of symbolic dance of images, a mishmash of colors, music, emotional revving, and fragmented insights. For Elisabeth, these weird creatures had names and spoke in ways to betray quite distinct personalities. One of the personalities only spoke in singsong rhyme and was often the author of Elisabeth's annual Christmas greetings. Another personality, claiming to be an Oriental Sage of some long distance disincarnate pedigree of Taoist background, had a long conversation with me about the nature of psychic geography, and the real meaning of the Theosophical root races.

I feel that Elisabeth Valentine Bacon is an important personal link in my appreciation of tarot reading. She did tell me, though, that I would have a rich and varied career in the occult arts and that my life was not going to be as conventional as I may have wanted it to be. Unfortunately she also turned out to be reasonably right about my rocky road with women. Of course, I have had many readings by many tarot readers over the years, and every now and then, I will find one that insists upon certain things that do not at the time makes sense and later even make less sense. I usually just dismiss it as new readers trusting to remember associations than in actually reading the symbolic flow of the cards. Likewise I have had some readings, when some things were predicted, that I had no reason to think would occur, and they did! These, of course, are the ones that I find worthy of comment and am sure to tell the reader that their predictions worked out in ways that I could not and did not expect.

I thought that sociological account was yours! Sorry for the misunderstanding.

That essay makes reference to Jason Lotterhand's 'Thursday Night Tarot', which I believe is still on. I confess that a few years back I had a book on these lectures on my hands and I couldn't make too much of it. I liked the idea of these lectures more than its contents. Something similar happened when I read Cabaret Místico, *by Alejandro Jodorowsky. The book is a transcript of some of the free lectures he gave every Wednesday in Paris, for about 20 years. I sympathize with these sustained efforts. Especially with Jodorowsky's custom of sitting at a coffee shop every*

Wednesday to read the tarot for free. I am told he doesn't do that anymore, but he did it for about 20 years. People who had been there say they had to take a number, and there was a little lotto to see if you got your reading with Jodorowsky or with one of his assistants. I also met a filmmaker to whom Jodorowsky read the tarot in private. He regards the event as one of the key moments in his life.

I am mentioning all this because you said you were interested in Jodorowsky's work. I went to see him here in New York when he came to give a lecture on the tarot. The event was mesmerizing due to Jodorowsky's great showmanship, but also because of the mix of irony and reverence he had while working with the tarot. After that I read everything he wrote. I was especially interested in his work with 'Psicomagia', which is his secular form of shamanism in which he prescribes metaphorical actions to heal people from their problems. Two things that interest me about Jodorowsky's approach are his focus on a magical experience where belief isn't necessary, and his idea of redefining magic to appeal to a contemporary audience. Recently, I watched a short video of a talk he gave in Italy. Here is a passage I would like to share with you:

> For me, to go out and do a gratuitous act every Wednesday… to read the tarot to anybody… It has changed my life; because every Wednesday I give advise to heal people, and by healing them I heal myself.

What do you think about Jodorowsky's practice in regard of only reading the tarot for free? As a matter of fact, he bases his practice on never charging and never predicting the future. Then there is this idea of healing yourself by healing others. I have given my fair share of readings to all kinds of therapists, and I am often terrified about how screwed are those we entrust our mental health to, but still, I understand the idea of being fed instead of being hungry. What do you think?

I must confess that I am limited to only what I can read in English. But I am happy that our conversation is turning toward topics that are keener to address. I already shared my disdain for Jason's approach to tarot. In retrospect I think it more my own youthful arrogance and a preoccupation with other aspects of the occult. A devotional understanding of the symbols of tarot as missives from the gods to remind us of their power and wisdom may well bring us to a measured appreciation of the archetypes of the major Arcana as icons. And I am willing to recognize in some cases an almost hypnotic connection between works of art and the ineffable relations they intimate.

I have in the past spent time in local coffeehouses reading the tarot for free to anyone I could interest. I found I tended to spend more time shuffling the cards than actually reading for anybody. (My counter-charisma at work, no doubt) I read for free and for a fee depending upon how the invitation is broached.

Soul work tarot is usually gratis. As a spiritual exercise I feel that the reading of tarot is a way of doing soul work with someone. It means I should be careful with what I say and also truthful. I notice that when I do not know a person very well, and I read their cards getting indications of difficulties and major stresses in their life, I will interpret the cards in a gentle way, almost protecting them from the more stark possibilities the cards portend. However, if I know someone better, and have a sense of their own story and how they manage their affairs, I tend to be more direct in telling of difficult news.

My experience as a reader is the way a reading is accepted, as an alternative story, as heartfelt advice, as revelations of the secrets of the heart, as healing old wounds and offering new insight in areas of incomprehension. My reading depends upon the psychic predisposition of the client and not my intention as a reader. The symbols heal, I do not heal. I may help activate the symbol in someone's psyche but they need to have the receptivity to accept the consequences.

Unlike Jodorowsky, I do not make a fetish out of one's position in time and will speak of future outcomes in probable terms. If someone wants to know an outcome of something that they are worried about, I will look into the cards and see what they say. However, I do not claim to foretell the future so much as saying that according to these cards the outcome looks one way or another, or that the way the cards are configured I cannot say for sure either way.

Jodorowsky's book on *Psicomagia* is scheduled to be published in English at the end of this year. I read his spiritual autobiography, which read like a mixture of humble self-confession and braggadocio. But perhaps this is a mere envy in that my own escapades in self-knowledge were not so pleasantly enthralled with erotic adventures. I still have not studied with the thoroughness that I want his views on tarot. But like yourself, I find his 'mix of irony and reverence' a refreshing view of the cards.

I am also be inclined to agree that magical experience does not rely upon belief. Several of my visionary experiences, including my visual take on the astral entities that were the companions to Elisabeth Valentine Bacon, occurred spontaneously and without any effort on my part. Likewise other visionary experiences happened well before I became aware of ritual and magical practices that supported them. I think even Lakoff recognizes that metaphors have the power of magic especially those that are seemingly newly minted in the experience of the speaker or listener.

I don't think we could communicate with each other at all without some active participation in magical thinking that allows us to make the truth lies and lies of the truth. This brings me round to aspects of my own tarot investigations that are still in the works, still undiscovered, still in potential. If I assume that the current core of what I call tarot hermeneutics is the reflexive meaning of tarot cards and patterns as read by the community of tarot readers, first off then is my wish to have some of my fellow tarot readers understand what this means and how it is of crucial significance to the creative practice of tarot. I do not mean that my work in particular is crucial to the future of tarot, but that this insight is important to keep the magic alive.

Beginning with dream work, tarot icons are a stylized form of natural symbols. Natural symbols are those spontaneous images that occurr to us in our dreams. If we attempt to understand these images, we find that they open us up to a panorama of interconnecting experiences that have significance to us. Our ability to speak is one of the ways that we have formalized natural symbols. One aspect of natural symbols is that there is associative significance as additive without limit. Languages and systems are formalized by imposing limits. When I speak of the language of the birds I speak of the natural symbols before we have formalized them with artificial limits.

Now, the images on tarot cards are derivative of mythical and iconic stories and assumptions which does frame them in ways to make them limited. But the images in themselves never lose hold of their natural propensity to escape into the wild. The active imagination developed by Carl Jung and his school is a form of running wild with the symbols. Needless to say I want to encourage tarot readers to run wild with the symbols while at the same time learning their historical and mythical antecedents.

Even natural symbols exist within a context of experience which is ever in the process of correcting itself. This process is recursive. This means that it is self-referential and may learn from repetition and unusual circumstances. The reflexive meaning of tarot cards and patterns means that as we read them we continue to learn that the symbols can do more than what we thought they could. Every time we read the cards with a different situation in mind the cards offer us new understandings not only about that situation, but about the significance and potential of the cards themselves to tell us things that are new as well as things that we already knew. In the day to day practice of tarot reading most tarot readers are reading for people who have issues about their lives they wish to have commentary on. Plenty of this has to do with affairs of the heart, with the outcome of business deals, with the understanding of interpersonal dynamics and behaviors. Given how powerful this tool is as a potential source of deeper understanding, it seems like a waste of time when we could be attempting to understand the dynamics of quantum mechanics in our everyday life by closely questioning the tarot cards.

Let's take a far-fetched analogy. I am a plumber. I know how to plumb very well and have all the expected skill and knowledge of any competent plumber. I'm faced with a job of plumbing. I look at the job and see what needs to be done. Okay, now I consulted tarot cards to see what they say about this plumbing job. Because I am a plumber I will read the tarot cards in a way that can make the symbolic content of the cards relevant to the plumbing job. Will my consultation of the tarot cards help me do a better job? Will the cards perhaps alert me to aspects of things that I did not already see? I cannot answer these questions because this is not the context in which I consult tarot. Let me know if you know any plumbers or other trades people who might be willing to learn tarot to see if it can affect the way they ply their trades.

Applying my tarot hermeneutics, I want to know how the cards selected address the issue. Next, I want to know how this situation affects how I understand the cards, for each new context gives rise to new possibilities of the way the card may be understood. I would like to open up this reflexive insight more, but I have not yet discovered ways to do it that do not close down the open-ended possibility I am trying to entertain and remain in creative tension with.

Since my own interests are clearly concerned with literary aspects of the esoteric, I can easily see how I may proceed using the tarot as a way to interrogate about the tradition. However the way tarot could be developed as a useful tool of inquiry has not yet been breached in any of would-be possibility.

Jodorowsky is great at recounting his dealings with famous people, from André Bretón to Marilyn Manson. That's a self-promotional gimmick the Amazing Kreskin also uses very well. Perhaps that is what I both, admire and criticize most in his work: he is great at playing for the effect. Reading for free accomplishes two important things: it separates him from all the professional fortunetellers, and frees him from having to deal with questions he doesn't find interesting. In a way, he accomplishes what you call 'soul work' by making people feel the reading is a privilege, not a service. You are there, after waiting for a week, maybe more, you draw your number, you go to sit with him, and he actually won't see you if you don't have a question, but he will rephrase your question to make the whole conversation more transcendent. A great example of this would be: "I can't tell you when you are going to find a man, but I could tell you why you haven't found one yet".

I do free readings on Friday mornings, and I do think those are my best readings. By letting the tarot speak, and accepting what it says, one gets to experience its true magic. I think the tarot invites us to a receiver-oriented form of communication, in which things are hinted at us, instead of a sender-oriented communication, in which things are impressed upon us. What do you think?

Furthermore, you are touching a couple of fascinating ideas here. The language of the birds is about finding wonder in the finger that points at the moon. There is this idea from painter Francesco Clemente, who said that he paints to help images recover their memory. I like this in poetic terms. I like it as a way of making poiesis. But I suspect that sometimes we get too caught up in the magic of the process, and we forget that the finger was originally pointing at something else. It had an original purpose. There is this idea, for example, that if you look at the pips for days or years, you will uncover their secrets. I don't think this is true. If you look at the pips for days or years, you uncover 'your' secrets, but you may still have no clue about what these images are about. You may still have no clue as to the possibility that that these images may be about nothing!

I wonder to what extent a symbol can be natural, as you suggest. Symbols are representational limits we impose on an image, element, or shape, turning them into some common ground where we can meet with other people. Wherever we mark the ground, we create boundaries. It seems to me that all symbols are artificial. I mean, the idea of one thing standing for another one is a convention we all agree upon, but it is not objectively true. Nothing is intrinsically symbolic, but we use things as symbols. Could you expand here, please?

First let me acknowledge, that I am enjoying this opportunity in conversation with you to attempt to express the directions of my thinking about tarot, its future significance and possibility. I am happy that you recognize the necessity that successful artists in our commodity saturated global culture must court Dame Fame, with the ravenous attention of a possessive pimp or an obsessive, penniless lover. I really cannot fault the success of artists who must cater to the fleeting attentions of the *nouveau rich*.

Still this recognition of the necessity of linking creative work with publicity gimmicks in order to succeed as an artist in our culture gives me a moment to further reflect on the nature of tarot reading as an art form. One of the things that is central to tarot is that there are 78 blank panels which may be populated with various forms of abstract and mostly stylized representational images. It is a popular art form, because, potentially, it can be mass-produced and owned for a fraction of the cost of the incredible amount of creativity and time it can take to populate those 78 panels.

When I spoke before about my spontaneous visions of the astral entities of Elisabeth Valentine Bacon, I was somewhat tutored in Surrealism by a college friend who had grown up in the backdrop of the San Francisco Renaissance. The San Francisco Renaissance is most notably known as the poetic announcement of the beat generation by Allen Ginsberg reading of the first part of *Howl for Carl Solomon*. My friend introduced me to the writings of André Bretón and the general ethos of the surrealists, especially in its poetic, rather than representational, pictorial emphasis. Eventually this association, and in spite of my resolutely sticking to my metaphysical obsessions, led me to finding the parlor games of the surrealists and their materialistic obsession with the occult as a demonstration of the autonomous imagination, and consituted an important ongoing critique of my own, more traditional, unconscious strivings; it gave rise to my introduction to and long-term friendship with the San Francisco poet, Phillip Lamantia. Philip died a few years ago, and I had not had a good conversation with him for almost 20 years, even when I met him in my late 20s, he being 20 years older than myself. He was an obsessively private individual known for his mantic autodidactic rants on alchemy and mystical and hermetic topics. In him I had met a fellow traveler.

I believe that I had a formal and somewhat limited friendship with him which lasted from my point of view the rest of our lives, but I do not wish to exaggerate the intimacy of it, but rather emphasize that what we shared was not an interest in poetry *per se,* but in the occult classics. And it was discussing these and their implications that we spent many carefully crafted hours in private during the heyday of our association. When I was in my late 30s and Philip in his 50s, I would call him and we would arrange an appointment for me to meet at his apartment, and we would talk about whatever we wanted to. I very much appreciated the things Philip knew about as they were things that I had not necessarily strayed across in my readings. So I have to admit that I did learn much from these conversations.

After calling Philip we would arrange a time to meet at his place on Union Street, usually on a weekday afternoon. We would sit in a small room in his flat, windows facing north, and a soft light streaming in. We would exchange pleasantries and a bit of gossip, usually allowing some point to illustrate a principle. and from that we would begin to move. Among the topics would be Thomas Vaughan in his *Magia Adamica,* discussing the Three Mothers as the mediation between word and thing. The Three Mothers or Aleph, Mem and Shin, their elements corresponding to air, water and fire as precreate propensities of unseparated or undifferentiated motions; Shakti, if you will, before the threefold supernal field is laid out as love/will, awareness/knowing, act/motion after the Trika's tattva list. God weighed Aleph with all and all with Aleph, and so with the other Mothers. This shows how Adam as cosmos is both agent and patient; Jacob's ladder cited, because, as Waite's notes, the hermetic maxim 'as above, so below' signifies the bond of union, a union occluded, however, in the measure, the weighing, of representing the secret intending toward creation, the word about to be uttered. So Goethe's word is deed of Faust's bargain, and pausing at the yawning chasm of abysmal three mothers in the heart of the athanor. The inverted Tower or the Hanged Man.

Begin again: On our afternoon visits, sitting quietly surrounded by Philip's books, the conversation would begin with a sharing of topical concern and eventually turn toward some shared hermetic symbology or substance. There we might delve into its purport and family resemblances to Kabbalah, Masonic, Taoist, Sufi, Egyptian, alchemical, Trika, Hegelian, shamanic, Swedenborgian concatenation of correspondences and transmogrifications that tended to astound with scintillating insight and bafflement, perplexity and awe. With mystagogic disclosures jolting ideas out of their customary associations of habit we would rape words into immediate lived images that suspend the ordinary and provoke the extraordinary senses, the laws of space and time suddenly suspended and revealed novel dimensions that enfold into new pristine syntaxes and heretofore unsuspected causal nexuses in onomatopoetic juxtapositions of sound, word, affect, sensation, image and cognitive accident, disembodied sensations. During the talkfest, this world slip from its routine moorings into the ever fresh, living shoreless ocean of the *mundus imaginalis*. I believe Philip and I shared this dedication to the occult or surreal, if you will, moment which evoked more than literary concerns. He was a rare friend with whom to navigate these subtle waters that by degrees float and plunge the self in each moment into stark raw vulnerabilities that blink and blaze flashes, wordful and wordless, brinking toward cognitive annihilation and simultaneous apotheosis.

I am sympathetic with your hesitation of accepting my view of natural symbols. Language is an idiosyncratic development of natural symbols within the living social contexts of speakers who share it. The custom of sharing creates degrees of closure. For me natural symbols are only incidentally closed, and they are always wild and willing to become transformed by newly discovered metaphors in their expression and juxtaposition.

None of this thinking is particularly unique with me, as anyone who is reasonably well read in postmodern thinking knows that, critically speaking, there is almost an obsession with issues of identity and difference and the meaning of symbols and their integrity. All of which goes back to the dawn of philosophy and the father of philosophy, Socrates and his exaltater, Plato. For Plato to come to an understanding of resemblance in his idea of the forms we need to understand *eidolon* as a deformation, so that representation, or art must be a deformation of the originating *eidos*. As Cassirer notes in reference to the difference between *eidos* and *eidolon*, "it is a testimony to Plato's extreme linguistic power that he was able, in a single variation, and with subtle nuance of expression, to fix a difference of meaning which is unrivaled in its systematic incisiveness in pregnancy."

Gilles Deleuze's *Difference and Repetition* (1968, translated in 1994) attempts to revisit these distinctions with renewed vigor by indicating a 'model of recognition', as one of the four postulates supplied in that 'image of thought' which, in his opinion, philosophy uses as its own implicit presupposition, deduced from common sense. According to Deleuze, to the two postulates that consist in hypothesizing a 'goodwill on the part of the thinker' and an 'upright nature on the part of the thought', two others should be added. These are the two postulates that relate to the method that can guarantee the correct nature of thought: Deleuze designates these postulates as 'a model of recognition' and the 'form of representation'.

With us in his view, recognition constitutes the model of natural and free philosophical thought, implied by the image of thought that philosophy assumes as its own implicit presupposition. This model may be characterized as transcendental. I would characterize these distinctions as having some family resemblance to my natural symbols especially as generative in dream images as the biological basis for the building of semantic vocabularies. 'Recognition', Deleuze explains, "may be defined by the harmonious exercise of all the faculties upon a supposed same object: the same object may be seen, touched, remembered, matched and/or conceived." By making this assumption, Deleuze confirms that recognition — with regard to its own object – "aligns with the form of the Same", which is the form of representation insofar as it is defined on the basis of an "intrinsic relation to the model or foundation." Here I would be less tautological and recognize that the form of the same may very well be generated in the sensate combining of sensation with imagination in memory.

On the other hand – that which relates to the subject of recognition – the model in question, Deleuze continues, "relies upon a subjective principle of collaboration of the faculties for 'everybody'– in other words, a common sense as a *concordia faultatum.*" According to Deleuze, that paradigm and this model is also recognizable in the conception of "sensibility as a passive synthesis"– that is, as the originary correlation between the body as sentient and the world as sensible – which has been developed by phenomenology. Here I move away from Deleuze's fine mesh of distinctions because I do not hold, on the level of the esoteric, the valid distinction between the self as sentient and in the world as sensible. Esoterically I see the world and the self as equally sentient. However, from the level of the occult, one might maintain the phenomenological duality of sentient/sensible.

This idea drives Deleuze to affirm, in *Difference and Representation,* that recognition cannot be "a model for what it means to think" since, on the basis of such a model, "thought is thereby filled with no more than an image of itself, one in which it recognizes itself the more it recognizes things." Yet Deleuze limits himself to a characterization of recognition, which, one is forced to admit, is tautological on the basis that it would tend to reproduce and reaffirm only previously acquired knowledge, but inevitably also the 'values' that come to be 'attached to an object' when it becomes an object of knowledge; values that end up remaining, 'established values.' On the contrary, Deleuze replies, "the new – in other words, difference – calls for forces in thought which are not the forces of recognition, today or tomorrow, but the powers of a completely other model, from an unrecognized and unrecognizable terra incognita." For me, difference is never actual difference, so much as it is metamorphosis, or transformation that allows something to be itself and not itself simultaneously, for instance, seeing images of an old woman and a stylish model in the same perceptible image based on shifts of perspective. I do not know if this is just another way of claiming that *terra incognita* is really the world recognized anew as something other than what it seemed before. Difference then does not stand by itself but stands with connection.

Yet this contrast of new and same proves difficult to sustain for one who is attempting to think the image of difference and repetition together. More than the conception of recognition developed by Deleuze, it is rather the one proposed by Gadamer – to recognize is to know more than is already familiar – which seems more consistent with such an attempt if this conception is understood according to the double formulation of Freud's unconscious: "I did not know and 'I have always known it.'" Rather than opposing itself artificially to the Deleuzian concept of the encounter, Gadamer's definition refers precisely to an *eidetic* recognition.

This recognition of image is, after all, only an apparent paradox of art and literature. By paying attention to the virtues of resemblance by perpetual exercises of deformation, we have come to explore the mystery of this recognition. It is this paradox that is the play for the tarot reader. We are in some degree poised in questions that are addressed by a random draw of cards, which scrambles us to reframe by drawing on the interconnections of natural symbols to make sense for ourselves and the querent.

To return to Plato's understanding of the verbal slip that unites and joins primal formation with the deformation as a symbol, I guess it makes sense to reiterate that a deformation without preliminary form, namely an unprecedented deformation, may be the basis of that creative image. Indeed, if all art is, in its essence a deformation, then the peculiarity of the deformation that characterizes artistic, literary investigations, and investigations of the meaning of tarot, is more than just a critique aimed at the principle of representation. Insofar as a mere 'frontal-positioning' toward the world turns around upon itself to become simultaneously less and more of what it can be or what it has been, so tarot, if properly winnowed of the wild utterance and the sterile abstraction, may offer seeds of hermeneutical power not yet discovered/invented.

So for me symbols are middle terms that hold incompatibles as one and unique in the same, implosive/explosive mix that opens things as meaning and meaning as things. A classic poiesis that makes and remakes by saying, what no craftsman could do or would want to do.

Lately, I have been wondering about a difference of appreciation I perceive between the French and the Americans in regards of tarot. Around here, where I live, surrounded by art galleries, a person would happily spend a thousand dollars in a white shirt, because of its label, but they will shudder at the sole mention of tarot. We are talking about a whole different set of superstitions! For these high-end customers, the tarot is associated with bad taste. It is that simple. In France, people may believe in the tarot or not, yet there is a certain sense of pride in the Marseille tarot being some sort of vernacular tradition. I suspect the French are in debt to the surrealists for that. Breton and his group loved magic, and they were fond of tarot. Even their 'exquisite corpses' can be seen as a game whose logic mirrors the workings of tarot. One often finds people who would say "there has to be something about tarot if Breton was interested in it." Jodorowsky has profited from that connection wisely, not only because he is the first to tell you that Breton himself threw out his copy of the RWS in the garbage, while saying that the only true tarot was the Marseille tarot, but also because of his own artistic merits. Once and again I find people who would say "if a great filmmaker like Jodorowsky, who is also a great comic author, cares for the tarot, maybe there is something to it." Both Breton and Jodorowsky are artists that high-end customers feel no shame of being associated with, insofar as they lend their prestige to the tarot. I am not sure America has an equivalent to that.

Lamantia must have been parroting Breton too, when he told me the Marseille tarot was the only non-bogus esoteric tarot.

Do you recall in which context Lamantia told you that the only 'serious' tarot was the Marseille?

This one is pretty clear. We never talked Tarot or did divination. I saw he had a Marseille style deck around. We talked a little about the Trumps and their symbolism. I may have brought up the RWS or some GD stuff. As I recall he was not too interested. When I first began reading in the occult, A. E. Waite's stuff littered the remainder tables at bookstores. (That would have been when I was a teenager in mid 60s). Philip never used the cards. We never read the cards. He may have in other contexts that I am unaware of.

Philip was interested in the European occultist R. A. Schwaller de Lubicz, (a fascist, with strange elitist ideas). At the time, in late 70s, I did not know about his questionable political views, but I found his take on symbols interesting. Philip had the French Edition of *The Temple of Man;* I waited years for the translation to make its way into English. Neither Philip nor myself were too terribly political. We held for San Franciscans, strong liberal populist, leftist views. I eventually became a situationist anarchist *(in theory as a quietist).* Of course, we were well aware of Breton's Marxist views.

The thing with surrealism is that it was a technique to discover things without creating them. When I was in graphic design school, we were told that art history swings between two poles: on one side are those historical moments in which aesthetic breakthroughs are made and new things are proposed. On the other hand, there are those historical moments in which all creative endeavor is a recombination of what was already there. Surrealism was like that. It was about rubbing two objects against each other to get a spark. Again, this is very close to what we do with tarot. I often wonder if that isn't a limitation of tarot as an expressive medium.

In a conversation with the Balkan writer and fellow tarot lover Lena Stefanovic, I mentioned that I like to think of tarot readings in terms of anagramming. We have either 22 or 78 images which existed in a specific order and had a specific meaning, and we rearrange them over and over to create new orders and new meanings. 'Paul Nagy' is an anagram for 'play a gun'. The same letters that yet are pulled into a whole different semantic field. Le Pendu, card number XIII, and Temperance, in that order, may be saying, "only moderation triumphs over treason and Death"; but Temperance followed by Le Pendu and XIII may be saying, "if moderation has you stuck, defy Death!" I am not suggesting these are the only possible interpretations for these sequences, of course. My point is that even if we take each image as a constant unit of meaning, anagramming them creates new, unexpected messages. Nothing new there. Something I remember fondly about my first encounter with Vito Acconci was precisely when I told him that I use the tarot to find new words outside the verbal world, and he told me that you can also find new words inside the old words. That is what an anagrams is. That is something we do with tarot: we find new images inside the old ones.

I guess I get what you are saying, but let me use the alphabet to further illustrate my point. In itself, the letter A has no meaning. But here and now I see it as a suggestion to "spread my legs wide". I do so by mapping an analogy between the letter A and my body. That is a rather primal kind of analogy. Kids do it from a very early stage. It is called personification. Since you can verify the the letter A looks like a guy standing with his legs spread open, we can 'meet' in that analogy. But if I tell you the letter A is a seahorse, I would be inviting you to Map another analogy where the letter A is compared to an object. Again, you can visually verify the analogy. This second analogy doesn't invalidate the first one. Lettersa and images are like Necker's Cube. They never change, yet they show us different angles.

After I sent you my last comment I thought: "Paul seems to be talking about analogical thinking!"

Speaking of the letter A, as a man standing or as a seahorse, has us meeting at the level where forms prompt a direct realization in us. That is what I understand as the 'language of the birds'. All other languages are cages. When I say "manzana" I am kidnapping all these forms to create something incomprehensible for you, unless you speak Spanish. I would starve if I went around asking for an "apple" in Madrid! The thing is, occultism is another language, another cage. I tend to privilege a his-

torical understanding of the tarot that has it as a game, a product of late medieval Christian Europe, later misread as a repository of occult knowledge. That's another cage. I am not saying it is not historically verifiable. I am saying it may limit the possibilities for poiesis that tarot offers when taken at the fundamental level where form is meaning.

My suspicion, at the moment, is that to take tarot readings up the the level of an art form, we must get rid of cages. There is some peril in that, as art often transcends the original use of the objects it touches. Any doctrine that has incorporated the tarot into it has some ideas to foster, and these ideas define the social responsibility of its readers. If we take the tarot as an expressive medium, how far can we push it beyond what a client, or ourselves, expects from a reading? I hate the idea of the tarot becoming a Rorschach test. That is why I am so interested in 'tarocchi appropriati.' There seems to be a happy middle point there between formal expansion and edifying message. But I wonder, in your view, how and when is tarot reading an art form?

Yes, you have stumbled over the Achilles' heel of the self-taught, our constant rediscovery of the obvious which we belabor as the hidden insight of the ages! Of course I'm talking about analogical thinking! I have sort of known that all along. I am very clear about it once in a while and then it all goes back into the fog. Praise fog! What other excuse do I have for tripping over my own heel?

I discussed the axiom of identity, which for Aristotle was the initial base of material logic. However the recognition of analogy which is A=B C D..., from the point of view of a representation, or initial presentation, is primary for metaphors to work: the interlinking of them. The axiom of identity works for stuff, things as things. But for things to mean something, the analogic process is primary. I am sure somebody has talked up this view more elegantly than myself at this time. Still analogy, as you say, is just another cage, whereas if my posited natural symbols obtain, it is in their propensity to escape cages, or to inhabit unexpected cages.

I do agree that recognizing the historic context of tarot emblems, with their fabled or mythical relatives, tends to put some serious constraints upon free ranging natural symbols. Yes the *Exquisite Corpse* does open us to surprises, very much like tarot cards layout responds to questions.

I like the idea of art being locked between the poles of technical innovation as one-sided creativity and re-amalgamation of the previously created as the other side. Given the nature of the 20th century and the drift towards collective major art forms that, as they evolve, eventually filter into the repertoire of the individual. I'm thinking of children today, more easily composing moving image videos than writing an essay. One can see the rise of the digital reinvention of all the arts as a mass movement of surrealism, while at the same time we have intensifications of art forms such as 3-D imaging and other stuff I probably haven't paid any attention to that is creating a digital holism that has the stench of primitive, tribal, individual craftsmanship potential. In other words, poets are now performers, who are actors, who sing and dance and otherwise act out as far as the imagination lets them a variety of selves, involving scenarios that can bend time and space, displace class, and if anything, displaying a product of the available technologies and styles of the time. Specialization has become universal. We are all Jacks of all trades.

This brings up the shadow of the analog, which is the empty space between metaphors. Or perhaps another way of putting it, it is the context between cages. Perhaps another word is incongruity. There seems to be several ways that tarot deals with its limited random set field of 78 boxes, no matter how diverse the potential meaning of each box is. One of them is to invent spreads. Spreads are developed to create semantic units in which we place the random tarot card. They are preset. One card spread, two card spread, three card spread, etc. each of them reproducing elements of place, time, and condition that may be present in the structure of the tarot deck or extraneous to it. What we have is a way to deal a few cards to get a desired result. I have a tendency to see them as a way of pre-focusing a reading to give a certain kind of result.

When I read tarot, sometimes I work with a preestablished spread and provide people with the frame of each card's potential significance within that focus area. Sometimes I feel this is very artificial and I just read the cards as they appear without wanting to know the question or wanting to predefine how the card may address an issue that I do not know anything about. If I am reading in this intuitive way I will pull two or three cards and I will discuss them with the querent. I will say something like, 'so far does any of this have any relationship to the question you have in mind?' I say, 'you don't have to tell me your question if you do not want to, but does anything I'm saying about the cards seem to relate to it?' Generally there are three types of responses: an emphatic yes, an equivocal yes or no, and most rarely, and emphatic no. Sometimes the emphatic yes means that the reading is done. I have given them something and I don't know what it is or what its significance is because their question is still only spoken within themselves. If I get the equivocal yes or no I may then ask them to tell me about their question, or even state the question forthright. Usually an unequivocal yes or no means that the person had formulated their question as a yes or no question. I know most tarot readers tend to shy away from yes and no formulations. Personally I also do, because the cards are usually addressing what is between the cages. In other words, context. I don't think that spreads themselves are an answer to how we get around the context, or how we bring it into the conversation. Spreads seem to be developed as pre-formulated semantic units, a kind of cookie-cutter sentence into which we plug the words, here the words being that tarot card images. Also, it is a simple way to limit the number of cards we will interpret.

All of this is foreplay to the big question of whether tarot reading can ever approach a real art form. With artists who produce a series of paintings of 22 or 78 interrelated images in various ways acknowledging or ignoring the icons of the historic tarot, we definitely have a representational art form with many variants. Of course, what is also true is that very few of these artists' decks are taken up by mainstream tarot readers and discussed seriously in the literature. However, I have to acknowledge that it is in the artist rather than in the tarot reader that one can argue for some degree of art form.

Perhaps the tarot reader is the critic. As critics interpret works of art for the viewing public or potential patron, tarot readers act as docents to the idle curious somnambulate through the galleries of self-unknowing knowledge. Tarot readers as critics and as interpreters of people's life stories are reflected in the mirrors of their art and questions. It used to be that the artist was the shaman whose ritual became an artifact that intimated the transcendent. As the transcendent has become embroiled in the immanence of experience, one may very well need a shaman-critic to ferret out the transcendent and immanent blur through the adroit interpretation of a tarot spread. I think the art form for the tarot reader, then, is not so much in the creation of art, as it is in the display of art through spreads and contexts of interpretation that interweave a person's life story into the universal ur-story of the mysteries of ancient initiation. Ultimately in the tarot-reader as artist is the erasure of death in life and life and death.

To continue with the problem of contexts outside of the cards themselves and the spreads that we invent to limit them or to give them semantic form, I know that Walt Amberstone has a tendency to read the cards when he is inventing deeper meanings for them as an embrace of abstraction. Personally I avoid abstraction. I see abstraction as one of the ways we build cages around wild natural symbols. Like the surrealists, I want to subtract the abstract into the image, or sub-sound morsel of old words with new meanings and new sounds with haunting allusions. So, I guess, as much as I like analogy, the real cutting edge for tarot interpretation is not the work of art hanging on the wall, nor is it the knowledgeable docent prattling on about the craftsmanship and historic contexts of his piece, nor the vacant eyed crowds who drink in unknowing visions of labyrinths of layered possibility, nor is it the building in which all this is taking place. For me, the art of tarot must be on the wall that holds all this together. When all the walls are transparent, perhaps the cards will flutter away as doves become butterflies and butterflies, poppies.

I guess cognition is the ultimate cage, and under the light of current cognitive research, perhaps the body is the ultimate cage, since – as has been argued by George Lakoff and Mark Johnson – all the metaphors that compose our thoughts, both literal and abstract, seem to arise from our bodily experience of the world. Whatever we think the world is has been defined by the way the limits of our physical bodies delineate the kind of relationship we have with the world.

Let's say we have two cards: The Tower and La Papesse. We could say that The Tower is in front of La Papesse. In fact, if I tell you "here is La Papesse, sitting, with The Tower standing right in front of her", you can verify that statement with a single glance, yet it is not objectively true. Not only are these two pieces of cardboard not placed one on top of the other, but the whole idea of La Papesse having The Tower in front of her is the product of our embodied understanding of the world, elicited from the fact that we think of ourselves as having a front and a back. Since we understand space in terms of both, what is in front and what is behind us, we project backs and fronts into all the objects in the world. We also project a spacial relationship between them based on the terms 'back' and 'front'. There is no objective 'frontness' or 'backness' existing separated from our experience of the world. In fact, if we had the same body and spatial orientation of a tree, notions like 'back' and 'front' would be incomprehensible. If we had the same body and spatial orientation of a planet, notions like 'higher' and 'lower' would be unfathomable.

We usually speak of the "images in the cards." There we have another verifiable statement that isn't objectively true. We experience our body as a container: we put stuff into it, we take stuff out of it. We travel through space as if space were a container: we enter in and out of rooms, halls, buildings or caves; and therefore we map the notions of 'in' and 'out' into everything. We see the card's surface, the space inside the external frame, as a container. In truth, it isn't. We don't put the image inside of the card. We print them on top of it. We don't even print images! We print dots of magenta, cyan, and yellow whose different density across the surface of the card makes us see all the other colors. But even when I tell you: "the Hermit's cane is red" and you can visually verify that fact, we are talking of something that is not objectively true. There is no red, nor blue, nor magenta, nor cyan existing separately from our experience of the world. What we have is the wavelength of light being reflected under certain lighting conditions that is absorbed by the color cones in our retinas and processed by the neural circuitry of our brains. Perhaps, neural synapse is the ultimate cage!

In those graphics that illustrate a chemical synapse, the synapse in itself seems like a gap. Perhaps, this is that "space between metaphors" you so beautifully described. There is indeed something called the "synaptic cleft" that seems to bridge two neurons. Perhaps, the neurotransmitters released into these synapses are the only objective truth, and even so, I am only saying that for poetic purposes!

But neural synapse can also be seen as a relationship, an exchange, which takes me back to art. We live now in a culture that manages an extended notion of art. That extended notion surpasses the traditional definition of artwork as a specific kind of medium, like painting, sculpture, drawing or photography. Given that now image-makers have a whole new range of (mass)media at their disposal, contemporary artists base their practice in ways of imparting any activity they do with an aesthetic intention. As a result of that contemporary art is often about the relationship between the artist and the audience, through the artwork, and not about the objects themselves. Marcel Duchamp was the first to tackle the importance of context in our appreciation of art. By doing so, he put art back in the realm of magic. I am not saying he did so consciously, nor that he thought of art as magic. What I am saying is that his work made evident to what extent art is a system of superstitions based on evocation – as in sympathetic magic – and proximity – as in contagious magic. A couple of decades later, Joseph Beuys challenged Duchamp's crypticism with a whole body of work that was shamanic in nature. One interesting aspect of Beuys's work is that, while being shamanic, it was also absolutely contemporary. No one felt that Beuys was going 'native'. He wasn't. He was pushing the boundaries of what was possible in art.

Beuys's main tenet was that "every man is an artist." By this he meant that the creative impulse is natural in man, and it can be, and should be, expressed in all realms of human creation – from plumbing to dentistry – not only through what we understands as 'beaux arts.' He also used to say that if you want to become an artist, your first mistake would be to go out and buy a canvas and some paintings. If we fast forward a little to find Marina Abramovic saying the the art of the future will consist on the artist sending images from his mind directly to the audience's mind. Here we can get a sense of the whole scope of what Beuys started. He worked through performance art and sculpture, but not our average Joe's kind of sculpture. Beuys's theory of sculpture, which I find very useful to understand the Marseille tarot's pips, is based on understanding the natural transition of materials, from a contracted to an expanded state, and viceversa. For Beuys, as for any shaman, the symbolic power of a substance is more important than the objects you create with it. After all, his pieces are still decomposing, traveling back and forward from contraction to expansion. People like Duchamp or Beuys opened the possibility to see the artist's practice as an attitude, a way of facing life, inside and outside the artist's studio.

All this long-winded trip is my way of saying that I am not really interested in limiting the artistic aspect of the tarot to its images, even when my only faith goes to the images. To me, the expressive medium is the relationship we engage in through the use of tarot. Here, I feel the need to go back to the early uses of tarot in poetry via 'tarocchi appropriati.' 'Tarocchi appropriati' was a whole literary genre whose popularity survived for a couple of centuries. I even see Calvino's Castle of Crossed Destinies as a late example of it. Ross Caldwell's working definition of 'tarocchi appropriati' is: "using the trumps to describe something else". It is quite open. I see lots of freedom in there. The person who gives one trump to each lady in a room, and improvises a small poem comparing each lady to the card he gave her, is mapping analogies between these women and their respective images. The fact that this process is almost indistinguishable from reading the tarot is what makes me suspect that there is a relationship between the tarot and poetry that predates the relationship between tarot and divination, always within the context of parlor games. Obviously, the expectations a lady would have about such poetic usage of the tarot aren't the same as she would have of fortunetelling. Such a poet doesn't really run the risk of being told afterwards: "Oh! But you didn't say anything about Johnny. He left me seven years ago. He told me he despised me. But I want to know if there is any hope of getting back together with him". Telling someone "you are like The Tower" could be just amusing, but it can also be edifying. It is all in the telling. Artistry is in the telling.

That seems to be the real 'material' on which we could erect the 'art' of tarot. That seems to be the trampoline from where to jump forward. The problem with trampolines is that you have to find the right point of inflection if you really want to jump. Otherwise it won't take you where you need to go. I don't think I have found that point of inflection yet.

Now, allow me to contradict myself. Although I don't want to reduce the art of tarot to the crafting of tarot-like images, my love for tarot begins and ends with the images. Along all these conversations I have had, a question has unexpectedly emerged to become somehow fundamental. I am going to pose that question to you now:

What – if anything – do you expect from images?

Cognitive psychology became *au-courant* after I had done my survey studies of psychology. What I cut my cognitive teeth on was the language of psychoanalysis, and of course, analytical psychology. I also came of age, and I was studying cultural anthropology, when Claude Lévi-Strauss' structuralism was all the rage. In fact I met the taciturn anthropologist when he visited San Francisco. I remember a lecture he gave in which he tried to give a learned general audience an overview of structuralism. What I remember most from that talk was his extended analogy of his structuralism ('it's good to think') with music. It was an ornate comparison that showed that for Lévi-Strauss there is a natural movement, with repetitions, and other forms of self-referential architecture, that makes up his attempt to map the unconscious of the collective dreams of peoples in their myths and folk stories.

Part of the reason for this remembrance is that I never became fully or deeply fascinated with the results of cognitive psychology. But I do agree with you. On general evidence, our experience as bodies in the world sets the universal metaphors in our languages. One of my favorite reference books, still in print, is by Carl Darling Buck, *A Dictionary of Selected Synonyms in the Principal Indo-European Languages: A Contribution to the History of Ideas*, (1950). Here a number of simple words are shown in their variety of stems – to reveal certain general categories of human experience. Another good work is by a Hungarian psychoanalyst, Theodore Thass-Thienemann, *The Interpretation of Language: Volume 1, Understanding the Symbolic Meaning of Language and The Interpretation of Language: Volume 2, Understanding the Unconscious Meaning of Language*. Thass-Thienemann is drunk on the secret meanings of words and their primitive and infantile associations. For instance, secret, as to not divulge, is related to the bodily process of secrete that the effuse and effluvia of the body are not to be spoken of. These they carry with them energies, or effigies of the person who produces them.

I think cognition is not the pivotal point of symbol as you suggest. I tend to want to look a little more into the brain stem, the language of the id, unconscious processes that only thrive in the twilight of semi-cognitive ignitions. Something that is energetic, the throb of sensation that synthesizes into lived feelings and forms. In other words, the higher functions of discrimination, especially as refined through institutional learning and guilds of knowledge, may obscure their messy antecedents. Still, the body is the seat of natural magic.

Once at a Wiccan summercamp I gave a workshop on minimalist magic. Basically I said that witches have become too preoccupied with magical implements, herbs, stones, and other elements. But it is important to recognize that our body carries with it all the magical properties we actually need. I went through the senses showing how each is a body and an element that is already empowered with profound charisma. I showed how the fingers and arms, hands and feet and legs. They all represent magical relations with the earth and the air. That our spit, tears, and piss is water, our snot, mud, our skin, dirt. Our bones are stones. Our voice, the wind, our mouth, origin of the winds, etc. Our ears are wings. Sound is flight. Our eyes open the light. Eyes are globes like sun and moon. Smell is eating wind. Divination as minimalist magic, with an 'anal log' to the body alone, might very well be shit. And it may also be the light of the imagination. The fire is in the hearth of our skull.

And in minimalist magic, the imagination impregnates all elements of the body with the mana of magic. Even in this rankly materialistic view of magic, I am a Platonist at heart, which means that, for me, it is consciousness that consecrates; awareness that makes the wary quick; attention that touches our intentions into acts; that it is important to recognize that we should consecrate the unadorned body and even connect our ritual artifacts with the primal magic of the body rather than the other way around.

Thinking of the tarot and the example of the structural way you suggested in reading The Tower and La Papesse. I do not think of tarot so much as some element of our body; say patches of skin, as perhaps one removed from the body, an aspect of clothing. The naked body is not the social body, except in the intimacy of lovers or family or in the anonymity of orgy. (An orgy is a suspension of the usual decorum related to sexual congress.) Tarot cards are civilized in the way that clothing is. In the end you ask me what I expect of the image. To me, the image is the end product of the imagination which is the process of blending sensations into forms remembered and conjectured.

Unlike the entrails of chickens, the ripped open body of another, the tarot cards are a nice accoutrement to our clothing. Of course, clothing is an extension of our skin. But here our skin is hidden by the symbols of our gender, social class, occupation, and other advertisements and messages are clothing broadcasts. Perhaps we should consider the divination of tarot cards one remove from the primordial gist of the naked body. Here we are civilizing the sacrifice of the chicken into a shuffle of cards. The game of a flight or fight becomes the gaming analogy, which you are so fond of, where the risk of tooth and claw is tamed and reproduced in bet of risk in high or low draw. Likewise the *tarocchi appropriati*, where persons become cards and cards that personas of people. This is storytelling as make-believe. However make-believe is more thrilling once it seems real. Hence the gambling analogy holds the make-believe at bay by the gambler's honor to pay his debts. Gambling then is a sort of form of hunting, a ritualized style of hunting when game has become livestock. As much as our experiences ever wed to the basic infantile aspects of experience, slowly extended to the world, but always at core, our bodily experience at base, then the image is the reduction of all the extensions and possibilities back to the moment of inception, where it connects us with the first inklings of awareness that wrinkles out of our brow and sucking instinct.

In the tarot images we have their historic purport and we have our idiosyncratic projections of what the images seem at any particular reading. There are many levels that one can read some of the classic tarots. At this year's Readers Studio, Ruth Ann and Wald Amberstone demonstrated reading cards with only a few associative elements. In one case we were given the Golden Dawn official color designations and we related them to the RWS background colors. We were also asked to focus on the functional meaning of the clothes worn by the images in the RWS cards. Once we had our chart of range of elements of clothing, we could offer an easy reading of the cards just by referencing those associations and none other.

In another exercise, a sort of elaborate gestalt dialogue with the card images, where we isolate the various images in their individuality and have them speak to us and to one another in a free associating conversation I, through the nine of swords, had the palms of the hands on the face of the sitting up figure speak to the eyes that it was comforting in its shame and fear. The swords became Venetian blinds that were steps on Jacob's ladder and the quilt comforter was the Milky Way showing us our afterlife destination. The Satyr carved on the bench emphasizes that this shame was not personal but recognition of the soul that it does not know the extent of either its sublimity or its depravity. Sure, I think that it makes sense to discover the formal meanings of the card images, but I also think that it makes sense to allow them to become alive and tell us what they mean anew each time we see them. Because for me, ultimately, the images are not the fixed forms on the cards, but are rather vivid originals that are ever transmogrifying in our imagination.

Therefore I forgive images there fixity in the cards, because I know that they are there merely to remind and stimulate the ur-image in my mind-heart. And this mind and heart is full of learned nonsense and innocent wonder that will always seek to see the new in the image, not only on the card but in my mind, for it is in that linking that the real tarot reading/thinking takes place to reveal things that I might not otherwise know, and perhaps to revile knowledge into its unknowing.

I would like to know more about your meeting with Allen Ginsberg, and about the feeling of San Francisco.

Jodorowsky tells a story that may or may not be real, of him meeting Ginsberg twice. The second time was in San Francisco. Jodoroswky boarded a cable card and there he was: Allen Ginsberg sitting on the last row, playing some sort of small piano and saying poems. The driver told Jodorowsky that Ginsberg did that evey afternoon to "heal the city". Jodorowsky links that event to his own desire to give readings for free.

Let me remind you that my relationship was with the surrealist poet Philip Lamantia, and not, in any way, Allen Ginsberg. And I do not wish to exaggerate my friendship with Lamantia. It was a semblance as I eulogized it.

However, I did hang out as a adolescent in North Beach and parts of Skid Row, then around Third St. and Howard, and where my friends live was near Six Street and Folsom, not too many blocks from where my father was born and where he worked for many years as an accountant at a tire company. How I ended up there is a complex story that might seem deservedly unique, if I did not know how intensely other adolescents discover their lives. I had had a stormy childhood that was haunted by serious failures to socialize. One way I addressed this deficit was developing the dyadic, alter-ego friendship with another disturbed youth, and together we sailed through adolescence into young adulthood. My friend, Mike, and I discovered the necessity of creating a persona. Neither of us had fathers in our lives and we knew we needed the direction of men to help us grow into men ourselves. We were both precocious and read books well beyond our years. We discovered Sigmund Freud and psychoanalysis and knew that we needed a 'father-image'. We also discovered the Beats. This is about 1962, just before a North Beach went topless. My own father had spent a year in county jail and had some friends from jail that ran some of the nightclubs in North Beach. With my friend Mike I found a way to connect to the street people that hung out in the North Beach neighborhoods. For Mike, it was finding a connection for marijuana. For me, I discovered City Lights Bookstore, and both Mike and myself read the Beats, and *Howl*. I read many times to myself when I was around 13-14 years old. I thought of Allen Ginsberg as the 'conscience of America'. I would occasionally wait tables, at a little dive called, *The Coffee and Confusion,* which in the evenings served up a rag-tag selection of folk music. There was pre-Beatles, a slight wave of new folk music. I even stood up a few afternoons and read my exceptionally horrendous poetry. From some of the people that hung out at the *Trieste*, we met some people who lived on Six Street, which, if you know San Francisco geography, is quite a ways from North Beach. Also I did not grow up anywhere near North Beach, and it took a good 45 minutes on streetcar and bus to get to that part of the town. My friend Mike was the outgoing one. And I was profoundly shy and self-defended. The emphasis here is that, as adolescence, we were in a bric-a-brac way creating the legend of who we were to be as adults. We were going to be beatniks.

During that time in North Beach, there were not too many beatniks around. Bob Kaufman, very much a meth-head, was there. The first poetry reading I went to had Kenneth Rexroth, Kenneth Patchen, Michael McClure, and Lawrence Ferlinghetti as principal readers for the residents of Marin City. Mike and I met many street people in those days: winos, whores, hustlers, junkies, bluesmen, pimps, and queers. Mike was always chasing down the drug. First it was pot, and then other drugs, which were his talisman to charisma. I hung around as a shadow, an oracular voice that announced the Emperor had no clothes. I listened closely and watched fervently and thought deeply about what I saw and heard. And yet I was only there on the actions of my friend. Myself, that was a mystery I knew I would dance with for the rest of my life. The Haight-Ashbury was a neighborhood that we also visited many times, and even were in a street gang there, that would still like to attack hippies. When the Haight-Ashbury exploded upon the consciousness of America, I was already living in an ashram in Nevada. My friend Mike and I were drifting apart. He became a petty criminal and drug addict, not living past the age of 25. I think I saw him for the last time when he was 23. He had been imprisoned several times. And his body was much broken from drug abuse and beatings he had received in his criminal life. In fact most of the cohorts I hung out with did not survive the heyday of the Haight.

I cannot say that I made any inroads into beatnik San Francisco. By the time the hippie ethos arose, I was ready to leave the beat behind for a cloistered seeking of ultimate reality. By that time I was clearly a mystic, which is still the best adjective to describe myself. Of course, I am a mystic without religion, a mystic without a personal God, a mystic without fellow travelers, on a road of uncertain demarcations. After almost 2 years as a yogi, I set myself free from another myth. I was the myth of a baby beatnik, then the myth of a renunciation yogi, and later, after I met a mentor, I was involved for three years in a cult of Tantric Buddhist shamanic mountain climbing and fire walking, officially known as *Kailash Shugendo*. During this time I attended junior-college, and as I ended my exclusive cultic association with *Kailash Shugendo,* I met my college friend, Stephen Schwartz (see endnote), in around 1972, who introduced me to surrealism and who had grown up on the edges of the San Francisco Renaissance poetry scene. His father was a friend of Kenneth Rexroth. Friend enough, to be able to use Rexroth's name on a Union Street used bookstore called *Kenneth Rexroth Books*. My friend acted as a bridge for me from my early adolescence and legendary self-making as beatnik. I now have some initiations and a more solid sense of self direction in terms of interests. I was studying cultural anthropology and going to apply it to the study of the new religions that I had been so involved with in my post adolescence. My friend introduced me to Lamantia. He also introduced me to other people in and around North Beach in the early 70s.

Now, my friend knew Allen Ginsberg quite well, as he had occasionally attended parties that my friend's parents had thrown in the 1960s. So over the years I heard many stories about Ginsberg, Ferlinghetti, Kenneth Rexroth, and was given an oral history of the San Francisco literary scene, especially seen from the ghetto of North Beach. I had then no pretenses to being a poet or a writer, so I would listen to other people pontificate in that area. In the late 70s I lived in North Beach myself for about two years, just before I went to Scotland to study the mysticism of Muhyiddin Ibn 'Arabi.

In the mid 80s, I believe, I was at a poetry reading where Philip Lamantia was reading, and Allen Ginsberg, came up to introduce Philip to some aspiring young poets. I was introduced to Allen, who I had met several times before in noncommittal ways. I said to him something like "Nice seeing you again, Allen!" to which Allen replied, "I don't know you! I have never seen you before! I'm not going to let this pass. I despise people like you who claim to know me when I know that I do not know you!"

So my last and only memorable encounter with Allen Ginsberg is his insisting that he had never met me before and that I was a poseur! I was humiliated in front of Nancy and Philip. And I could read Philip well enough to know that he was embarrassed for me. Of course, I offered no defense. I did laugh the other day, when I read one scholar of the Beat Generation saying that one was a beatnik or not if Allen Ginsberg said you were a beatnik or not!

In my youthful, self-making, I embraced becoming a beatnik. Only in middle-age, to be denounced by the Pope of Beatitude himself, I am nothing, a mere poseur. Now as a mystic, being a mere nothing, is quite a comfort.

What does the tarot say? One card draw: Ace of Discs (Thoth Tarot). Allen was unknowingly releasing me from my youthful dream of beatnik becoming! Now I may well become a Tarot reader, a poseur, perhaps, definitely, a know-it-all! Of course I am not a true know-it-all, just an omnivorous hermeneut.

Before I ask you my final question, I want to thank you for what has been one of the most delightful dialogues I have had so far.

These days I am struggling to explainin a certain idea: I suspect that the magician's craft is founded in developing an 'epistemological humility' (To borrow a term from Michael Hurst). This is achieved by understanding and accepting the limits of cognition and the way cognition fails prey to a series of daily illusions we often cannot consciously control. To guard the boundary between reality and the other-world is to remain alert at the limits of perception. But the magician's craft would be incomplete, his aim would fail short, if he would devote himself to unmask our senses alone. For the magician to go around saying: "Don't trust your senses, they can be fooled. Half of what you remember, you made it up", is important, but it is also contractive and a little ungiving. The magician's craft becomes whole if he can use these cognitive illusions to create something with them. Something better than disenchantment. Otherwise one runs the risk of ending, as Serbian poet Milorad Pavic would say: "Neither a magus to yourself nor to us a prophet."

What do you want to be when you grow up?

You began our exchange with a simple but directive question: what did I want from Tarot? My first reaction was that I did not want anything of Tarot. I did not desire tarot to liberate me from the quagmire of myself or the marginality of my circumstance. I did not want to win friends or influence people by tarot reading, though I do enjoy the reading of tarot as a way to escape from incessant small talk. Nor did I want tarot's effect of generating impending discernment into people's lives and problems that seems like magic and invoke creditable sensations that demonstrate an almost proof of uncanny percipience for people who eschew the mystic, because, for me mystery, is matter-of-fact and a habit-of-understanding.

I want to see if I can find a way to let tarot speak on many levels at once so that the reader is challenged with every moment as unique and unlike any other. Perhaps like the phenomenologist, I want to teach myself and perhaps some other tarotists to read cards by bracketing the rote associations and opening to the effulgent symbolic in unique circumstances. I plan to explore the evolving significance of card readings as I apply it to the wisdom tradition from which tarot emerged. So far I claim no method for this inquiry, and I am not certain I am in search of one. I may perhaps discover or invent or borrow workable protocols to proceed with this project, but as of now it is just a pipe scheme.

Metaphors to Live By by George Lakoff and Mark Johnson and *Philosophy in the Flesh: The Embodied Mind and Its Challenge to Western Thought* by George Lakoff are remarkably successful expositions of how our language derives out of the fundamentals of universal experience based on living in the world through our senses. In many ways they do with modern linguistic theory integrated with behavioral and cognitive science what a previous generation attempted to do through phenomenology, psychoanalysis and logical positivism. Theodore Thass-Thienemann is now remembered for his two volume work, *The Interpretation of Language* that explores the cornucopia words as betrayed in semantic ambivalences and transmogrifications. The two volumes were composed to understand the etymologies of words as reflective of the development of the psyche and aspects of universal experience. The first volume is based on the conviction that understanding verbal symbolism is a basic form of knowledge. Understanding the roots of words, sort of like understanding images, opens us to linguistic symbolism, verbal representations that the author says is analogous to arithmetic that is the basis of the mathematics of the sciences. Thass-Thienemann claimed his etymologies and verbal symbols explore the root concepts and language. Experience of the human body represents the bedrock not only of human development individually, but also sets up the warp and woof by which words evolve their extended meaning. In his second volume, the author explores fundamental elements of human experience, again as reflected in core words that deal with the universals of culture, of course, in this case the culture is psychoanalytically informed. The reason I am referring to Thass-Thienemann's work is that he brings in elements of introspection and dream analysis that are more reductively dealt with by Lakoff and Johnson.

I do enjoy a good magic show. The stage illusionist, even the three-card-monty hustle, plays with my perceptions, as I daily demonstrate to myself if no one other, the passive attention that can be easily misdirected by the distracting movements and the false constructions of my own mind. Even being shown how the illusion works, my mind will not necessarily liberate me from the habits of my misperceptions. Am I so much addicted to the illusion? It must be a seductive delight. Beside myself, how many of us share this lemming-like inclination?

Some neuroscientists claim that our connecting things causally because of their near contiguous appearance is a false creation of perception that constructs continuity to our perceptions when reality may have no such causal connection. Much persistent prejudice is based on this. The belief that the skin pigment says something about the character of people is false though it is true people behave differently with one another based on perceived race, even when such people would not want to be racist.

One approach to the meaning of nirvana is explained as the ability to see how the magic lantern show of our misperceptions can be broken so we just see what is and do not chase false associative stories or causes by linking discreet instants as a flow.

Every instant is its own discreet universe which is complete as is, without being joined, attached, and entrained to its antecedent or subsequent instants. Even the great wheel of samsara suffering (meaning 'continuous movement' or 'incessant flowing') never stops until we recognize it never moves and never has moved and nothing has ever arisen or ceased arising because such a story is told by the barren woman's child who is blind and mute.

It is also true that the images on tarot cards may well be blind and mute yet they speak to some of us of universes of significance and possibility, hope and love, perhaps somewhere between the flame and the wind that snuffs it out. A wind so still it never blew and always promises to quench a flame indistinguishable from dark.

When I grow up? I want tarot to blow out the flame.

Thank you for engaging me in this conversation. I think through this process I have come to a better understanding of what I am trying to do. And I do not think I would have this perspective, if it hadn't been for our exchange of ideas. I have tried to clarify my understanding of how tarot may become a valid way for people to recognize occult phenomena in their lives. Another less arcane way of putting this is to say that recognition of the occult can be awakening to the effects of the unconscious in our life. As we awaken to the possibility that there are aspects of our selves that are permanently never seen directly, and yet whose effects are felt and manifest in our everyday life, we may come to an appreciation that our consciousness is much more than directed ego awareness. Furthermore I hope that awakening to the unconscious, through learning how to interact with natural symbols, which are fundamentally imaginative interjects of our sensate life recombined in our reflective life of memory and experience, I hope some tarot readers will become aware of how the occult can evolve into a profoundly transforming experience of the unity of the self and the world through the esoteric. The esoteric is fundamentally a holistic grasp of awareness as it is in itself. This awareness is transcendent and immanent beyond any duality. One could say that the human mind and reason are but shadows to esoteric realization. No set of tarot cards can in themselves awaken us to our own root mind, much less the root of the root of pure awareness without a second and without qualification. Even with this obvious point, study of the tarot, when done in conjunction with other hermetic exercises, can offer some of us the liberating possibility of being transformed by the esoteric.

When I grow up? Tarot will blow out the flame.

The flame blows out.

There is no flame.

No flame ever was or ever will be.

There never was a flame.

Nor tarot.

New York / North Carolina, June 2010.

NOTES:

In the course of the above conversation, Stephen Schwartz was kind enough to make the following precision about some of Paul Nagy's comments:

Hello Mr. Enriquez

I am the person mentioned by Paul whose father was involved in a book-selling enterprise with Kenneth Rexroth. Rexroth and my father, Horace Schwartz, had been friends for a long time. My father published the first edition of R's long poem THOU SHALT NOT KILL of which I always believed Gins's HOWL was imitative. My father also knew Lamantia well and in 1968 or 1969 I was introduced to Lamantia, with whom I was close for some years.

Kenneth Patton should be Patchen. I had grown up closer to the midst of the SF poetry scene than to its edges – my father also published Ferlinghetti's first poems to appear in print. Ginsberg did not attend parties held by my parents – rather, my parents attended dinners hosted by Rexroth at which Ginsberg and all the rest were guests. I met Ginsberg in the company of Ferlinghetti around 1966.

I did not consider myself a beatnik. I would say that given his publication enterprise through City Lights Ferlinghetti had more authority to decide who was or was not a beatnik but I don't remember anybody competing for the title who was in the original circle. Rexroth's group, Robert Duncan's circle, and the friends of Jack Spicer were influential but did not consider themselves beatniks.

The small instrument Allen G. carried around with him was a harmonium, which, as I understand it, he had picked up in India.

Best wishes,

Stephen Schwartz

§

Paul Nagy's web site is at *www.tarothermeneutics.com*

www.ingramcontent.com/pod-product-compliance
Lightning Source LLC
Chambersburg PA
CBHW031249230426
43670CB00005B/108